UNIVERSITY COLLEGE
WINCHESTER

Martial Rose Library
Tel: 01962 827306

- 1 NOV 2011

2 4 FEB 2012

To be returned on or before the day marked above, subject to recall.

WITHDRAWN FROM
THE LIBRARY
UNIVERSITY OF
WINCHESTER

KA 0205135 4

D1145840

Technical Design Solutions for Theatre
The Technical Brief Collection
Volume 2

Bronislaw J. Sammler, Don Harvey

Focal Press

Boston Oxford Auckland Johannesburg Melbourne New Delhi

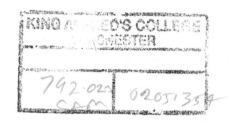

792.02
SAM   0205135

Focal Press is an imprint of Butterworth–Heinemann.

Copyright © 2002 by Yale University School of Drama

A member of the Reed Elsevier group

All rights reserved.

No part of this publication may be reproduced, stored in a retrieval system, or transmitted in any form or by any means, electronic, mechanical, photocopying, recording, or otherwise, without the prior written permission of the publisher.

∞ Recognizing the importance of preserving what has been written, Butterworth–Heinemann prints its books on acid-free paper whenever possible.

Library of Congress Cataloging-in-Publication Data

ISBN 0-240-80492-9

British Library Cataloguing-in-Publication Data
A catalogue record for this book is available from the British Library.

The publisher offers special discounts on bulk orders of this book.
For information, please contact:

Manager of Special Sales
Butterworth–Heinemann
225 Wildwood Avenue
Woburn, MA 01801-2041
Tel: 781-904-2500
Fax: 781-904-2620

For information on all Focal Press publications available, contact our World Wide Web home page at:
http://www.bh.com

10 9 8 7 6 5 4 3 2 1

Printed in the United States of America

Table of Contents

RIGGING HARDWARE

RIGGING TECHNIQUES

SAFETY

SCENERY

The following excerpt is taken from Mark Shanda's article "The *'Essential'* Technical Direction Library," which appeared in the August, 2001, issue of *TD&T*. From time to time we have discussed moving *Technical Brief* to an electronic format. But, like Mr. Shanda, we always decide that electronic media are complements to — not replacements for — print media, and we consequently recommit ourselves to the *Technical Brief* mission: to document technical solutions in such a way that others need not reinvent them — and to do it in a form that invites repeated contemplation and further invention. Actually, Mr. Shanda puts it quite elegantly . . .

A thin blue wire is an important feature in my office. The wire extends from a phone jack on the wall and is attached to my computer, providing a connection to a promised world of ideas and information. A private off-ramp on the information superhighway with instant access to data from around the globe is mine. The blue wire has changed the way I work. I have come to deeply appreciate and rely heavily on e-mail. Communicating with colleagues throughout the world with the ease of typing a few lines and hitting the send button has made many a recent project go smoothly. A list of favorite web sites has been developed and, on several occasions, I have turned to the web to track down a vital piece of information.

However, despite occasionally getting lost for hours surfing the net, discovering the ridiculous and the sublime, there has been something missing. I long for the feel of a real book in my hands.

There is nothing quite so pleasurable as leafing through the pages of a trusted volume in search of ideas to address a current technical challenge. The bookshelf at the east end of my office is loaded with literally hundreds of books ranging from course textbooks to out-of-print treasures I have purchased at used book stores.

They are in a jumbled assortment of both vertical and horizontal stacks for which only I have the retrieval and storage code. Just around the corner from the book stacks, I have another floor-to-ceiling bookshelf which holds nothing but catalogs. As I survey my over-20-year-old collection of "text-based resources," identifying those most valuable proves an easy task. The essential ones are all dog-eared, scribbled in, and, in fact, rather limited in number.

My momentary observation of my "priceless" collection launched my first and possibly last search to identify the essential technical director resource library. In that pursuit, I conducted a wholly unscientific and biased survey, which was "snail" mailed to 20 academic and commercial theatre technical directors.

Each was asked, "If marooned on a desert island and forced to continue to be a technical director for the Desert Island Repertory Theatre (not a pleasant thought, although I hear they do good work), what are the three primary text-based resources you would want with you?"

Sixteen responses were received from the illustrious group. Not surprising, most respondents could not limit their answers to only three choices, but there was consensus on several selections. The survey responses were supplemented with direct conversations and with several technical types at the recent [2001] USITT Annual Conference & Stage Expo.

What follows is an annotated list of the resources identified as indispensable by the group . . . .

We're honored that Mr. Shanda and so many other professionals recognize *Technical Brief* as an essential part of the "The *'Essential'* Technical Direction Library . . . ."

The Technical Brief Collection

Yale's published collection of new and occasionally reinvented theatrical wheels is useful not only for the particular problems the articles solve, but for providing ideas about how to approach similar challenges. *Technical Brief* continues to be an excellent publishing source of simple solutions to a wide variety of technical problems. These short, detailed solutions often can serve as springboards for developing parallel solutions. The compilation volume has brought all the illustrations into a similar format and is well indexed. *Technical Brief* continues to be published . . . .

Whenever a production problem arises, *Technical Brief* is the first resource to which my students and I turn. While most theatre-related resources speak in general terms, *Technical Brief* speaks in specifics, providing clear illustrations, narrative, and in some cases even a bill of materials. It's pretty common for me to receive phone calls from past students asking about "that tech brief we used on such and such production." I fax them a copy of the brief and encourage them to get a complete set for themselves since the series, in many instances, features multiple approaches to solving similar problems. While, thankfully, there are now a growing number of similar experiential publications, *Technical Brief* remains the granddaddy of them all. Any serious theatre technician should be sure to have the complete collection within an arm's reach of their desk.

— Dennis Dorn, Director of University Theatre
University of Wisconsin-Madison

Now that I have over 20 years' experience in academic, professional, and educational theater I can safely declare that I DO NOT know everything. I approach each new production with the same sense of excitement, anticipation, and apprehension that I had when I was just learning the trade. Only now I know full well that each production will challenge me in ways I have yet to imagine. It is this constant challenge that makes Technical Direction an often exhausting but always rewarding profession.

One of the most valuable lessons that I have learned thus far is to rely on a library of resources I have collected over the years. Of these, I turn often to Yale's *Technical Brief*. On many occasions I have found the perfect solution to a production problem in its pages. The clear and concisely written articles often allow me to simply hand the task to a student and have it produced with minimal supervision. On many other occasions, *Technical Brief* has "jump started" my thinking by providing ideas that I could change, modify, or build on to suit my particular needs.

Both educators and students need forums where we can share ideas and solutions to specific production challenges. *Technical Brief* provides just that. It has proven to be an indispensable tool for both teaching and learning.

— Tim Francis, Technical Director
Trinity University, San Antonio, Texas

I look forward to each issue of Yale's *Technical Brief*, not because I expect to find the solution to an immediate need (although that has often been the case), but because I admire innovation. As a fellow practitioner in the black art of technical theatre, a brief description and a drawing or two is all I need to recognize a good idea. I am a connoisseur of invention and I savor the clever morsels that appear in the pages of *Technical Brief*. These concise descriptions of applied research and development are even more compelling when one realizes that they are created in concert with immutable deadlines and ridiculously small budgets. If necessity is the mother of invention, then we are a needy group indeed. Yale's *Technical Brief* is one of the very few publications that attempts to meet the needs of theatre technicians, both as a resource and means of expression.

The demands of technical theatre are often daunting. We work with our heads down, focused on the problem at hand and with little consideration for recording our solutions for posterity — there simply is no time. An idea may be sketched on a napkin, or, more likely, a piece of 1x3, which later ends up in the scenery and the documentation is lost forever. Few editors appreciate receiving a chunk of lumber and a scribbled note as the germ of an article, but Ben Sammler and Don Harvey are the exception. They, too, are connoisseurs of invention who can recognize a good idea and understand the constraints under which we labor. That napkin sketch, that drawing scribbled on a cornerblock, becomes a polished article in *Technical Brief* and the technical theatre community is richer for it. Too often we have worked feverishly to solve an intractable problem only to have someone say, "Oh yeah, I saw one of those over at Theatre x. They call it 'the wheel.'" *Technical Brief* reduces redundancy, and that saves our most precious commodity — time.

Thumbing through *Volume I, The Technical Brief Collection: Ten Years of Solutions to Recurring Problems in Technical Theatre*, is like walking down the aisle of a good hardware store. I find myself mumbling, "Now isn't that clever . . . oh, I could use that for this . . . I wonder if that would work for . . . ." I like hardware stores. I can't wait to wander down the aisles of *Volume II.*

— Loren Schreiber, Technical Director
San Diego State University

Acknowledgements

Twenty years have passed since the first issue of *Technical Brief* was mailed to approximately fifty subscribers. Since then over two hundred forty articles have been written by more than two hundred colleagues and our publication has reached nearly three thousand subscribers in twenty-three different nations.

With the compilation of Volume II of *The Technical Brief Collection,* our successes are even more accessible to generations of technical designers to follow. Their tasks will be easier as they use your methodologies and techniques as the foundation for their solutions to new problems.

Don and I are privileged to have had the opportunity to work with so many talented people and are pleased to have facilitated this unique communication. I thank both our writers and our readers. Together we have all made a profound difference to our profession.

— Ben Sammler

There are all sorts of good reasons for not writing a *Technical Brief.* There's almost never enough time to work up carefully detailed text and graphics. The solutions we develop — like the problems they address — are often idiosyncratic enough that they may never have to be repeated or so familiar that we're not likely to forget them. And it's certainly not the money: *Technical Brief* has never paid for a single contribution. So just exactly why anyone (our own students included) ever submits an article remains something of a mystery to me. Yet, 208 individuals have found some good reason for writing a *Technical Brief.*

Whatever their different, private motives, these 208 authors have earned my profound respect and gratitude. Their articles have provided the profession with a record of problems solved. But more importantly from my point of view, the record they've provided is the foundation of an enduring professional legacy from which all of us can draw — and to which all of us are invited to contribute.

— Don Harvey

TECHNICAL BRIEF

Costumes

When a costume design calls for armor, hoopskirts, bustles, novelty metal costumes, or oversized animal suits, the costume shop can use the expertise of the scene shop's metal worker to advantage. Tracing the development and construction of the metal corset described here will help clarify the primary concerns of the costumer — the actor's safety and comfort — and the potential contribution of the metal worker. The approach used to build this corset could be used in building armor or any other metal costume.

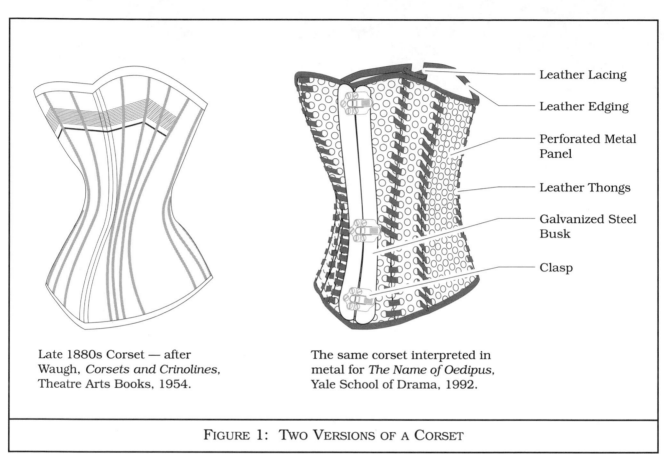

Late 1880s Corset — after Waugh, *Corsets and Crinolines*, Theatre Arts Books, 1954.

The same corset interpreted in metal for *The Name of Oedipus*, Yale School of Drama, 1992.

Leather Lacing

Leather Edging

Perforated Metal Panel

Leather Thongs

Galvanized Steel Busk

Clasp

FIGURE 1: TWO VERSIONS OF A CORSET

DESIGN CHOICES

Pattern and material choice is critical. Metal doesn't stretch like most traditional costuming materials, but it does come in a variety of weights (gauges) and styles. Some styles of perforated metal even seem able to mimic fabric's bias stretch capability to a limited degree, making them potentially useful materials for costumers. The metalworker can describe materials and their advantages and disadvantages to the designer and draper, and can help them make a workable selection. Pattern choice also requires collaboration: working together the metalworker and costumer can best determine which patterns will translate to the new medium.

As Figure 1 illustrates, the costume plot for *The Name of Oedipus* included a late-1880s-silhouette corset, to be built of metal and worn over a cotton camisole. Through research, the costume designer and the draper established that straight-boned corsets, such as the original iron corsets, Elizabethan or late-1880s corsets, are appropriate for translation into metal; spiral-boned corsets are not. To find a lightweight metal which could negotiate the compound curves of the human body, the designer and draper worked with the props craftsperson and chose perforated steel for the outer corset panel, galvanized steel for the busk (the rigid fastening mechanism on the front of corsets), and fiberglass door-screening for a decorative middle layer between the lining and the outer cover. See Figure 2.

PATTERN MAKING AND CONSTRUCTION

Working as usual, the costume shop built a muslin mock-up of the corset and fitted it to the actor. The mock-up determined the final pattern pieces which, in this case, would be used by two shops. The costume shop used the pattern to create the inner two layers of the garment: the lining and the fiberglass-mesh interfacing. The interfacing was purely decorative, while the lining, built of heavy muslin and fully boned with $\frac{1}{4}$" steel bones, supported the actor and kept her from being injured by the metal.

The metal shop used the costume shop's original pattern pieces on the perforated metal, cut-

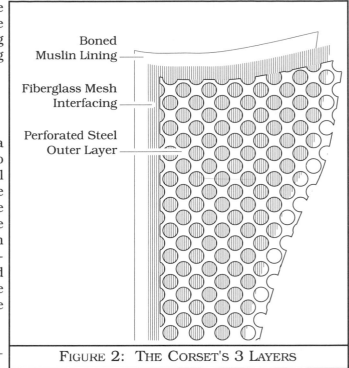

FIGURE 2: THE CORSET'S 3 LAYERS

Boned Muslin Lining

Fiberglass Mesh Interfacing

Perforated Steel Outer Layer

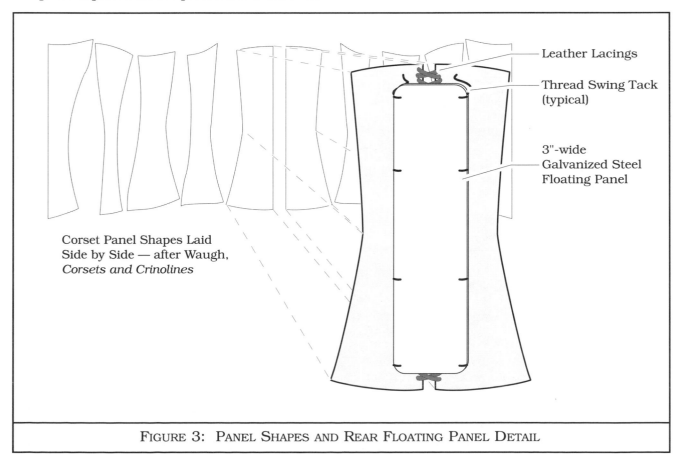

Leather Lacings

Thread Swing Tack (typical)

3"-wide Galvanized Steel Floating Panel

Corset Panel Shapes Laid Side by Side — after Waugh, *Corsets and Crinolines*

FIGURE 3: PANEL SHAPES AND REAR FLOATING PANEL DETAIL

ting it to shape on the bandsaw, and grinding off its burrs. The pieces were hand-bent over a table edge to form the compound curves necessary to mimic the shape of the torso. The rear lacings of the corset were backed by a floating panel of galvanized steel and leather, held in place with sewn swing tacks. The floating panel, shown in Figure 3, protected the actor from metal edges left exposed for lacing. The costume shop laced the steel panels together and, after assembling the corset's three layers, edged the top and bottom of the corset with leather strips to bind the layers together and to protect the actor. The galvanized steel busk on the corset's front provided a base for the 3 metal chest latches, which served as clasps.

CONCLUSIONS

Metal costume construction is best approached through the collaboration of two shops. The costumer is concerned with the silhouette of the garment and the safety and comfort of the actor; the metalworker, with the possibilities and limitations inherent in the choice of material and fabrication technique. Realizing that these concerns are mutually supportive rather than mutually exclusive is the key to a productive partnership.

The metal corset described here was designed by Elizabeth Fried and built by Yale Rep's draper Robin Hirsch in consultation with the Props Craftsperson David Schrader.

ελελελ

Knowing that poor copies of the Elizabethan figure-eight just don't work on stage, draper Kay Hirsch did a great deal of painstaking research before she began building ruffs for the Guthrie Theater 20 years ago. After she had turned to paintings and sculptures throughout the British Isles to define the look, she developed a way to replicate these ruffs in modern materials — Petersham, bias-woven nylon horsehair, and chiffon. This article describes her method, which can be used to build a wide variety of durable, yet lightweight and easily maintained Elizabethan figure-eights.

DESIGN PRINCIPLES

No two figure-eights are identical. Each has its own peculiar width (the distance between its neckband and its outer edge), height (the distance between the tops and bottoms of its eights), and fullness (the density of the eights), none of which

can be established except through fittings. A few generalizations do, however, apply to all figure-eights. First, they are almost never as wide as they look. A ruff only 4" wide can easily make its wearer's head look as though it were sitting on a plate — effective in comedy, but not necessarily in drama. Second, whatever their widths, figure-eights are typically at least $\frac{1}{3}$ as tall as they are wide (despite the illusion in the drawing below). Thus, the eights of most 3"-wide ruffs are, for instance, 2" tall or more. Finally, proportionately taller ruffs look more graceful, for their eights are more open along their outer edge and tend to fill up the space under the wearer's chin.

With these guidelines in mind, you can quickly establish the best width and height for a figure-eight during a muslin fitting by using a simple, brown-paper mockup. The mock-up, nothing more than a flat donut deliberately cut $\frac{1}{2}$" over-wide and placed over the draped muslin, reveals how a proposed width will look in the context of the entire costume. Once width has been gauged, a good height can be eyeballed by holding a tape measure under the actor's chin at the edge of the mock-up. The ruff's fullness can best be judged by folding a length of the nylon horsehair into a ribbon-candy-like strip, its eights set at the height you found with the tape measure, and then squeezing one side of the strip's eights together as though they were gathered at a neckband. The tighter you need to squeeze to get the right look, the closer together and more numerous the ruff's eights will be. In general, a ruff's eights will be between $\frac{1}{8}$" and $\frac{1}{4}$" apart at the neckband, and in most cases between $\frac{1}{4}$" and $\frac{1}{2}$" apart. Make a note of your spacing-at-neckband estimate, and before you release the strip, mark the bottoms and the tops of four adjacent eights for reference later on.

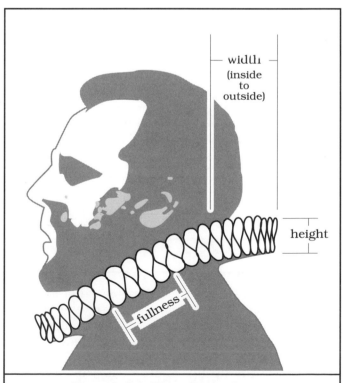

FIGURE 2: RUFF DIMENSIONS

MATERIALS AND MEASURES

The neckbands of Kay's ruffs are made of Petersham strips, cut 3" longer than the wearer's neck measurement. Part of the excess becomes a base for the ruff's skirt-hook fastener; the rest allows for adjustments. The stiff nylon horsehair gives the eights their shape. Though optional, dressing layers of silk chiffon or lightweight lace sewn on top of the horsehair can reflect light onto the wearer's face, and edgings of spiky lace, cording, or flat trim can help stabilize and decorate the eights.

As far as the materials' width is concerned, both the Petersham and the horsehair are used in their stock widths. Stock Petersham widths make convenient neckbands, and since the horsehair is bias-woven it will simply fall apart if cut lengthwise. The chiffon or lace used for the dressing layer is bias-cut into strips $1\frac{1}{2}$" wider than the horsehair and pieced together as necessary. The table below lists the materials the author used in building two figure-eights for Yale Repertory Theatre productions and indicates the lengths of the pieces involved in each.

	Hamlet	*The Duchess of Malfi*
Petersham	1" wide, 19" long	$\frac{1}{2}$" wide, 20" long
Horsehair	3" wide, 6 yards long	1" wide, 3 yards long
Edging	flat, shiny braid, 6 yards long	$\frac{1}{2}$" spiky lace, 3 yards long
Chiffon	silk, $\frac{1}{2}$ yard	silk scraps

TABLE 1: MATERIALS USED IN TWO YALE REPERTORY THEATRE FIGURE-EIGHT RUFFS

CONSTRUCTION SEQUENCE

1. Prepare the Neckband. Make two marks on one edge of the Petersham, one at 1" in from an end, and the other $\frac{1}{2}$" farther away from the first than the wearer's neck measurement. Then mark off the spacing-at-neckband increments you noted during the fitting. Make an identically spaced series of marks along the other edge of the Petersham, but offset this series of marks so that connecting the dots would result in a zig-zag as in Figure 3. Fold the Petersham back against itself at your first mark and stitch it down as a base for the neckband snap.

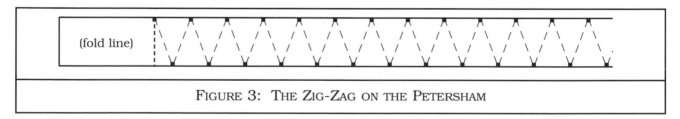

FIGURE 3: THE ZIG-ZAG ON THE PETERSHAM

2. Prepare the Eights. Taking care not to distort the horsehair, pin and hand-baste the strips of dressing layer material to it, turning $\frac{3}{4}$" under along each edge. Machine stitch the trim in place along one edge (now, the outside edge). Using a button-and-carpet bobbin thread, run two lines of machine gathering about $\frac{1}{4}$" apart along the ruff's inside edge, as close to that edge as possible. Trim away any excess chiffon. Next, referring to the sample strip you marked during the fitting, and starting about 2" in from the end of the horsehair, mark the spacing between adjacent eights on both edges of the horsehair with "00" brass pins located directly opposite each other.

3. Gather and Stitch the Eights to the Neckband. Gathering the horsehair and chiffon gradually and removing the pins as necessary, align the pins in the horsehair with the appropriate marks on the Petersham and stitch the materials firmly together at the marks with double button-and-carpet thread. After you've fastened the first 8 or 10 eights to the neckband, pin them to each other along the outside edge to establish their shape and check your progress with a second fitting.

4. Finishing Off. After you're satisfied with the ruff's proportions, finish stitching the eights to the neckband and pinning them together. Next, with the ruff lying flat, adjust the eights as necessary and stitch them firmly together. Then form some of the excess horsehair next to the very first eight into the upper half of an eight and some of the excess next to the last eight into the lower half of an eight. Stitch these half-eights to their adjacent full-eights, and finish off the gathering threads solidly. Fold the unfinished end of the Petersham back against itself $\frac{1}{2}$" or $\frac{3}{4}$" from the last half-eight, stitch it down, and add skirt hooks to complete the neckband. Add two clear plastic snaps to join the free ends of the ruff invisibly.

No matter how endearing or frightful, realistic, or fantastic, good theatrical masks share a single basic aim: the actor's comfort. A mask that's too heavy is exhausting to wear. One that fits awkwardly demands far too much of its wearer's attention. A good theatrical mask, on the other hand, is somewhat like theatrical makeup in that it weighs next to nothing and it moves exactly as its wearer does.

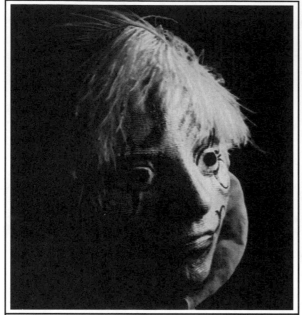

FIGURE 1: RUSTIC

FIGURE 2: DEMON

Borrowing materials and techniques from millinery, maskmaker Katherine Snider has perfected a way to build lightweight, face-hugging masks. As Figures 1 and 2 demonstrate, each of her masks is a testament to her artistry. Just as importantly, each of them is the result of an approach that uses inexpensive and entirely non-toxic materials. This article, the first in a two-part series, describes the crafting of the base that is common to all her masks. Its sequel will address more advanced issues including the use of non-traditional materials and ways to finish a mask.

MATERIALS

Buckram, the basic material in all of Ms. Snider's masks, comes in different plies numbered 1 through 4 ranging from very coarse to very fine. Number 1 buckram, the coarsest, has holes nearly $\frac{1}{4}$" apart; the smoothest, Number 4, resembles lightweight muslin. The coarseness of the buckram determines how smooth a mask can be. The only other materials this approach uses in giving a mask its basic shape are water and Sobo® glue.

CONSTRUCTION

Like other maskmaking approaches, this one involves bending the mask material over a form that reproduces the desired contours, the best choice being a plaster casting of the intended wearer's face. Construction is fairly simple:

Step 1. Cut the buckram roughly 2" larger than the casting. Soak the cut buckram in warm water for a few minutes until it is so flexible that it will drape easily over the casting.

Step 2. While the buckram is soaking, cover the casting with a light coat of Vaseline®. The Vaseline® helps the buckram stick to the mold and is especially helpful around prominent features like the eyes and nose.

Step 3. Stretch the buckram over the casting, pushing the excess material toward the top of the head. This will help keep the buckram to a single layer, preventing the creation of unwanted wrinkles. Because buckram has a bias, several attempts at discovering the best way to lay the material over the casting may be necessary. Fortunately, the buckram can be repeatedly soaked and stretched as necessary.

Step 4. Push the buckram into the eyes, nose, and mouth as illustrated in Figure 4 until it sticks to the casting and lies flat.

Step 5. When the buckram is at last conforming to the casting's contours, let it dry. Since buckram is not flammable, you can use a hair dryer to speed the drying.

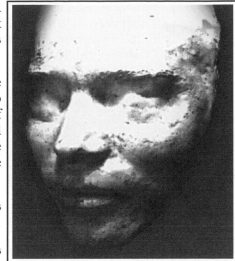

FIGURE 3: A FACE CASTING

Step 6. Brush one or two layers of the Sobo® over the exterior of the dried buckram as a base for finish and texture materials to be added later. Brush a layer of Sobo® over the interior, as well. This coating will make the buckram feel more comfortable. Let the Sobo® dry completely — 10 to 30 minutes.

Step 7. Cut out the eyes, nose, mouth, and any other necessary holes. Trim any excess buckram off the edges of the buckram, and the base for your mask is finished.

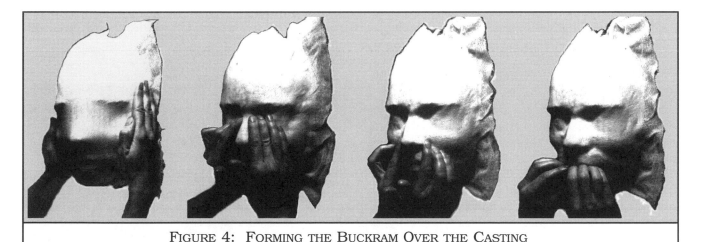

FIGURE 4: FORMING THE BUCKRAM OVER THE CASTING

FINAL COMMENTS

Katherine Snider's approach to maskmaking is a simple, forgiving process that permits re-working as necessary to correct mistakes. It uses non-toxic materials, and the masks that it produces lie comfortably close to the face, allowing performers the freedom of movement their craft requires.

❧❧❧

The key to maskmaker Katherine Snider's art lies in the creation of non-toxic, form-fitting mask bases which conform ideally to the actor's face.   Part one of this two-part series introduced her process for creating lightweight masks, an approach that uses milliners' techniques and a favorite millinery material — buckram — to establish each mask's basic shape.   This article describes the use of non-toxic materials and methods to produce a wide variety of looks and finishes.   Every mask's design presents a new challenge, but whether it is to be a three-foot radiating star point or an oversized Einstein mustache, any feature can be built from materials that are lightweight and that present health hazards to neither the builder nor the wearer.

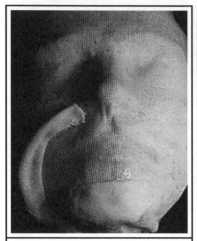

FIGURE 1: CHIN PAD & CHEEKBONE ROLL

FIGURE 2: THE SKULL MASK

ADDING BASIC FACIAL FEATURES

All facial features are made from tissue or from buckram or other fabrics. Buckram is good for longer, pointy shapes, and tissue is good for more delicately defined shapes lying closer to the base. While features can be built independently and then sewn or glued to a base, most are formed and attached simultaneously.   This process involves coating both the feature and the mask base with Sobo®, and then shaping the feature in place. Figure 1 shows a buckram chin pad and cheekbone roll molded in this manner, and Figure 2 shows how such simple structures look on a finished mask. The rims of The Skull's eye sockets are rolls of tissue; the cheekbones, rolls of buckram. Figures 3 and 4 below show the various degrees of relief that this technique can produce.

Whenever folds or rolls of material would be unnecessarily heavy, Ms. Snider bends buckram over other objects and sizes it with a half Sobo® half fabric stiffener mixture. Ping-pong balls, tennis balls, and other found objects are among the likeliest forms, but when necessary, Ms. Snider carves forms out of Styrofoam® or foam-rubber, or sculpts them in modeling clay.

To create unusually large projections, Ms. Snider frequently begins with a base made of window screening. This method produced the elaborate crest of the *Romeo and Juliet* Fantasy Mask in Figure 5.   Buckram stretched over a window-screening form and treated with a mixture of Sobo® glue and fabric stiffener easily followed and reinforced the contours bent into the screening. The

FIGURE 3: THE SAGE

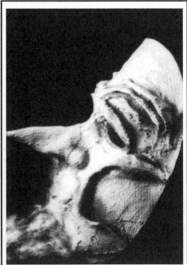

FIGURE 4: THE THE SAGE IN PROFILE

FIGURE 5: FANTASY MASK

coating for this particular crest used a fairly high proportion of fabric stiffener. Fabric stiffener shrinks material, and if used on the mask's base would probably have made the mask uncomfortably tight. But since the crest shown here was simply attached to the forehead of the buckram mask base, the amount of fabric stiffener used on the crest did not alter the shape of the form-fitting base.

Adding features to a mask base, whether by sewing or by hot-gluing them to the buckram, creates visible seams. Such seams can emphasize the rough, scraggly texture or the sharply chiseled features that some masks should have. But when necessary, the seams can be disguised with little effort. Stretching a layer of four-ply buckram over a mask's base and features and then coating the whole with several layers of Sobo® can produce a nearly bone-smooth surface. Any darting necessary in such a final layer can usually be hidden high on the forehead or underneath the chin.

FINISHING

The last steps in maskmaking are the application of surface texture and facial details. A number of different textures can be achieved by coating masks with Latex or with sawdust, feathers, gesso, straw, leaves, or anything combined with Sobo® glue and brushed over the mask.

FIGURE 6: THE DEMON & THE RUSTIC

The facial details of Ms. Snider's masks are made from an odd assortment of materials and objects, some bought, some found, all commonly available. Figure 6's Demon and Rustic (both of which appeared in the earlier article as well) hint at this approach. The Demon's eyes are ping-pong balls. His teeth are simple plastic store-bought teeth cut and glued to fit the mask, and then covered with a fine buckram, Sobo®, and paint. Both masks make liberal use of feathers, and The Rustic also has a flowing, chiffon neckerchief. Sooner or later, all the traditional maskmaking details, such as hair made from unraveled rope, find their place on Ms. Snider's masks.

A MONUMENT TO AN APPROACH

Parade-scale masks can also be built out of buckram and window screening, but creating them proceeds a bit differently. To form the gigantic head of Albert Einstein shown in Figure 7, Ms. Snider used a spoon and gloved hands to mold window screening itself into a mask base. Then she stiffened the screening by sewing a heavier-gauge wire around its edge, covered the screening with

FIGURE 7: DR. EINSTEIN

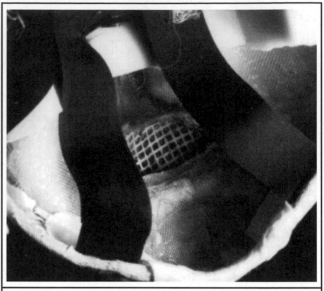

FIGURE 8: DR. EINSTEIN'S HARNESS & SHELF

buckram, and coated the buckram with her usual Sobo® and fabric stiffener mixture. Ms. Snider painted unraveled hemp with gray, black, and silver spray paint to create Einstein's hair. Similar pieces of hemp sewn and glued over hooking rug created the mustache while allowing enough vision for the actor to move on stage. This "window" appears in Figure 8.

Figure 8 also shows the nylon-webbing harness and foam-rubber shelf Ms. Snider built into this mask to hold it up. The webbing was sized to fit the performer, and the shelf rested on a hardhat that became part of the performer's costume. As the performer moved, the hardhat bounced against the foam rubber, producing a highly desirable puppet-like bobbing action,

Making provisions for quick changes is often among the last items on a TD's to-do list. Having one or more of the easily stored, inexpensive quick change booths described here can help make the countdown to tech rehearsals less frantic. These booths are modeled after an equally useful item common to most shops — the welding screen.

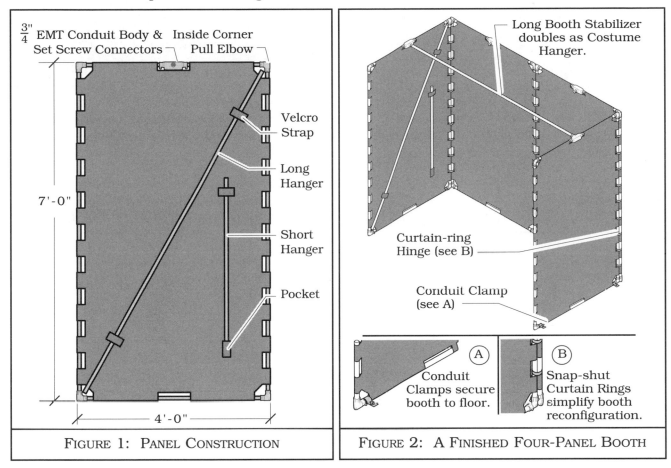

$\frac{3}{4}$" EMT Conduit Body & Inside Corner Set Screw Connectors — Pull Elbow

Velcro Strap

Long Hanger

Short Hanger

Pocket

7'-0"

4'-0"

FIGURE 1: PANEL CONSTRUCTION

Long Booth Stabilizer doubles as Costume Hanger.

Curtain-ring Hinge (see B)

Conduit Clamp (see A)

(A) Conduit Clamps secure booth to floor.

(B) Snap-shut Curtain Rings simplify booth reconfiguration.

FIGURE 2: A FINISHED FOUR-PANEL BOOTH

MATERIALS AND DIMENSIONS

The booth is made up of four identical panels hinged together. See Figure 1. Each panel consists of a 4'-0" x 7'-0" frame of $\frac{3}{4}$" EMT conduit and a fabric cover. The tabbed pipe pocket sewn into the perimeter of the screen provides multiple opportunities for joining panels into booths like that shown in Figure 2. Velcro® straps and two sets of pockets sewn onto the fabric covers provide storage locations for two sizes of stabilizer/costume-hanger conduits. A list of the parts needed for a four-panel booth is laid out in Table 1. Table 2 presents a cut list of the framing members.

ASSEMBLY NOTES

Assembling the booth is very simple. Still, a few suggestions may be helpful. Before assembling the frames, paint all the pipes black and then wrap their ends with Teflon® tape. Painting the pipe will make the booth less visible. Keeping the joints loose allows for quick modification or reconfiguration of a setup and is particularly important at the tee in the top of each frame. After the individual frames are assembled and covered, they are hinged together with shower curtain rings or cable ties. The hinge joint doesn't have to be particularly snug: the stabilizer/costume-hanger pipe makes up for the slop inherent in the hinge. Nevertheless, since an entire four panel booth weighs only a few pounds, securing it to the stage floor with conduit clamps or tying it off to walls or scenery backstage is recommended.

8 ea.	duvy panels with 2" x 4" tabbed pocket in each edge, $3'-1\frac{1}{2}"$ x $6'-1\frac{1}{2}"$ finished size
1 ea.	2" x 4" duvy pocket for short stabilizer
12 ea.	$\frac{1}{2}"$ conduit
16 ea.	$\frac{1}{2}"$ conduit
4 ea.	$\frac{1}{2}"$ conduit
1 ea	roll of Teflon® tape
27 ea.	shower curtain rings or cable ties
3 ea.	2" x 4" Velcro® hooks and loops

TABLE 1: LIST OF BOOTH COMPONENTS

8 ea.	$6'-10\frac{1}{2}"$ (uprights)
4 ea.	$3'-10\frac{1}{2}"$ (bottom member)
8 ea.	$1'-10\frac{1}{2}"$ (top member)
1 ea.	$7'-10\frac{1}{2}"$ (long stabilizer)
1 ea.	$3'-10\frac{1}{2}"$ (short stabilizer)

TABLE 2: FRAME CUT LIST

VARIATIONS ON A FOUR-PANEL THEME

The modular structure of the frames allows for various configurations. Folding the frames into a 4' x 4' booth and using a short stabilizer between the top T-joints produces a compact, one-person dressing area. In this setup, you may want to turn one panel's cover into a loosely hung tab curtain that can be quickly pushed aside.

CONCLUSION

Whether the reader chooses to build the panels exactly as described here or to modify the design to suit particular needs, the basic design of this booth has a few key advantages: it's inexpensive; it's easily built; it stores compactly; and, best of all, it can be set up for use in just a few minutes.

TECHNICAL BRIEF

Lighting

In smaller theatre departments like mine, keeping electrical cable organized is as tiresome as it is essential. The cables pulled down in haste during a strike are often tossed onto a jumbled pile in a corner until they can be collected in a laundry hamper and rolled out of the way just before the last sweep. During the next load-in, having to search for just the cable you need in the resulting spaghetti pile makes the work just that much harder.

LABELING

When I arrived at Antelope Valley College, I found a total of 54 cables measuring anywhere from 1'-0" to 80'-0". None were marked as to length, and they had no designated storage area. My first chore was to mark each one. Following the example of Master Electricians everywhere, my stage-craft students and I coded each cable with colored spike tape. In our system, a band of yellow tape indicates 25'-0"; red indicates 10'-0"; green, 5'-0"; and blue, 1'-0". Some electricians suggest standardizing the cables' length by cutting each cable down to the nearest 5 or 10 feet. At times I have considered doing so, but whenever I find that the last available cable is just barely long enough to reach the light being hung, I'm glad I've never cut any of them. Besides, with very little practice, even the newest students know that a cable marked YRGBBB is 25'+10'+5'+1'+1'+1' or 43'-0" long.

STORING

The next step was to create a storage area for the cable. Since our theatre is a black box with an overhead grid, it made sense in terms of storage and ease of access to build a rolling cart. I developed the design illustrated on the following page as a shop project for my beginning students, deliberately making the cart easy to build. I also made certain that it could be built from existing scrap material and that it would store tucked out of the way in any odd corner in our crowded space that happened to be available at the time. Labels and strips of colored spike tape on the shelves' edges clearly indicate where the various cables should be stored.

The original cart has been in use for several years now with almost no modifications, and it certainly stores our cable more efficiently than a laundry hamper would.

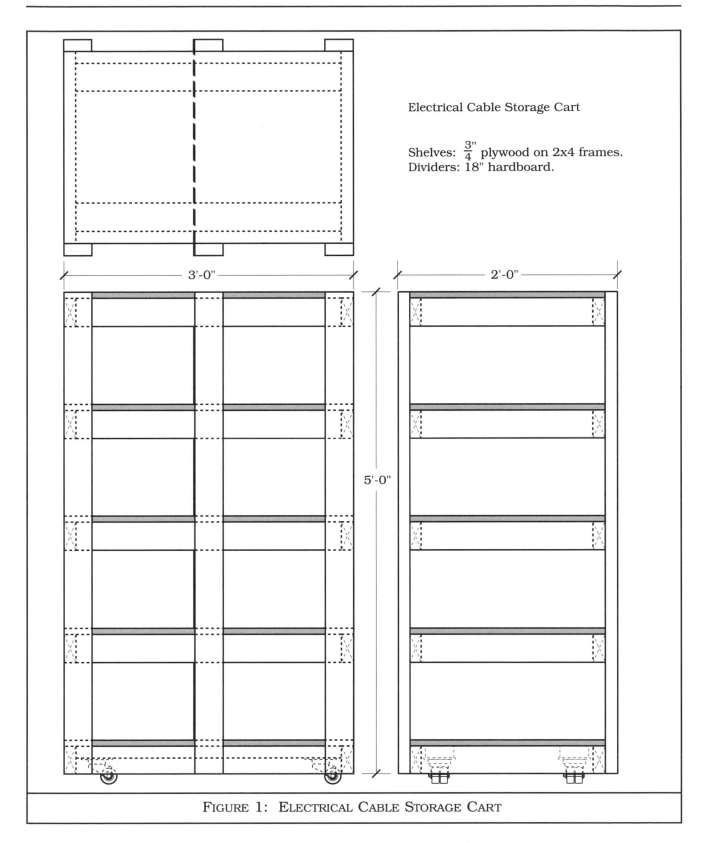

Electrical Cable Storage Cart

Shelves: $\frac{3}{4}$" plywood on 2x4 frames.
Dividers: 18" hardboard.

3'-0"

2'-0"

5'-0"

FIGURE 1: ELECTRICAL CABLE STORAGE CART

There are occasions when it is nice to use really saturated colors in strip lights, yet a flat filter too close to the lamp will bubble and eventually burn through with prolonged use. Technicians repeatedly face the problem of prolonging the life of such filters, and one solution is to vacuform the flat color media into convex or arched shapes. In this form the filters are distanced from the heat source and burnthrough is no longer inevitable.

In most instances, the first step is to mold flat filters over an appropriate form. Glass roundels and hardware-cloth "roofs" like those shown below make good forms for vacuforming filters. You could, of course, use a heat gun instead of a vacuform machine.

Filters that have been shaped by heat will need support during use, or heat from stage lamps will flatten them out again. To keep that from happening, I often use the hardware-cloth molds pictured here as filter spacers. Both models shown are easy to make, and both have worked well.

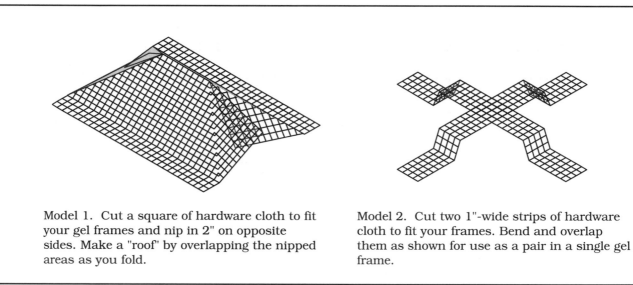

Model 1. Cut a square of hardware cloth to fit your gel frames and nip in 2" on opposite sides. Make a "roof" by overlapping the nipped areas as you fold.

Model 2. Cut two 1"-wide strips of hardware cloth to fit your frames. Bend and overlap them as shown for use as a pair in a single gel frame.

FIGURE 1: TWO HARDWARE-CLOTH FILTER MOLDS / SPACERS

Typically, I put them in individual gel frames (almost a necessity in overhead striplights). For floor use, though, I sometimes prefer to make a single, arched piece of hardware cloth big enough to cover an entire striplight, lay unshaped filters on top of it, and tape adjacent filters to each other.

After three weeks of almost continual use (prep and performance for a musical review and lighting class projects), a set of filters I had vacuformed had not bubbled up or burned through, though they had become as brittle and dry as the flat filters I had used in the past. This is the longest period of sustained use (several hours daily) I have tried to date.

❧❧❧

In a recent production involving a bar as a set piece, the lighting designer wished to place small lamps in a false ceiling. MR16 lamps were chosen because of their small size and low price. Since budget was a major constraint, purchasing lamp holders was out of the question. After pondering the problem, this solution was developed.

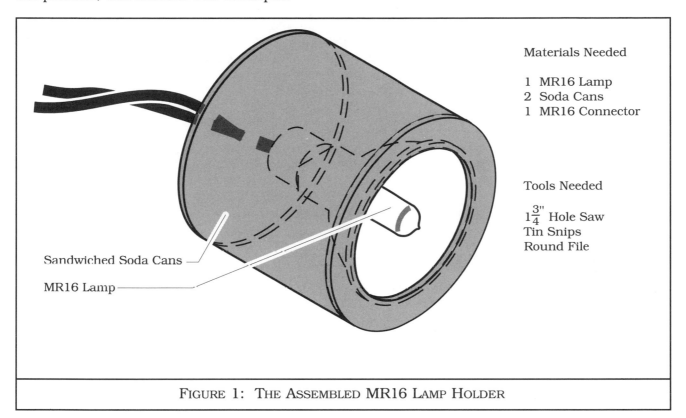

Materials Needed

1 MR16 Lamp
2 Soda Cans
1 MR16 Connector

Tools Needed

$1\frac{3}{4}$" Hole Saw
Tin Snips
Round File

Sandwiched Soda Cans

MR16 Lamp

FIGURE 1: THE ASSEMBLED MR16 LAMP HOLDER

CONSTRUCTION SEQUENCE

1. Adjust the centering bit in the hole saw so that the blade protrudes farther than the bit.

2. Turn one soda can upside down and center the hole saw over the can's stacking ring. Gently drill out the bottom of the can. Repeat this step on the second can. Lacking a drill press, the drilling can be done by hand since the saw tends to center itself on the can.

3. Smooth the edges of the drilled-out cans with the round file.

4. With the tin snips, cut halfway down each can from its top. Then cut away the top half of each can, being careful not to leave a jagged edge on the bottom half (the part you want to keep).

5. Place one of the cans, bottom up, on a table. Place the MR16 lamp, base down, on the cutout of the can with the lamp's flange resting on the can.

6. Using steady and even pressure, carefully push the second can over the first until the lamp's flange is sandwiched between the two cans.

7. Connect the MR16 connector to the lamp pins.

MOUNTING

Fastening the completed lamp holders to a set piece depends largely on the piece itself. Hose clamps have been used to attach the lamp holders to dowels mounted in the set piece. Overhead mounting techniques can involve cutting a hole slightly smaller than the diameter of the cans into the set piece. This way the stacking rim protrudes slightly, and the cans rest on the piece itself. Gaffers tape has been used, though the heat of the lamps tends to gum the adhesive fairly quickly. Holes drilled in the cans will allow them to be screwed or bolted to the edge of a set piece.

WIRING NOTES

In our production, 12-volt, 50-watt lamps were used, wired in series to avoid having to use a transformer. Three strings of five lamps each were connected to their own proportionally patched dimmer in order to prevent overpowering them. Wiring five 12-volt lamps in series produced a load of 60 volts. Connecting them to a 120-volt dimmer proportionally patched at 50% insured that they would be powered correctly. If the dimmer allowed the lamps to see a full 120 volts, they would burn out, very quickly.

FIRE SAFETY PRECAUTIONS

MR16 lamps generate a great deal of heat. Users should take care that the lamp holders themselves and the surrounding scenery are designed and treated appropriately. Specifically, in building the lamp holders, cut away as much of the can as possible to minimize the amount of confined space. Use THHN wire rather than zip cord in wiring them. In installing them, do not allow them to be completely enclosed within a set piece. Any surrounding scenery should be designed to promote rather than inhibit the free circulation of air and must be flame-proofed.

FINAL COMMENTS

The major drawback to this design is losing a lamp. If the lamps are wired in a series, all lamps in that string go out if one goes bad. Once the bad lamp has been identified, the entire holder must be removed from the set piece and thrown away since it is next to impossible to disassemble the holder and keep the cans usable. It is recommended that a few spares be made at the time of constructing them in case of emergencies.

As to cost, though building them seems labor-intensive, these lamp holders are obviously cost-effective from a materials standpoint, and some organizations will find them cost-effective in time as well. Drilling the cans takes mere minutes; cutting them around the middle takes a bit longer but is still relatively quick. Assembly takes almost no time at all. Though soda cans tend to crush easily, one learns how to pressure fit the cans quickly after just a little practice. Thus, theatres with limited budgets and inexpensive labor forces will find these lamp holders doubly attractive.

¿∂¿∂¿∂

TECHNICAL BRIEF

Lighting Effects

A Schmitt-Trigger Practical Switch   *Alan Hendrickson & Patrick Seeley*

A production of *Search and Destroy* at the Yale Repertory Theatre required that a practical be turned on and off along with other light cues. For several reasons, though, cabling the practical to an offstage control unit was impractical, and actors found it impossible to trigger the unit consistently because of the nature of the action. We solved the problem by using the electronic circuit diagrammed below.

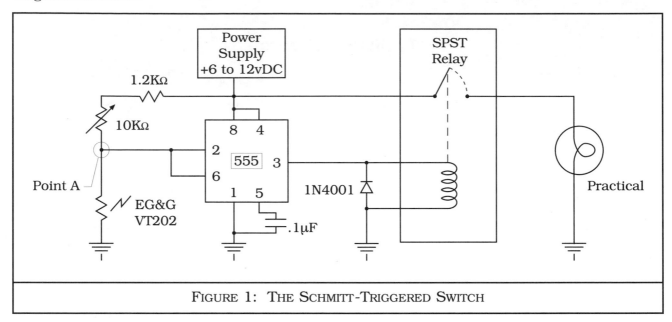

FIGURE 1: THE SCHMITT-TRIGGERED SWITCH

SYSTEM OPERATION

Increasing the amount of ambient stage light reduces the resistance of the photocell, reducing the voltage across point A. Wiring the 1.2KΩ resistor and the 10KΩ variable resistor in series with the power supply and the photoresistor creates the limits of sensitivity of the circuit and allows for adjustment. Within the circuit's limits, changes in the voltage trigger a single-pole, single-throw (SPST) relay, turning the practical on and off.

Wired as illustrated above, the 555 timer chip acts as a Schmitt trigger, a circuit which creates a range of operation with two distinct ends. This particular Schmitt trigger is activated only when changes in ambient light cause the input voltage (at pins 2 and 6) to cross either end of the range. Changes in ambient light which fall within the range are, of course, passed on to the Schmitt trigger but do not trigger the practical on or off.

The output voltage at the bottom of the range of operation energizes the coil inside the relay, creating a magnetic field and closing the SPST relay. Once this has happened, current flows to the practical and it is turned on. When the stage lights dim beyond the high end of the range of operation, the voltage at point A is raised, releasing the relay switch and turning the practical off.

The other components are needed to protect the circuit. The diode wired in parallel with the relay's coil prevents the inductive spikes created during deactivation of the relay from reaching the 555 timer chip. The 1µF capacitor filters noise from the inputs. The photoresistor, EG&G VT202, is available from Newark Electronics or Allied Electronics. All other components are readily available at local electronics shops.

Lighting designers are constantly faced with the need to mimic nature's lighting on the stage. Template breakup patterns or gobos are often used to simulate the effect of natural light as it passes through leaved tree limbs. The result, while a good start, is never complete, for in nature the patterns of light change as the wind moves the limbs, and the stage lighting equipment available to simulate movement like this is often prohibitively costly.

THE RIG

Described here is one device which can give ns the movement produced in nature. As the figures show, the rig consists of two simple additions to standard lighting equipment: a spring mounted between the C-clamp and the yoke of a lighting instrument (see Figure 1); and an operating line attached to the front of the instrument's barrel and reeved offstage through any number of batten-mounted offset sheaves. Operation requires only that a stagehand pull the operating line on cue.

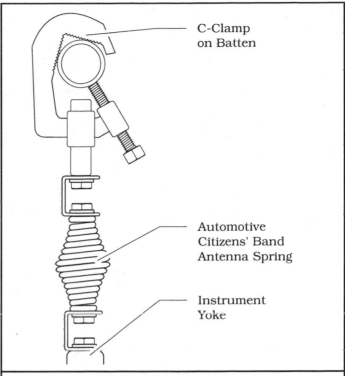

C-Clamp
on Batten

Automotive
Citizens' Band
Antenna Spring

Instrument
Yoke

FIGURE 1: DETAIL OF ANTENNA SPRING MOUNT

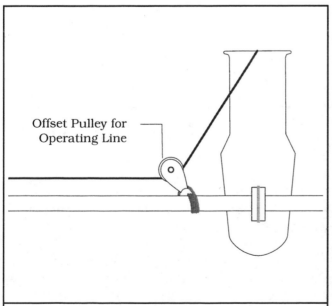

Offset Pulley for
Operating Line

FIGURE 2: SCHEMATIC OF OPERATING LINE RIG

COMPONENT AND CONSTRUCTION NOTES

The size of the instrument dictates the strength of the spring required, of course. In some cases, a spring made of or cut from the base of a locally purchased citizens' band car antenna will work quite well. Appropriate alternatives are available overnight from national distributors
-Carr.

Designers who plan to use such rigs should remember that they impose two important constraints. First, the placement of the offset sheaves will probably be adjusted during tech rehearsals regardless of what the plot shows. Thus, the location of nearby instruments, cable, and hardware should take such a likelihood into account. Second, the batten or ladder or boom base which carries such an instrument will need to be tied off so that it doesn't move when the operating line is pulled.

A Ground-Fog Generating System

Erik Walstad

Generating a scene's worth of ground-hugging fog is tricky business. Dry-ice fogs hug the ground well enough, but they don't last very long, and storing and handling sizable blocks of frozen CO_2 is awkward at best. On the other hand, the longer-lasting fogs produced by theatrical fluid-based foggers are pretty easily generated, but they tend to rise rather than hug the ground, dispersing more or less evenly as general hazes. The ground-fog generator described here capitalizes on some of the strengths of both approaches by producing a mixture of very cold CO_2 and relatively long-lasting fluid-based fog.

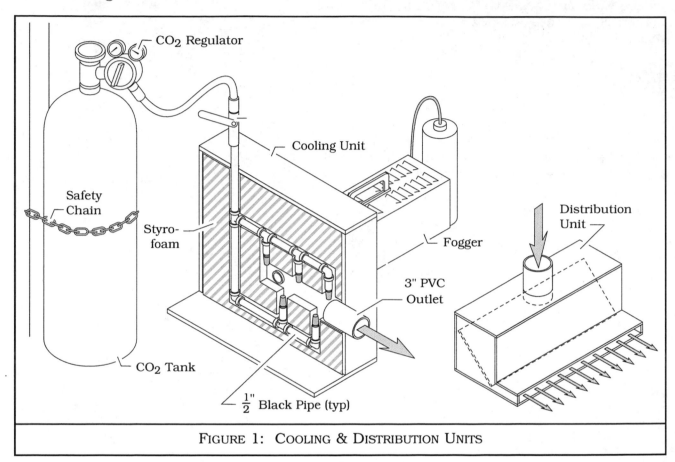

FIGURE 1: COOLING & DISTRIBUTION UNITS

Figure 1 illustrates this generator's key components: a cooling unit and a distribution unit. The cooling unit consists of a plywood shell surrounding blocks of styrofoam positioned to create a well-insulated mixing chamber. Relatively warm fog from a fluid fogger is pumped into the chamber through a 2"-diameter PVC pipe. Cold CO_2 gas, bleeding at a controlled rate from a commercially available pressurized tank, enters the same mixing chamber through a five-jet manifold of $\frac{1}{2}$" black pipe fitted with pneumatic system exhaust mufflers. The fog and CO_2 combine in the chamber, and the chilled vapor mixture is pushed through a 3" PVC outlet into dryer-hose transmission lines, escaping onto the stage floor through one or more distribution units. Each distribution unit is simplicity itself: a $\frac{1}{4}$" plywood box with an internal baffle angled toward a slit-like vent at the unit's base.

Though the units pictured in Figure 1 can be modified in some ways to suit particular needs, builders should keep a few requirements in mind. First, though the fog mixture is somewhat pressurized, this is essentially a gravity-fed system. Thus, the cooling unit should be located above the distribution unit, and if multiple distribution units are to be used, all hoses between them and the cooling unit should be about the same length to balance the flow of fog. Second, since the valves on CO_2 tanks are back-seated and must be fully open during use, the line from tank to manifold must include a regulator to reduce the pressure to about 20psi. The line should also include a ball-type shutoff valve for flow control and faster system activation. Third, and most important, the CO_2 tank must be securely mounted or chained in an upright position near the cooling unit itself. The solidness of the mount is important because even though CO_2 is inert, the tank is highly pressurized and dangerous if damaged. Further, the tank's position is important because if the tank is laid on its side, the entire system will freeze up. And finally, of course, the shorter the CO_2 hose, the less chance there is that it will be damaged, and the greater the likelihood that all system controls will be conveniently close to each other.

As it did for the University of Wisconsin's production of *Evelyn and the Polka King*, this system can generate a pleasing and relatively long-lasting ground fog. Since it is tempting to overdo a good thing, the reader is reminded that fluid-based fogs can irritate the human respiratory system, and that Actors' Equity and others recommend them for "intermittent use in moderation." Before you plan to use this or any other fluid-based fog generator, obtain the relevant MSDS (Material Safety Data Sheet) from the manufacturer and use the product responsibly.

ನಾನಾನಾ

Each year, many shows are performed in front of translucent cycs lit to simulate a night sky. Many of those cycs hide moon boxes whose front openings are cut to resemble one of the moon's phases. The effect is often lovely — even striking — but no matter how artfully the lighting designer manages subtle shifts in color and intensity, most of these moons remain stubbornly static: usually in the same place in the sky and nearly always in the same phase. This article describes a simple rig that lets a scenic moon sweep across the sky in a gentle arc and simultaneously change phase. The rig uses no motors, no gears, no sophisticated control circuitry: its operation is powered by a stagehand and by gravity.

COMPONENTS AND OPERATION

The design incorporates two pendulums. One of them is the spotline-hung moon box itself, whose circular opening represents a full moon of the desired size. This pendulum is equipped with an operating line that is used to change the moon's position in the sky. The second pendulum, a simple, mostly circular panel, is a cover for the opening in the moon box. Cut a little larger than the moon box's opening and attached to the face of the moon box at a single pivot point, the cover is gravity-driven and gradually reveals more or less of the moon's face as a stagehand hauls the moon box out or lets it in. Figure 1 illustrates the rig's operation.

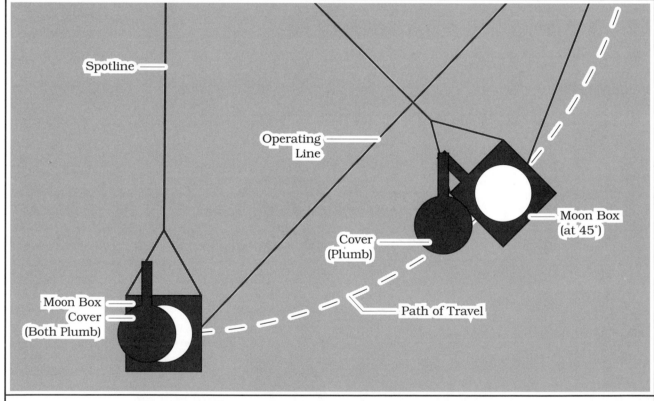

FIGURE 1: COMPONENTS AND OPERATING PRINCIPLE

DESIGNING THE RIG

The designer's drawings provided most of the information we needed to plan the rig for a dance concert at Northern Illinois University. Figures 2 through 4 illustrate our use of drafting to derive the one missing piece of data: the location of the cover's pivot relative to the front of our moon box.

Though this rig has the potential to hide or reveal all of a moon's face, a given theater's structure may limit the possibilities. Gently sweeping paths of travel require long spotlines, for instance, and some grids are simply too low to accommodate them. Technical Designers are well advised to do the drafting before promising the moon . . . .

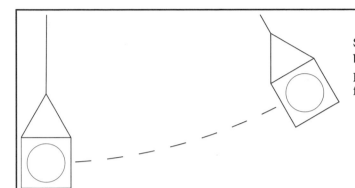

Step A: Lay out a front elevation of the moon box's path of travel, showing the box in position at both ends of the path. Draw the full-moon face on the box in both positions.

FIGURE 2: PLANNING – STEP A

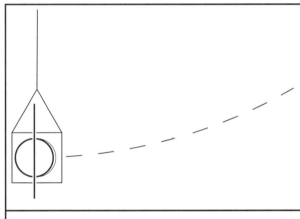

Step B: Referring to the designer's drawings, draw the cover on the low-trim representation of the moon box, positioning it to produce the desired crescent shape. Erect a vertical line through the center of the cover.

FIGURE 3: PLANNING – STEP B

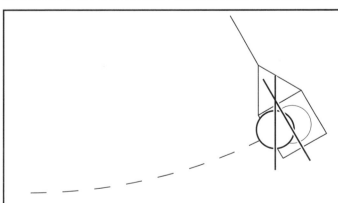

Step C: Transfer the recently erected vertical line to the high-trim representation of the moon box, rotating and locating that line accurately. Draw the cover on this view, again positioning it to produce the desired shape. Erect a new vertical through the cover's center. The intersection of the two erected lines represents the location of the cover's pivot.

FIGURE 4: PLANNING – STEP C

VARIABLES TO CONSIDER

The length of the spotline is only one of the variables that affect the way the moon looks throughout its travel. Figure 5 illustrates, for instance, that the distance between the cover's pivot and its center affects the relative quickness with which the moon changes from crescent to full. And Figure 6 shows the changes in the moon's attitude that result from subtle shifts in the cover's pivot location.

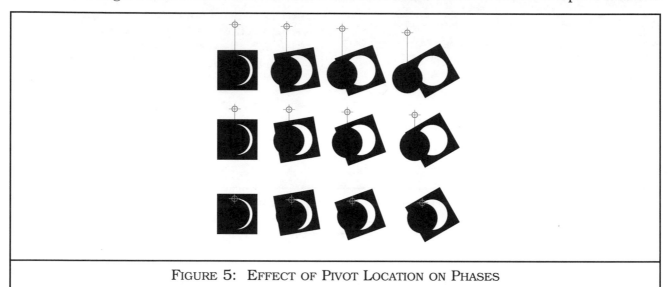

FIGURE 5: EFFECT OF PIVOT LOCATION ON PHASES

FIGURE 6: EFFECT OF PIVOT LOCATION ON ALTITUDE

CONCLUSION

Though it produces very believable crescent moons, this approach doesn't accurately simulate all lunar phases. In fact, any serious astronomers in the audience will probably grumble that, once more than half the moon's face is revealed, the effect resembles a lunar eclipse rather than a gibbous moon. The lapse is, however, astronomical in a scientific sense only, and even the physical scientists in the audience will welcome the variety, spectacle, and life that this rig can give a scenic moon.

In reviewing the requirements for a dance piece dealing with the life and music of Jim Morrison and the Doors, Northern Illinois University Resident Lighting Designer Mark C. Williams casually remarked, "and then the dancer holds up 'The World's Brightest Glowing Thing.'" Mark's objective was to symbolize the short, bright candle of Morrison's life with an effect that had the intensity of burning magnesium. But the Lighting Designer's objective left the Master Electrician (me) with two questions: "What is The World's Brightest Glowing Thing?" and "How is it powered?"

The Thing was to be smuggled onstage by a dancer in the corps and passed to the crouched Morrison figure, while the rest of the dancers formed a people-pile around him. Then "Morrison" would slowly stand, holding the Thing out in front of him as though offering it to the World. Suddenly, the Thing would throw a brilliant light that would silhouette the dancer against the cyc for just a few moments. Then the light would suddenly go out, and the Thing would be passed to another member of the corps, who would spirit it offstage.

What I needed was an extremely safe and compact source of brilliant light that a dancer could easily trigger and that my novice crew could comfortably and confidently prepare for each show. With all the action of the dance, paging a cable around scenery and through the people-pile would be a major headache, so I was reluctant to use a cabled source. Similarly, given the dancers' proximity to the effect and the need for multiple handoffs, using a small pyro device was out of the question. My standard stage lamp catalogs offered a few battery-powered possibilities, but the prices were quite prohibitive — and when I examined the potential cost of high-amperage battery packs, I could hear my budget scream.

Just as I was wondering how to tell the Designer "It can't be done," one of my former students arrived, needing some help in replacing her burned-out headlight. The replacement lamp didn't look much like a "normal headlight" to me. It was just an ordinary-looking lamp — you know, like an FEL. I've been driving too many old trucks . . . .

While installing the lamp and cursing the engineer who had designed the headlight housing, I realized that I was holding a perfect, low-voltage, high-intensity point source. If only the power supply could be more convenient than the one that was currently acidifying my elbow. As I washed up, I thought of the 12v cordless drill I had recently purchased. Surely, driving screws required a healthy amperage. Besides, the effect I needed to power wouldn't last more than a minute, and my Panasonic EY9001's battery could be recharged in 15 minutes. So, a few hours later, after convincing a counterperson that "I Really Don't Care What Car It Fits," I emerged from the local auto parts emporium $15 poorer but with a 12v 65/45-watt halogen headlamp, type 9004, in my possession.

CONSTRUCTION

After cutting away the lamp's protective plastic skirt to access the contact pins, I determined the appropriate pin-out with my VOM and then soldered both the hot leads and the common to short lengths of 12-gauge wire. I formed some battery connections by soldering pieces of brass shim stock to more 12-gauge wire and then folded them to provide large, flat surfaces to mate with the battery contacts.

Figure 1 illustrates the wooden project box I built from 1x3 and $\frac{1}{4}$" lauan. Each side of the box was stapled to the 1x3 base, but the joints between adjacent sides and between the sides and the top were just gaffers-taped so that the crew could easily get to the battery if the need should arise. The dimensions noted in Figure 1 left just enough room for the battery, the bases of the lamp, and a toggle switch. I wired the lamp to the battery and switch through a hole in the box's lid, and to

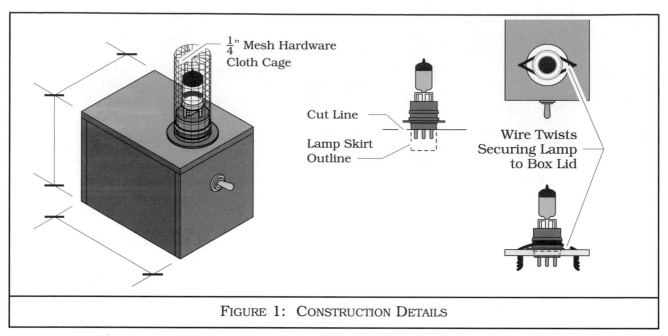

FIGURE 1: CONSTRUCTION DETAILS

secure the lamp, I replaced its O-Ring with two pieces of wire that I wrapped around the lamp's base and twisted together underneath the lid as shown. To protect the envelope from finger contact and to prevent anyone's being injured if the lamp shattered, I encased the lamp in a cage made of $\frac{1}{4}$" mesh hardware cloth, fastening the cage in place with a nylon wire-tie.

COMMENTARY

No practical could have been easier to build, and even the steps I took to allow for trouble-shooting proved unnecessary: I never had to replace the lamp, and the battery never needed a re-charge. Best of all, the unit really did look like "The World's Brightest Glowing Thing."

A Yale School of Drama production for which I was the Master Electrician called for a 10'-long foot-light unit at the front edge of the deck to disappear quickly after the first scene and remain hidden throughout the rest of the play. The simple and inexpensive two-part device we used allowed ten Pro-cans to swing downward simultaneously and then be hidden behind a specially rigged commando-cloth masking panel. Assistant Technical Director Jim Kempf developed the conceptual outlines of the rig. Building and installing this rig took only a few hours, and (not counting the Pro-cans themselves) the components cost less than $50.

THE MAIN COMPONENTS

Figure 1 represents a centerline section through the overhanging deck, the footlight unit, and the masking rig. The ten pivot arms that carried the Pro-cans were made of $\frac{3}{16}$" x 1" bar stock bent to suit the relationship between the deck and the studwalls. The arms extended from the Pro-cans'

mounting position to a common shaft mounted to the upstage side of the deck's first studwall, 18" back from the edge of the deck. The shaft was located high enough above the house floor that the arms could swing through the near-90° arc that would guarantee their being masked.

The pivot arms were welded at 1'-0" intervals along the length of an 11'-0" shaft of $1\frac{1}{4}$" schedule 40 black pipe. Three simple, shop-built bearings of bar stock and $1\frac{1}{2}$" schedule 40 black pipe screwed to the upper ends of convenient studs carried the shaft. Figure 2 on the next page illustrates the shaft and bearing details. Figure 3 offers a closer look at the rig.

THE OPERATING LINE

We used a $\frac{1}{16}$" aircraft-cable operating line to drive the rig. The weight involved was so light, however, that we used screw-eyes instead of sheaves to mule the operating line to its tie-off. We weighted the operating line for our convenience in re-setting, but since the rig posed no safety threat we terminated the operating line in a simple dog clip. The essential features of the operating line are shown in Figure 3.

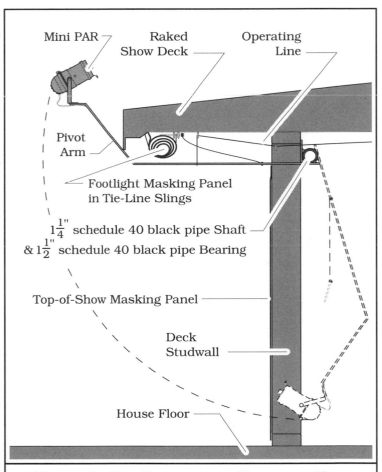

Mini PAR · Raked Show Deck · Operating Line · Pivot Arm · Footlight Masking Panel in Tie-Line Slings · $1\frac{1}{4}$" schedule 40 black pipe Shaft & $1\frac{1}{2}$" schedule 40 black pipe Bearing · Top-of-Show Masking Panel · Deck Studwall · House Floor

FIGURE 1: THE DISAPPEARING FOOTLIGHT UNIT

MASKING

As Figure 3 shows, the Footlight Masking Panel was suspended, neatly rolled, in a pair of tie-line slings below the deck. Underneath the footlight unit, another panel, the Top-of-Show, Masking Panel was gaffers-taped to the studs and masked the deck studwall while the footlights were up.

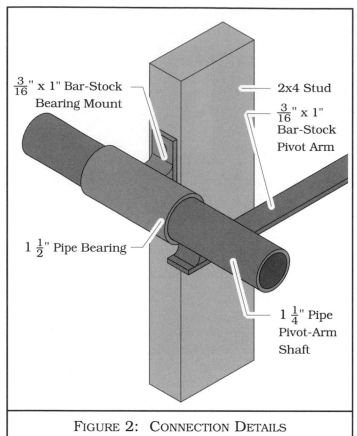

FIGURE 2: CONNECTION DETAILS

- $\frac{3}{16}$" x 1" Bar-Stock Bearing Mount
- 2x4 Stud
- $\frac{3}{16}$" x 1" Bar-Stock Pivot Arm
- $1\frac{1}{2}$" Pipe Bearing
- $1\frac{1}{4}$" Pipe Pivot-Arm Shaft

When the footlight unit was tripped, the pivot arms broke the Top-of-Show Masking Panel's taped connections, letting it fall to the floor. A little farther in their travel, two of the ganged pivot arms pulled the pins of two nail-and-screw-eye catches, and the Footlight Masking Panel unfurled, covering the Pro-cans, pivot arms, studwall, and the heap of commando cloth that the Top-of-Show Masking Panel had become. The trick happened so quickly that the Footlight Masking Panel always unfurled with an audible "thwop." But the insignificant noise was easily covered by a relatively quiet music cue.

FINAL COMMENTS

The mechanism operated reliably, and its reset never took more than ten minutes. One run crew member rolled up the Footlight Masking Panel and held it and the pivot arms up while another secured the operating line's dog clip. Next, after resetting the tie-line slings, one or both people re-taped the Top-of-Show Masking Panel to the deck studwall.

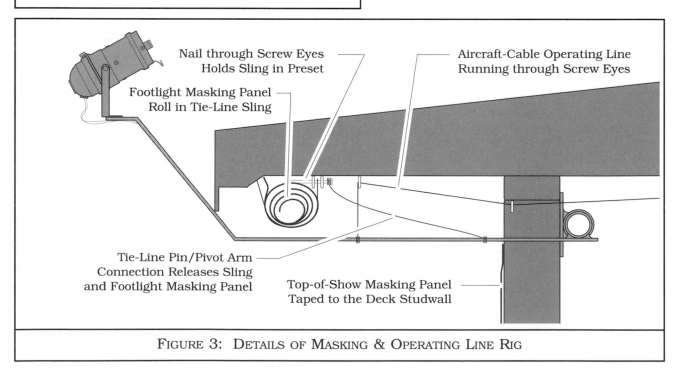

- Nail through Screw Eyes Holds Sling in Preset
- Aircraft-Cable Operating Line Running through Screw Eyes
- Footlight Masking Panel Roll in Tie-Line Sling
- Tie-Line Pin/Pivot Arm Connection Releases Sling and Footlight Masking Panel
- Top-of-Show Masking Panel Taped to the Deck Studwall

FIGURE 3: DETAILS OF MASKING & OPERATING LINE RIG

Twice during each performance of the University of Toledo's production of *The Actor's Nightmare*, a recorded voice sternly warned the audience that the taking of pictures was not permitted. Those warnings were immediately followed by a sequence of flashes — from cameras hidden on the set and triggered remotely. Toledo student Lino Stavole's suggestion that we might be able to use Kodak's "throw-away" cameras for the flash effects was a gold mine! The tiny, inexpensive Kodak Fun Flash® has great potential for achieving many types of flash effects.

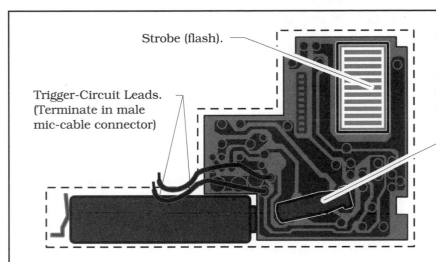

Strobe (flash).

Trigger-Circuit Leads.
(Terminate in male
mic-cable connector)

Broken line surrounds essential circuitry (capacitor, battery, and strobe), which would fit in an opening $2\frac{3}{8}$" tall, 4" wide, and $1\frac{1}{4}$" deep.

Charging contact.
Provide alternate switch or
solder contact down and
remove battery.

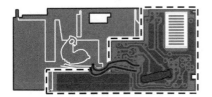

Lightest grey at right indicates case parts that could be cut off and discarded. Essential parts are detailed above.

FIGURE 1: FRONT VIEW OF KODAK'S FUN FLASH®, CASE REMOVED

After prying a Fun Flash® apart, we found it needed only the two modifications illustrated above. First, to achieve remote firing, we terminated the strobe's trigger-circuit leads in a male mic-cable connector. We plugged this connector into one end of a 25' cable, whose other end terminated in a normal-open pushbutton. Second, having decided we would remove the battery between uses, we soldered the camera's spring-steel charging contact down. (We could certainly have installed a remote switch instead.) With that, the unit was ready for installation and use. We found that the unit worked reliably with trigger cables up to 40' long and that, with a good battery, capacitor charging took only about 10 seconds. Not bad for a $20 investment!

"My computer is out to get me!" It's not an uncommon suspicion in today's PC-saturated world. But for the characters of *Murder by Numbers*, that vague suspicion becomes chilling conviction as an apparently ordinary desktop computer takes over the lives (and deaths) of its human housemates. The plot of this play requires a "computer with personality" — a machine able to engage in dialogue with other characters and to exhibit human-like emotional shadings and timing on cue. For the director of the 1995 production at Brisbane (Australia's) Playhouse, the decision to use an offstage actor to speak the computer's lines was immediately clear; but for the company's technical staff, the means of giving life to the inanimate desktop computer onstage was decidedly less so.

Our solution was to synchronize sound with pulses of light to produce the necessary illusion. A small incandescent light hidden in a gutted computer monitor was wired to glow brightly when lit. A small, powered speaker, which would provide amplification and sound localization for the audience, was also housed in the empty monitor.

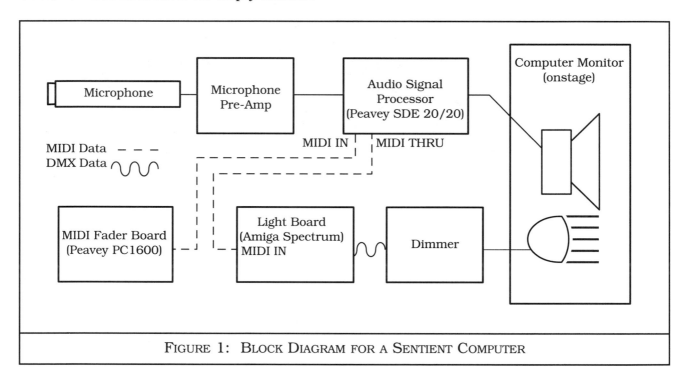

FIGURE 1: BLOCK DIAGRAM FOR A SENTIENT COMPUTER

AUDIO PROCESSING

The block diagram above describes how the computer voice was produced. A microphone signal was sent via a preamplifier into a digital multi-effects processor (a Peavey SDE 20/20). The complete processing patch comprised two pitch shifts — one an octave lower than the actor's vocal pitch; the other, six tones higher (with regeneration applied) — followed by a variable low-pass resonant filter. Using the processor's internal mixer, a small amount of the original voice signal was mixed back into the processed signal to enhance dialog intelligibility.

The actor was given expressive control of the processor through use of a backstage Peavey PC1600, a MIDI (Musical Instrument Digital Interface) fader board which was programmed to generate MIDI controller #6 in response to the actor's movement of a fader. The MIDI data was fed to the audio processor's MIDI IN, which was set up to respond by opening the low-pass filter and increasing the resonance. With this variable control, low fader values produced a sedate, smooth voice, and high fader values generated shrieking, angry tones.

CONTROLLING THE LIGHT

It was decided that, whenever the computer spoke, the light in the monitor case should flash or dim in response to changes in the actor's voice. If the computer were to seem truly sentient, changes in the sound and light would have to be neatly synchronized. It was logical to give real-time control of both elements to the actor, so that he could modulate them as the dramatic moment required. The use of the MIDI protocol permitted simultaneous adjustment of both sound and light with the use of a single fader.

MIDI data was fed from the MIDI THRU on the Peavey PC1600 audio processor to the MIDI IN of an Amiga Spectrum, a software-based light board, one of whose dimmers was set to respond to MIDI controller #6. The resultant DMX output of the board was routed to a dimmer which controlled the brightness of the lamp in the computer monitor.

THE RESULT

The ultimate effect of this setup was that the actor could ride the MIDI fader as he pleased during his dialogue, causing the computer's tone of voice and its flashes of emotion to vary simultaneously. Combined with the actor's natural variations in delivery from performance to performance, this produced a highly effective "computer presence" on the stage.

This technique can be readily adapted for many situations in which multiple events need to be controlled simultaneously from a single location. Two words of advice for would-be MIDI users: do not attempt to run MIDI data cables more than 50 feet without installing a MIDI line driver; and do check carefully any devices that you wish to control via MIDI, for not all devices respond to MIDI, and those that do, vary considerably in the way they respond.

ﻉﺍﻉﺍﻉﺍ

The director of PCPA's *Damn Yankees* wanted the devil character, Applegate, to pitch a flash-paper fireball like a baseball — a neat trick for performer and technician alike. For the trick to be effective and safe, Applegate would need control over its ignition and trajectory. Figures 1 and 2 show the launcher we built which met both needs. Its circuitry allowed instantaneous firing at any time during the actor's wind-up and delivery, and its barrel provided at least reasonable control over the flash paper's flight path.

THE COMPONENTS

The launcher consists of two distinct assemblies — an Arming Unit and a Firing Unit — joined by arm's-length leads of 28-gauge wire sewn into the actor's costume. The Arming Unit consists of 4 AA batteries lying side by side in a shallow plastic case for maximum concealability. A recessed slide switch mounted on a separate case is the launcher's arming switch. (The tab of electrician's tape over the switch in the photo helped keep our Applegate's movements from accidentally disarming our launcher.) The LED "armed" indicator above the slide switch lights up whenever the circuit is on.

Figure 1 also shows the parts of the Firing Unit: a $3\frac{1}{4}$" barrel made of $\frac{3}{8}$" brass tube and fitted with a 6" length of $\frac{1}{2}$" brass strap. The strap wraps around the actor's first and index fingers, holding the firing pushbutton, as well as the barrel, securely in place.

Figure 2 shows how easily and comfortably the Firing Unit can be concealed by an actor's hand.

CONSTRUCTION NOTES

All dimensions noted in Figure 3 should be treated as guidelines only, for launchers of this sort are "actor-specific." The length of the brass strap for the finger mounts and the length of the barrel will depend on the size of a given actor's hand.

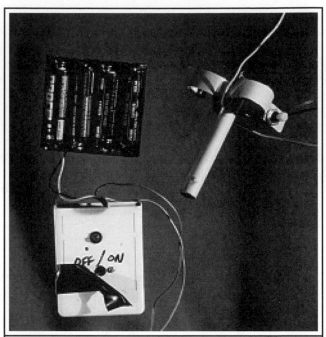

FIGURE 1: ARMING UNIT & FIRING UNIT

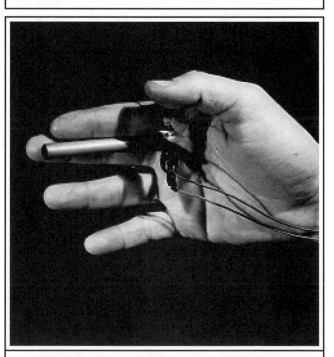

FIGURE 2: PALMING THE FIRING UNIT

It is also helpful to know in advance whether the actor involved is right-handed or left-handed, for the pushbutton is thumb-operated. We secured the two sides of the strap together with a small brass screw whose point we then ground smooth.

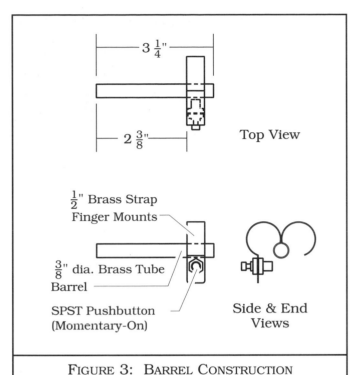

½" Brass Strap
Finger Mounts

3/8" dia. Brass Tube
Barrel

SPST Pushbutton
(Momentary-On)

Top View

Side & End
Views

FIGURE 3: BARREL CONSTRUCTION

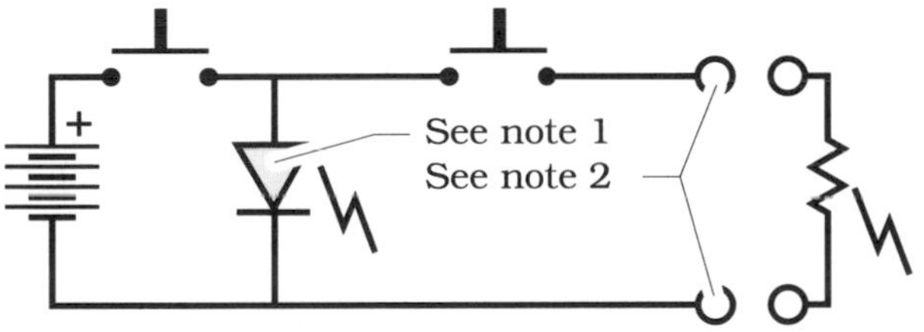

See note 1
See note 2

Arming Circuit:
4 AA Batteries
SPST Sliding Switch
LED

Firing Circuit:
SPST Momentary-On
Pushbutton Switch
Estes Model Rocket
Igniter

Notes:

1. Use an LED like Radio Shack 276-208 that will
not burn out at the voltage supplied by the
batteries.

2. One lead from the firing switch and one from the
arming switch are fitted with male disconnect
terminals to facilitate connection to the igniter leads.
See Figure 5.

FIGURE 4: CIRCUITRY

Figure 4 details the assembly of the launcher's circuitry. To assure instantaneous ignition, we used Estes Model Rocket Igniters instead of the more common electric matches to fire the effect. Estes, located in Penrose, Colorado, can be reached at (719) 372-6565.

PREPARATION AND LOADING NOTES

Before loading the launcher, make sure the arming switch is off and the batteries are removed. See Figure 5 for a step-by-step guide to preparation and loading.

A single igniter would fire the effect, but ganging a pair of them and heat-shrinking the ganged leads has advantages. Ganging igniters provides a form of assurance — at least one of the two is likely to fire. The heat shrink reinforces the igniters' leads and defeats the possibility that they will short out against each other or the brass barrel. A collar of electricians' tape wrapped just below the igniters' heads provides strain-relief against wishboning.

The amount of flash paper used and the diameter of the launcher's barrel together govern how big a fireball will be, how far it will fly, and how loud the effect's popping sound will be. Needless to say, experimenting in the shop prior to tech is recommended.

The last steps before making the electrical connections are to bend the protruding igniter leads down so they will fit comfortably in the performer's hand, and to carefully seal the rear of the tube with electrical tape. This seal must be sound enough to protect the performer's hand from the brief but quite intense "blowback" firing the launcher produces.

ELECTRICAL CONNECTIONS

After sealing the flashpaper wad and the igniter into the barrel, bend the ends of the igniter leads through the holes in the male disconnect terminals coming from the Arming Unit and the "fire" pushbutton. Wrap these contact points in electrical tape to provide strain relief and prevent electrical shorting. Then lay them on top of one another and bind them together to provide further strain relief. Before reloading the batteries, double check that the Arming Unit's switch is off.

FINAL NOTES

A director's desire to produce pyrotechnics from a performer's person is something no Master Electrician or Properties Master likes to hear. This device offers a production a reliable and safe solution that can be made for as little as $20 with parts obtained at Radio Shack or any other hobby store. Over the course of a 24-performance run, the device achieved a 96% success rate. Safety is enhanced by the control gained over exactly when the device fires and therefore over the direction in which the burning flash paper is sent. Nevertheless, state or municipal fire regulations would prohibit the use of this device in many localities. Before planning to build one, check with the local Fire Marshal.

The author would like to thank PCPA's Lighting Director Mike Peterson and Properties Director Tim Hogan for their help in developing this device.

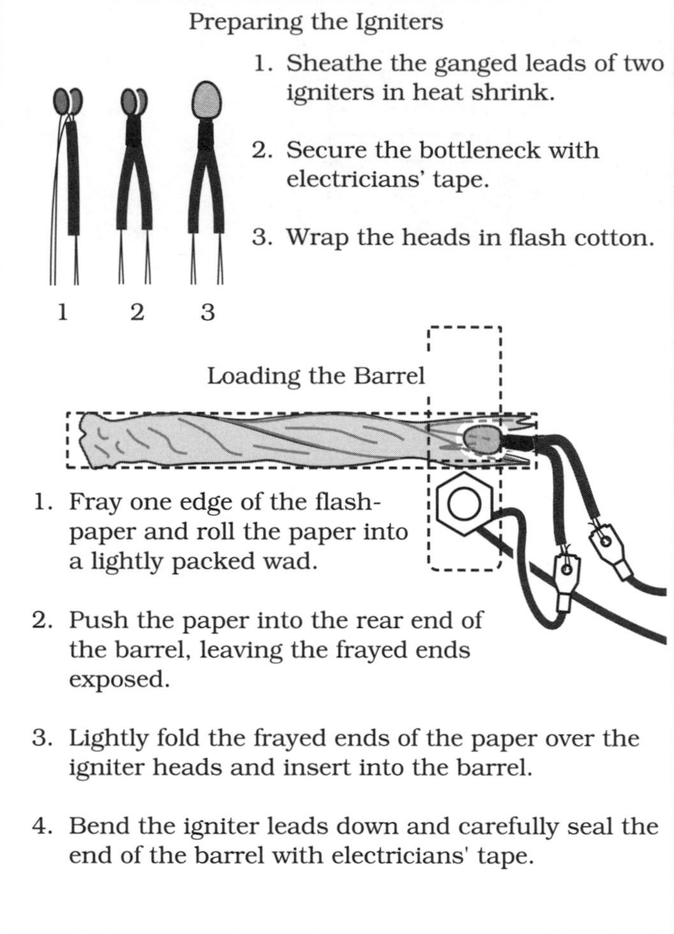

Preparing the Igniters

1. Sheathe the ganged leads of two igniters in heat shrink.

2. Secure the bottleneck with electricians' tape.

3. Wrap the heads in flash cotton.

1   2   3

Loading the Barrel

1. Fray one edge of the flash-paper and roll the paper into a lightly packed wad.

2. Push the paper into the rear end of the barrel, leaving the frayed ends exposed.

3. Lightly fold the frayed ends of the paper over the igniter heads and insert into the barrel.

4. Bend the igniter leads down and carefully seal the end of the barrel with electricians' tape.

FIGURE 5: PREPARATION AND LOADING

For the Yale Repertory Theatre's 1997 production of *The Skin of Our Teeth*, Director Liz Diamond and Lighting Designer Jennifer Tipton wanted to create a 5-minute stylized lighting effect to simulate the downpour during the flood. Since renting a scene machine was beyond the budget allocated for this effect, we looked for alternative solutions. Harking back to the days of disco, we experimented with the mirror-ball method of reflecting light. We worked with a lighting instrument and a drum covered in mirrored tiles — a rain drum. By changing the arrangement of the tiles, the angle of the light, and the rate of rotation, we were able to produce the effect we wanted. Though this article describes the drum built for our production, the details can be modified to fit your specific needs.

POSITION AND LIGHTING

For our effect, we placed 3 rain drums on the Yale Repertory Theatre's first-beam catwalk, positioning them as shown in Figure 1. Each drum was lit by an Altman 6x16. The lens of the instrument was roughly 24" away from the drum and we did not shutter or gel the instruments as we did not want to cut down on the light output. Since the reflected light had a taller spread than we wanted, we hung a sheet of tin on the catwalk pipe in front of the drum to act as a shutter.

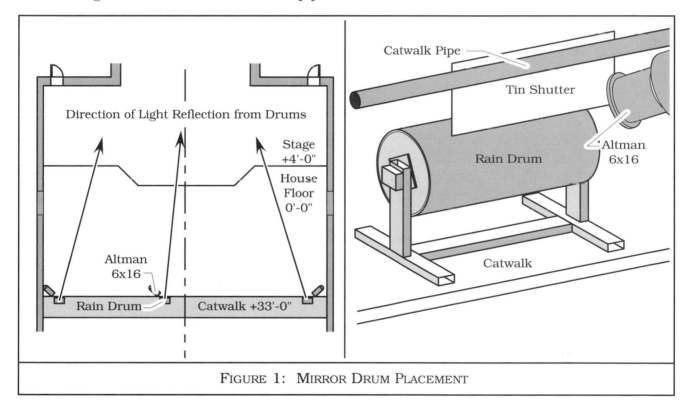

FIGURE 1: MIRROR DRUM PLACEMENT

MATERIALS AND CONSTRUCTION

To build each drum, we used a 20" length of 9"-diameter Sonotube®. Each end of the tube was plugged with a $\frac{3}{4}$" plywood disc. In the center of each disc, we drilled a hole for a 24"-long, $\frac{3}{4}$"-diameter steel drive rod. After drilling out one end of the drive rod to receive the shaft of a small motor, we tapped a hole for a set screw that would join the two. This design made the use of any belt or chain drive assemblies unnecessary. We welded a steel plate to the drive rod, as in Figure 2, and screwed it to the plywood plug to connect the drum and the drive rod.

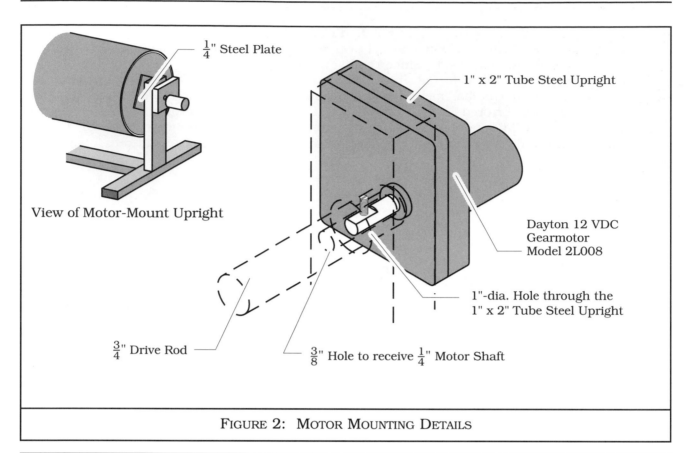

$\frac{1}{4}$" Steel Plate

1" x 2" Tube Steel Upright

View of Motor-Mount Upright

Dayton 12 VDC
Gearmotor
Model 2L008

1"-dia. Hole through the
1" x 2" Tube Steel Upright

$\frac{3}{4}$" Drive Rod

$\frac{3}{8}$" Hole to receive $\frac{1}{4}$" Motor Shaft

FIGURE 2: MOTOR MOUNTING DETAILS

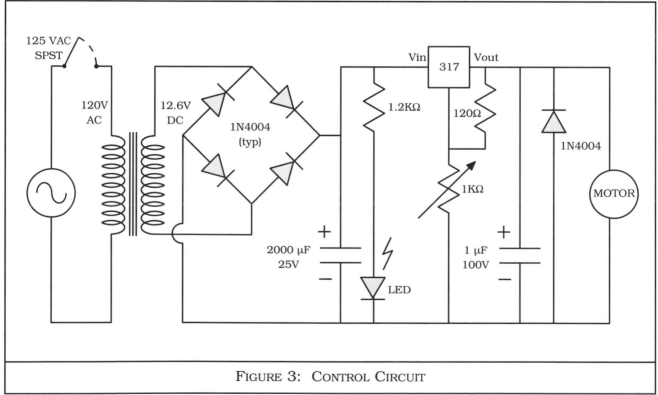

125 VAC
SPST

120V
AC

12.6V
DC

1N4004
(typ)

Vin   317   Vout

1.2KΩ   120Ω

1N4004

1KΩ

2000 µF
25V

1 µF
100V

MOTOR

LED

FIGURE 3: CONTROL CIRCUIT

Local craft stores sell small packages of $\frac{1}{4}$" square mirror tiles, but we purchased ours in bulk from a Disco Supplies Dealer. We hot-glued each tile onto the drum in a random fashion, covering approximately 50% of the drum's surface, making sure to leave spaces between the tiles and to orient them in different directions. The density and the randomness of the tiles' placement affected "how hard it was raining" onstage: the more tiles we added, the harder it rained.

The frame was built out of 1x2 tube steel. The base measured 12" x 22"; the uprights, 12". We mounted a Dayton 12VDC gearmotor (model 2L008) that we bought from Grainger onto the frame, centering its shaft in a 1" hole that we had previously drilled in the center of one upright. To the other upright, we attached a UHMW block with a $\frac{3}{4}$" hole in the center to act as a bearing. The drive rod fit snugly into the UHMW block on one end of the frame and was secured to the motor with a set screw on the other end.

CONTROL

Rather than buy a more expensive controller, we built the control circuit (see Figure 3) for the effect and ran control cables from the motors to the booth. The control box allowed us to plug into a 120VAC outlet and vary the motor's speed from a remote location. To achieve the look we wanted, we slowed the motors to 2 to 4 RPM, causing them to become very noisy. Higher motor speeds cut down on the noise, but blurred the specks of light, ruining the effect. Our sound effects masked the motor noise, but you may want to choose a different motor if noise is an issue.

❧❧❧❧

I've always fancied myself a good campfire builder, but I never thought I'd put this skill to use in the theatre! For The Bread Loaf Theater's recent production of Shakespeare's Henriad series, our designer asked that each show include six large outdoor bonfires. The shows were going to run for 12 days straight in rotating repertory, and every show involved bonfires at some point. In each show, both actors and audience members were close to the fires when they were lit and while they burned. The fires were burned in 5' tall braziers, which were used in different locations each night. The huge fires were to be started by an actor carrying a torch and had to instantly ignite. Once lit, the fires needed to burn brightly for 45 minutes, at which point they were extinguished. The fires were untouched for at least 15 minutes prior to being ignited, which meant that any accelerant used needed a low volatility so it didn't evaporate, or cause an explosion when lit. The fires needed to be predictable, light immediately in wind or rain, and be safe for actors and audience — in short they needed to be everything fire usually isn't!

The solution, after many hours of trial and error, culminated in the following recipe for the perfect fire. The braziers were made of steel mesh wrapped into a shallow cone, onto which square tube steel legs were welded. We then ripped down 1x4 to $\frac{3}{4}$" x $\frac{3}{4}$" x 8" sticks. These were placed in the brazier oriented like petals on a flower radiating out from the center. We placed them close enough to block nearly all airflow to the fires from underneath.

Making fire burst safely and reliably into flames is difficult. In our early experiments, the accelerant either evaporated, caused a giant fireball, or didn't burn hot enough to light the wood. The solution was to fold a 36" x 48" piece of butcher paper into quarters and form it into a bowl by rolling the outside edges inward. The bowl, 4-paper-layers thick, was placed in the brazier and filled about a third full with charcoal lighter fluid. Once it had

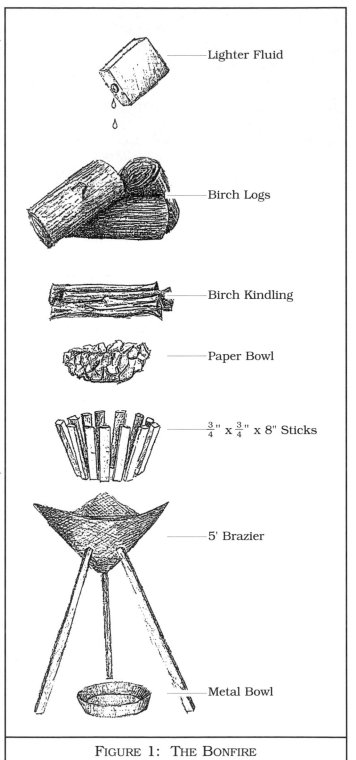

Lighter Fluid

Birch Logs

Birch Kindling

Paper Bowl

$\frac{3}{4}$" x $\frac{3}{4}$" x 8" Sticks

5' Brazier

Metal Bowl

FIGURE 1: THE BONFIRE

become completely saturated, the paper held a reservoir of the lighter fluid. With fewer than four layers, the bowl burned too quickly, and the lighter fluid fell out of the bottom of the brazier, creating a flaming puddle.

The bulk of the fires' fuel was birch kindling and logs. We experimented with pine, oak, cherry, and maple logs, but settled on the birch because it exploded the least, lit the easiest, and burned sufficiently long and brightly. It was crucial for the kindling and logs to be thoroughly dry and seasoned. Unseasoned logs were a complete failure. The best results were achieved when approximately twelve 1" thick kindling pieces were laid in a brazier, all oriented in the same direction with a few birch logs placed on top.

After adding the logs, the entire assembly was given a thorough dousing of lighter fluid. The lighter fluid tended to run off the logs and drip onto the ground, which would be problematic if burning embers fell from the fire into the flammable puddle. Therefore, before the final dousing each night, we laid a scrap of plywood under the brazier to catch drips of accelerant. Once the braziers had finished dripping (about 60 seconds), we removed the plywood and placed a metal bowl, about 12" in diameter with 2" of water, under the brazier to extinguish any of the larger embers that might fall. The plywood, now soaked in lighter fluid, was removed from the area and placed flat on the ground, damp side up, to dry safely.

In addition to careful assembly, we took a few more safety precautions. Each night we thoroughly hosed the ground around each brazier. Also, there was a fire attendant standing inconspicuously near each fire with a fire extinguisher filled with water and a wet towel. In the unlikely event that a spark landed on an actor or audience member's clothing and began to singe, it could be easily and undramatically extinguished with the wet towel.

All in all, the fires were a huge success. They were predictable, reliable, and safe.

ঙ৳ঙ৳ঙ

A Free-Falling Ball of Light

Donald W. Titus

For each performance of a recent production of *Heaven,* we needed an "astrological ball of light" to fall, roll, and bounce freely down a 20' commercial plastic trash chute into an onstage dumpster. After considering and discarding several alternatives including chase effects and battery-powered light sources, we settled on the lighting fixture described here.

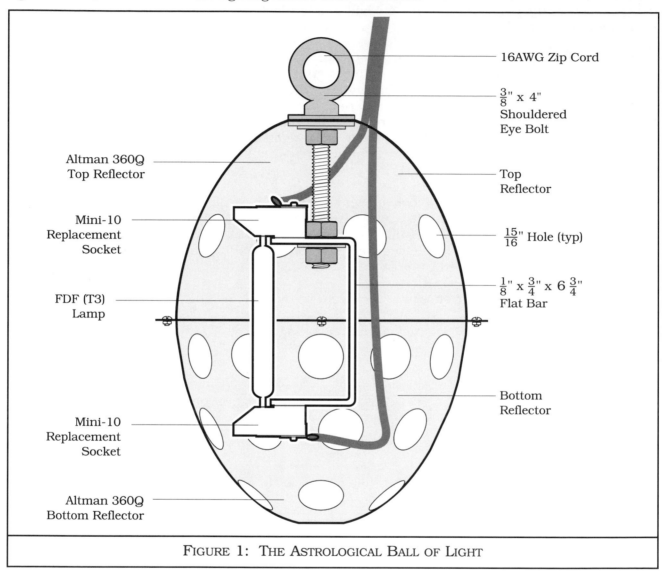

FIGURE 1: THE ASTROLOGICAL BALL OF LIGHT

THE SHELL

To form a protective shell, I modified two Altman 360Q reflectors. Their durability and the fact that their lamp-base holes are centered made them ideal for this use. After drilling a series of $\frac{3}{8}$" pilot holes, I used a Greenlee punch to make rings of $\frac{15}{16}$"-diameter holes around both reflectors as shown in Figure 1. Different sizes and/or patterns of holes would certainly work, but for the record, I gave the bottom reflector three rings of holes: a 5-hole ring near the lamp-base hole; a 12-hole ring near the rim; and a 9-hole ring about halfway between them. Adding holes after initial testing would be fairly simple, so I gave the top reflector only 1 ring of 9 holes. Testing showed that punching more holes was unnecessary. Near the top reflector's lamp-base hole, I drilled a $\frac{3}{8}$" hole for the wiring. After finishing the shell, I began work on the lamp assembly.

LAMP ASSEMBLY

I chose an FDF (T3) lamp as the light source for its availability and low cost. In building the lamp assembly, I used only a $6\frac{3}{4}$" length of $\frac{1}{8}$" x $\frac{3}{4}$" flat bar, a $\frac{3}{8}$" x 4" shouldered eyebolt, and two mini-10 replacement sockets. Measuring in $\frac{1}{4}$" from each end of the flat bar, I drilled and tapped a hole for a #4 screw for socket attachment. I also drilled a $\frac{7}{16}$" hole $1\frac{3}{16}$" from one end of the bar to receive the eyebolt. I then bent the flat bar $1\frac{3}{4}$" from each end, attached the sockets, and connected them to the crimped ends of a 30' length of 16awg zip cord.

I passed the eyebolt through the lamp-base hole in the top reflector and secured it with a nut and washer. I then screwed a second nut and washer onto the end of the eyebolt and adjusted this second nut so that the lamp's filament would be roughly centered in the assembled shell. Next, having attached the lamp assembly to the end of the eyebolt, I passed the zip cord through the $\frac{3}{8}$" hole in the top reflector and wire-tied it to the eye of the eyebolt for strain relief. Once I had installed the lamp, assembled the reflectors, and attached a pin connector to the end of the zip cord, our astrological ball of light was complete except for its rigging pickup.

THE RIGGING AND RELEASE MECHANISM

I rigged the ball to be dropped from the rod of a $\frac{1}{2}$"-19# pull-type solenoid (Grainger number 2X662). Since the ball's out-trim was 2' lower than the grid on which the solenoid was mounted, I split the zip cord leads about 2' above the ball and installed a circle cotter (McMaster-Carr 95390A318). If the ball had been heavier, I could have tailed-down to the eyebolt, but doing so proved unnecessary.

Simultaneously powering the lamp and solenoid with a non-dim created the desired illusion while preventing the audience from anticipating the effect. The zip cord was flexible enough not to hamper the free-fall look as the ball fell all the way into the dumpster, where it landed on a 3"-thick foam pad. The effect — which had taken less than two hours to build — operated spectacularly for twenty-five performances (plus techs) and we lost only two lamps to burnout.

≈≈≈

TECHNICAL BRIEF

Painting

For a production of *The Imaginary Invalid* at the University of Wisconsin LaCrosse, we gave our shop-built French Baroque furniture the necessary low-relief surface decoration with appliqués of Anaglypta®, an embossed wallpaper manufactured by British Crown Relief, Ltd. The following list outlines the steps we followed.

1. Cut lengths and shapes of the desired pattern from a roll of embossed wallpaper.

2. Soak pieces of wallpaper in clean, room-temperature water for one minute.

3. Allow the wallpaper to shed excess water.

4. Apply a thin coat of flexible glue and water (2 parts glue: 1 part water) to the surface of the piece to be covered.

5. Adhere the wallpaper to the glue-coated area, and then top coat the paper with more of the glue and water mixture. Let all surfaces dry thoroughly.

6. Base paint the surface with a latex paint thinned as much as possible. (Thicker base paint will obscure the pattern.) The base color should be a tint since it will be revealed in step 7 as the highlight color. Let the paint dry.

7. Apply the shadow color, lightly wiping the paint from raised areas of the pattern with a damp sponge, leaving the paint in the recessed areas. Let the paint dry.

8. Brush the raised areas with a coat of bronzing powder suspended in clear latex to create an effective gilded appearance.

9. Apply a gloss latex or other finish coat.

Since Anaglypta® is a 100% cotton product, the coat of flexible glue which is applied to its surface in step 5 is crucial. On samples without this coating, the wallpaper was damaged by the application of multiple coats of paint.

Anaglypta®, an imported wall covering which may be a bit difficult to find in some locales, ranges in price from $20.00 to $40.00 per roll depending on the supplier. Treating the Invalid's spinet and bench, armchair and matching ottoman, changing screen, side table, and two side chairs took less than half of a single roll. Anaglypta® is available from the following vendors among others:

Budget Paint & Wallpaper
4009 Minnehaha Avenue South
Minneapolis, MN 55406
(612) 724-7676

Norton Blumenthal, Inc.
979 Third Avenue
New York, NY 10022
(212) 752-2535

None of the materials used in this relief technique are toxic, and no special tools or skills are required. Perhaps one of this technique's most attractive aspects is the fact that it can be accomplished by a relatively unskilled work force. Our staff is always looking for construction and finishing techniques which can be effectively undertaken by students fulfilling crew requirements in the shop. A noteworthy bonus is the fact that those students who applied this technique to our furniture felt a great sense of accomplishment — "Beats sweeping floors!"

Technical Director for this production was Ron Stoffregen.

The marble patterns that sooner or later every scenic artist paints on wood can now be created quite quickly on fabric. The simple technique involves swirling a pattern into dye as it floats on a specially thickened water base and then floating pre-treated fabric on top of it. In mere seconds, the pattern is picked up by the fabric. After rinsing and drying, the fabric can be used on scenic elements such as narrow wall panels, on props and upholstery, and, of course, in costuming.

EQUIPMENT

Stretching the fabric on a frame will yield the best results, especially if the fabric pieces are relatively large. In addition to one or more fabric frames, you will also need two shallow, waterproof troughs — one for dyeing and one for rinsing — slightly larger than the dimensions of the frames. A pair of children's wading pools can be made to work in some instances; but I have also used troughs made of simple 1x3 Hollywood frames laid on the floor and lined with 4-mil plastic drop cloths. However the trough is made, the inside should be light and uniform so that you can see the dye pattern. You will also need a vat or sink large enough for soaking and rinsing the unframed fabric, as well as a washer and dryer, an iron, one or more large buckets, mops and other cleanup tools, rubber gloves, a respirator, and footwear with non-skid soles.

METHOD

Several manufacturers market competing lines of marbling colors, and you should follow the instructions written specifically for the dyes you use. The notes below summarize the typical method and offer the cautions and suggestions which apply regardless of dye choice.

PREPARING THE FABRIC

Wash the fabric to remove dirt, oils, and finishes. Special soaps are available from dye suppliers for this purpose and should be used for the best results. Some suppliers suggest adding a dye activator to the wash water. After washing the fabric wring it out well, but while it is still damp place it in whatever pre-soak the manufacturer recommends to insure that the fabric will absorb the dye. After the fabric has been pre-soaked, wring it out and hang it up to dry. You can use the spin cycle of a washing machine to wring the fabric out — as long as you're careful not to rinse it inadvertently. Rinsing reverses the effect of the pre-soak. Dampness, wrinkles, and folds result in unevenly dyed sections. Therefore, after the fabric is completely dry, iron it to remove any wrinkles. Rather than fold it, roll it on a tube for storage if you're not ready to dye it right away.

PREPARING AND USING THE DYEBATH

Mix the marbling base in a bucket. It will need to sit for anywhere from 15 minutes to 24 hours depending on the product you use, but it can be mixed in advance and stored in closed containers. Pour the base into the dye trough when you're ready for dyeing. Set up the rinse trough as close to the dye trough as is practical, and fill it with water. Working quickly, gently float the dyes on top of the base. If you work too slowly or if you agitate the base, the color can sink and/or combine with the base. Using a comb, rake, or other similar tool, gently swirl the dyes across the surface of the base without letting the tool dip so deep that it disturbs the base. Hold the framed fabric perfectly horizontal above the trough and lower it straight onto the dye. Float the fabric on the surface of the dye bath for a second or two. Do not allow it to sink into the dyebath. This is the most difficult part of the process and may require two or more people depending on the size of the fabric and its frame. Immediately after its removal from the dyebath, dunk the fabric and frame in the rinse trough to get rid of most of the excess dye. Take the fabric off the frame and move it to a sink or washer for a more thorough rinsing. If you're lucky enough to be working outdoors, you can simply hang the fabric on a line and hose it off. The marbling base is often reusable, but each pattern is literally lifted off the base with the fabric and can be used only once. Before "re-inking" the marbling base for the next piece of fabric, clean its surface of any dye residue by using sheets of newspaper as blotters.

FABRIC HANDLING AFTER DYEING

Instructions about post-dyeing processes vary from product to product. Typically, after the fabric has been rinsed and dried, the dye will need to be set, either by soaking it in a chemical solution or setting it with the heat of an iron or dryer. After that, it will need to be washed again to remove any remaining chemicals.

SAFETY

Many people are more sensitive to dye chemicals than they realize. If you're using powdered chemicals, wear a respirator with a dust/mist filter while you work. It is all too easy to inhale minute, airborne particles of powdered dyes; and relying on general ventilation is foolhardy. Fortunately, most marbling dyes come in a ready-to-use liquid form.

Regardless of the dye type, wear rubber gloves at all times when handling the fabric and dye. The chemical pre-soak stays in the fabric until the final wash, and even when the fabric is dry these chemicals can irritate the skin.

The marbling base is extremely slippery. It is almost impossible not to drip or spill some of the marbling base on the floor — especially while moving the fabric from the dye vat to the rinse vat. Wear non-skid footwear and clean spills up as soon as possible to prevent accidents.

FINAL NOTES

Manufacturers' claims that the marbling base can be reused indefinitely are not entirely true: it eventually becomes clouded with excess dye and produces a muddy pattern. When this happens the base should be discarded and the trough should be thoroughly cleaned before being refilled.

The marbling dyes I used work best on cotton and wool. I got fairly good results on silk, acetate, polyester, and cotton-polyester blends. Rayon and nylon gave poor results. A veritable rainbow of colors is available, including neon, pearlized, and metallics. The pearlized and metallics are somewhat disappointing, as the shimmering particles tend to separate out and sink faster than you can manipulate the fabric into position.

This technique's main drawback is that a continuous pattern, without breaks or seams, cannot be achieved on more than a few yards of fabric. Therefore, it is not particularly useful for treating large elements such as drops or groundcloths. On the other hand, dyeing the fabric is quite easy compared to fabric painting — and it's certainly faster. Many yards of fabric can be patterned in a few hours rather than in the days needed to hand-paint patterns. The cost is reasonable, too: ten yards of fabric can be patterned for about $30.00.

❧❧❧

There's no shortage of information about the ingredients used in texture coatings for scenery and props. Every stagecraft text offers detailed recipes, nearly every shop has a favorite "house blend," and of course there's always the wisdom of the Internet. Nevertheless, many of the texture coatings used in theatre suffer from two shortcomings: they can't easily be built up into rich relief; and they tend to be fairly fragile. This article addresses those problems.

THE PROBLEM AND SOLUTION

The "Shadow Dance" segment of California State University–Pomona's 1993 production *Bends in the Road* was set in a five-thousand-year-old tomb. The challenge was to give the wagon-mounted unit an inexpensive coating that looked like rough stone and that would not break or chip during scene changes.

Figure 1 illustrates the texture we achieved by using mixtures of three readily available materials: vermiculite, joint compound, and white glue. The

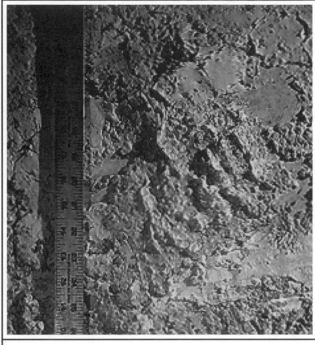

FIGURE 1

vermiculite provided the actor-friendly and realistically rough surface texture we wanted. The joint compound gave the mixture substantial body, letting us build up the depth of the coating. Ordinary white glue provided enough adhesive strength to keep the texture in place on our tomb's walls.

PREPARATION AND APPLICATION

We built standard Hollywood flats for the tomb's basic structure. But rather than apply the texture material directly to the flats' lauan skins, we first applied a single layer of theatrical gauze. We rolled white glue onto the flats as they lay on the floor and then "wallpapered" them with the gauze, which we smoothed into the glue as evenly as possible. We immediately top-coated the gauze with another roller application of glue and then let the flats dry overnight.

Covering the flats with gauze served two very useful purposes: it gave the lauan a useful amount of tooth, increasing the chances that our texture coat would stay in place, and it gave us an effective means of hiding any holidays in the texture coatings.

Merely combining the joint compound, glue, and vermiculite in four different proportions yielded the rich texture we needed. The individual possibilities are shown on the next page. The texture at the upper left in Figure 2 results from a 1:1:1 blend (joint compound:glue:vermiculite). Doubling the amount of joint compound in the mix for a 2:1:1 blend yields the chunkier texture shown at the lower left, which is largely responsible for giving the finished product its impressive depth. The pancake-batter-like texture at the lower right is produced by doubling the glue (1:2:1); and the contrasting granular texture in the upper right corner is produced by doubling the vermiculite (1:1:2).

We troweled all four mixtures onto the flats simultaneously, aiming more for visual effect than for even coverage. We let the coating dry overnight and then used brushes and sponges in painting the hard, deeply textured surface.

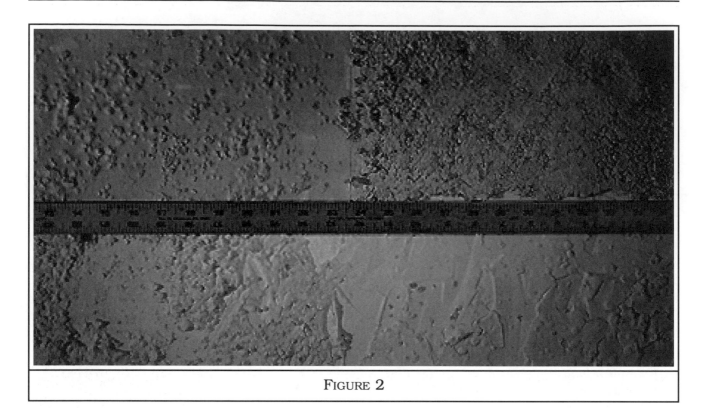

FIGURE 2

FINAL NOTES

This combination of materials becomes quite rigid and is probably suitable for use on continuous and sturdy surfaces only. We have not tested whether the addition of a plasticizer or the use of a flexible glue would allow application directly over hardware cloth, window screening, or other similarly "open" armatures, but it seems an interesting possibility.

Certainly, other texture materials such as sawdust or sand can be used instead of vermiculite. Vermiculite, however, has the advantage of being cleaner than sawdust, less abrasive than sand, and lighter than either of them.

❧❧❧❧

All the action in a recent production of *A Ride Across Lake Constance* at the Yale School of Drama took place within a single box set made with 26'-tall walls and fitted with an elaborate grand staircase, a suitably massive chandelier, and little else. Nothing in the set moved: there were no traps or turntables or elevators; there was no flying scenery. In fact, aside from two doors upstage painted with the same stenciled pattern as the walls, the audience had essentially nothing to look at for two hours but the same 5 actors and the set decoration. Thus, the set designer was intent that the furniture looked just so. Figure 1 illustrates the Naugahyde®-upholstered look that Set Designer Michaela Strumberger wanted and that we achieved, within budget limits.

FIGURE 1: THE SHOP-MADE-NAUGAHYDE UPHOLSTERED SOFA

The set, a hotel lobby, was to be furnished with two sofas and two stuffed chairs — all matching. Buying four new pieces would have been beyond our budget, as would recovering four stock pieces in Naugahyde®. Though vinyl would have cost less, using it would have limited the designer's color choices and might have been quite troublesome for me, an inexperienced upholsterer. Thus, in the end we adopted Michael Yeargan's suggestion that muslin could be painted and finished to look exactly like Naugahyde® — from an audience's vantage point anyway. The technique is quite simple and for us was cost-effective enough that we were able to afford two good sofas and two solid chairs in a hotel liquidation sale.

THE PROCESS

Our first step was to cut lengths of 68" medium-weight muslin roughly to size for reupholstering the two sofas. (We intended to deal with the two stuffed chairs separately.) Though we did not sew the muslin pieces together right away, we did label them before taking them to the paint shop and laying them out in preparation for their paint treatment.

The first step in painting consisted of wet blending three colors of paint on the fabric. We used a number of browns and rust colors, but whatever the color palette and no matter how many different tints or tones are used, all the paint must be thinned until it is just slightly thicker than water. After our wet-blended base coat was thoroughly dry, we sewed the fabric as necessary and tacked it onto the furniture.

Our next step was to touch up the few holidays in our base coat, using the original wet-blend technique and paints. We also worked in a fairly elaborate set of painted shadows and highlights, and at this point the tinting and toning were essentially done. Finally, we were ready to begin turning the muslin into Naugahyde®.

As it turns out, this entirely straightforward process produces some unbelievably spectacular results. We used High Gloss Acrylic Polyurethane for Floors and Trim, obtained from a local paint store, to seal the paint and simulate the texture of Naugahyde®. Applied with a brush and allowed to dry completely between coats, the polyurethane initially looked somewhat milky, and it did tend to darken the colors a bit, but in the end it dried essentially clear. The trick, though, is to be patient — and to plan enough time for the application of multiple coats. Before tackling the sofas, we worked up a test strip of fabric measuring about 1' x 5'. After painting the whole strip and letting it dry (as noted above), we left the first square foot of fabric unsealed, and then added progressively more layers of polyurethane as we worked down the test strip — 5 layers to the second square foot, 10 to the third, 15 to the fourth, and 20 to the last. Predictably, that test gave each square foot its own particular tone and shine. It turned out that 10 coats of the polyurethane produced the finish shown on the sofa in Figure 1.

NOTES

Adding multiple layers of acrylic makes fabric progressively "crisper." Should you try this treatment on fabric other than muslin, you might end up with something very much like sandpaper, as we did when we painted and sealed the lighter colored and somewhat worn original fabric on two stuffed chairs. Finally, though the involved sequence of steps in this process takes a long time, it is quite affordable, allows for custom colors, and actually requires less effort than upholstering with vinyl or Naugahyde®.

ဆပဆပ

The Yale School of Drama's production of Soyenka's *The Road* featured a wonderfully simple and yet effective stained glass window. It consisted of a single piece of clear plastic vinyl sheeting stretched over an open frame with self-adhesive foam weather stripping as "leading." With three different painting techniques used in finishing the window, the overall effect, shown in Figure 1, was excellent both up close and at a distance.

CONSTRUCTION

The window's 4' x 10' frame was made from $1\frac{1}{2}$" x $1\frac{1}{2}$" angle iron to eliminate the need for internal toggles. Lauan nailing strips tek-screwed to the steel provided a stapling surface for a 54" x 10' piece of 32-mil clear PVC vinyl sheeting. Since the sheeting could not be sized like muslin, it was stretched as taut as possible as it was stapled. Once the vinyl had been framed, the pattern of leading was laid out with a marker, and the $\frac{1}{8}$"-wide adhesive-backed weather stripping was applied to separate the window into panes. The process is illustrated in Figure 2.

PAINTING

The vinyl sheeting was flexible even when taut, and the window was to be painted while laid out flat on the floor. To keep the paint from pooling, the scenic artists supported the vinyl with scraps of plywood stacked $1\frac{1}{2}$" high. The paint mixture for the glass was a combination of tints, Rosco Supersaturated Paints, and Benjamin Moore Clear

FIGURE 1: FULL VIEW

Acrylic. For single-color panes, the scenic artists simply poured on thin layers of the mixture, thus avoiding brush strokes which would have been noticeable when backlit. The foam leading kept the poured paint from leaking from one pane to the next.

In a second technique, an air brush was used to apply successive layers of watered-down paint on the more detailed areas. As Figure 3 shows, this technique was particularly effective for the face and hands. Our scenic artists found adding a top coat of clear acrylic to be unnecessary, but one could be added, if desired, to give all sections a glossy look.

After the glass painting was completed, the weather stripping was painted with a mixture of graphite powder and black paint, applied with a brush.

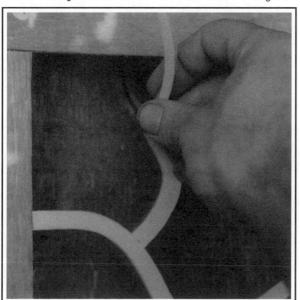

FIGURE 2: LAYING IN THE "LEADING"

NOTES

The common alternatives to the vinyl and foam materials suggested here are Plexiglas® and pre-made leading paste. It is difficult, however, to acquire Plexiglas® in sheets larger than 4' x 10', and even in that size, it is costly. Other rigid sheet goods are also quite pricey. A 4' x 10' sheet of $\frac{1}{16}$" PETG, for instance, would have cost $32.00. The PVC vinyl sheeting cost $6.00 per yard for a 54"-wide piece. The vinyl can also be cut with a matte knife, avoiding the health hazards caused by sawing Plexiglas®.

Foam weather stripping is comparable in price to both the homemade and the pre-made leading paste (a mixture of paint and flexglue) available at many craft shops. It is, however, much easier, faster, and cleaner to correct mistakes made with the foam. The weather stripping is widely available, inexpensive, reads well at a distance, and requires no preparation or cleanup.

FIGURE 3: PAINT DETAIL

For a production of Moliere's *The Misanthrope* at the Yale School of Drama, the set designer wanted to emulate a piece of research he had found. The picture showed an aged eighteenth-century mirror with the reflective particles peeling off. Where the reflective particles had peeled away, the mirror had become translucent. Scenic Artist Tobin Ost and I used the technique described here to treat Plexiglas® to achieve the same look.

PAINTING AND ERASING THE DYE

The first step, after cutting and cleaning the Plexiglas®, was to apply Fiebings Leather Shoe Dye which is sold by the quart. We cut it by about 10% with denatured alcohol to stretch it as far as possible. As it turned out, the dye went much farther than expected. We applied the dye with wads of cheesecloth, and at the same time pulled the dye up with dry cheesecloth, allowing the dye to create natural puddle edges without obscuring the translucency entirely.

We followed this step immediately with a light spattering of denatured alcohol which erased the dye completely, permitting us to fix mistakes. The light spattering helped reduce opacity and created random patterns. We repeated the alternate application of dye and alcohol until we were satisfied with the panels and then left them to dry overnight. Figure 1 shows how a panel looked as we neared the end of this process.

BRUSH EFFECT AND SILVER LEAF

We prepared the imitation silver leaf by peeling it from its backing paper and tossing it as though it were a salad. Since the silver leaf tends to stick to fingers, we used the handles of our brushes to toss, rip, and separate it. This helped to eliminate straight edges and corners and gave the silver a less controlled look.

After preparing the silver leaf, we painted the dyed side of the Plexiglas® with polyurethane, applying it with brushes to help achieve the brushed look of antique glass. Once the polyurethane became tacky (about 20 minutes) we applied the silver leaf by sprinkling it over the Plexiglas®, and brushing it on. The silver leaf adhered to the polyurethane wherever it touched, so it was not necessary to brush every bit of it down. In fact, leaving some of it loose and brushing it off after the polyurethane had dried only improved the look. After

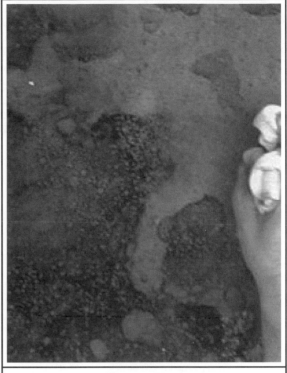

FIGURE 1: PAINTING AND ERASING COMPLETE

FIGURE 2: SILVER LEAF APPLIED

leaving the panels to dry overnight, we removed the excess silver leaf with brushes, a vacuum, and rags.

For the other side of the Plexiglas®, we mixed 1 part denatured alcohol with 4 parts shoe dye in a sprayer. We then lightly sprayed areas of the Plexiglas® while we spattered denatured alcohol to give it a more organic and less opaque look. Once the panel dried (4 to 5 hours), we brushed on a coat of polyurethane to create the finished product.

The materials proved to be good choices. This technique worked well because the denatured alcohol's incompatibility with the other materials produced the desired puddling. Furthermore, the polyurethane was tacky enough to attach the silver leaf and did not leave a haze when it dried.

SAFETY

Every material used in this process is toxic. Proper respirators are necessary for every stage of this process.

FIGURE 3: FINISHED SURFACE

❧❧❧❧❧

TECHNICAL BRIEF

Props

It has to flow, it has to be safe for the actor, it should look real, and it shouldn't stain, but there is no one perfect stage blood recipe. Both *Technical Brief* and *Theatre Crafts* have previously addressed this common and complex problem, but neither has published the two recipes printed here.

RECIPE 1: SMALL-VOLUME, REALISTIC BLOOD

In its edible form, this first recipe realistically simulates the results of mouth injuries, and its sweetness is an incentive for the actor to spit it out.

1.   Mix together $\frac{1}{3}$ to $\frac{1}{2}$ bottle corn syrup and $2\frac{1}{2}$ tbsp. peanut butter, the more processed, the better.

2.   Add 1 tsp. corn starch, a little less for a thinner mix.

3.   Mix well and add 1 tbsp. red food color.

This recipe has been used without harm to costumes: the peanut butter bonded with the food color well enough to prevent the white cotton shirts on which it was used from becoming stained. Immediately after rehearsals and performances, a thorough cold-water rinse removed most of the blood from the shirts, and the remaining traces disappeared with normal laundering.

If this mixture need not be edible, it can be thinned by adding a small amount of Foto-flow®. With this addition, however, it is not suitable for use in blood packs under clothes: the Foto-flow® is absorbed into the fabric more rapidly than the peanut butter and corn syrup, leaving a watery-looking red spot.

RECIPE 2: BIG-VOLUME, SYMBOLIC BLOOD

For a production which required a mixture to flow down Plexiglas® walls every night and stain them for the rest of the show, a different recipe was needed. The stain, of course, could not be permanent, and the blood had to be cheap enough that we could use five gallons each night.

Being careful to avoid creating bubbles, mix together 75 parts Pink Pearl® dishwashing liquid, 15 parts chocolate syrup, and 10 parts red food coloring. Obviously, the consistency can be varied by altering the proportions of the components.

For another recipe, see the October, 1986 issue of *Theatre Crafts*. The Pink Pearl® recipe was developed at Shakespeare/Santa Cruz in 1988; and the peanut butter recipe, by Abe Morrison, a Technical Intern at the Yale School of Drama, in 1989.

For a production of *Blythe Spirit*, Klaus Holm, Technical Director at Wilkes College, needed a way of toppling a chair on a thrust stage. As the chair had to move from one location to another during the play, wires could not be used. Instead, Klaus converted a small section of a platform beneath the chair leg into a small trapdoor — a "flipper" — which would open and close quickly, tipping the chair over in the process.

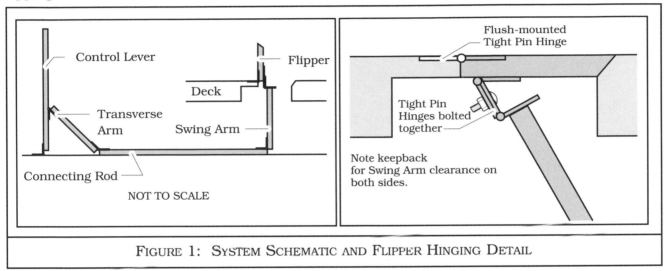

FIGURE 1: SYSTEM SCHEMATIC AND FLIPPER HINGING DETAIL

Figure 1 illustrates the essential parts of the chair-tipping mechanism: an offstage control lever, a connecting rod, a swing arm, and the flipper, and details the flipper/swing arm hinge connection. When the operator pulls the control lever back (or pushes it forward) quickly, the flipper pops up momentarily and then reseats itself.

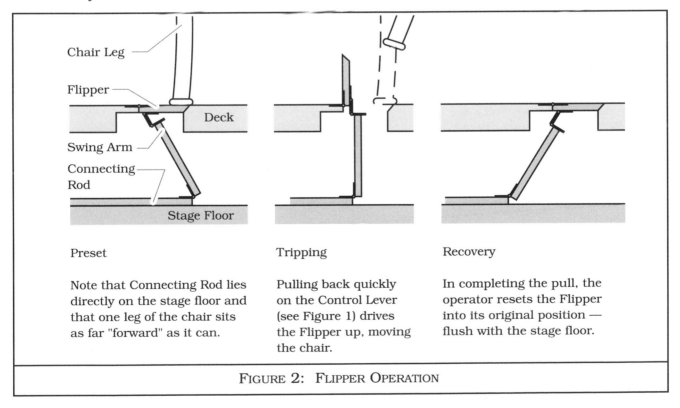

Preset

Note that Connecting Rod lies directly on the stage floor and that one leg of the chair sits as far "forward" as it can.

Tripping

Pulling back quickly on the Control Lever (see Figure 1) drives the Flipper up, moving the chair.

Recovery

In completing the pull, the operator resets the Flipper into its original position — flush with the stage floor.

FIGURE 2: FLIPPER OPERATION

CONSTRUCTION NOTES

1. The connecting rod must be secured to the floor in such a way that it can slide back and forth easily without lifting off the floor.

2. The transverse arm shown in Figure 1 was useful in gaining speed because it let us join the connecting rod to the control lever farther away from the lever's pivot. Some deck and connecting rod hardware designs will permit direct connection between the control lever and the connecting rod — and some will need no separate control lever at all.

Most of the components in this system can be replaced with alternatives which may better suit other applications. The hinges shown bolted together in Figure 2, for instance, could be replaced by a double-swing hinge. Similarly, neither the control lever nor any part of the linkage need be made of lumber, and a solenoid-controlled pneumatic cylinder could be used at the flipper. In our case, however, Klaus decided to use lumber and hardware already on hand in order to save money and time in both the shop and the theatre.

❦❦❦❦

A particular scene in a November 1990 production of *Little Shop of Horrors* at SUNY Binghamton called for a "simple, lightning-fast change" of several shelves filled with potted plants. In an instant, actors working in full view of the audience would have to replace "live" plants with their "dead" counterparts.

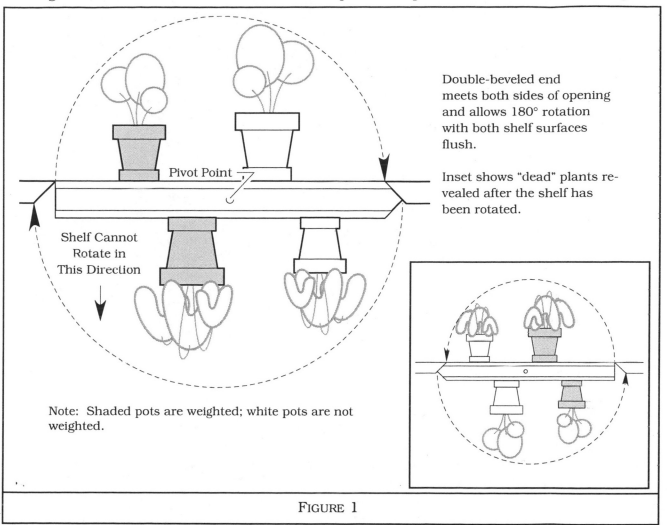

Double-beveled end meets both sides of opening and allows 180° rotation with both shelf surfaces flush.

Inset shows "dead" plants revealed after the shelf has been rotated.

Pivot Point

Shelf Cannot Rotate in This Direction

Note: Shaded pots are weighted; white pots are not weighted.

FIGURE 1

To make sure the change could happen as quickly as possible, I developed a double-sided shelf which could pivot from one position to another and would then rely on the distribution of its weight to keep it in place. Figure 1 illustrates the shelf's construction and operation.

The shelves we built were rectangular, lauan-covered frames of 1x3, but the shelves' shape and the choice of shelf material is fairly arbitrary, as long as the pivots can be installed accurately and no material on the shelves is allowed to cross the arc of the unit's swing. Precise pivot location is critical to the smooth functioning of the units. The figures also illustrate the placement of weighted and unweighted pots.

The two sets of plants were attached to both shelf surfaces which would be flipped around at the appropriate time. The plants were weighted as noted in the drawing, and their weight provided the necessary stability in either position. Once installed on the set, the shelves consistently worked well.

Many properties managers and craftspeople use rat traps as quick and reliable methods in rigging stage tricks. The application described here will create the illusion of a gunshot shattering a plate resting on a shelf.

The trick is achieved by first cutting approximately 1" from the end of a rat trap and removing all hardware except for the spring-loaded "guillotine." Next, a $1\frac{1}{2}$" hex head bold "firing pin" is brazed to the guillotine. The rat trap is then attached to the back of the hard-covered flat behind the plate. A hole slightly larger than the diameter of the firing pin is drilled through the flat to allow free passage.

The trap is loaded by placing a stiff wire (*i.e.,* coat hanger) "release pin" through two screw eyes and over the guillotine. The free end of the release pin is attached to a solenoid with a $\frac{3}{4}$" stroke and an 8-oz pull.

The effect is fired from a remote location, typically the stage manager's booth. The one drawback in this otherwise foolproof design is timing. The actor and the effect's operator need to develop a signal so the gunshot and the trick occur simultaneously. The noise caused by the guillotine slamming into the back of the flat is a non-issue because it will be masked by the gunshot. Also, any additional noise will only augment the spectacle. Once the effect is triggered, the firing pin will show through the flat. Painting the tip of the firing pin can help disguise it to appear as though the "bullet" actually chipped the plaster, brick, or stone wall.

SAFETY WARNING

This rat trap trick can be used to shatter window panes, and it can also be rigged under a table to shatter glasses, bowls, bottles, eggs, and the like. Flying shards of glass and certain other materials are serious safety hazards, and users must insure that actors and crew are not endangered by the operation of this device.

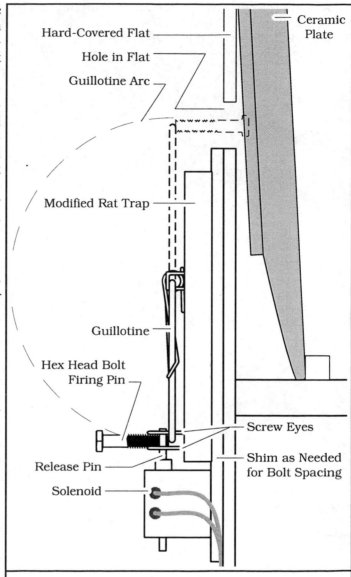

FIGURE 1: RAT TRAP IN PLACE

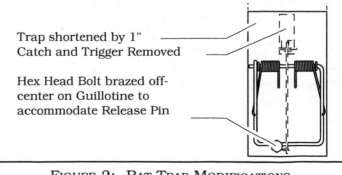

FIGURE 2: RAT TRAP MODIFICATIONS

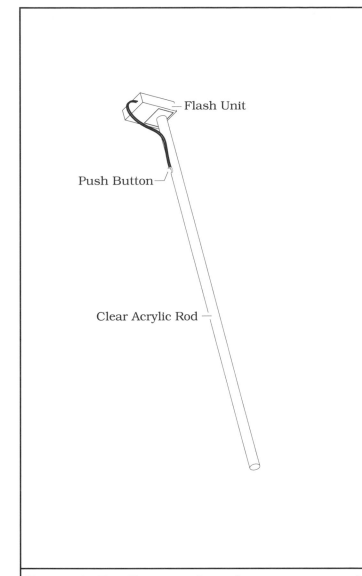

Flash Unit

Push Button

Clear Acrylic Rod

FIGURE 1: THE FLASHING CANE (DRESSING OMITTED)

One of the special effects I designed for Theatreworks' 1992 production of *Into the Woods* was built into the witch's light-emitting cane. Many times throughout the action the witch uses her cane to "flash her victims" as she casts a spell. To avoid having to reload a flash-paper device of some sort, I investigated other ways to produce flashes of light. Ultimately, I discovered that a small commercially available photo flash mounted at one end of a solid acrylic rod would generate what can be best described as a "lump of light" which travels down the rod.

As the light source, I used a Phoenix® flash unit measuring $2\frac{1}{2}$" x $3\frac{1}{2}$" x 1", bought at a local camera supply shop. I glued the flash unit to the end of a 3'-long $\frac{7}{8}$"-diameter clear acrylic rod with warm-water-soluble Friendly Plastic®, disguising the unit as part of the cane's handle. In dressing the assembled handle, I was careful to preserve access to the flash unit's battery compartment so that we could replace the two AA batteries periodically. I also wired a small momentary push-button switch into the flash trigger circuit and mounted the switch to the cane's shaft at a convenient location.

In a dimly lit "woods" setting, the cane produced an impressive effect each time it flashed during the show's 40-performance run. It also took a lot of abuse without needing repair, except that I had to expand the batteries' spring contacts from time to time: they tended to flatten a bit whenever the unit was inadvertently dropped.

Sometimes we're so attracted to one of a material's uses that we're blinded to its other possibilities. We commonly use sheet Plexiglas® as a safe substitute for panes of glass because it's transparent and shatter-resistant. Most of the time, we want it to remain rigid, planar, and transparent — just like glass. Perhaps that's why, when the Yale Summer Cabaret needed a distorting fun-house mirror, it took us so long to realize that mirrored Plexiglas® is exactly the right material.

Mirrored Plexiglas® comes in 4x8 sheets costing about $200, but smaller low-cost/no-cost scraps can be found at large-volume glass or plastic shops that have no use for small pieces. Experimenting with some cost-free scraps of mirrored Plexiglas® that we found in a glass store, we were surprised to find that we were able to build an entirely convincing mirror simply by bending $\frac{1}{8}$" mirrored Plexiglas® over an irregular surface and fastening it down securely. Eighth-inch mirrored Plexiglas® is much more flexible than we had anticipated: we found that we could easily bend a 2'-wide strip into a 9"-diameter cylinder. And it's easy to cut as long as you use an appropriate blade.

As far as this particular use was concerned, once we had cut the mirrored Plexiglas® to the right size and shape, we pushed it into place against a "terrain" we had built out of scrap lumber fastened to the back of a hollow-core door with screws and glue. We experimented with three different mounting techniques: pin-mounting by means of screw-in mirror mounts that clamped down over the edge of the mirrored Plexiglas®; pin-mounting by means of screws through holes in the Plexiglas® itself; and continuous-edge mounting by means of hot-melt glue. Ultimately, we used a combination of screws through the mirrored Plexiglas® and a bead of the hot-melt glue. The mirror took little time to build, cost next to nothing, and distorted images just as we wanted it to.

A health-and-safety postscript . . . . It is possible to squeeze a slightly tighter bending radius out of Plexiglas® by heating it carefully and evenly with a heat gun. But heating Plexiglas® (and even machining it) releases noxious gases. Craftspeople are warned to work in a ventilated area and to wear appropriate respirators as well as safety glasses whenever they work with this wonderfully versatile material.

&⚬&⚬&

Few experienced theatre technicians would have trouble assembling the lights and sound equipment necessary to simulate the flash and noise of an explosion. But what about generating the flying debris that an explosion should cause? When such a need arises, a pneumatic debris cannon may offer the best solution. Figure 1 depicts the essential components of such cannons.

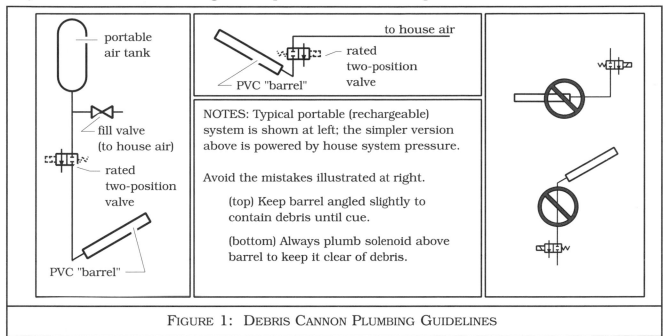

FIGURE 1: DEBRIS CANNON PLUMBING GUIDELINES

SYSTEM COMPONENTS AND DESIGN CONSIDERATIONS

All pneumatic debris cannons include a source of pressurized air, a release valve of some sort, assorted hoses and fittings, and a cannon barrel. But there the similarities end, for the design of each cannon depends on the nature of the debris to be thrown and the amount of pressure required, as well as on the installation possibilities inherent in a given set. The following discussion will illustrate some of the many differences.

A DRY-MIX CANNON

A 1991 Berkeley Rep production of *McTeague* used a debris cannon to simulate the effect of a mine-shaft collapse. The stage was set as an exterior, with the entrance to the shaft located upstage and facing the audience. The cannon's 3'-long "barrel" of 3" schedule 40 PVC was hidden in the shaft and was aimed directly toward the playing space. So that the debris would appear to include some "dust" and some "rocks" the mix consisted of two parts Pearlite®, one part tinted sawdust, one part dried peat moss, and a few chunks of painted Styrofoam®. During preset the barrel was filled with enough of the mix to last for a 10-second effect. The mix was poured, rather than packed, into the barrel, and the mouth of the barrel was tilted upward at about 30° to keep the debris in place. The effect was triggered by throwing a non-dim to open a two-position solenoid valve. As soon as the valve opened, air compressed to 120psi threw some of the larger Styrofoam® chunks onto the stage, along with some of the "dust." The shape of the "mine shaft" magnified the eddies that the relatively large barrel had induced in the air stream, and the dust billowed out onto the set very much as it would in reality. Since the cannon's 10-gallon air tank was not attached to a compressor, air pressure in the system began to drop immediately, but it continued to blow the lighter material into the air until the valve was closed. The tank was recharged for each performance.

The effect was very impressive and the system worked reliably, but its results were not exactly predictable. Not all of the debris material left the barrel in every cue, and there was no way to control which chunks of Styrofoam® would be shot out first or where any of the debris would settle. The director's blocking had to accommodate that uncertainty. Further, the effect was very loud. The hiss of the escaping air resonated inside the cannon's oversized barrel and produced a roar loud enough to require masking by an extended sound cue.

Finally, finding the right combination of ingredients for the debris mix took a lot of experimentation. This cannon was not particularly powerful, and the right mix for this effect consisted of the lightest of materials. Materials such as confetti, fake snow, and shredded paper or mylar seem likely candidates for other types of dry-mix debris.

A WET-MIX CANNON

Chris Darland designed a much more compact debris cannon to simulate the results of a suicide by gunshot for a 1995 Collaborative Workshop Production of *The Philanthropist* at the Yale School of Drama. The cannon's barrel was an 18" length of 1" schedule 40 PVC, fastened to the back of an armchair and aimed upwards at a point on the wall behind the victim. Chris added oatmeal to a standard blood mix to simulate brain tissue, and he kept the mix from fouling the two-position normally closed solenoid valve by loading a piece of wadding into the barrel before pouring in the mix. Since he needed a sudden air burst, Chris triggered the solenoid with a pushbutton.

This effect was impressively convincing, and it looked simple enough, but Chris's experimentation demonstrated how much trickier the use of a wet mix can be. Air pressure settings must be higher, and the preset can't be done too carefully. Load the cannon too soon, and the mix turns into crusty chunks or a solid mass; make the mix too wet, and the effect resembles heavy blobs of mud being blown not too far into the air; tilt the cannon's barrel too little, and the mix flows out onto the floor.

SAFETY NOTES AND CONCLUSION

Building a debris cannon should not be undertaken without the full cooperation of everyone involved, from general manager and director to cast member and stagehand. While compressed air is fairly safe compared to other propellants, pneumatic debris cannons can be dangerous and are potentially life-threatening. The use of a barrel makes the trajectory of the debris generally, but not precisely, predictable, and the cannon designer must work closely with the director, the cast, the crew, and stage and house management to insure that no one will be in the way when the cannon is fired.

The designer must also determine the lowest air pressure settings that an effect will require and must carefully choose the ingredients of a debris mix. The materials must be kept as light as possible so that they land with little force. And they cannot generate fine dusts that could harm or irritate eyes or respiratory passages.

Dealing with all of the logistical and safety-related issues involved guarantees that building, installing, and teching a debris-cannon effect will take a great deal of time. Yet, despite these difficulties, few other theatrical effects can match a debris cannon's ability to produce this particular type of explosion effect.

ᘓᘓᘓᘓ

Sometimes, achieving the effects of animated cartoons in live theater is difficult — and then sometimes it's not. Take, for instance, a director's desire to see a puppet "zing" out over the audiences' heads (like Wile E. Coyote so often does) after a character explodes onstage. With some ingenuity and a handful of scavenged hardware, Jim Kempf arranged just such an effect for the Yale Repertory Theatre production of *Le Bourgeois Avant Garde.*

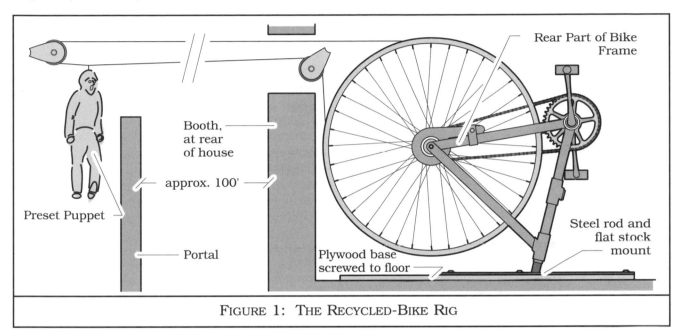

FIGURE 1: THE RECYCLED-BIKE RIG

Jim strung a loop of $\frac{1}{16}$" aircraft cable around a sheave hung just behind the show portal. The cable cleared the top of the portal and extended to the back of the house, where it ran over a second sheave and then into the booth. In the booth it was wrapped once around the tire-less rear wheel of a junked, coaster-brake bicycle. Jim had cut the frame of the bike in two just in front of the seat stem. He discarded the front part of the frame, the seat, and both tires and kept the rest intact. He mounted the rear half of the bike frame upside down on a scrap of $\frac{5}{8}$" plywood by slipping the seat-stem over a $\frac{1}{2}$" rod that he had welded to flat stock and bolted to the plywood. The rig assembled quickly, and the cable was tensioned merely by pulling the plywood/bike assembly into place and then screwing it to the booth floor.

At the top of the show, the puppet was preset behind a portal on the bottom line of the loop. On "go," a crew member spun the bike pedals, and the puppet flew over the heads of the audience at an amazing speed. The effect worked so well, in fact, that the operator had to work on not spinning the pedals too quickly — and using the coaster brake was essential.

❦❦❦❦

A Simple Approach to Complicated
Theatrical Sculpture

Chris Van Alstyne

Faced with the challenge of creating a 14'-tall, commendatory statue for Mozart's *Don Giovanni* at Brooklyn College and lacking any formal training in sculpture, I needed a plan. I chose an approach I had used in the past — a plywood armature covered with carved, white bead foam — to achieve the high level of detail and lifelike quality Set Designer John Scheffler required.

FIGURE 1

FIGURE 2

My introduction to the project was a sketched front elevation of an existing sculpture. After confirming the Designer's intent, I located a book that showed many different views of the statue and a book on horse anatomy that gave me all the information I needed to plan the armature. The front elevation gave enough information about the silhouette of the legs, torso, head, and rider. The book on horse anatomy gave actual cross-section views through the body of a horse at various locations.

Because of the size and expected weight of the finished piece, I used $\frac{3}{4}$" plywood for the armature. After transferring the outline of the torso and legs to the plywood in scale, I cut them out with a jigsaw. I blocked individual parts out with ripped-down 2x6 as needed to achieve appropriate depth between body parts and added a floor plate made from 2 layers of $\frac{3}{4}$" plywood to stabilize the unit. See Figure 2.

The slight twist of the horse's head was achieved by cutting two identical plates of plywood to match the scaled cross section. I attached one to the torso using the armature as a centerline and the other to an outline of the horse's neck and head that I had prepared as described in the preceding paragraph. Next, I attached the two built-up plates with drywall screws. See Figure 3. I used the same process in building the armature for the rider's waist and neck, estimating the cross section from measurements of my own body. Since the entire structure would be covered, I was not overly concerned about the joinery. I attached the arms with small nailing blocks and modified corner braces. Finally, referring to the anatomic views of horses and detailed views of the original sculpture to create scaled profiles, I attached pieces of $\frac{1}{4}$" lauan and 1x1 pine nailers to the armature wherever necessary as illustrated in Figure 3. Though not structural, these profiles would later allow me to carve the foam in a kind of "connect-the-dots" fashion by guiding the saw and rasp.

With the armature and profiles assembled, the next task was to attach the white bead foam. To glue the foam to the armature, I used a standard panel adhesive that required that the foam pieces

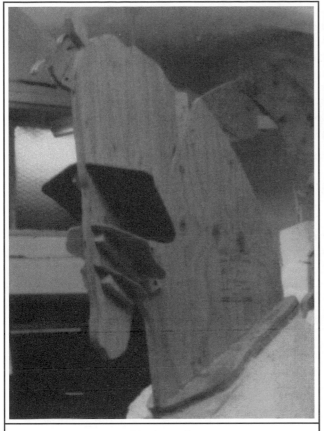

FIGURE 3

FIGURE 4

be held in position until the glue set. If I were to do a similar project, I would use "green glue" instead.

Once the glue had set, I started hacking away with a handsaw, Surform®, rasp, and — my personal favorite — a keyhole saw. Carving was easy and fast because I really did not have to make any decisions: the profiles had taken care of that. (See Figure 4.) Once the carving was completed, I covered the entire surface with brown craft paper that had been soaked in wallpaper paste. I chose craft paper because I wanted to be able to sand the surface to get it truly smooth.

At this point the designer came back and, together, we added the necessary details. Twisted craft paper, $\frac{1}{4}$" foam rubber, feathers, and to-go coffee lids were added where needed — as well as Licorice Sombreros®, Lifesavers®, and Nilla Wafers®. Three coats of paint finished the work: a brown base, bronzing powder in clear acrylic, and, finally, a green sponge glaze.

Although the added detail was extremely effective, the overall impact of the statue was firmly based in its scale and in the accuracy of the underlying structure. With careful research and measurement, any carpenter should be able to build profiles like these, and consequently to turn two-dimensional information into three-dimensional objects.

Theatrical designers often desire chandeliers in uncommon sizes — typically, larger than life. This was certainly true of the chandeliers that Set Designer Hee Soo Kim envisioned for a production of *Life Is a Dream* at the Yale School of Drama. Though the chandeliers themselves were of a fairly standard design, they measured 7'-0" tall by 5'-0" wide and would obviously not be available from any local building supply. Having decided to build them in house, we developed the approach described here, which was more than satisfactory and could be duplicated by any theater with a welder and a wood lathe.

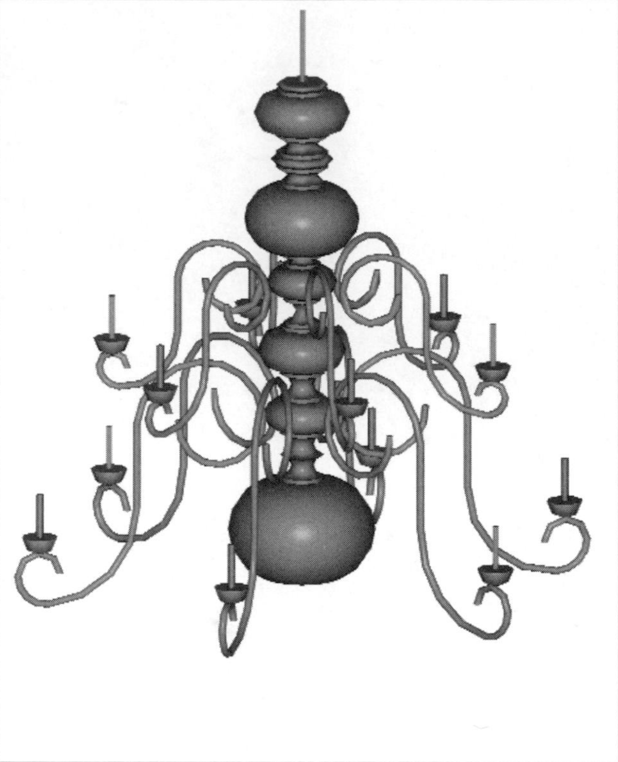

As shown in Figure 1, the chandeliers consisted of two tiers of six arms mounted on a central column. Each arm was adorned with a drip cup, candle holder, and flicker candle. For the purposes of this brief I will discuss the three phases of construction: building the skeleton, building the central column, and finishing.

BUILDING THE SKELETON

The skeleton was accomplished with a steel frame. The biggest challenge being that of the arms. We decided on $\frac{3}{4}$" round mechanical tubing with a 0.049" wall. The thin wall was to aid in bending, and the choice of steel was due to cost and weldability. The center column was $1\frac{1}{4}$" schedule 40 pipe and the candlestick holders were $\frac{1}{2}$" round mechanical tubing.

The design called for two different sized arms each with a pair of curves. The bending process is illustrated in Figures 2-4. The steel for the arms was cut long and filled with sand to discourage

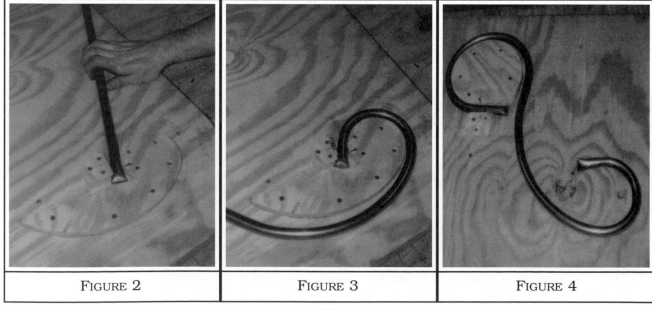

FIGURE 1

FIGURE 2

FIGURE 3

FIGURE 4

FIGURE 5

FIGURE 6

the walls from crushing. We began by plugging the steel with small corks, but found it easier and faster to crimp the ends in a vise. Drafting the two arms full scale was helpful in cutting the jig blocks, and testing the shape afterwards. Remember to cut the blocks a little small to allow for "backlash." This may require some trial and error for the first one, but it becomes quickly apparent. We screwed the jig blocks for each end of an arm to opposite ends of a table, so that while we bent one end of an arm, the jig blocks for the other end did not interfere. We bent the twelve small arms, and then refitted the table with the jig blocks for the large arms. Bending all 24 arms was accomplished in only four hours, the uniformity of which can be viewed in Figure 5. The ends were then cut to size with a portable band saw, and the sand drained. Before assembly, $\frac{1}{4}$" holes were drilled in each arm where the candle would sit and just above where it would attach to the center column. This allowed for internal routing of the electrical cable. Pieces of 1" pipe $\frac{1}{2}$" long were used to reinforce the arms where they would attach to the center column.

The size and shape of the designed center column required the arms to sit away from the $1\frac{1}{4}$" schedule 40 black pipe. This was accomplished by bending 6" diameter rings out of 1" strap steel, and welding them to the center pipe with $\frac{3}{8}$" rod spokes. The arms were then welded to this ring (Figure 6). The arms were placed correctly by capturing the top and bottom of the center column so that it stayed vertical but rotated freely. One arm was welded every 60° on the top and bottom tier, and the tiers were offset 30° to one another. Before going any further the cable needed to be run, which was accomplished by snaking a piece of $\frac{1}{4}$" aircraft cable through the arm, taping on a length of zip cord, and pulling it back through. This was without a doubt the most tedious step in the process.

The last pieces to be added to the skeleton were the short lengths of steel tubing that the candlestick holders would later sleeve over. This called for care in order not to destroy the zip cord while welding. One possible solution is to run the zip cord long, so that after welding you can pull the cord out far enough to cut off the damaged section. At this point the steel skeleton was finished and set aside.

BUILDING THE CENTRAL COLUMN

There are of course, an infinite number of possibilities for the shape of the center column, however the idea remains constant. The various balls, coves and beads this particular design required were made out of EPS foam. The larger balls (6", 10", and 12") were purchased, and the smaller sections were turned on a lathe. Laminating three layers of 2" foam in manageable lengths (about 18"), and capping the ends with $\frac{1}{4}$" plywood worked well. After the sections were turned, they and the balls were cored with an extended $1\frac{1}{4}$" spade bit. Because the foam for the candlestick holders was so small (2" x 6"), we inserted a $\frac{1}{2}$" dowel through the center to give it some rigidity on the lathe. This worked well because when the dowel was removed, the candlestick holder slipped nicely over the $\frac{1}{2}$" mechanical tubing that we welded to the arms earlier. The larger pieces were fitted over the $1\frac{1}{4}$" center column (Figure 7) to give the chandeliers their overall shape.

FINISHING

At this point the chandeliers did not look like much, but at the same time they were not very far from completion. The foam was covered with Foam Coat®, but could be covered with any suitable product, and sanded smooth. Specific to this design was the call for foliage on the arms. We found weldable stamped leaves, in a variety of sizes, from a

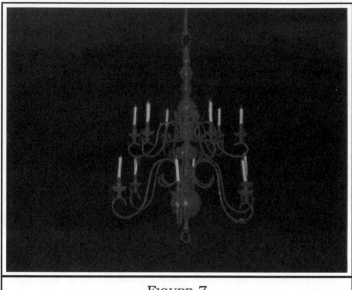

FIGURE 7

fencing manufacturer that worked great. Six-inch-diameter wooden bowls substituted for drip cups, and pre-owned flicker candles were used. The final touches were a turned wooden finial epoxied to the bottom, and bent steel rings epoxied to the top and bottom. The chandeliers were coated with a thick primer, to provide a uniform finish, and sent to the paint shop.

The chandeliers, while time consuming, were relatively easy to build. From start to finish, including painting, they took about 45 hours each. While this represents a significant amount of time, the material cost was fairly low, about $200 per chandelier less the cost of the flicker candles. It is also a project that can be accomplished by one carpenter, with the exception of the four-hour bending time. The finished product worked well for the show and is a useful stock item.

This article details a method for designing and building sturdy and attractive masks using ATL75, a plastic-impregnated felt. These lightweight, water-resistant, tough masks are custom fit to the actor's face providing maximum comfort, visibility, and breathability, as proven by Southern Illinois University's production of *The Good Woman of Setzuan.* The set was fraught with actor traps including heights of over twenty feet and numerous obstacles navigated by masked actors frantically running around the stage. The several steps involved in building such successful masks takes careful preparation and requires approximately 40 hours of work. A list of the tools and materials used appears at the end of this article.

CREATING THE MOLD AND THE CASTING

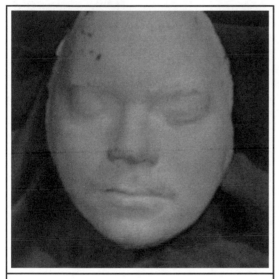

FIGURE 1: THE CASTING

Building a casting like that shown in Figure 1 requires creating a negative mold that duplicates the contours of the actor's face. To make them, we used dental alginate, mixed according to the instructions on the package. With the actor leaning back or lying face up, apply a $\frac{1}{4}$"–thick layer of alginate over the entire face with plastic spatulas. In covering the nostrils, have the actor first take a deep breath to be held until after the nose is completely covered. Then have the actor exhale quickly through the nose. The resulting holes will be filled later. After the dental alginate has dried, reinforce the nose area with 1" x 6" strips of plaster bandage extending from the forehead downward. Next, apply a layer of horizontal strips over the entire face, overlapping the strips by about $\frac{1}{4}$". Follow this layer with a layer of vertical strips, again covering the face completely. After the bandage layers have dried, gently release the mold. Any tears or cracks that occur in the mold can be fixed by applying small amounts of dental alginate with an artist's brush. Complete the mold, sealing the nostrils with plaster bandages and building up the perimeter so that the mold forms a sort of bowl for the plaster of Paris. Line a sturdy box with loosely wadded newspaper and lay the mold face down in the box.

Mix enough plaster of Paris to make the casting in one pour. Insert a loop of mechanic's wire into the back of the wet casting so that it can be hung later for storage. Allow the casting to harden for at least twenty-four hours.

CREATING THE MASK

Creating the mask takes time and patience; there is a learning curve involved, but creating a second and subsequent masks should move progressively faster. The complexity of the design will also dictate how much time it will take, and the scale of facial detail is important. Exaggerated features read better on stage and are more easily built.

Carefully pull the casting from the mold and prop it up on a table or hang it at a comfortable working height by its embedded wire loop. Next, apply modeling clay to the casting and sculpt it into the desired features. (This took us approximately three hours per mask.) After sculpting the desired features, cover any prominent protrusions, such as horns or exaggerated noses, with appropriately sized pieces of aluminum foil. With a spoon or similar tool, rub the foil into the clay and burnish it until smooth. Next, cover the entire face with a single piece of aluminum foil. Smooth and burnish this final foil layer. This last layer of aluminum foil serves as a sacrificial release agent, and yet provides a base that the mask material can cling to. Do not spray any release agents on the foil.

Applying the mask material, ATL75®, to the aluminum foil is the most time-consuming part of the process — approximately thirty hours per mask. It also involves a health hazard since it uses methyl ethyl ketone (MEK) as a solvent. Always work in a well-ventilated room and wear chemical-resistant gloves and splash goggles while using it. Cut the fabric into $\frac{1}{4}$"-wide strips more than long enough to cover the face from crown to neck. Working one strip at a time, soak the fabric in a glass bowl of MEK until it is limp. Starting along the center-line of the nose, apply the strips, using wooden spoons as necessary to push the fabric snugly into hollows under the nose and lips. Because the ATL75® will want to stick to the spoons, you will need to dip the spoons

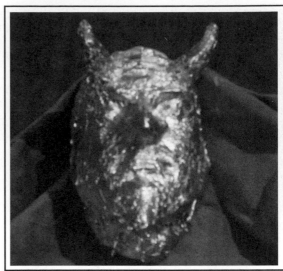

FIGURE 2: BURNISHED MASK

in the MEK repeatedly as you work. The strips of fabric need to be applied quickly because the ATL75® sets up as the MEK evaporates. You cannot re-soak a strip after you start to apply it.

Working from the first strip, apply adjoining strips, tightly butting their edges together like wallpaper without overlapping them. Leave the occasional gaps that occur for patching later. Continue with the vertical strips until the mask is completely covered. Fill any gaps in the layer with custom cuts of the fabric. After the layer of vertical strips is complete, apply a layer of horizontal strips. After both layers are completely dry (about 24 hours), pull the hardened fabric off the plaster casting and peel any scraps of aluminum foil off the mask.

Trim the edges of the fabric and bind the perimeter of the mask with mechanic's wire to prevent fraying and splitting of the edges and to strengthen the mask. Cut the mechanic's wire and a 1" strip of the fabric 2" longer than would be enough to go around the edge of the mask completely. Bend the wire to conform to the mask's edge and cover it with the MEK-soaked fabric strip, leaving $\frac{1}{2}$" of fabric on either side of the wire. Let this dry.

FIGURE 3: MASKS WITH PRIMER COAT

Next, cut out the desired eye shape with an Exacto knife, making sure the eye holes are large enough to accommodate the actor's peripheral vision. Then drill out the nostrils with a regular twist bit. Drill two additional but smaller holes just above each ear to attach elastic bands. Rub vinyl spackle into the fabric with your finger to create a smooth, durable, and paintable surface. Sand the dried spackle smooth, starting with 80-grit and working up to 400-grit sandpaper. Finally, rinse the spackle dust off the mask with cold water, dry the mask, and apply a primer coat to both sides. See Figure 3. It is better to paint and clear coat the mask before adding hair or appliqués of jewels or fabric. If

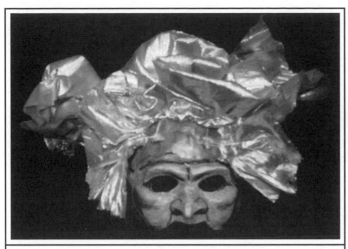

FIGURE 4: FINISHED MASK

hair is required, drill small holes in the mask, feed the hair through to the inside of the mask and secure it with hot glue. This allows for a more natural lay of the hair and gives a better overall appearance.

This type of mask has many advantages. Because the mold is taken right from the actor's face, it provides maximum comfort. Its light weight reduces the number of complaints from actors, and its strength and durability ensure that it can also take quite a lot of hard use with little or no damage. Enjoy and be creative!

TOOLS AND MATERIALS

Caution: While using ATL75 and MEK, work in a well-ventilated area, and wear chemical-resistant gloves, a respirator, and splash goggles.

For the Mold

Plaster bandages (any medical supply store)
Dental alginate
Mixing containers
Plastic spatulas

For the Casting

5 lbs. figurine-grade plaster of Paris
2" loop of mechanics' wire
Newspaper
1 box large enough to hold the casting

For Building the Mask

Modeling clay
Aluminum Foil
ATL75®-impregnated fabric
methyl ethyl ketone
Wooden spoons
Glass bowl

For Finishing the Mask

Mechanics' wire
Vinyl spackle
Sandpaper (80-400 grit)
Primer
Latex enamel paint
Clear coat polyurethane

Looking for an alternative to real glass block, we developed the cost-effective technique described here. Using Plexiglas®, spike tape, and Saran Wrap® or other plastic wrap as materials, the process involves only a few simple steps.

Cut the Plexiglas® to the desired size. Then, before framing it, apply strips of beige $\frac{1}{2}$" cloth spike tape to the back of the Plexiglas® to simulate grout lines. Don't use colored spike tape — especially if it's not all the same color — because it will show through the Plexiglas®. Next, paint the same side of the Plexiglas® with a coat of clear acrylic sealer and lay strips of clear plastic wrap on the wet surface. Working quickly, crinkle the wrap to produce the desired texture. You can leave any big bubbles as they add to the glass block effect.

FIGURE 1: MAKING PLAIN "GLASS BLOCK"

Poking holes in the plastic wrap will help in the drying process. A simple hole puncher can be built by drilling screws through a block of wood until the tips of the screws protrude through the wood. With this or a similar tool, gently pounce the plastic wrap to let air hit the sealer. Figure 1 shows how various stages of the technique should look.

❧❧❧

Making it snow for Villanova University's production of *Angels in America*, I faced several difficulties: it had to snow at several onstage locations; we didn't have a few thousand dollars to spare; and my crew consisted of unskilled student labor. The biggest obstacle, though, was that, since the grid of our black box theatre is close to the ceiling, there was no room to mount a snow cradle, and the snow would have to be stored and loaded into a distribution system that started in the wings. In response, I designed and built an inexpensive, very workable, and nearly foolproof snow machine.

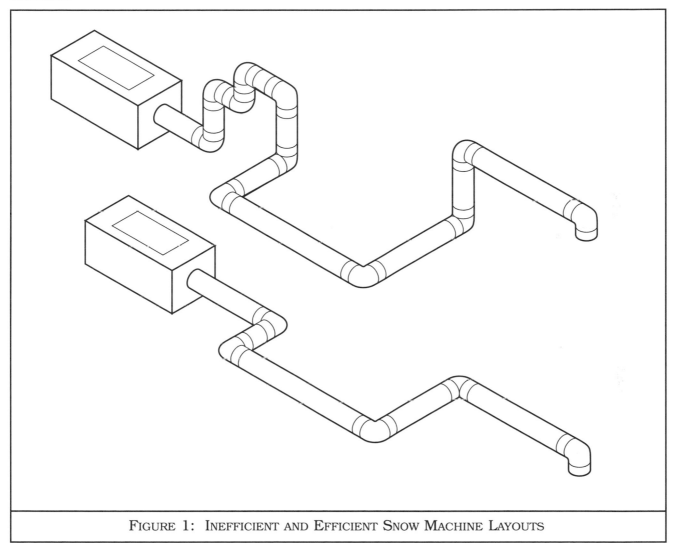

FIGURE 1: INEFFICIENT AND EFFICIENT SNOW MACHINE LAYOUTS

The snow machine consists of a bathroom exhaust fan, several lengths of PVC, and an assortment of PVC fittings, all joined by gaffer's tape to facilitate any unclogging that might be necessary. In use, plastic snow is manually fed into the bathroom fan and is blown through the PVC to the desired exit port(s) onstage.

THE FAN

Buy a ducted bathroom exhaust fan without a light, taking two factors into consideration: the cfm rating and the sones rating. Most bathroom exhaust fans move 50 to 70 cfm with more expensive models moving as much as 110 cfm. The sones rating is an index of noise generated during operation. The lower the number, the quieter the fan. A fan with a 0.6 sones rating is practically noiseless; a 4.0 sones rating will remind you of the fan in a cheap apartment building bathroom. I have found that all work effectively, but the air/snow stream from more forceful fans can be unacceptably noisy at the exit port(s). I recommend using an economy exhaust fan with ratings of 50 cfm and 2.5 sones. Its air stream is relatively quiet, and you can build a sound-insulating plywood box around the fan if necessary. Ratings aside, all bathroom fans come with a plug, and, therefore, no wiring is needed.

THE DUCTWORK

Flexible ducting is not a good choice for snow delivery because of its tendency to clog. The amount of PVC piping and the number of fittings will vary with the length of snow run(s) and the number of turns required to reach the destination. Within reason, any length of PVC run can be employed. We have had runs up to 60' with few problems. In laying out the system, plan to mount the fan as high as or higher than the distribution runs, and keep in mind that the straighter the path, both horizontally and vertically, the more efficient the system will be. See Figure 1. Design a route that minimizes the number of elbows required. Remember that elbows that change the horizontal direction of an air stream are less prone to clogging than "vertical" ones.

Most bathroom fans are designed to receive a 4" duct. For most of my snow runs, I attach a reducing coupling at the fan and "step down" to 2" PVC. I do not recommend using anything smaller. The runs' exit ports do not have to be increased in order to obtain a nice spread of falling snow. The air currents of the theater will provide that for you. Keep in mind that this type of snow system is for the specific aiming of the snow, but it will never look like a blizzard.

USE AND MAINTENANCE

Feeding plastic snow directly into an inverted exhaust fan may seem strange at first, but it truly is the best method. The fan housing should be vacuumed at the end of each performance for maintenance.

CONCLUDING NOTES

Plastic snow can be bought at a local theatrical supply store or through any mail order theatrical supply company like Mutual Hardware, (278) 361-2480. Not only have I used one snow machine to generate snow effects in a half-dozen shows, I have also used it with Mylar® and different types of paper to produce successful showers of blue rain and yellow drops of sunlight.

❧❧❧

TECHNICAL BRIEF

Rigging Hardware

A production of *The Crucible* at the University of Cincinnati, College–Conservatory of Music used a couple of two-fold purchase block and falls to help along some counterweight lines that changed load during set moves. One out-of-weight line needed to be hauled out and the other needed to be slipped in. In both cases the moving block was attached to the eye under an arbor, and the static block was attached to structural members at deck level. Both lines needed to be controlled and tied off at the locking rail.

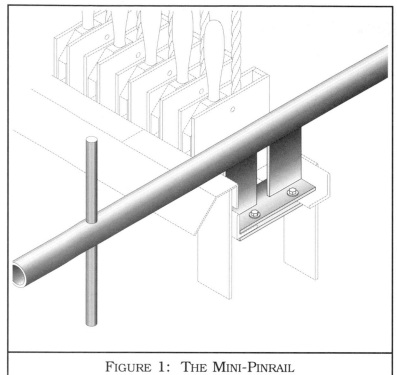

FIGURE 1: THE MINI-PINRAIL

After I spent the requisite time in the moaning chair staring at the problem, the light bulb flickered on overhead. The solution lay in the modular construction of our locking rail. Adopting the same modular approach used in attaching the rope locks to our locking rail, I built a two-part steel base which could sit in line with the rope locks and be bolted down just as our locks are. A two-leg pedestal welded to the base supports a welded-on mini-pinrail pipe at a height which just clears the top of the locking rail. Pedestal and base parts are made of $\frac{1}{4}$" x 3" steel strap. The pin is a piece of $\frac{3}{4}$" solid round bar inserted through a hole in the $1\frac{1}{2}$" schedule 80 black pipe and welded in place. As installed, the mini-pinrail extends far enough past the locking rail so that a fly operator can face the mini-pinrail straight on (perpendicular to the locking rail) and operate the hemp line in normal fashion.

A great advantage of these mini-pinrails is that they can be kept on hand and quickly bolted on anywhere along our locking rail where there is a 3" space. A quick safety warning, though: Look out! These mini-pinrails project out from the locking rail a fair distance. Woe to the fly operator rushing between rail cues who forgets to take the wide route.

Kibitzing credit goes to Steve Miller of Sapsis Rigging.

❧❧❧

Scenery bumpers are invaluable in tightly packed lofts. The standard bumper, an 18" strap-steel ring, is adequate for deflecting soft drops, but as Stage Carpenter for a Yale School of Drama production, I learned that it does not always work well on hard-covered, irregularly shaped scenery. Our production featured an x-shaped lauan railroad-crossing sign, hung on a batten directly upstage of an electric. The standard bumper we installed to protect the scenery caught on the sign, damaging it and causing focus problems. In response, I made a new type of scenery bumper from a paint can. Too wide to catch the arms of the sign, the paint-can bumper worked well throughout the run. Figure 1 illustrates both the standard strap-steel bumper and its shop-built replacement.

MATERIALS

For the scenery bumper I used a standard one-gallon paint can for the body, but other sizes of buckets or lengths of

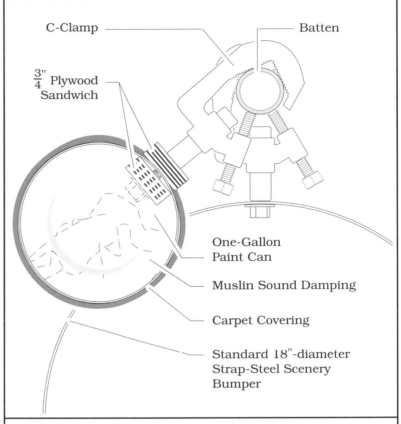

FIGURE 1: 18" STRAP STEEL AND PAINT CAN BUMPERS

PVC pipe will work, and can be chosen to suit the circumstances. If you are using a piece of PVC pipe, you may need to buy or make end caps, which are needed to keep the body from deforming while it does its job. Silicone or epoxy secures the can lids or end caps to the body of the bumper. Plywood provides a secure base for attachment of the inevitable C-clamp, a sound damper of loosely packed muslin or foam scraps fills the bumper, and its outside is covered with carpet to guard the piece of scenery against abrasion.

SCENERY BUMPER CONSTRUCTION

Paint-can bumper construction is fairly self-evident. One side of the body needs to be flattened to nest snugly between the pieces of the plywood sandwich. Alternatively, of course, the plywood could be sanded to conform to the bumper's body. Drywall screws work well in fastening the halves of the sandwich together once they're in place. After drilling a $\frac{1}{2}$" bolt hole through the sandwich and the body, attach the C-clamp, using fender washers on both sides of the wood. Fill the inside of the cylinder with loosely packed sound-damping material, run a bead of silicone or epoxy around the end(s) of the body, place the lid or end caps in position, and use a mallet to seat them properly. Secure a piece of low-pile carpet around the body with gaffers tape and/or contact cement.

A FURTHER POSSIBILITY

Though they are padded, the bumpers could damage some scenery finishes by rubbing. If that possibility exists, you may want to build a scenery roller rather than a scenery bumper.

SCENERY ROLLER CONSTRUCTION

Building a roller is similar to building a bumper. Simply add an axle of threaded rod and an $\frac{1}{8}$" strap-steel bracket to the materials listed above. Instead of sandwiching the body of the paint can between pieces of plywood, attach one piece of $\frac{3}{4}$" plywood on the inside of the lid and another on the inside of the bottom with drywall screws and drill holes for the threaded-rod axle. Lay in the sound-damping material and secure the ends of the cylinder as you would on the bumper. Then attach carpet to the outside of the roller.

Make a bracket of $\frac{1}{8}$" strap steel, leaving a minimum of $\frac{1}{2}$" clearance on both ends of the roller and 1" between its side and the bracket. Drill axle holes in each arm of the bracket, and drill a hole in the center of the bracket for the C-clamp. Mount the C-clamp on the bracket and assemble the roller to the bracket by means of the threaded-rod axle. Use washers to fill the gaps between the bracket and the roller, centering the roller on the bracket. Double-nut the ends of the axle.

CONCLUSION

Though we happened to use one-gallon paint cans, other cylinders — smaller or larger — could be used on either the bumper or the roller. The choice is best made in light of a specific application. Regardless of that choice, however, both of these simple scenery guides present useful opportunities for recycling materials that would otherwise be thrown away.

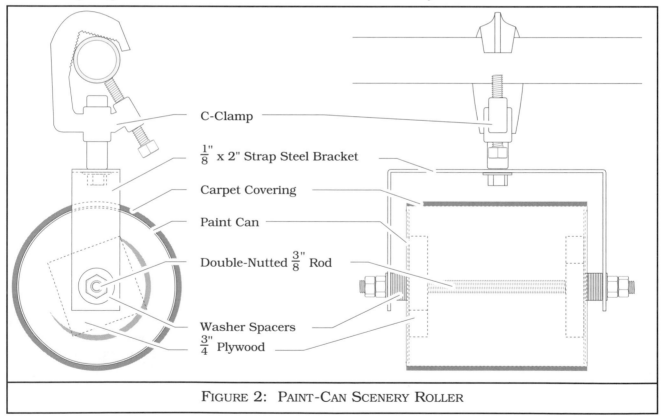

C-Clamp

$\frac{1}{8}$" x 2" Strap Steel Bracket

Carpet Covering

Paint Can

Double-Nutted $\frac{3}{8}$" Rod

Washer Spacers
$\frac{3}{4}$" Plywood

FIGURE 2: PAINT-CAN SCENERY ROLLER

Usually when we hang a drop, we expect it to stay hung until strike. We're so used to keeping drops in the air that most of us are at least momentarily stumped when we have to rig one to fall off a batten. This article describes a quick-release device that will let drops fall to the floor on cue.

OPERATING PRINCIPLE

The quick release is essentially a shop-built continuous hinge as long as the drop is wide. As Figure 1 illustrates, it hangs barrel-down beneath a lineset, with one of its leaves fixed in position by pipe-clamp attachment to the batten, and the other left free to swing down whenever the device's three restraining pins are pulled.

The leaves are made of lengths of 1x3, fastened together end-to-end by scabs of $\frac{1}{2}$" plywood screwed to the non-barrel edge of each leaf. These leaves pivot on a set of carefully aligned 2" tight-pin hinges spaced about 2' apart along the quick release's length.

The quick release's free leaf carries a series of $\frac{1}{4}$" flat head stove bolts, their heads countersunk into the plywood scabs and sandwiched between them and the 1x3. Spaced as far apart as the drop's grommets are, these bolts are the mounting pins on which the drop hangs until released.

The shop-built restraining pins operate very much like familiar barrel bolts. Their barrels are made of short lengths of bar stock and $\frac{1}{4}$" pipe; their bolts, short lengths of $\frac{1}{4}$" round stock with an eye formed at one end. Figure 3 best details their construction.

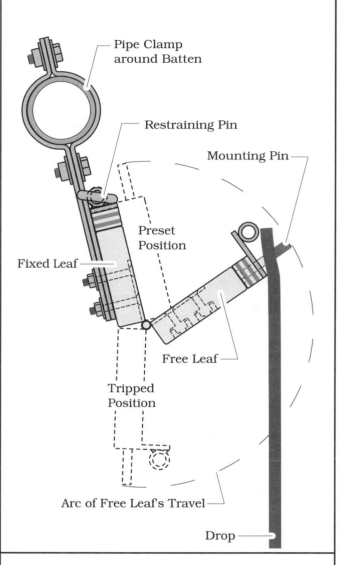

FIGURE 1: QUICK RELEASE IN OPERATION

The restraining pins are rigged with aircraft-cable leads which are clewed together and joined to a single operating line. We intended that the quick release we rigged for a Yale School of Drama production would be driven by a pneumatic cylinder, whose use we thought would minimize batten swing. We found during techs, however, that the batten's movement was not noticeable. For performances we triggered the quick release by means of an offstage handline: the lower-tech approach was simply more reliable.

The weight of the drop and the quick release itself tends to rotate the batten toward the drop. If the batten rotated too far, of course, the drop would slip off its pins. Rigging the batten as though it were to be used for an overhung electric pipe prevents such rotation. The most familiar technique — and the one we used — involves clamping sidearms to the batten, next to the batten's pickups and with their arms pointing straight up so that their arms can be tied to the batten's pickups.

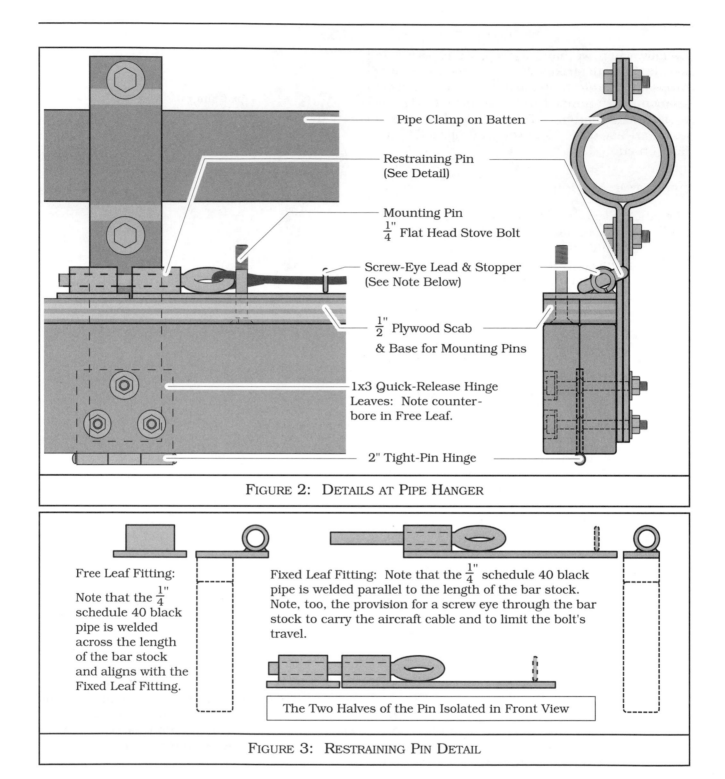

Pipe Clamp on Batten

Restraining Pin
(See Detail)

Mounting Pin
$\frac{1}{4}$" Flat Head Stove Bolt

Screw-Eye Lead & Stopper
(See Note Below)

$\frac{1}{2}$" Plywood Scab
& Base for Mounting Pins

1x3 Quick-Release Hinge
Leaves: Note counter-
bore in Free Leaf.

2" Tight-Pin Hinge

FIGURE 2: DETAILS AT PIPE HANGER

Free Leaf Fitting:

Note that the $\frac{1}{4}$" schedule 40 black pipe is welded across the length of the bar stock and aligns with the Fixed Leaf Fitting.

Fixed Leaf Fitting: Note that the $\frac{1}{4}$" schedule 40 black pipe is welded parallel to the length of the bar stock. Note, too, the provision for a screw eye through the bar stock to carry the aircraft cable and to limit the bolt's travel.

The Two Halves of the Pin Isolated in Front View

FIGURE 3: RESTRAINING PIN DETAIL

For the most part, curtain rigs used in theatre are not technically difficult. But a curtain that needs to be paged around a circular track and then drop gracefully to the floor as if released by magic is an unusual challenge. Add to that challenge the absence of fly space and a limited budget, and the rig seems almost sure to be cut. Those were the challenges we faced in mounting our 1998 production of *Cymbeline* at the Yale School of Drama. Our solution worked extremely well, was almost noise free, and, since most of the parts were in stock, cost very little to accomplish.

THE BASIC RIG

Figure 1 shows a general view of the rig we built. The curtain was a panel of nylon netting held up by small wooden balls that glided along a circular traveler track. The track, C-clamped to the fixed lighting grid, was made up of two rings, the bottom one of which could be lowered on cue by actuating three pneumatic cylinders. When that bottom ring was lowered, the wooden balls holding the curtain slipped out of the track.

TRACK & RELEASE MECHANISM

Figure 2 shows the construction of the track. Angle-iron-reinforced quarter-ply was sufficiently light and rigid for the rings. The 5'-diameter top ring was banded by a strip of $\frac{1}{8}$" tempered Masonite®, glued and stapled in place as shown, smooth side in. The bottom ring was made $\frac{1}{2}$" smaller in diameter than the top ring, and its outside edge was beveled, filled, sanded, and then coated with paraffin wax to ease movement of the wooden-ball glides. The glides, $\frac{3}{8}$" in diameter, were drilled through to receive the pieces of monofilament line that served as curtain ties. With their $\frac{9}{16}$" bore and 1" stroke, the Clippard Minimatic 9SD cylinders we used extended less than $2\frac{1}{2}$" above the rig.

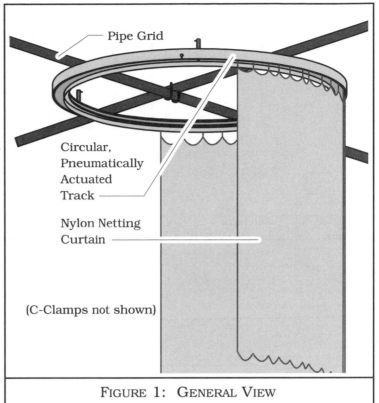

Pipe Grid

Circular, Pneumatically Actuated Track

Nylon Netting Curtain

(C-Clamps not shown)

FIGURE 1: GENERAL VIEW

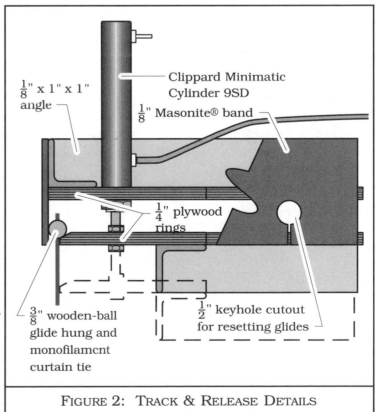

$\frac{1}{8}$" x 1" x 1" angle

Clippard Minimatic Cylinder 9SD

$\frac{1}{8}$" Masonite® band

$\frac{1}{4}$" plywood rings

$\frac{3}{8}$" wooden-ball glide hung and monofilament curtain tie

$\frac{1}{2}$" keyhole cutout for resetting glides

FIGURE 2: TRACK & RELEASE DETAILS

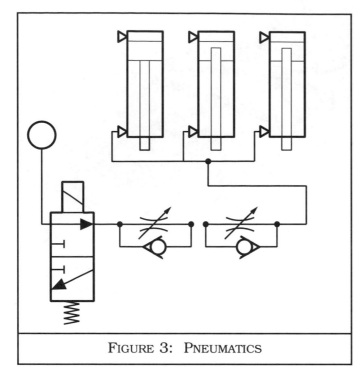

FIGURE 3: PNEUMATICS

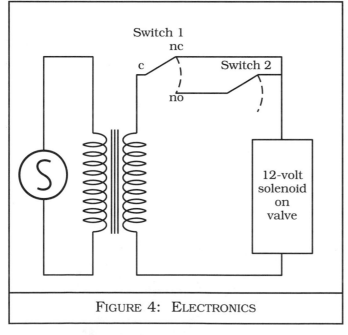

FIGURE 4: ELECTRONICS

THE ACTUATING SYSTEM

The actuating system was plumbed as shown in Figure 3. The components included one 12-volt-solenoid-actuated, two-position, three-way control valve, one 3-way coupler, and two flow control valves. The cylinders' retract ports were coupled and powered; the extension ports were left open.

Wired to two switches as shown in Figure 4, the solenoid-actuated valve kept the cylinder rods retracted, holding the bottom ring in the up position. In its normal position, the first switch, an SPDT momentary pushbutton, kept the second switch disarmed and the solenoid energized. On the "warn" cue, the first switch was thrown, arming the second switch, a normally closed SPST momentary pushbutton. On the "go" cue, the second pushbutton was pushed, dropping the curtain to the floor.

FINAL NOTES

The whole rig was bench-built and then mounted to the lighting grid with two standard lighting C-clamps. After a few minor adjustments to fine-tune the system, the effect ran reliably throughout tech rehearsals and performances.

Purchased new, the needed cylinders, valves, and switches could easily cost $200 or more. Since all the pneumatic and electronic parts were pulled from our stock, however, building this rig cost only about $25 in plywood, Masonite®, and angle iron.

For an industrial in Puerto Rico an 80'-wide x 20'-tall muslin drop needed to go away in the blink of an eye. The solution, a variation on the design featured in "A Quick Release for Drops," was developed by Ben Thoron and Peter Ballenger for the Old Globe Theater. The concept of the rig is simple. Each module consists of two lengths of aluminum angle hinged together as shown in Figure 1. Each module is hung from a batten or truss by three lighting C-clamps bolted to a fixed angle, and the modules are interlocked to form a single rig by $\frac{1}{4}$"-diameter bolts passed through the connector sleeves. Three release pins joined to a common linkage hold the swinging angle and the fixed angle back to back until the rig is triggered. A line of studs along the free flange of the swinging angle holds the grommets of a hanging drop. When the "go" button is pushed, a pneumatic cylinder attached to the linkage pulls the release pins, the swinging angle rotates downward, and the drop is released.

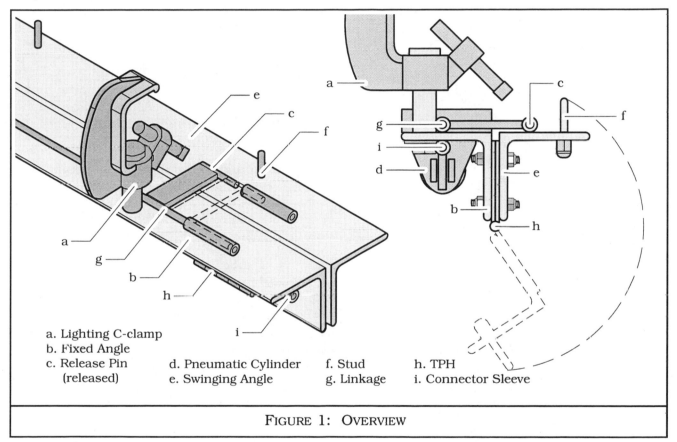

a. Lighting C-clamp
b. Fixed Angle
c. Release Pin   d. Pneumatic Cylinder   f. Stud   h. TPH
   (released)   e. Swinging Angle   g. Linkage   i. Connector Sleeve

FIGURE 1: OVERVIEW

CONSTRUCTION DETAILS

Figures 2, 3, and 4 detail the construction of a 10' module. The 80' rig comprised nine modules, each built under 10' long to satisfy air-freight restrictions. To allow them to operate individually, each module was given its own double-acting pneumatic piston, mounted on the fixed angle and plumbed to move the linkage on the pull stroke only so that each module could be closed independently by hand. That choice simplified hanging the drop: once the 80' rig was assembled and hung, one person walking along its length could preset the modules one at a time.

The 3" x 3" x $\frac{1}{4}$" aluminum angle was a good material to use because, in addition to being light-weight and locally available, it provided sufficiently wide surfaces on which to mount the hardware. The use of aluminum also minimized machining time. For instance, the $3\frac{5}{16}$" slot (see Figure 3) cut

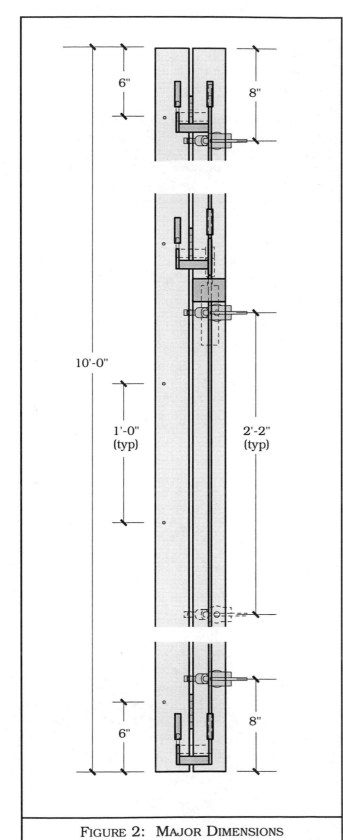

FIGURE 2: MAJOR DIMENSIONS

in the fixed flange of each module to join the cylinder to the linkage began as two $\frac{5}{16}$" holes drilled 3" apart. Two quick passes with a saber saw turned them into a slot. Drilling the five holes that provided mounting options for each module's C-clamps also went quickly, as did drilling and tapping the ten holes that received the studs and the eighteen holes for the 2" TPHs that joined the angles. Note that the hinges' bolt holes were oversized so that the hinges could be finessed into proper alignment during assembly.

Making the studs from $\frac{1}{4}$" x 2" hex head bolts was also a good choice. After their heads had been cut off and the plain-shaft ends had been rounded over on the belt-sander, they provided a nice smooth edge for the drop's grommets. The thread that protruded through the flange of the swinging angle allowed the studs to be secured with nylon-insert nuts for safety's sake.

Using $\frac{1}{2}$" aluminum tube with a wall thickness of 0.125" as sleeves and the shop's stock of hot-formed $\frac{1}{4}$" steel rod as the material for the linkage and release pins was somewhat less successful. Rust and other surface imperfections had to be sanded off the hot-formed rod before the linkage and release pins would slide easily through the aluminum sleeves. Even after the sanding, a block of UHMW had to be added to counter the piston-induced torque that caused the linkage to bind. Using sleeves made of UHMW and/or linkage-and-pin assemblies made of aluminum or cold-rolled steel rod would probably have worked better.

FINAL NOTES

Though more expensive in both labor and material than its predecessor, this rig provides a fine looking finished product ideal for traveling shows. The modules are rugged and can be used individually or fastened together through their connector sleeves to form batten-long rigs. In the end this rig proved to be a lightweight and reliable solution to release a drop.

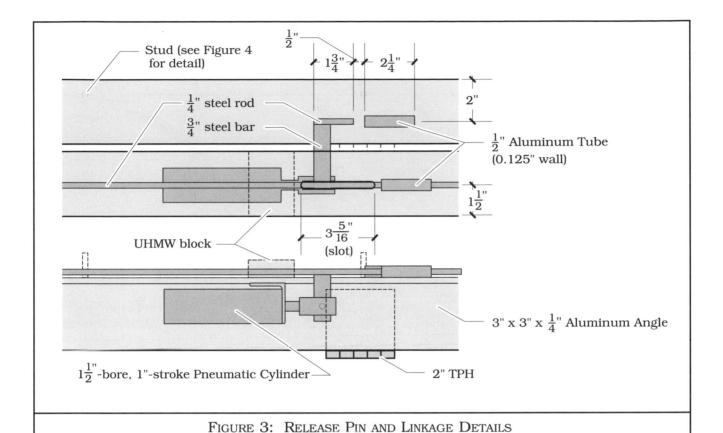

Stud (see Figure 4 for detail)

¼" steel rod

¾" steel bar

½"

1¾"

2¼"

2"

½" Aluminum Tube (0.125" wall)

1½"

UHMW block

3 5/16" (slot)

3" x 3" x ¼" Aluminum Angle

1½"-bore, 1"-stroke Pneumatic Cylinder

2" TPH

FIGURE 3: RELEASE PIN AND LINKAGE DETAILS

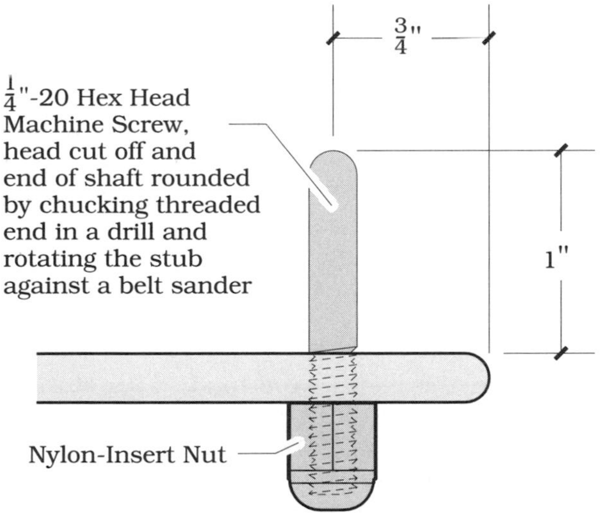

¼"-20 Hex Head Machine Screw, head cut off and end of shaft rounded by chucking threaded end in a drill and rotating the stub against a belt sander

¾"

1"

Nylon-Insert Nut

FIGURE 4: STUD DETAILS

To avoid the noise typically associated with traveler tracks, the technical designers for the 1997 Yale Repertory Theatre's *A Midsummer Night's Dream* developed a system that used P1000 Unistrut® in place of standard traveler track and UHMW glides in place of wheeled carriers to support a pair of tube steel framed flats. This article details construction of the glides.

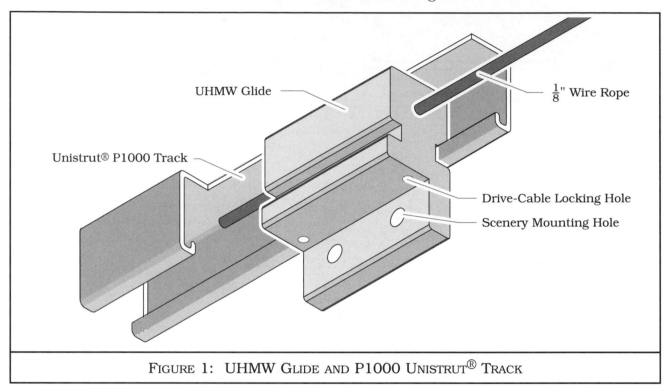

FIGURE 1: UHMW GLIDE AND P1000 UNISTRUT® TRACK

UHMW was chosen for its low coefficient of friction and machinability. In constructing the glides, blocks of UHMW were cut to 1½" x 1½" x 12" and then machined down to the section pictured in Figure 1. The section was designed not only to act as a glide, but also to incorporate all of the hardware connections for hanging the legs and securing the drive cables. Blanks were cut to 3" lengths and then the holes for the cable, set screws, and leg hardware were bored and tapped as necessary. The tapped holes were intended for setscrews which would secure the glide to the drive cable. Though ultimately not used for that purpose in this application, their effectiveness to hold onto the cable was tested. In repeated tests, significant damage was done to the cable before the glide was harmed.

Figure 2 shows the ideal dimensions for the glides. Most of the glides were made with standard woodworking tools (table saw with dado blade, radial arm saw, and drill press), and tolerances were fairly relaxed. One pair of glides, however, was produced using the school's machining tools: vertical mill, drill press, and lathe. The more precisely machined set of glides performed better, but the sets made with woodworking tools worked well enough to be used in this application.

The 6'-0" x 16'-0" legs supported by the glides were framed in 1" x 1" x 0.035" tube steel to reduce weight. Weld-nuts inserted through the front of the top rails accepted $\frac{5}{16}$" flat head stove bolts inserted through the back of the glides. Covered with Duvetyn®, the legs weighed approximately 60 pounds each. Each leg was fitted with two glides and no friction problems were ever experienced. Initially, the designers anticipated that a pair of glides could not carry more than 100 pounds. Though no ratings can really be applied, subsequent experience has shown that they perform

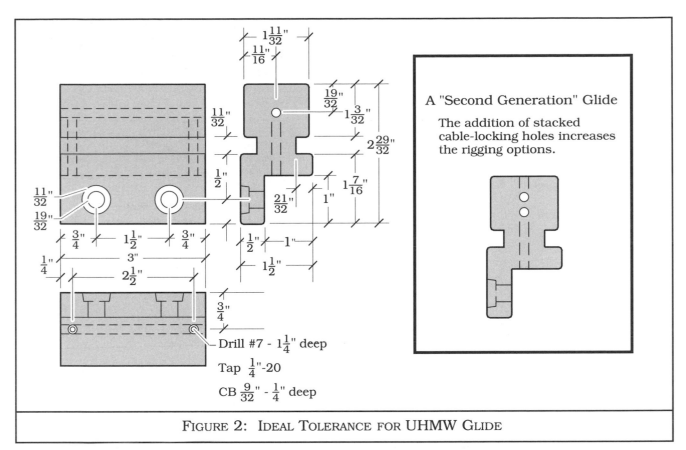

A "Second Generation" Glide

The addition of stacked cable-locking holes increases the rigging options.

Drill #7 - $1\frac{1}{4}$" deep

Tap $\frac{1}{4}$"-20

CB $\frac{9}{32}$" - $\frac{1}{4}$" deep

FIGURE 2: IDEAL TOLERANCE FOR UHMW GLIDE

beyond this limit with no problems. For one production, two carriers were used to support a 3'-0" x 18'-0" flat framed in $\frac{5}{4}$x3 pine, covered with $1\frac{1}{4}$" medium density fiberboard, and stiffened with $1\frac{1}{2}$" x $\frac{1}{8}$" angle iron. That unit weighed upwards of 150 to 200 pounds.

Since the first round of glides was machined, several more have been made, each customized to improve on the design. Typical changes have included changes in the cable/rope location in the carrier, number of cables running through the carrier, and mounting details between carrier and scenic element. The most effective of these variations, one in which two $\frac{1}{8}$" cables are used, requires the stacking of the cables and the addition of a second set of locking screws as shown at the right in Figure 2. This has necessitated the use of P1000HS slotted Unistrut® to allow access to the top of the glide, which has the added advantage of reducing the weight of the channel by a noticeable margin. It is also important to note that glides have been developed for use with rope, which are useful in manual operations. I recommend that glide "blanks" be made in quantity, and that mounting and cable/rope holes be added as necessary. Requiring only basic machining tools and skills, and using relatively inexpensive materials, the glides have been a great success and will undoubtedly be useful in future productions.

❧❧❧

Drop boxes are often used in theater to achieve a sudden and dramatic scene change. They may contain a drop, banner, or loose material such as confetti or ticker tape. The chief challenge in engineering drop boxes is to ensure that the effect is quiet and repeatable. The designer for the Yale Repertory Theatre's production of *Measure for Measure* wanted four, grid-high, orange china silk banners to be released behind the actors at a specific moment. Technical Director Mario Tooch achieved this through a set of pneumatic drop boxes that a single operator could trigger simultaneously.

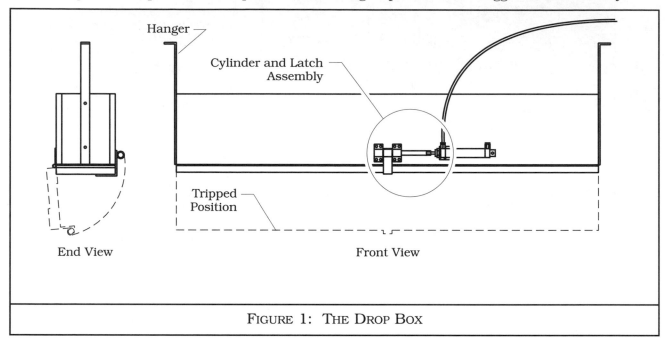

FIGURE 1: THE DROP BOX

RIGGING & OPERATION

The drop boxes had hinged bottoms and open tops to facilitate loading and were hung from battens. Connected to a pneumatic manifold as shown in Figure 2, the four cylinders were actuated by a single toggle switch. The retraction of the cylinder pulled the latch pin. To reset the effect, the crew flew in the battens, swung the boxes' bottoms back up, and pushed the latch pins into the latch by hand. After a little experimentation, we discovered that air pressure settings as low as 40 psi would open the latch reliably and without much noise.

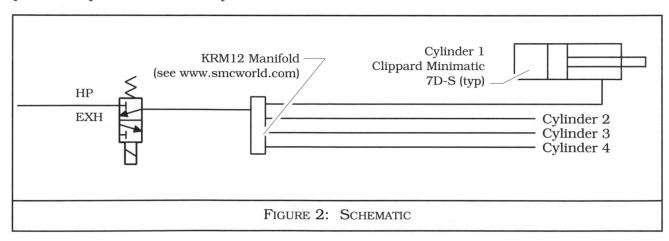

FIGURE 2: SCHEMATIC

CONSTRUCTION

Our drop boxes were $9\frac{1}{8}$" tall, $6\frac{3}{4}$" deep, and 4'-0" long, but boxes of other sizes could use the latch design we developed. The latch components are detailed in Figure 3. Regardless of box size, there are a few fundamental considerations in latch design and construction. To speed construction, we used only one size of bar stock for the latch pieces, and, for this particular cylinder, the angle iron had to be $\frac{1}{16}$" thinner than the bar stock. All steel was laid out, drilled, then bent. Due to the small pieces, it is important to drill the holes before bending the steel since drilling bent steel is time consuming and difficult. Deburring all the holes and reaming the pipe allows for smoother operation and assembly. The release pin, a $\frac{1}{2}$" UHMW rod drilled, tapped, and threaded onto the piston rod, operated almost silently.

The next step was to build the boxes. The boxes had simple 1x3 framing with a lauan skin. The door was attached using tight pin back-flap hinges and $\frac{3}{16}$" flat head stove bolts. The hanging brackets and the cylinder bracket were also attached with flat head stove bolts.. The latch pieces were attached using drywall screws.

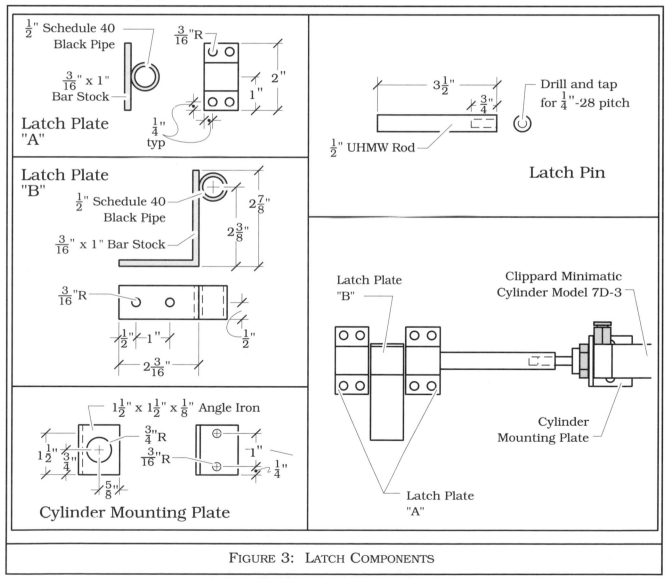

FIGURE 3: LATCH COMPONENTS

CONCLUSION

This system is easy to assemble and can essentially be used by any theater with an air compressor or built-in air system. The only specialty items are a pneumatic solenoid, pneumatic cylinders, and a simple light switch.

I found this drop-box mechanism very useful. A theater could easily adapt the process to make one long box or several smaller boxes, depending on the specific needs of the production. The units are easy to build and install. They are also less likely to jam or catch than the traditional trickline and pin drop box. The repeatable behavior and ability to activate multiple units simultaneously are by far the most appealing aspects of these drop boxes.

≈•≈•≈

The traditional adjustable floor pulley has two drawbacks when installed in a traveler system that flies. If it is flown out with the traveler, it poses a safety hazard. If it is detached from the system and left fastened to the deck, re-rigging the traveler's run line and reattaching the pulley takes time. Developed for the 1999 tour of Yale Repertory Theatre's *Geography II: Tree*, the alternate design described here solves those problems. In addition to a base plate and two trapezoidal gussets, each pulley comprises two similar but not completely identical sheave plates. Each sheave plate consists of two pieces of bar stock: one, a rectangle: the other an L-shaped piece which "surrounds" the rectangle, leaving a $\frac{1}{2}$"-wide L-shaped slot between the two pieces. This slot allows quick loading of the run line. Figure 1 shows how the run line is installed; Figure 2 illustrates the relationship between the sheaves, spacers, and plates; and Figure 3 details construction of the floor pulley components.

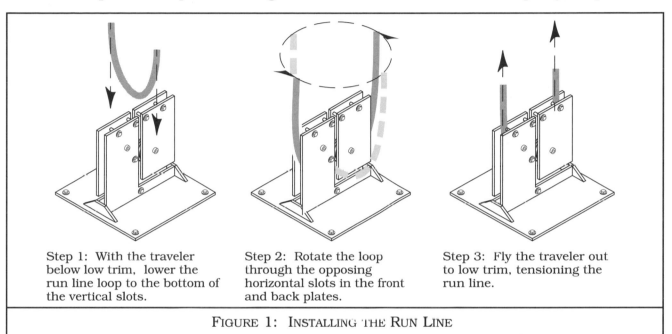

Step 1: With the traveler below low trim, lower the run line loop to the bottom of the vertical slots.

Step 2: Rotate the loop through the opposing horizontal slots in the front and back plates.

Step 3: Fly the traveler out to low trim, tensioning the run line.

FIGURE 1: INSTALLING THE RUN LINE

NOTES

Though originally designed to expedite load-in during a tour, this floor pulley would also serve as a useful addition to stock rigging hardware. It can be attached to the stage floor with $\frac{1}{4}$"-diameter lag bolts or, alternatively, held in place by stage weights. Milling the holes for the sheaves' axle bolts into horizontal slots and fitting the axle bolts with wing nuts would make the tension this style of floor pulley supplies adjustable.

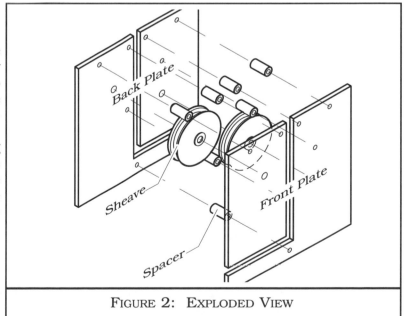

FIGURE 2: EXPLODED VIEW

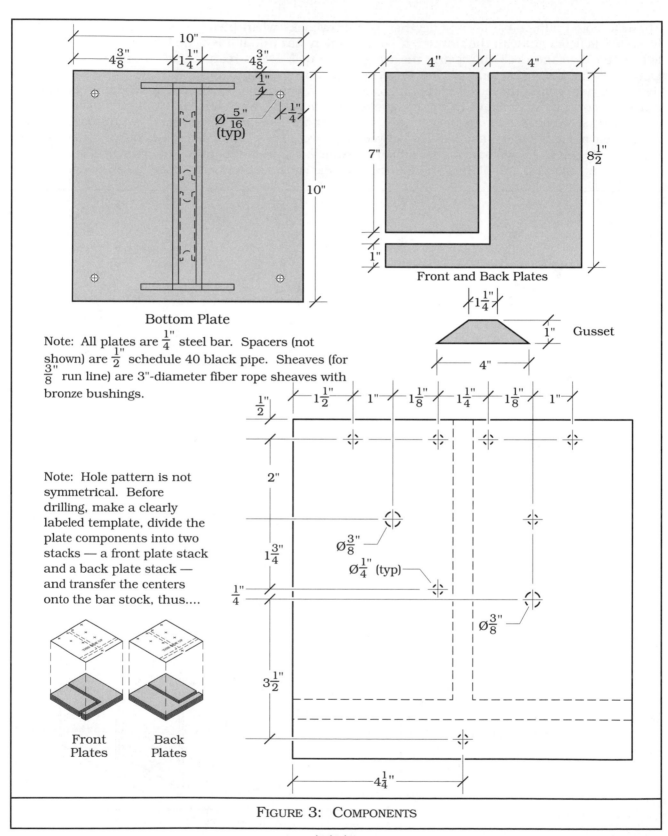

Bottom Plate

Front and Back Plates

Gusset

Note: All plates are $\frac{1}{4}$" steel bar. Spacers (not shown) are $\frac{1}{2}$" schedule 40 black pipe. Sheaves (for $\frac{3}{8}$" run line) are 3"-diameter fiber rope sheaves with bronze bushings.

Note: Hole pattern is not symmetrical. Before drilling, make a clearly labeled template, divide the plate components into two stacks — a front plate stack and a back plate stack — and transfer the centers onto the bar stock, thus....

Front Plates   Back Plates

FIGURE 3: COMPONENTS

TECHNICAL BRIEF

Rigging Techniques

Large hanging drops often sag, wrinkle, or ripple. Solutions include the use of sandwich boards, cables, or steel trusses along the edges to stretch the drops. All of these offer one disadvantage or another: sandwich boards can be used only on stationary drops, hour-glassing can occur when using cables, and steel trusses are heavy and construction is time-consuming. A different solution that stretches drops tight with readily available materials while still allowing for vertical travel uses TJI® joists as stretchers.

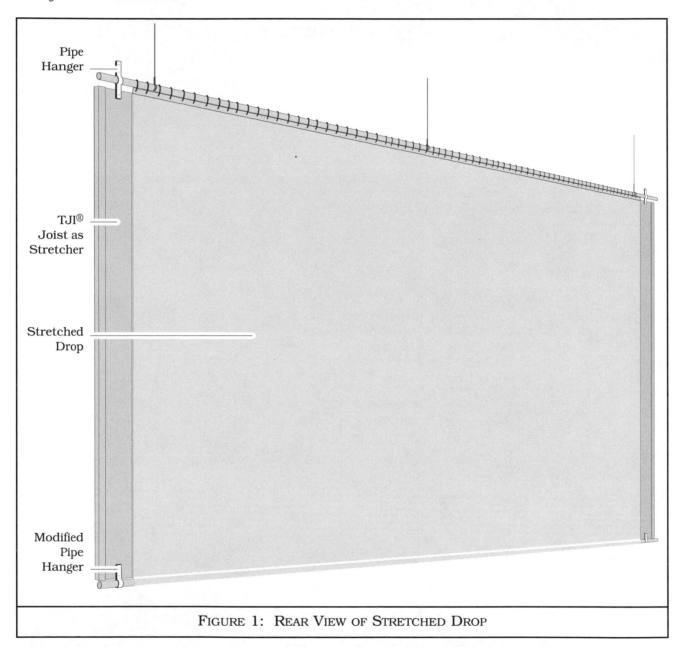

FIGURE 1: REAR VIEW OF STRETCHED DROP

TJI® joists, wooden I-beams manufactured by the Trus-Joist Corporation, are commonly used in place of solid lumber beams in wood construction. Their flanges are made of laminated pine; and their webs, of plywood. They come in various widths ranging from $9\frac{1}{2}$" to 16" and are readily available in lengths up to 60' from most full-service lumber yards.

For use as drop stretchers, a pair of TJI® joists is attached to a batten and bottom pipe. The TJI® joists themselves stretch the drop vertically and provide an attachment point for the edges of the drop after it has been stretched horizontally. The connections are pictured in Figure 2. The hardware at the batten is a simple pipe hanger fastened to one side of a joist's web with a single bolt. The bottom connection is a second pipe hanger with one pair of its flanges cut off so that the flown drop can rest on the floor.

In installation, the drop and its TJI® stretchers are attached to a batten which has been flown in to working height. See Figure 3. (Counterweighting the system involves balancing the weight of both the drop and the stretchers.) As the batten is raised, the stretchers pivot into position. Finally, the bottom pipe is run through the drop's pocket, the joists are clamped to it, and the drop is stretched horizontally and attached to its stretchers.

Because TJI®s are made of wood, it is easy to staple the fabric directly to them. Alternatively, an extra piece of muslin sewn onto a drop's edge will provide a "stretching handle" and spare the drop from staple damage. It is equally easy to sandwich the drop between the TJI® stretchers and additional pieces of lumber, eliminating the use of staples entirely — a very handy approach to stretching scrims and other similarly valuable soft goods.

Admittedly, TJI® joists are somewhat costly, but because they are so long and because they are made of wood they make almost perfect drop stretchers. We've successfully used $9\frac{1}{2}$" TJI®s to stretch drops as tall as 40'. And, of course, those same TJI®s found their way into subsequent productions — not always as drop stretchers, either.

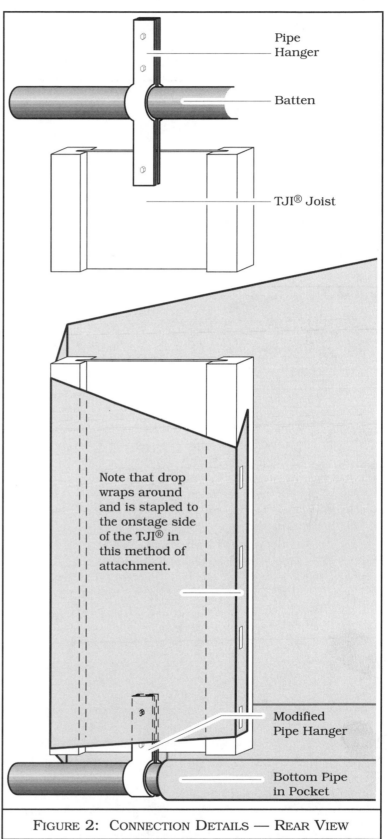

Pipe Hanger

Batten

TJI® Joist

Note that drop wraps around and is stapled to the onstage side of the TJI® in this method of attachment.

Modified Pipe Hanger

Bottom Pipe in Pocket

FIGURE 2: CONNECTION DETAILS — REAR VIEW

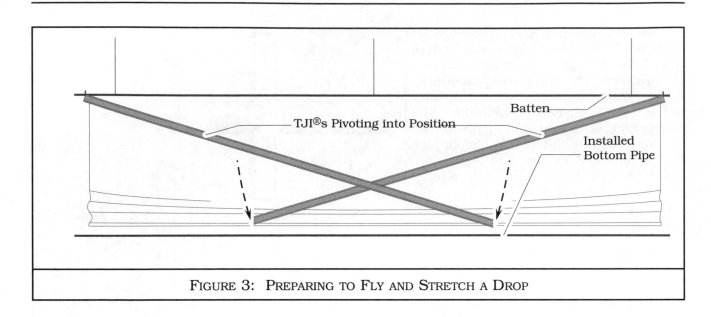

FIGURE 3: PREPARING TO FLY AND STRETCH A DROP

For an Arizona State University production, I designed the rig illustrated below to tilt a panel from its initial vertical position to an angle of 45° over the acting area. The rig used two lengths of traveler track hung parallel to each other and perpendicular to the two system pipes that supported them. Each track carried a single traveler trolley, and the ends of both tracks were fitted with single-sheave blocks. The panel's top was hung directly from the trolleys. Its bottom was picked up by a pair of lines that were run over the tracks' upstage sheaves and then connected to the trolleys. A pair of wire-rope control lines run under the downstage sheaves connected the trolleys to a third batten, the control batten. Raising the control batten pulled the trolleys downstage, simultaneously shifting the panel's top forward and lifting its bottom. This rig was easily run by a single fly operator, and produced little of the batten swing that moves like this so often generate.

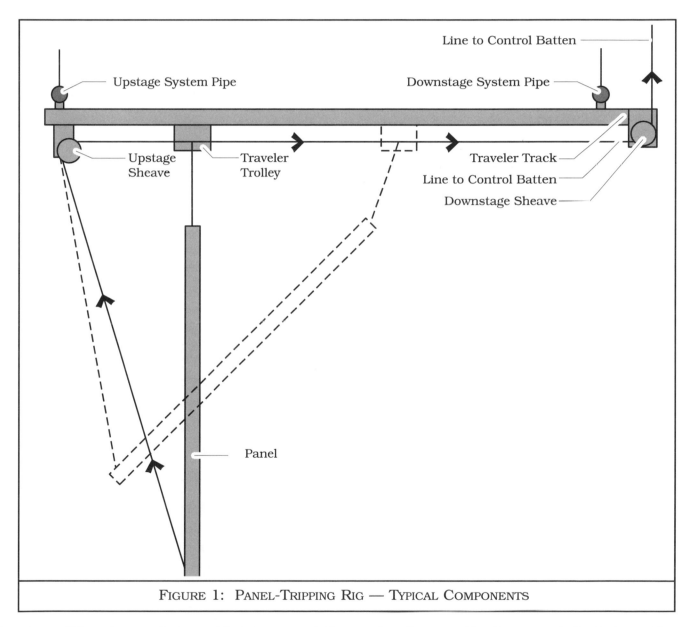

FIGURE 1: PANEL-TRIPPING RIG — TYPICAL COMPONENTS

Many different manufacturers' hardware could be used in this rig. For the record, the lists on the following page describe the materials we used and the steps we followed in rigging the panel.

MATERIALS

Two P1000 Unistrut® channels
Two P2950 Unistrut® trolley assemblies
Four $3\frac{1}{2}$" phenolic resin sheaves for $\frac{1}{8}$" aircraft cable
Four shop-fabricated brackets for the sheaves
Four lighting instrument C-clamps
$\frac{1}{8}$" aircraft cable and hardware

ASSEMBLY

1. Cut tracks to length.

2. Bolt C-clamp hangers to track.

3. Place trolleys in track.

4. Mount sheaves at ends of tracks.

5. Clamp tracks to system pipes and fly to working height.

6. Run top pickups from panel to the center holes on the trolleys.

7. Run the bottom pickups from the panel over the upstage sheaves and connect them to the upstage holes on the trolleys.

8. Run control lines from the downstage holes on the trolleys, under the downstage sheaves, and to the control batten.

NOTES

1. The weight of the panel shifts toward the downstage system pipe during the move. Tie off the system pipes securely and provide appropriate safeguards to keep their handlines from slipping through the rope locks.

2. The minimal batten swing this rig generates can be further reduced by tying the system pipes off downstage and upstage.

✿✿✿

Standard traveler track manufactured for the theatre industry, such as ADC Models 170 and 280, perform their intended functions of providing for the movement of soft goods across the stage quite well. However, when heavy scenic elements must effect similar motions, these tracks may not perform satisfactorily. Common problems include excessive noise, loads exceeding the track's design, and sagging draw cables. Further, the hardware typically available for these tracks is designed for $\frac{1}{2}$" or $\frac{5}{8}$" rope operation, making the connection of $\frac{1}{8}$" or $\frac{3}{16}$" aircraft cable for winch-driven operation difficult and cumbersome. In an effort to discover an improved traveler track design, I surveyed a number of manufacturers and developed the design detailed here.

First, it is useful to identify the primary concern which led to this investigation — noise. Typical traveler track consists of a sheet metal tube, bent to allow the wheels of a carrier inside and connection of other hardware outside. This design results in a megaphone in which the primary noise, caused by the small carrier wheels, is amplified in a resonant chamber. Increasing the mass of the track, using larger wheels, and moving the wheels from the inside to the outside of the track are three ways to reduce the noise. Any of these steps alone produces good results, but since the lat-

ter two necessitate abandoning the standard track anyway, we opted to incorporate all three in designing a track to carry two heavy wall units in the Yale Repertory Theatre's 1996 production of *First Lady*.

Atlas Silk's Models 801 and 1001, the acknowledged inspiration for our design, is sold as heavy-duty (but non-rated) curtain track and proved too expensive. Our adaptation incorporates two pieces of Unistrut® P1000 that, held parallel by custom hangers as shown in Figure 1, serve as rails for our custom carrier wheels. Unistrut® is constructed of a heavier gauge steel than ADC 280, and by running the carrier wheels on top of the Unistrut®, we achieved all our design objectives. To distinguish our track Unistrut® from other pieces and to protect it over time, we purchased the P1000 with Unistrut®'s Perma-Green II, baked-on finish.

To suspend the track we constructed a set of brackets like those detailed in Figure 2 whose design incorporates not only track support, but also dresses the draw cable neatly above the scenery. Spacing of the brackets for any track is a factor of the size and weight of the load. For our first use of the track — moving a pair of 500#, 12'w x 20'h steel-framed hard-covered flats — bracket spacing of 5' worked well.

The carriers we built consist of $\frac{3}{16}$" plate bent as shown in Figure 3, fitted with two all-thread bolts from which to hang the scenery, and featuring a pair of in-line skate wheels to roll along the top of the Unistrut®. The all-thread bolts

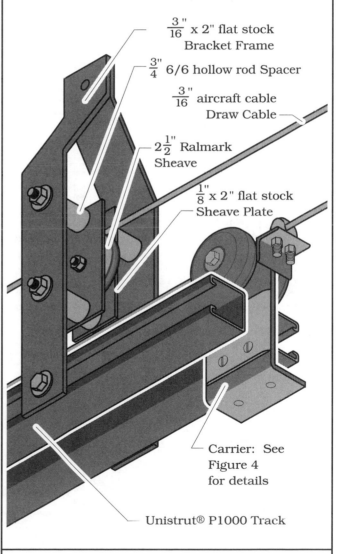

$\frac{3}{16}$" x 2" flat stock
Bracket Frame

$\frac{3}{4}$" 6/6 hollow rod Spacer

$\frac{3}{16}$" aircraft cable
Draw Cable

$2\frac{1}{2}$" Ralmark
Sheave

$\frac{1}{8}$" x 2" flat stock
Sheave Plate

Carrier: See
Figure 4
for details

Unistrut® P1000 Track

FIGURE 1: BRACKET, TRACK, & CARRIER

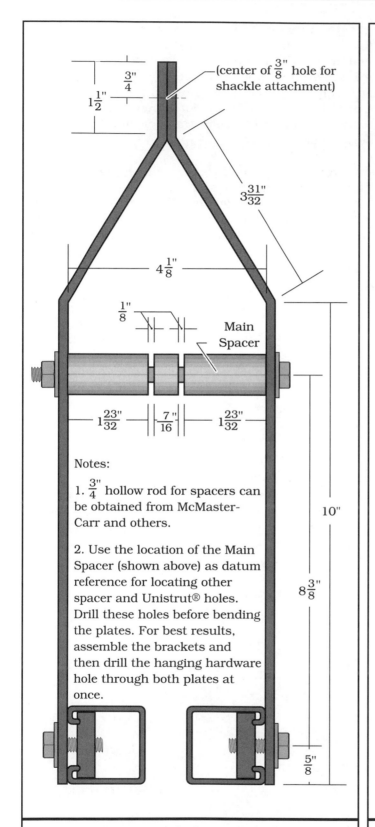

Notes:

1. $\frac{3}{4}$" hollow rod for spacers can be obtained from McMaster-Carr and others.

2. Use the location of the Main Spacer (shown above) as datum reference for locating other spacer and Unistrut® holes. Drill these holes before bending the plates. For best results, assemble the brackets and then drill the hanging hardware hole through both plates at once.

FIGURE 2: NOTES & COMMON DIMENSIONS

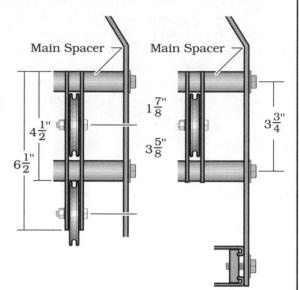

Live-End Bracket   Standard Bracket

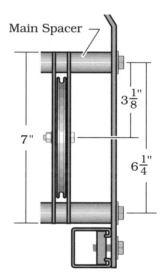

Main Spacer

Dead-End Bracket

All sheaves align with brackets' centerlines.

Live-End and Standard Brackets use $2\frac{1}{2}$" Ralmark sheaves; the Dead-End, a 5" Ralmark sheave.

Spacer/Track connectors are $\frac{5}{16}$" hex head bolts. Sheave Axles are $\frac{1}{4}$" hex head bolts.

FIGURE 3: BRACKET DETAILS

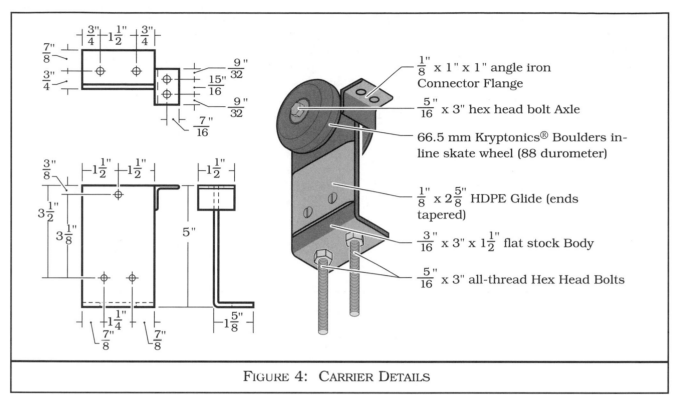

FIGURE 4: CARRIER DETAILS

allowed us a couple of inches of trim adjustment. We used 66.5mm Kryptonics® wheels (88 durometer) with low-grade bearings. The sides of the carrier plates are covered with HDPE to minimize both noise and the chance of the carrier snagging at a joint between sections of Unistrut®. The small angle flange added to the lead carriers on each piece of scenery allowed for attachment to the draw cable with a wire rope clip.

In its inaugural production, the track performed well. Scenery tracked smoothly and nearly silently, thus satisfying our goals for the project. Future implementations will no doubt benefit from continued consideration of the design.

❧❧❧

Bringing flown units to a gentle stop as they touch down on a stage floor is usually a simple task. But the results of a botched "in" are as ugly as they are familiar. Stop short of the floor, and the units hang in mid air, twisting or swinging back and forth in response to the slightest movement nearby. Overshoot the low-trim spike, and they bang into the floor and then lean crazily out of plumb. Normally, rig trimming and operator training will eliminate most such possibilities. But when they don't, the best solution may be to give each unit a self-masking and trim-correcting foot like those developed by University of Virginia Technical Director Jeff Dennstaedt.

HANGING-FLAT-AND-FOOT DESIGN

The University of Virginia's rigging system is hydraulically driven. During long rehearsals for the University's 1993 spring musical *Babes in Arms*, fluid viscosity changes made the system's trims increasingly unreliable. To compensate, Jeff re-designed a pair of profiled-tree flats as two-part mechanical systems. The upper part of each tree, the hanging flat, was conventionally rigged. The lower part, the foot, was attached to the hanging flat by means of an ordinary screen door closer mounted vertically on the back of the hanging flat. Figure 1 identifies the parts and outlines their operation.

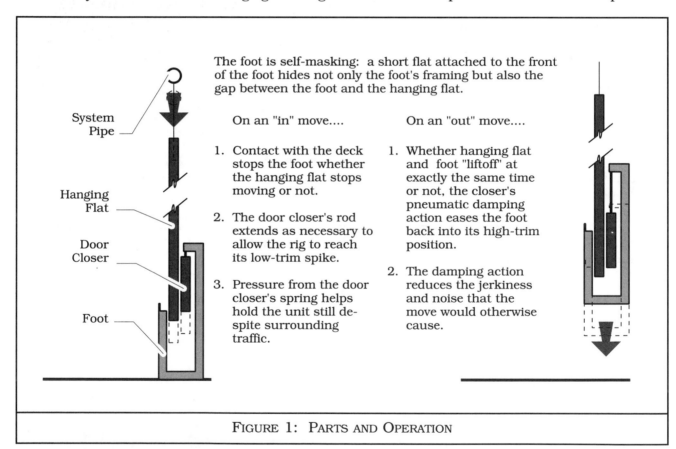

The foot is self-masking: a short flat attached to the front of the foot hides not only the foot's framing but also the gap between the foot and the hanging flat.

On an "in" move....

1. Contact with the deck stops the foot whether the hanging flat stops moving or not.

2. The door closer's rod extends as necessary to allow the rig to reach its low-trim spike.

3. Pressure from the door closer's spring helps hold the unit still despite surrounding traffic.

On an "out" move....

1. Whether hanging flat and foot "liftoff" at exactly the same time or not, the closer's pneumatic damping action eases the foot back into its high-trim position.

2. The damping action reduces the jerkiness and noise that the move would otherwise cause.

System Pipe

Hanging Flat

Door Closer

Foot

FIGURE 1: PARTS AND OPERATION

"FOOT NOTES"

Figure 2A shows a closer look at the original hanger-and-foot design. Set designer Michael Allen was happy to add a small shrub to the base of each tree as the foot's masking. The technique is a good one, but note that the heavier a foot becomes, the more carefully the technical designer must balance it upstage-downstage and right-left to avoid bending the screen door closer's rod.

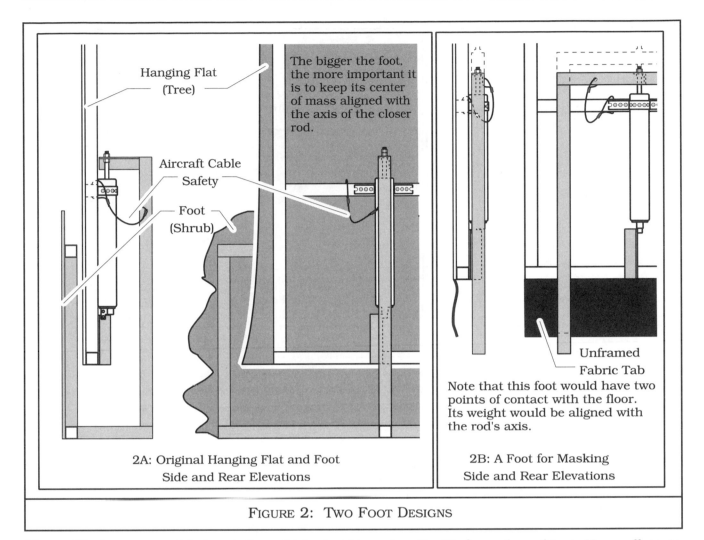

The bigger the foot, the more important it is to keep its center of mass aligned with the axis of the closer rod.

Hanging Flat (Tree)

Aircraft Cable Safety

Foot (Shrub)

Unframed Fabric Tab

Note that this foot would have two points of contact with the floor. Its weight would be aligned with the rod's axis.

2A: Original Hanging Flat and Foot
Side and Rear Elevations

2B: A Foot for Masking
Side and Rear Elevations

FIGURE 2: TWO FOOT DESIGNS

Figure 2B shows an untried variation which should work well with framed masking. Here, all parts of the foot would be upstage of a hung masking flat. The foot would anchor the flat against movement. The unframed fabric tab at the bottom of the hanger would mask the foot and any gap between the masking flat and the floor.

CONNECTIONS AND HARDWARE

Figure 3 illustrates the typical connections between the door closer and the flattage. Whatever door closer is used, a strip of plumber's strap and a short piece of angle iron will probably be all the hardware needed to mount the cylinder to the hanging flat. Figure 3A represents a hard-covered, tube-steel-framed flat, but the connections would be essentially the same for a wood-framed flat.

The plumber's strap is bent over the upper end of the cylinder and screwed to a toggle. The angle iron (the "rail angle") connecting the door closer to the hanging flat is either screwed or welded to the flat's bottom rail. A hole bored near the top end of the rail angle offers a convenient mount for the lower end of the cylinder.

Connecting the closer's rod to the unit's foot is fairly simple if the door closer's rod has a threaded end. Nutting the rod on either side of the rod angle as shown in Figure 3B will "fix" the connection

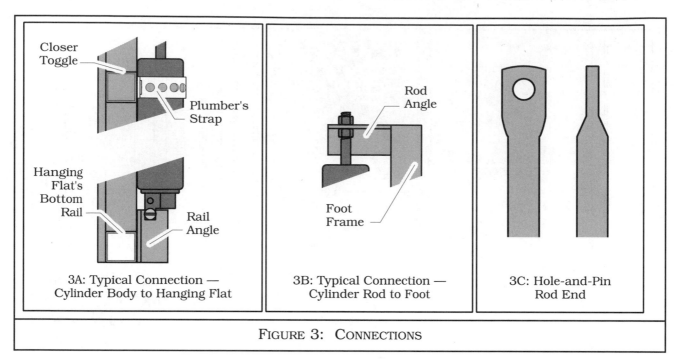

| 3A: Typical Connection — Cylinder Body to Hanging Flat | 3B: Typical Connection — Cylinder Rod to Foot | 3C: Hole-and-Pin Rod End |

FIGURE 3: CONNECTIONS

well enough to keep the foot from swinging. Not all door closer rods have threaded ends, however, and attaching the foot to a rod that has a hole-and-pin end like that shown in Figure 3C would be somewhat trickier. Obviously, balancing the unit would also be much more critical.

FINAL NOTES

Hanging-flat-and-foot units are neither expensive nor difficult to build. After several stages of refining his design, Jeff built and installed the first pair of them in half a day at a cost of about $15. Though developed for use with a hydraulically driven rigging system, they should be useful in trimming and anchoring flown units regardless of rigging system type.

෧෧෧෧

Like many theaters around the country, the stage at Iowa State University's Fisher Theater has a relatively low ceiling and has neither a grid nor a loading gallery. Furthermore, though the proscenium opening is 18'-0" tall, the first lineset (the highest of 20 single-purchase linesets) flies out to only 31'-0". The design for the 1992 production of *The Merry Wives of Windsor* called for three 10'-0" high by 16'-0" wide flats to fly in and out during the show. To move out of sight, the flats had to fly 20'-0"; but to stay out of sight, the batten that carried them could travel only 10'-0". Obviously, we'd need to use a double-purchase rig. Figure 1 illustrates the type of rig we used.

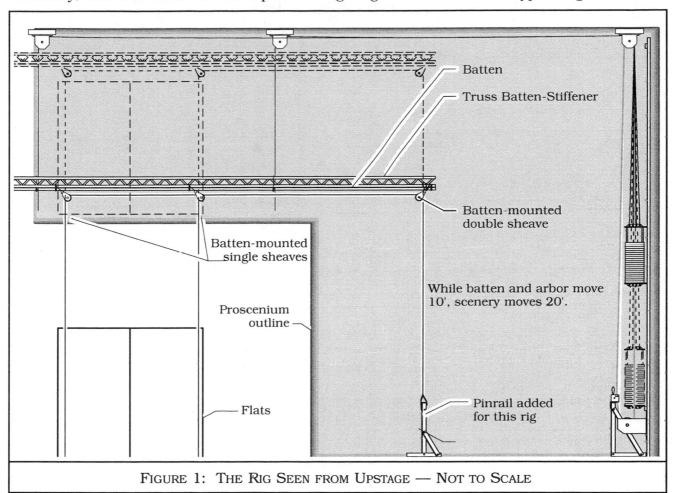

Batten

Truss Batten-Stiffener

Batten-mounted double sheave

Batten-mounted single sheaves

Proscenium outline

While batten and arbor move 10', scenery moves 20'.

Flats

Pinrail added for this rig

FIGURE 1: THE RIG SEEN FROM UPSTAGE — NOT TO SCALE

ESSENTIALS OF THE RIG

We achieved the 2:1 ratio by attaching additional sheaves directly to the batten and running the flats' lift lines over those sheaves and then offstage, where they were shackled to a pinrail we mounted on the floor directly under the end of the batten. Rigs like this can be easy to install and operate, but only if care is taken in their design, for they impose unusual loads on various parts of the rigging system. Figure 2 illustrates those loads.

This type of rig makes the stage floor itself part of the rigging system. For every 100# of scenery, the pinrail connection to the floor will have to supply 100# of force — multiplied by an appropriate safety factor — just to keep the scenery in the air. Getting it there takes even more force. Next, like any other muling sheaves, the set of sheaves mounted on the batten will bear more than the weight of the scenery in the form of resultant forces like those illustrated below. In this rig, the worst case occurs in the worst place — at the end of the batten — where the lift lines are ganged and pulled down toward the floor. We stiffened the end of our batten with a truss to keep it from deforming at the shortline pickup. Finally, for every 100# of scenery there will have to be 200# of counterweight in the arbor. It's just a logistical issue, but arbors aren't always tall enough to take the amount of counterweight this rig may need. Finally, it is important to remember the other logistical issue: the scenery's lift lines will have to tie off directly under the end of the batten, where they may be in the way of entrances, exits, and scene changes. Despite the careful planning it takes, this rig has undeniable advantages in low-ceiling stagehouses.

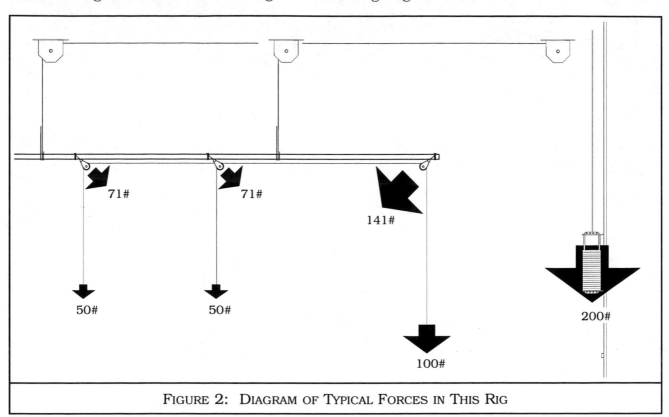

FIGURE 2: DIAGRAM OF TYPICAL FORCES IN THIS RIG

During the final, climactic moments of the last act, the false proscenium for the Yale School of Drama's production of *The Fatty Arbuckle Spookhouse Review* had to fly out of view — along with the rest of the scenery and the show's lead actress. The 500# false proscenium was a muslin-covered tube steel structure consisting of two legs measuring 2'-6" x 22'-0" and a header measuring 2'-6" x 33'-0". Because it was designed with a 1'-3" reveal, we built the unit as three triangular trusses to be assembled at load-in and picked at four points. Rather than try to pinpoint the upstage-downstage location of its center of gravity, we decided to fit the unit with the adjustable pickpoints and guides described here. That way, no matter how the weight was actually distributed, we could fly the proscenium out perpendicular to the stage floor. Figure 1 illustrates how the picks worked.

PICK AND GUIDE CONSTRUCTION

The picks were built of $1\frac{5}{8}$" P1000 Unistrut®, $\frac{1}{4}$" x $1\frac{1}{2}$" flat bar, Unistrut® nuts, two $\frac{3}{8}$" hex head bolts, and a rated $\frac{3}{8}$" shouldered eyebolt. The flat bar was cut 3" long and drilled with holes for the eyebolt and the two bolts that connected the bar to the Unistrut® nuts.

The guides were 3" x 3" blocks of $\frac{1}{4}$" UHMW drilled with three holes: two $\frac{3}{8}$" holes for the Unistrut® nuts and a $\frac{1}{2}$" hole which guided the $\frac{3}{16}$" aircraft cable pick lines. UHMW was substituted for flat bar in order to protect the wire rope, although a $\frac{3}{4}$" plywood plate would have achieved the same results.

Both pieces of Unistrut® were welded to the proscenium legs' 1" square tube steel frames, but the Unistrut® for the guide was set $1\frac{1}{2}$" further offstage so that the guide hole was directly above the shouldered eyebolt.

SOME CONSIDERATIONS

The weight of the false proscenium was distributed over four pick points, one on each leg and two on the header. Once trimmed, none of them was expected to carry more than 200#. But in keeping with safe practice, we chose hardware

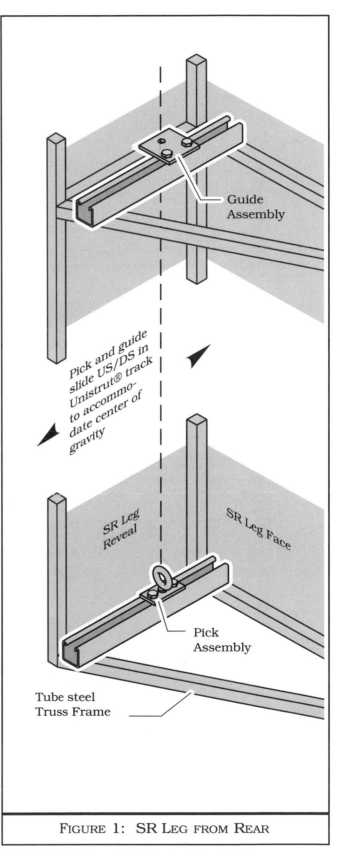

FIGURE 1: SR LEG FROM REAR

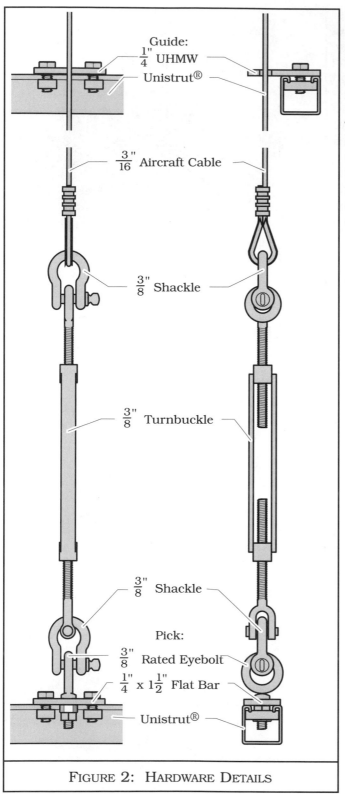

that would provide a 10:1 safety factor, and we assigned construction of the unit built to our most experienced welder. It is always important to look at all of the connections and the rating of each piece of hardware in flown units such as this.

The entire system was built of stock hardware and materials, and the cost was negligible. The adjustability in the pick points allowed us to fly the unit perpendicular to the stage floor after minimal adjustment. All in all, this was an effective and simple solution that allowed for easy, accurate adjustment in place.

Guide:
$\frac{1}{4}$" UHMW

Unistrut®

$\frac{3}{16}$" Aircraft Cable

$\frac{3}{8}$" Shackle

$\frac{3}{8}$" Turnbuckle

$\frac{3}{8}$" Shackle

Pick:

$\frac{3}{8}$" Rated Eyebolt

$\frac{1}{4}$" x $1\frac{1}{2}$" Flat Bar

Unistrut®

FIGURE 2: HARDWARE DETAILS

The design for the 1997 Yale Repertory Theatre's *A Midsummer Night's Dream* featured a soft-covered full-stage portal that opened, like an iris, for a scene change. The designer wanted the portal legs and header to form a single plane, and the audience's proximity required that the rig operate quietly. Meeting these objectives produced the rig described here.

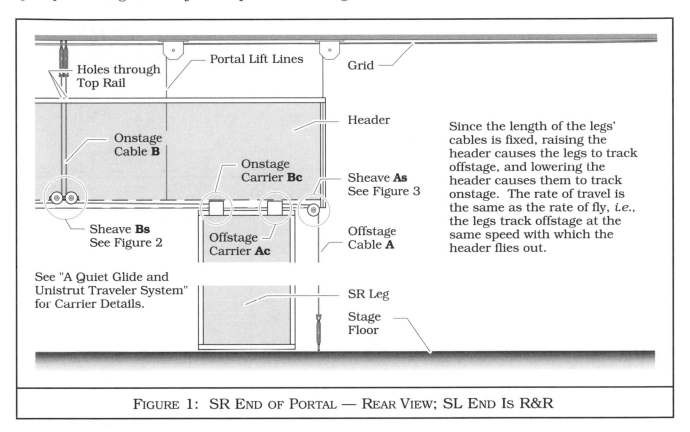

Since the length of the legs' cables is fixed, raising the header causes the legs to track offstage, and lowering the header causes them to track onstage. The rate of travel is the same as the rate of fly, *i.e.*, the legs track offstage at the same speed with which the header flies out.

FIGURE 1: SR END OF PORTAL — REAR VIEW; SL END IS R&R

Though the unit needed only to iris out, we rigged it to work in both directions to speed resetting. As shown in Figure 1, the portal legs traveled on a track that was built into the header as its bottom rail. Each leg was fitted with two drive cables: an offstage cable **A** and an onstage cable **B**. Each offstage cable was dead-tied to carrier **Ac** and to the stage floor. Between these two connections, each offstage cable was reeved over sheave **As**. The offstage cables pulled the portal legs farther apart whenever the header flew out. Similarly, each onstage cable was dead-tied to carrier **Bc** and to the grid. Between these connections, each onstage cable was reeved around sheave **Bs**. On the way to the grid, cable **B** passed through holes drilled in the header's top rail. As the header flew in, it pulled the legs closer to their top-of-show positions. Crosby® clips and turnbuckles at the grid and floor allowed for adjustment. The cables were initially tensioned with the unit irised in.

Using Unistrut® P1000 channel for the track offered three distinct advantages. First, it was strong enough to be used as the header's bottom rail though it was supported only at 4' panel seams. Second, since Unistrut® will accept a variety of fittings, bolting and welding other rigging components to it was simple. Since welding was involved, we specified a plain finish on the Unistrut®. Finally, Unistrut® is inexpensive — $3.00/ft. vs. standard traveler track's $12.00 to $15.00/ft. cost.

We built the header as two separate flats that we joined together during load-in. We milled a slot at the onstage end of each Unistrut® rail to allow mounting of two $2\frac{1}{2}$" Ralmark® sheaves as shown in

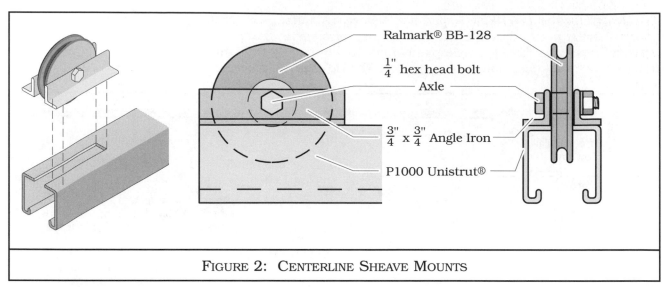

FIGURE 2: CENTERLINE SHEAVE MOUNTS

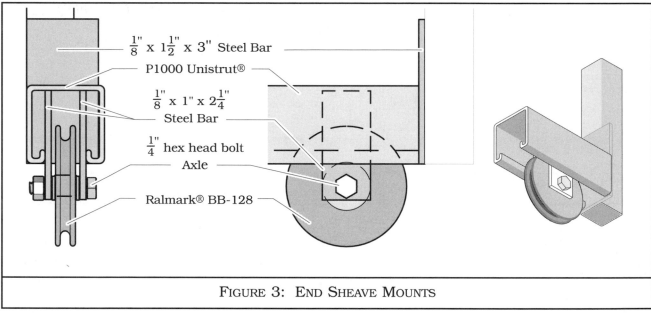

FIGURE 3: END SHEAVE MOUNTS

Figure 2. We ground down the horizontal flanges of the angle iron mounts to maintain the "finger-friendliness" of the rail. At the rail's offstage end, two pieces of $\frac{1}{8}$" x 1" x $2\frac{1}{4}$" steel bar were drilled as axle plates for the sheaves' $\frac{1}{4}$" hex head bolt axles and then welded into the slot of the channel. The $\frac{1}{8}$" x $1\frac{1}{2}$" x 3" steel bar tabs which were welded to the ends of the tracks served both as stops and as a means of joining the header's bottom rail to its stiles.

❧❧❧

TECHNICAL BRIEF

Safety

Safety rails for escape units are often assembled as an afterthought. After load-in, when attention focuses on finishing the set, finishing these rails often takes a low priority compared to the notes from tech rehearsals. At the University of Southern California we built a modular safety rail system that bolts together quickly and fits our stock escape units regardless of how they happen to be laid out for a given show. In addition, the system includes a type of foot connection that allows the stair rails to fit either side of our escape stair units.

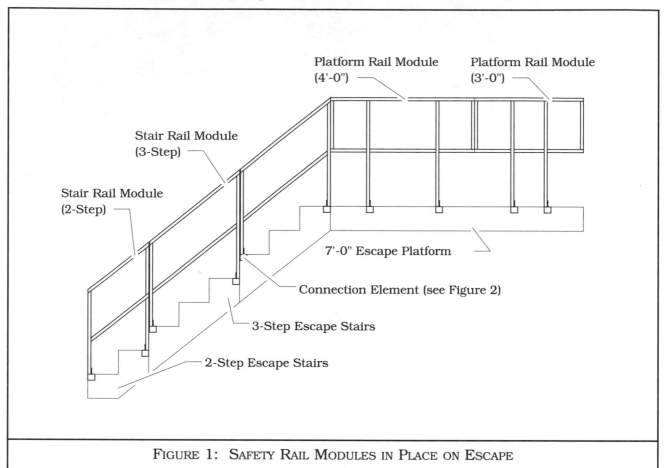

Platform Rail Module (4'-0")

Platform Rail Module (3'-0")

Stair Rail Module (3-Step)

Stair Rail Module (2-Step)

7'-0" Escape Platform

Connection Element (see Figure 2)

3-Step Escape Stairs

2-Step Escape Stairs

FIGURE 1: SAFETY RAIL MODULES IN PLACE ON ESCAPE

RAIL MODULES

We built several platform rail modules 3'-0" and 4'-0" long to accommodate various platform lengths, as well as some 2'-11" and 3'-11" modules for use at 90° corners. Each platform rail module, made of 1" tube steel, has an upper and a lower rail spaced 18" apart; and each has two 36" verticals, set in 1'-0" from its ends. The stair rail modules were built to fit our stock 2-step and 3-step escape stairs, all of which have an 8" rise and 10" run. Made of 1" tube steel like the platform rail modules, the stair rail modules are also 36" tall with upper and lower rails and two verticals. The stair rails' verticals, however, are set flush with the ends. Figure 1 illustrates the various modules.

Carefully spaced $\frac{3}{8}$" holes allow all the modules to be bolted together quickly with $\frac{5}{16}$" hex head bolts. The standardized location of bolt holes in all rail modules assures easy end-to-end and 90° connection. We used a plywood jig to make sure all holes would line up.

CONNECTION ELEMENTS

The reversible connection elements, which join both types of modules to the escape units, are made from two pieces of steel: a piece of $\frac{1}{8}$" x 2" x 2" steel angle cut $2\frac{1}{4}$" long, and a 2"-long piece of $\frac{1}{4}$" x 2" flat stock welded to the angle as illustrated in Figure 2. The angle's length allows for the thickness of the $\frac{1}{4}$" flat stock and creates a flush edge between the verticals and the connection elements. The flatness of the fillet weld which attaches the flat stock to the angle insures that the railing's verticals will bolt nearly flush to the angle iron. The angle iron is drilled and countersunk to allow drywall screw connections to the escape units, and the flat stock is drilled to accept two $\frac{5}{16}$" hex head bolts for attachment to the railing's verticals.

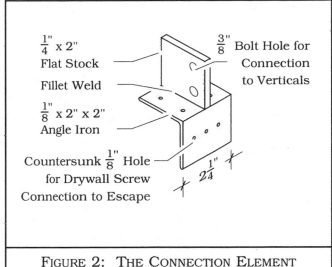

FIGURE 2: THE CONNECTION ELEMENT

MODULE INSTALLATION

After the connection elements have been attached to rail modules, each rail module is stood in place and attached to the escape units with $1\frac{1}{2}$" or longer drywall screws. As Figure 3 illustrates, a $\frac{1}{4}$" gap occurs between stair risers and the connection elements where the hex head bolts' heads protrude, but bolting the railing verticals of adjacent modules together eliminates the gap above the treads. Bolting a $\frac{1}{4}$" shim between each top stair rail module and its adjacent platform rail module solves the gap problem at stair/platform transitions. Once all the railings have been screwed down, the rail modules are bolted together. Gaffer's tape across any gaps between adjacent modules creates a smooth surface for a sliding hand.

CONCLUSION

The addition of a stock safety rail system to the scenery inventory provides a time-saving alternative to many last-minute escape rails, and these modular units will adapt to most stock platform and stair unit configurations which are based on a standardized pitch. This safety rail system provides efficient, quick installation and a greater measure of safety for actors and technicians alike.

Thanks to Ann Johnson for collaborating in the design.

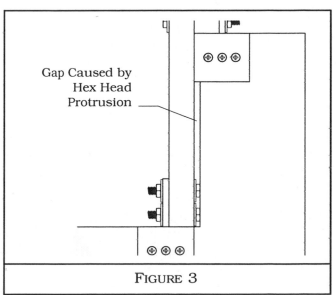

FIGURE 3

CO₂ Fire Suppression System for Theatrical Fire Effects

Jens McVoy

For every director who wants to use live fire, there is a fire marshal ready to refuse. The reluctance is, of course, rooted in a legitimate concern about the difficulties of controlling live fire onstage. Probably no live-fire effect can be made foolproof, but an effective CO_2 fire suppression system like the one described here can help reassure everyone involved in a production.

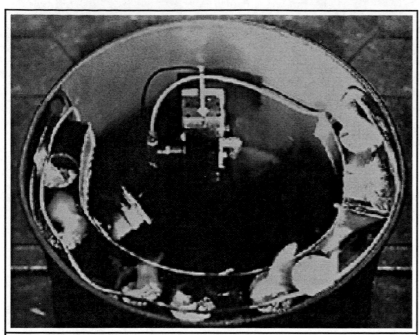

FIGURE 1: THE CO₂ FIRE SUPPRESSION SYSTEM

CONSTRUCTION

Figure 1 shows how this suppression system was integrated into a trash-barrel fire effect for a Yale Repertory Theatre production. As part of that production's action three "street people" build a fire in a 55-gallon drum and stand huddled around it for warmth. The effect was fueled by Sterno® mixed with various amounts of kosher salt to produce a convincingly realistic reddish-orange flame. The fuel was contained in several individual cans spaced at random around a steel trough welded inside the barrel's rim. A piece of wicking material extended from each can of Sterno® toward a knot that tied all of them together, and an actor started the fire by lighting the knot.

The parts of the suppression system that was built into this effect consisted of a few feet of $\frac{1}{4}$" OD copper tubing, a pneumatic hose and plunge valve, a 10-pound tank of CO_2 fitted with a flow regulator, and an assortment of fittings.

In this installation, the CO_2 tank was mounted out of sight on the frame of the lift that carried the barrel. The plunge valve was attached to the upstage side of the barrel, and its handle protruded through the side of the barrel so that an actor could activate the system if necessary. Both the valve and the pneumatic hose connecting it to the tank were located well away from the heat source.

Both ends of a large loop of copper tubing were attached to the valve at a tee by $\frac{1}{4}$" compression fittings and $\frac{1}{2}$" machine thread nipples. The loop of copper tubing was hand-bent to sit just above each can of Sterno® and then $\frac{1}{8}$" holes were drilled in the tubing at an angle that would dump CO_2 into the cans if necessary, displacing the oxygen and extinguishing the fire.

NOTES

This simple system can be modified for integration into many different live-fire-effect designs. For instance, the manual valve described above could be replaced by a solenoid-activated valve to be triggered remotely. Alternatively, both types of valves could be installed so that either an actor or someone offstage could respond to a problem. Finding the right regulator settings will take time. As a benchmark, a pressure of 40psig worked well in our effect, extinguishing all flame in approximately 2 seconds; but other designs may require different settings. Whatever changes are made, however, anyone who assembles a system like this should observe the following points:

- Seal all threaded fittings with Teflon® tape, and check all fittings for leaks.

- Keep all non-fireproof materials and parts away from the flames.

- Form the copper tubing as a loop and connect both its ends to the valve. Feeding gas simultaneously into both ends of a loop ensures the consistent and unimpeded flow of gas through all the ports.

CONCLUSION

This system effectively puts out fires based on Sterno® and similar fuels. It is not, however, appropriate for use with all types of fuels. Specifically, it will not necessarily work on paper or wood fires or on any other fires whose embers remain hot long after the flame has been extinguished. Theatrical fire effects rarely use such fuels, of course, but for safety's sake the local fire marshal should review the appropriateness of any fire suppression system you propose to build.

᠅᠅᠅

TECHNICAL BRIEF

Scenery

Although adults take the portability of modular set pieces, often known as "acting cubes," for granted, small children would be hard pressed to maneuver a 15" cube of standard $\frac{3}{4}$" plywood construction. The Seattle Children's Theater designed a lightweight solution to this problem for the youngest student actors to use in their summer instructional program. A thin plywood shell with a minimal pine frame served to reduce weight, and beadboard supplied intermediate support inside the cubes. The combination of strength and portability was soon appreciated by the adults as well as the kids who used the cubes.

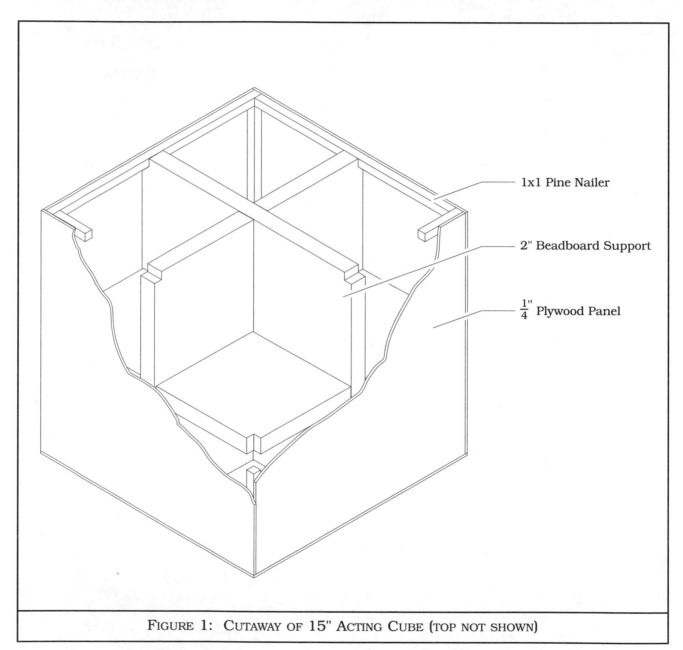

1x1 Pine Nailer

2" Beadboard Support

$\frac{1}{4}$" Plywood Panel

FIGURE 1: CUTAWAY OF 15" ACTING CUBE (TOP NOT SHOWN)

The cutaway view in Figure 1 shows the construction of a single cube, part of a set designed as a magnified version of a child's play blocks. Six panels of $\frac{1}{4}$" plywood liberally glued and bradded to 1x1 nailers form a shell with strong joints. Notched blocks of 2" beadboard perpendicularly span

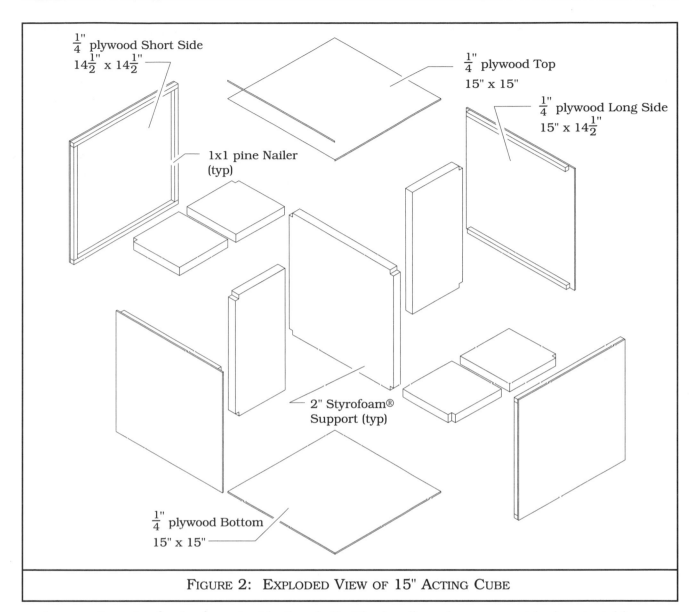

FIGURE 2: EXPLODED VIEW OF 15" ACTING CUBE

each opposite pair of cube faces inside the shell. The beadboard proves an ideal material because of its light weight and ability to withstand the compressive load of an adult standing on one of these $\frac{1}{4}$" plywood boxes.

The shell of the cube is assembled first, as it is easiest to construct the cube from the outside in. Starting with the beadboard supports requires an awkward glue-up of the beadboard pieces to one another, and can be eliminated by installing them after the plywood panels have been joined. The shell should be built as an open-ended box, with one of the opposing long sides left off to accommodate the seven cuts of beadboard shown in Figure 2. Applying adhesive to each plywood/beadboard and beadboard/beadboard joint guarantees stability of the internal supports. Common construction adhesive serves this purpose well, although the thickness of the glue-line may necessitate some judicious trimming of the beadboard slabs to allow a good fit. During the construction of a second set of cubes at The Children's Theater, a polyurethane-foam-based adhesive available in spray cans solved the glue-line-thickness problem, but was unfortunately messier. To seal the cube slide the remaining long side into place and nail it home.

A rugged and splinter-free finish is essential given the hard use for which the cubes were designed. After a thorough sanding to round off the sharp corners, the plywood edges and voids at the joints need to be filled. The Children's Theater shop found Bondo® to be the sturdiest putty in protecting the edges. A final sanding to remove the excess is all that is required to prepare the blocks for a paint finish.

A 15" cube built from $\frac{3}{4}$" plywood weighs approximately 21 pounds. This alternative construction weighs only $9\frac{1}{2}$ pounds: 7 pounds for the plywood; 1 pound for the pine framing; and $1\frac{1}{2}$ pounds for the beadboard supports. Materials for each of the heavier cubes cost approximately $5.80, as compared to $6.50 for the lightweight version. The slightly higher cost and longer construction time, about twice as long, involved in fabricating these lightweight cubes are relatively low if the benefits of portability are desired. It is worth noting that other block configurations are easily adapted from this plan. The Children's Theater built double (15x15x30), triple (15x15x45), and quadruple (15x15x60) blocks, as well as assorted round and triangular shapes for its collection.

Silas Morse at the Seattle Children's Theater deserves the credit for inspiring this design.

Of the many stock scenic systems I have read about or seen, there have never been any for stock stair-cases apart from saving old step units in hopes that they are reusable. This is impractical and requires a considerable amount of storage space since stair units often do not stack conveniently. In addition, with environmental issues taking on ever-greater importance we are constantly reminded of the phrase "reduce and reuse" and should strive to apply such philosophies to scenic construction.

This article describes the construction and use of a simple step module that can be used to form staircases of either a 6:12 or an 8:10 rise-to-run ratio. These modules can be mass produced and neatly stored for future use. They can be assembled into a staircase of any desired length, and, at strike, can be returned to storage rather than tossed into a dumpster.

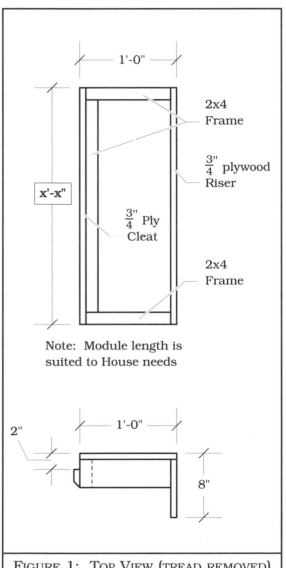

Note: Module length is suited to House needs

FIGURE 1: TOP VIEW (TREAD REMOVED) AND END VIEW OF STEP MODULE

THE STEP MODULE

Figure 1 shows the components of a typical step module: 2x4 framing supports three sides of a $\frac{3}{4}$" plywood tread; the fourth side is supported by a plate of $\frac{3}{4}$" plywood that doubles as the riser. The riser and tread are 8" and 12" wide, respectively, and their length is determined by the theater's typical needs. A $\frac{3}{4}$" plywood cleat is glued and screwed to the outside of the 2x4 framing member opposite the riser. The bottom of this cleat is beveled at a 45° angle so that an edge of the 2x4 to which it is attached will sit directly on a stringer. Because the placement of these cleats dictates the slope of modules assembled into a 6:12 staircase, it's important that the top of each cleat be located exactly 2" below the top of its module's tread.

TYPICAL ASSEMBLY

We frequently stand the modules on their ends for convenience during assembly. Once we've assembled as many as we need, we lay one of two pre-cut stringers in place "under" the staircase and use a $\frac{3}{4}$" plywood plate to join the stringer to the 2x4 framing of each module. We then flip the unit over and attach the second stringer in a similar manner. Finally, we attach the assembled staircase to its platform.

In a 6:12 staircase, the riser of each step module sits on the $\frac{3}{4}$" plywood cleat of the next-lower module and is screwed to its mate's 2x4 frame. (See Figure 2a.) In a 6:12 staircase, the lowest step must be custom made with a 6" total rise. In an 8:10 staircase, the riser of each module sits on top of the tread of the next-lower module and is screwed to a $\frac{3}{4}$" x $1\frac{1}{4}$" cleat, leaving only 10" of each tread exposed. In order to maintain the correct slope, the top module in an 8:10 staircase is typically level with the platform to which the staircase rises. Alternatively, it is possible in some platforming systems to allow for a 2" recess under the platform.

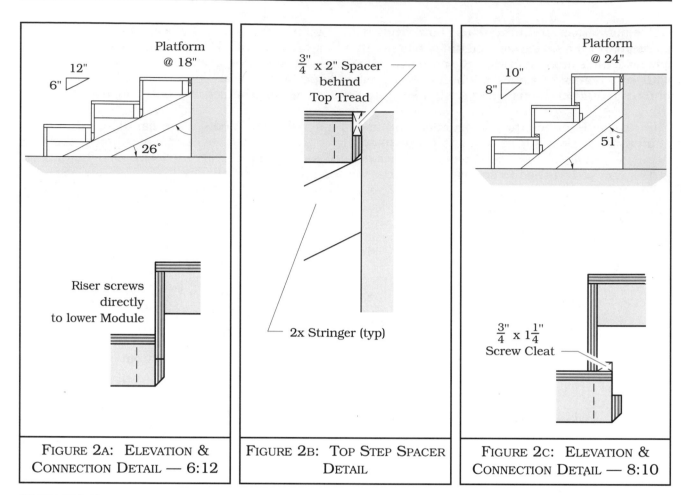

FIGURE 2A: ELEVATION & CONNECTION DETAIL — 6:12

FIGURE 2B: TOP STEP SPACER DETAIL

FIGURE 2C: ELEVATION & CONNECTION DETAIL — 8:10

VARIATIONS

The modules described here assemble into a pretty "boxy" staircase. If a more formal look is desired, a nosing can always be added. Whether a nosing is to be applied or not, however, the butt joint between each module's riser and tread should be treated to render it invisible since, as often as not, the audience will see the front of the stairs. Decorative tread facings and sound deadening materials such as Masonite® and Homasote® can be added as long as a custom bottom step is built to dimensions which account for the thickness of the additional material. Building allowances for any such materials to the modules themselves would create too weak an attachment point for the 6:12 ratio.

SUMMARY

Like all stock scenery, staircases built of these step modules should never be allowed to limit a designer, and they cannot easily be used in set designs which call for staircases with a distinctive look. Nevertheless, stock scenery is very useful when it meets commonly recurring needs with practical and expedient solutions, and whenever a staircase needs only to be useful rather than useful and decorative, this system of step modules can be a valuable addition to any theater's stock scenery.

Up to a point, saving time and money by using stock escape stairs is a good practice, but too many fixed-pitch escapes are pressed into service even when they aren't exactly the right height. Such practice is inelegant at best and unsafe at worst. Furthermore, as many technicians and manufacturers have discovered, it is ultimately unnecessary. This article describes a design for a variable-pitch staircase.

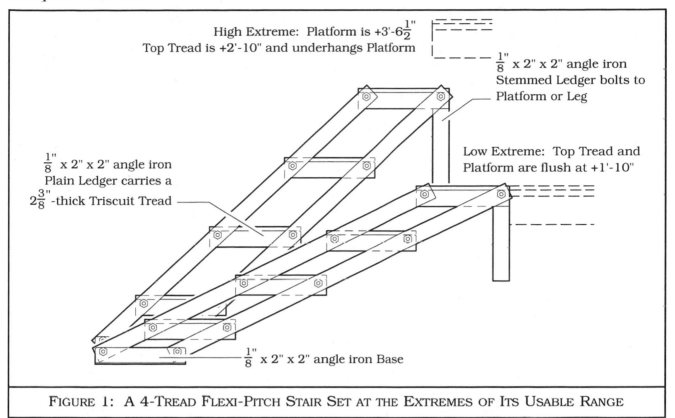

High Extreme: Platform is $+3'\text{-}6\frac{1}{2}"$
Top Tread is $+2'\text{-}10"$ and underhangs Platform

$\frac{1}{8}"$ x 2" x 2" angle iron
Stemmed Ledger bolts to
Platform or Leg

$\frac{1}{8}"$ x 2" x 2" angle iron
Plain Ledger carries a
$2\frac{3}{8}"$ -thick Triscuit Tread

Low Extreme: Top Tread and
Platform are flush at $+1'\text{-}10"$

$\frac{1}{8}"$ x 2" x 2" angle iron Base

FIGURE 1: A 4-TREAD FLEXI-PITCH STAIR SET AT THE EXTREMES OF ITS USABLE RANGE

GENERAL DESCRIPTION

The carriages of these open-riser stairs consist of two parallel lengths of tube steel which serve as stringers, and a number of pieces of angle iron which support the treads. The single bolt connections joining the carriage components are essentially pin joints. As a result, a fully formed stair folds nearly flat for storage and its treads remain uniformly level and evenly spaced regardless of the angle at which they are set for a specific use. As Figure 1 and the tables at the end of this article illustrate, this design allows a single stair to be angled to suit a wide range of platform heights.

HARDWARE SPECIFICS

Figure 2A details the fabrication of a carriage's stringer: a length of 1x2 steel tube with a series of $\frac{7}{16}"$ diameter holes drilled along the centerline of its 2" walls. Figure 2B depicts the typical base or plain ledger: an $11\frac{1}{4}"$ piece of $\frac{1}{8}"$ x 2" x 2" angle iron drilled with $\frac{7}{16}"$ diameter holes, each centered 1" in from the end and $1\frac{1}{2}"$ away from the angle's spine. Uniform hole spacing makes all base and plain ledgers reversible and interchangeable. Figure 2C depicts the distinctive stem of the stemmed ledger: a $9\frac{1}{4}"$ long upright of $\frac{1}{8}"$ x 2" x 2" angle iron drilled to allow bolting to a leg or a platform. Note that one hole in the stemmed ledger's horizontal member is inset 3" rather than the typical $1\frac{1}{2}"$ from the end to provide clearance for any leg that might be used with the stair.

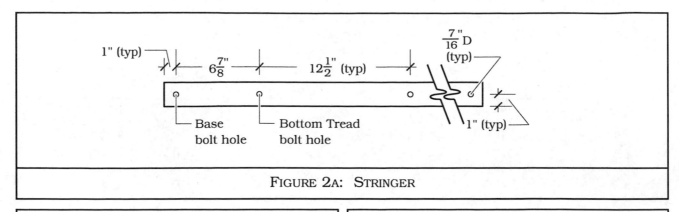

FIGURE 2A: STRINGER

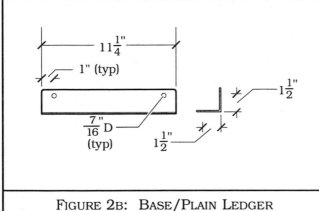

FIGURE 2B: BASE/PLAIN LEDGER

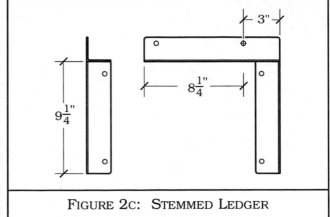

FIGURE 2C: STEMMED LEDGER

Figure 3 details the construction of the triscuit (stressed-skin) tread intended for use with this carriage design. Tread width is set at $11\frac{1}{4}$"; tread length must be calculated to suit particular stock platform legging requirements. Since at steeper pitches the stair needs to underhang the platforming in order to maintain consistent tread width, the tread length must allow the entire carriage to stand between the legs of a stock platform.

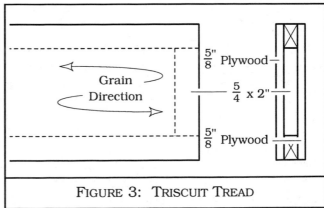

FIGURE 3: TRISCUIT TREAD

GEOMETRY

This stair design is based on three constants: an $11\frac{1}{4}$" tread width, $2\frac{3}{8}$" tread thickness, and a $12\frac{1}{2}$" normal hole-to-hole spacing between tread bolt connections along the carriage. All other values are derived for each pitch as shown in Figure 4.

The tables below summarize the design data for five different stair units. Note particularly that at the gentlest pitch, the stairs' bases sit directly on the floor. At any other pitch, however, the base must be shimmed up in order to provide the right riser height for the first tread.

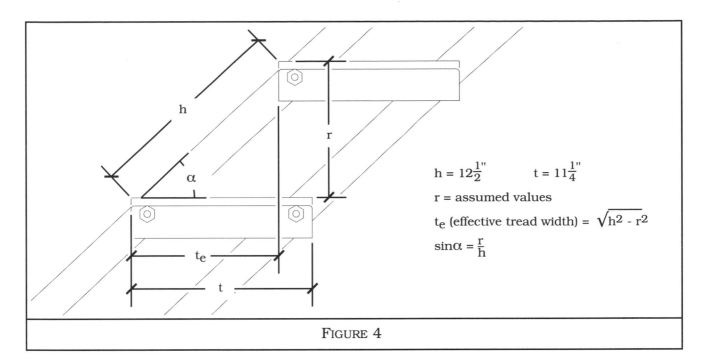

$$h = 12\tfrac{1}{2}" \qquad t = 11\tfrac{1}{4}"$$

r = assumed values

t_e (effective tread width) $= \sqrt{h^2 - r^2}$

$\sin\alpha = \dfrac{r}{h}$

FIGURE 4

FLEXI-PITCH STAIR DESIGN DATA

Number of Treads	@ r = $5\tfrac{1}{2}$" (a)		@ r = $8\tfrac{1}{2}$" (b)		Carriage Length
	Total Rise	Total Run(c)	Total Rise	Total Run(c)	
2	11"	1'-10$\tfrac{1}{2}$"	2'-2$\tfrac{1}{2}$"	1'-6$\tfrac{1}{2}$"	1'-9$\tfrac{3}{8}$"
4	1'-10"	3'-9"	3'-6$\tfrac{1}{2}$"	3'-1"	3'-10$\tfrac{3}{8}$"
7	3'-3$\tfrac{1}{2}$"	6'-6$\tfrac{1}{2}$"	5'-8"	5'-4"	6'-11$\tfrac{7}{8}$"
12	5'-6"	11'-11$\tfrac{1}{2}$"	9'-2$\tfrac{1}{2}$"	9'-2"	12'-2$\tfrac{3}{8}$"
18	8'-3"	16'-10"	12'-0"	14'-11"	18'-5$\tfrac{3}{8}$"

@ r = $8\tfrac{1}{2}$" (b)			
r	t_e	pad	α
$5\tfrac{1}{2}$"	11$\tfrac{1}{4}$"	na	26°
6"	10$\tfrac{15}{16}$"	$\tfrac{3}{4}$"	29°
7"	10$\tfrac{3}{8}$"	1$\tfrac{3}{16}$"	34°
8"	9$\tfrac{5}{8}$"	1$\tfrac{5}{8}$"	40°
$8\tfrac{1}{2}$"	9$\tfrac{3}{16}$"	1$\tfrac{7}{8}$"	43°

(a) Top tread flush with platform
(b) Top tread underhung
(c) Rounded to nearest $\tfrac{1}{2}$"
(d) Max vertical distance between landings: 12'-0"

Minimum riser height = 5"
Minimum tread width = 9"

A No-Weld Spiral Staircase

David A. Griffith

Though center-column spiral staircases are structurally simple, they are not particularly easy to build. The fact that they are generally made of metal makes them especially challenging for any shop not equipped for welding. As a university Technical Director faced with this problem, I turned to physics lab technicians for help. With their advice (and the use of some of their equipment) my carpenters turned out a sturdy 10'-tall spiral staircase that uses plywood and PVC pipe instead of metal as the main components. Other non-welding shops should find the design described here just as useful as I did.

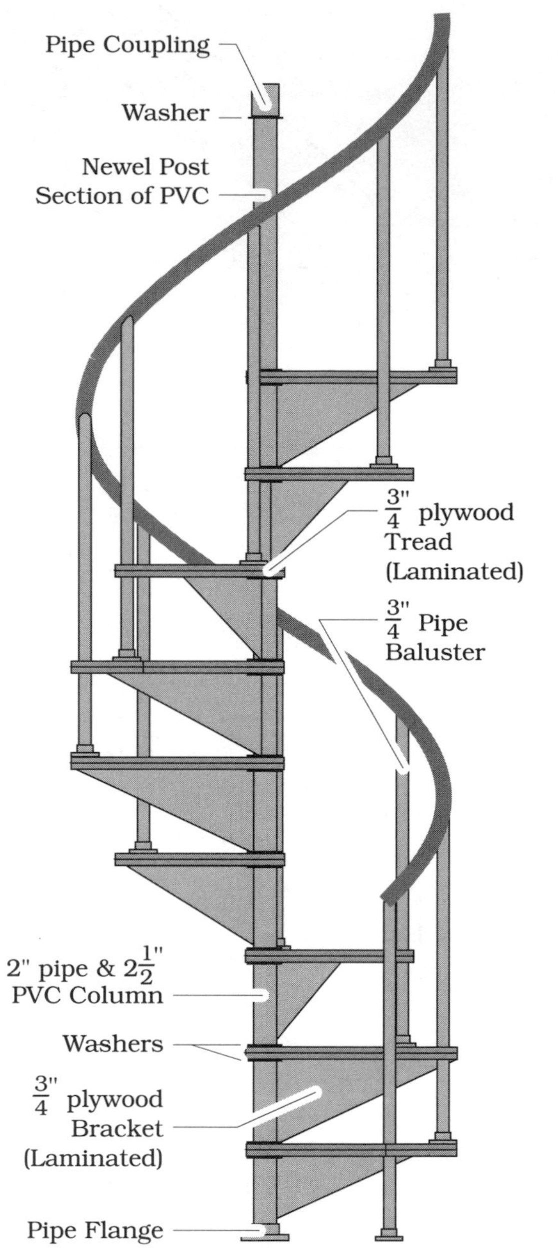

CONSTRUCTION

Figure 1 identifies the parts and materials this staircase uses. The treads are made of double layers of $\frac{3}{4}$" AC plywood glued and stapled together, and drilled at their inside ends to fit the core of the staircase's column. A plywood bracket stiffens each tread. These brackets, cut as right triangles and mounted in $\frac{1}{2}$" dados in the bottoms of the treads, bear against the staircase's column. Like the treads themselves, the brackets are two-layer laminates of $\frac{3}{4}$" AC plywood.

Along their outside edges, each tread is joined to the next lower tread by a $\frac{3}{4}$"-pipe baluster. The balusters screw into flanges bolted to the tops of the treads, and, where each one passes through a hole near the nosing of the next-higher tread, it is fixed in place by an 8d duplex-nail tread-pin.

The core of this staircase's central column is a length of 2" schedule 40 black pipe, and the sleeves that surround that core are lengths of $2\frac{1}{2}$" PVC. For the original model of this staircase, we used schedule 80 PVC, laboriously reaming out each sleeve on a lathe. I have since learned, however, that schedule 40 PVC would have worked just as well, and its use would completely have eliminated all machining.

The sleeves in this staircase are not permanently fastened to the treads. Unlike their counterparts in metal staircases, they are independent components whose basic functions are to maintain a consistent rise, and to help the treads stand straight out from

FIGURE 1: PARTS & MATERIALS

the central column. During assembly, the column's 2" schedule 40 black pipe is screwed tightly into the flange that will ultimately connect it to the floor. Next, the first PVC sleeve is slid over the pipe, followed by an unusually large steel washer, then the bottom tread, and another oversized washer, in that order. The sequence of adding sleeve, washer, tread, and washer, illustrated in Figure 2, continues until the last tread is in place and topped by a washer.

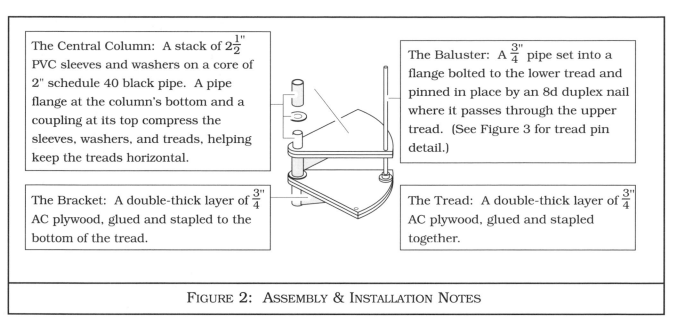

The Central Column: A stack of $2\frac{1}{2}$" PVC sleeves and washers on a core of 2" schedule 40 black pipe. A pipe flange at the column's bottom and a coupling at its top compress the sleeves, washers, and treads, helping keep the treads horizontal.

The Baluster: A $\frac{3}{4}$" pipe set into a flange bolted to the lower tread and pinned in place by an 8d duplex nail where it passes through the upper tread. (See Figure 3 for tread pin detail.)

The Bracket: A double-thick layer of $\frac{3}{4}$" AC plywood, glued and stapled to the bottom of the tread.

The Tread: A double-thick layer of $\frac{3}{4}$" AC plywood, glued and stapled together.

FIGURE 2: ASSEMBLY & INSTALLATION NOTES

In our staircase, the top 3' of the column served as a newel post for the staircase. A final section of PVC sleeved over the pipe above the top tread and washer was cut just long enough to leave room for one last washer and the pipe coupling that served as the newel's cap.

INSTALLATION

During installation, the pre-assembled column and treads are stood up and the column is lagged to the floor and secured at its upper end. The lowest tread is then rotated into its playing position and fitted with its baluster, which is fed through the hole in the tread's nosing and screwed into a flange. Next, the duplex-nail tread-pin, pictured in Figure 3, is inserted into the edge of the tread and through the baluster. Lagging the baluster's flange to the stage floor completes the installation of the first tread, a sequence of operations that is repeated with each of the other steps. After all treads and balusters have been fastened together, the newel-cap coupling at the top of the column is tightened, compressing all the treads, washers, and PVC sleeves and stiffening the whole unit.

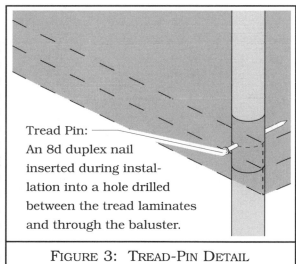

Tread Pin: An 8d duplex nail inserted during installation into a hole drilled between the tread laminates and through the baluster.

FIGURE 3: TREAD-PIN DETAIL

CONCLUDING COMMENTS

The design of the handrail for spiral staircases I will leave to others. The original model of this design used flexible PVC tubing, a material too flexible to be satisfactory, even though the balustrade of $\frac{3}{4}$" pipes offered enough in the way of actor safety. I was very pleased with the rest of the design. It played well, trucked easily, and continues to store compactly under some shelves in the scene shop, ready to be used again.

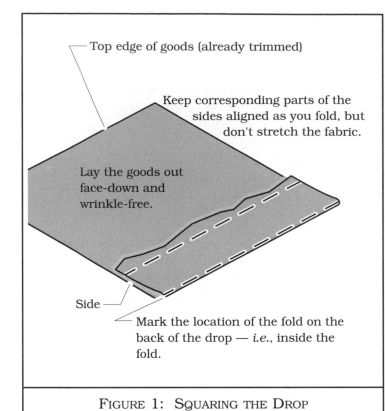

Top edge of goods (already trimmed)

Keep corresponding parts of the sides aligned as you fold, but don't stretch the fabric.

Lay the goods out face-down and wrinkle-free.

Side

Mark the location of the fold on the back of the drop — *i.e.*, inside the fold.

FIGURE 1: SQUARING THE DROP

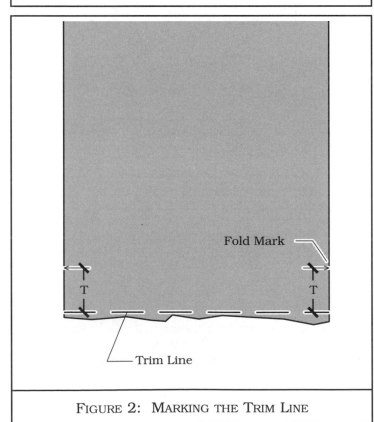

Fold Mark

T   T

Trim Line

FIGURE 2: MARKING THE TRIM LINE

Shop carpenters who balk at sewing hems or pipe pockets in soft goods should find this article helpful. The two methods described here require little or no pinning, probably the most tedious and time-consuming part of any large sewing project. Aside from a sewing machine, the only tools needed are a fabric pencil, a snap line, and a tape measure. While only the "three-snap" method is suitable for opaque fabrics, those who are working with semi-transparents may use either the "three-snap" or the "four-snap" method. Either can save considerable time.

FIRST THINGS FIRST: DEFINING A STRAIGHT POCKET

If you're working with a piece that has horizontal seams, you can probably trust the bottom selvage as a good reference in measuring for a pocket. If you have doubts, though, or if you're working with a seamless piece or one with vertical seams, here's an easy way to insure that a hem or pipe pocket will be both straight and perpendicular to the sides of the piece.

Lay the goods out flat and face down, taking care to avoid stretching the fabric as you work. Fold 2' or 3' of the bottom end back on the rest of the piece, lining up the edges of the fabric as shown in Figure 1. The fold is perpendicular to the sides of the goods. Open the ends of the fold just enough to mark its location on the back of the goods with a fabric pencil. Now unfold the goods. If the end of the piece were left too uneven, bulky flaps of fabric could fill the pocket. Measure down from the fold marks to establish a Trim Line (see Figure 2) as close to the bottom end of the goods as possible. Make sure that the distance (T) between the trim line and the fold marks is the same at both vertical edges. Snap the Trim Line and cut off any excess fabric, leaving the trim line clearly visible.

THE THREE-SNAP METHOD (ALL FABRICS)

Note: these dimensions produce a 3" hem.

Using a fabric pencil on one vertical edge (side) of the goods, lay in marks **A** and **B** at $\frac{1}{2}$" and 7" from the Trim Line, respectively, as in Figure 3. Lay in corresponding marks **A'** and **B'** on the opposite vertical edge of the piece.

Using a chalk color with minimal contrast to the fabric (blue chalk on black fabric, for instance, or red on natural or white fabric), snap line **b** between marks **B** and **B'** on the back of the goods. Then fold the fabric back and snap line **a** on the front of the goods between marks **A** and **A'**. Use no more chalk than is necessary. Draw tick marks at regular intervals along both these lines. They will warn you about fabric "creep" during sewing.

If you must bundle the marked goods for transport to a different location for sewing, keep in mind that you'll be sewing with the fabric good side down. Use Figure 3 as a guide for stitching, and keep the tick marks aligned as shown to prevent fabric creep.

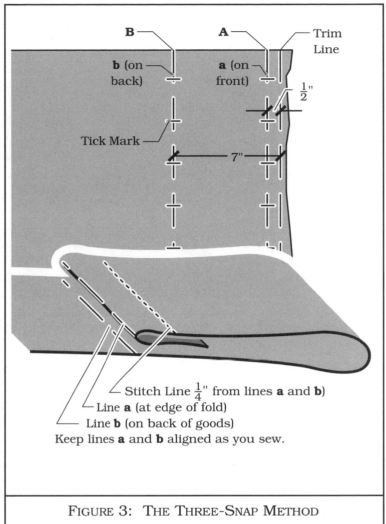

FIGURE 3: THE THREE-SNAP METHOD

THE FOUR-SNAP METHOD (SCRIMS AND OTHER SEMI-TRANSPARENTS ONLY)

This method uses a similar alignment procedure to produce a 3" hem. It requires a little more preparation, but it provides guides for the stitches themselves. The notes refer to Figure 4. On one of the vertical edges (sides) of the goods, draw marks **A**, **B**, and **C** at $\frac{3}{8}$", $1\frac{1}{8}$", and $7\frac{1}{8}$", respectively, from the Trim Line. Draw corresponding marks **A'**, **B'**, and **C'** on the opposite vertical edge. Using a chalk of greater color contrast than that suggested for the three-snap method (*e.g.*, red chalk for black fabric and blue for natural or white), snap line **a** and line **c** (at $\frac{3}{8}$", and $7\frac{1}{8}$", respectively) on the back of the goods, then fold the fabric back to snap line **b** on the front. To prevent the chalk from marking the lower layer of fabric, you may want to separate the two layers with a strip of brown paper before making this last snap. Snapping line **b** on the front guarantees that all three lines will be face up (and therefore more easily seen) during sewing. As with the three-snap method, mark perpendicular tick marks along the snap lines at regular intervals. As you sew, align all three snap lines and the tick marks and let your needle follow the stacked lines. Be particularly careful to correct for fabric creep.

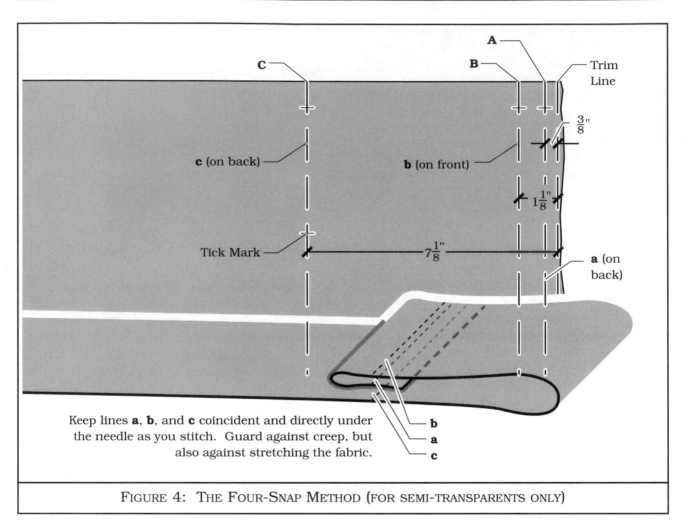

FIGURE 4: THE FOUR-SNAP METHOD (FOR SEMI-TRANSPARENTS ONLY)

FINAL COMMENTS

Powdered charcoal snap lines might be more appropriate than chalk in some cases. On the other hand, chalk certainly "stays put" better than charcoal — something to keep in mind if the goods must be bundled and moved before sewing. In any event, the results of these methods are certainly comparable to more traditional methods and they take far less set up and sewing time than those that require the use of pins.

❧❧❧❧

While working as TD for the Opera Festival of New Jersey, I hung the company's black scrim late in load-in to prevent accidental damage, only to find a series of half-dollar sized holes like the one shown in Figure 1 at the right. Time and money precluded scrim replacement, and although we made a determined attempt, no one on the crew proved capable of professional-quality reweaving. We also vainly tried two other approaches — sewing the holes shut, and stitching patches over them. All three techniques were tediously slow, and our repairs, while better-looking than the holes, were not satisfactory. Still, lacking better alternatives, we persevered in our efforts.

One afternoon, Stephan Olson, one of our designers, noticed what we were doing and told me about a "fix" an old Broadway hand had shown him: rather than sew a patch in, Olson suggested, we could "spot-weld" it with Sobo® glue. I was a bit skeptical, but decided to try this method, which proved easy, fast, and effective.

FIGURE 1: A CANDIDATE FOR SPOT-WELDING

MATERIALS AND PROCESS

Spot-welding scrim with Sobo® is simplicity itself. For most repairs all you need is glue, some scrim scraps, a pair of scissors, and one or more embroidery hoops. Some repairs will require a helper and one or more small scraps of clear acrylic sheeting.

The process has only four steps:

    tension the damaged area
    trim away any untensioned flaps
    cut a patch and lay it in place
    spot-weld the patch in place with Sobo®

The notes and photos on the following pages provide the necessary details.

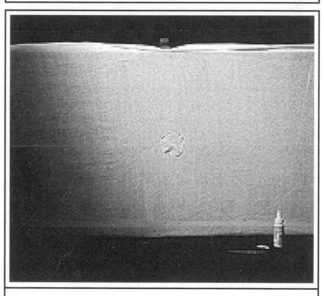

FIGURE 2: A SUCCESSFUL SPOT-WELD

STEPS 1 AND 2: TENSION AND TRIM THE DAMAGED AREA

The damaged area must first be tensioned. An appropriate amount of tension can be provided by the weight of the scrim's bottom pipe if the piece is hanging and the holes are within easy reach, or by the use of an embroidery hoop if the scrim is down. For readers unfamiliar with the device, an embroidery hoop is a set of two wooden or plastic circles, one of which nests inside the other, trapping and stretching fabric between them. Shown in use in Figures 3, 4, and 5, they range from 3" to 12" and more in diameter, are very inexpensive, and are available at any fabric shop. With the damaged area tensioned, cut away any loose flaps, trimming the tear into a rough circle.

FIGURE 3: ALIGNING A PATCH

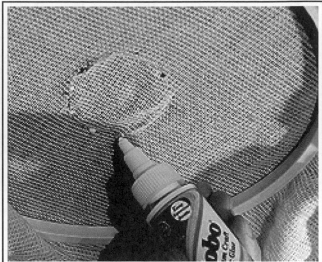

FIGURE 4: GLUING BY THE NUMBERS

STEPS 3 AND 4: PREP AND SPOT-WELD THE PATCH

Trim a patch from scrap scrim. Size the patch to fit inside the hole without overlapping the threads around it. Align the weave of the patch with that of the weave of the scrim as shown in Figure 3, and "spot-weld" the patch in with Sobo® as in Figure 4, applying small dots of the glue at positions corresponding to the numbers on a clock. Do not stretch the patch into position. Sobo® spot-welding works because while the scrim is under tension, the patch is not: all the patch has to do is fill the hole. Because there's no tension on the patch, a few small dots of glue are sufficient to hold it in place. The fewer dots you use, the fewer spots there will be to reflect stage light. Once the glue has dried, the repair is complete and the goods can be put back into service.

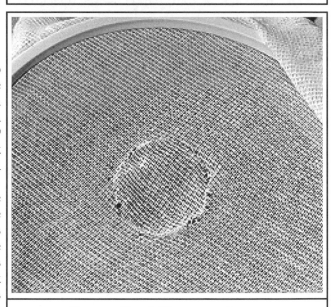

FIGURE 5: A FINISHED PATCH

NOTES

Sobo® seems the best glue for this purpose. It "tacks" quickly, remains reasonably flexible when dry, and isn't very shiny. We tried some other glues — including some designed for fabric — but the results were not as good. All of them became more brittle, and some of them were too shiny.

There is certainly room for experimentation, but we found that tears trimmed to a circular shape resisted the tension well, and round patches are easy to make. Obviously, if you used embroidery hoops as tensioners, the trimmed tears would have to be significantly smaller than the hoops. Other limits seem likely: I doubt that long tears, for instance, could be repaired with this approach. In any case, long tears are fairly easy to sew.

If you're repairing a scrim that's already in the air, you'll need a helper working behind the goods. The helper must first push the "back" half of the embroidery hoop toward you to help you capture and tension the fabric, and then hold a "backing plate" behind the damaged area so that the scrim doesn't drift away from you while you're working.

If that backing plate is transparent, your helper will be able to see what you're doing; if it's non-porous, it won't get glued to the goods. Glass might do, but a scrap of clear acrylic sheeting probably works best as a backing plate.

FINAL COMMENTS

Spot-welding scrim with Sobo® is a handy technique in situations where time or money is short. Its results are far less likely to be visible

FIGURE 6: "BACKING" A REPAIR WITH CLEAR ACRYLIC SHEETING

from the house than are the repairs other techniques produce. Conveniently, it can be done whether the scrim is in the air or on the ground. Last, though it is neither as permanent nor as elegant as professional reweaving, "'tis enough, 'twill serve."

The grand staircase for the Yale School of Drama's spring 1997 production of *A Ride Across Lake Constance* (see Figure 1) was designed to impress. But the staircase was more massive than complicated: only its handrails presented an unusual technical challenge. Beginning as straight sections along the top landings and upper staircases, they curved in broad, sweeping descents that began at the mid-landing and ended in tight volutes at the bottom.

Building curved handrails from ordinary scenic materials is usually difficult and time-consuming. Fortunately, the cross-section of this particular handrail was a simple oval closely resembling one of the pre-formed handrails that Julius Blum & Co., Inc. sells as Colorail®. See Figure 2. A Colorail® handrail has two parts: an armature and a sleeve. The armature is a custom-fitted and installed length of steel or aluminum stock. Julius Blum & Co., Inc. sells several styles of armatures, but designs the sleeves to fit over commonly used bar stock shapes. The solid-color PVC sleeves, when heated, can easily be molded around the armatures. After cooling, the sleeves conform to the shape of their armatures.

FIGURE 1: THE LAKE CONSTANCE STAIRCASE

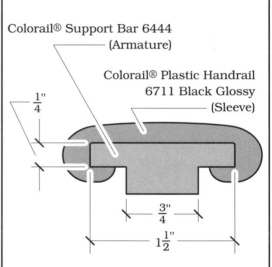

Colorail® Support Bar 6444 (Armature)

Colorail® Plastic Handrail 6711 Black Glossy (Sleeve)

$\frac{1}{4}$"

$\frac{3}{4}$"

$1\frac{1}{2}$"

FIGURE 2: HANDRAIL CROSS SECTION

TWO ARMATURE DESIGNS

Since the Colorail® sleeves would completely hide the armatures we built, we let the handrails' geometry influence material choice. Lengths of $\frac{1}{4}$" x $1\frac{1}{2}$" steel bar worked well along the upper landings and the upper straight-run staircases. But rather than try to bend that same bar around the handrail's compound curves, student Robin MacDuffie developed an open-framework armature consisting of two lengths of $\frac{1}{4}$" x $\frac{1}{4}$" steel bar held 1" apart by steel tabs. The steps he followed in laying out a table jig to build the sweeps of handrail are described in Figure 3.

With the jig complete, Robin screwed plywood blocks on the inside of arc **b** and the outside of arc **c** and then bent pre-cut lengths of square stock around them. After clamping the steel in place, he welded the lengths of square stock together with short tabs of $\frac{1}{8}$" x 1" bar stock spaced about 8" apart. With the same approach and a smaller jig, he made the volute. Since the staircase was symmetrical, one pair of jigs produced handrails for both sides of the unit.

1. Measuring from line **A-A'** parallel to the staircase's centerline, locate the center ✛ of each baluster.

2. Connect the dots between baluster centers with freehand arc **a**.

3. At each baluster center, lay in the tangent **T-T'** to arc **a** and erect radial line **R-R'** perpendicular to **T-T'** (see detail at right).

4. At the baluster centers, mark point series **b** $\frac{3}{4}$" inside arc **a** on **R-R'** and point series **c** $\frac{3}{4}$" outside arc **a** on **R-R'** (see detail at right).

5. Connect point series **b** with freehand arc b and point series **c** with freehand arc c.

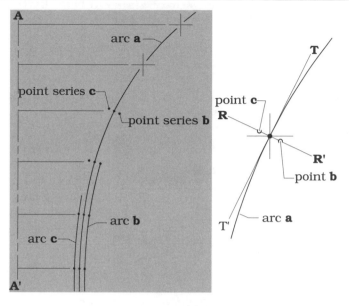

FIGURE 3: JIGGING UP FOR THE LARGE SWEEPS

HANDRAIL INSTALLATION

Installation proceeded quickly at first. After lagging the 1" tube steel balusters to the staircase, we clamped the straight bar-stock armatures to the balusters of the straight-run staircases and upper landings and welded the pieces together.

The large sweeps went on almost as quickly as the straight bar stock. Hand pressure and a number of C-clamps were enough to persuade the sweeps to follow the staircase's rise. After aligning the square stock with the top of a baluster as in Figure 4, Robin tack-welded that joint and moved on to the next.

The volutes were also quick and easy. After welding them to the ends of their sweeps, Robin used a pry bar to develop their "drops" and to align them with the stage floor. The results are shown in Figure 5.

In fact, only one section of the handrail — the transition between the straight bar stock and the sweeps — was at all time-consuming. The transition pieces had to be built in place because jigging them up would have been more troublesome than worthwhile. However, the $\frac{1}{4}$" square stock was too stiff to be bent by hand. To solve this problem, Robin made a model for the square stock out of $\frac{1}{4}$" round stock, which is quite easy

FIGURE 4: SWEEP JOINT READY FOR WELDING

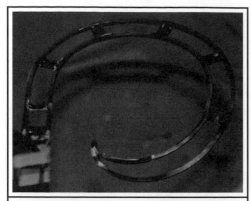

FIGURE 5: VOLUTE ARMATURE

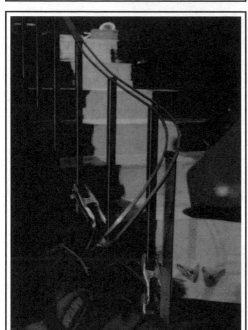

FIGURE 6: TRANSITION PIECE

to bend by hand. He then used a Hossfeld Bender to make the square stock match his round-stock model. Figure 6 shows the resulting transitional pieces in place, ready to be welded to the the stage right balusters.

Applying the Colorail® sleeve was as simple, fast, and fun as Julius Blum & Co., Inc.'s catalog had promised. Feeding the PVC through a heat-gun-powered heating sleeve made it quite pliable, and it stayed easy to work with for many minutes. Even so, the volutes proved troublesome: the sleeve's "plastic memory" would not allow it to stay wrapped around such a tight curve. Rather than risk leaving it permanently dented by spring clamps, we wrapped wide strips of muslin around it like first-aid bandages to help it hold its shape until it could cool enough to stay in place.

CONCLUSION

The twin-bar armatures made these railings strong enough for a person to slide down, and though developed specifically to work with Colorail®, they could easily be modified for use with other "overcoats". Those who would use the techniques outlined here are advised to plan their jigs carefully. Simple plan-view jigs like the ones we used make no allowance for staircase rise and will not produce good results for steeper stairs or for handrails with tight sweeps.

On the other hand, any type of jigging may be a form of overkill. If round stock can be hand bent for a model, why can't it be hand bent to work as the finished rails in at least some cases?

Colorail® sleeves and armatures are available from

> Julius Blum & Co., Inc.
> P.O. Box 816
> Carlstadt, NJ 07072
> 201-438-6003, 800-526-6293, fax: 201-438-6003

The ceiling for the Yale Repertory Theatre's 1997 production of *Candida* was essentially a large trapezoid that covered most of the set. See Figure 1. It had to look as nearly seamless as possible, and it needed to load in quickly and be raised out of the way so that the set's walls could be assembled underneath it. Moreover, for scheduling reasons, the ceiling's cover had to be delivered to paints before the carpenters officially began building the show. The obvious solution was a muslin cover that could be sewn together and painted early, and then stretched over one or more separately built frames during load-in. The approach is an old one, but the framing system deserves review because it is simple and efficient.

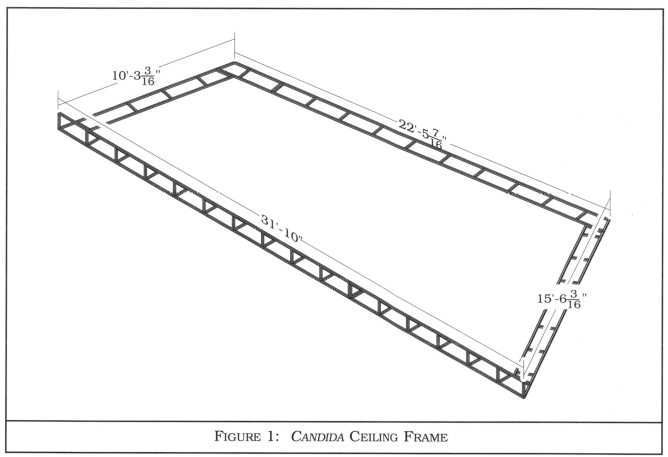

FIGURE 1: *CANDIDA* CEILING FRAME

Figure 1 illustrates the ceiling's frame, not an assembly of independent flats but rather a single built-up tube steel frame that was covered by a single piece of fabric. The different cross sections of the frame's sides met different structural requirements. The "L"-shaped downstage side was designed to span 31'-10" from stage right to stage left and to resist bending laterally under the pull of the taut ceiling fabric. Figure 2 shows that three parallel lengths of 1" x 1" x 0.049" square tube formed the rails of the downstage side of the frame. Held 10" apart by 1x1 tube steel toggles welded at 2'-0" intervals, the over/under rails were strong enough to span the opening without noticeable deflection. The similarly spaced upstage/downstage rails effectively countered the bending force of the sized fabric.

Because the other three sides of the ceiling frame rested directly on scenery walls, they did not need the downstage "L"-shaped cross section. Their simpler design is shown in Figure 3. On all four sides of the frame, a $\frac{1}{2}$"-plywood nailing strip tek-screwed to the outside styles provided the surface to which the fabric was stapled.

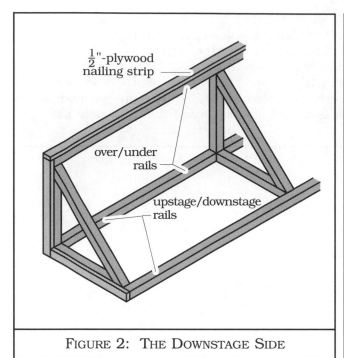

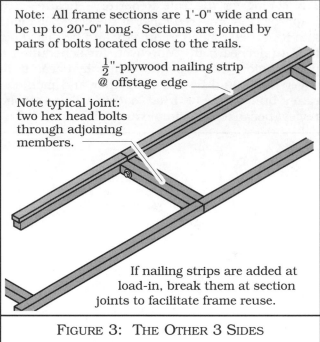

½"-plywood
nailing strip

over/under
rails

upstage/downstage
rails

FIGURE 2: THE DOWNSTAGE SIDE

Note: All frame sections are 1'-0" wide and can be up to 20'-0" long. Sections are joined by pairs of bolts located close to the rails.

½"-plywood nailing strip
@ offstage edge

Note typical joint:
two hex head bolts
through adjoining
members.

If nailing strips are added at
load-in, break them at section
joints to facilitate frame reuse.

FIGURE 3: THE OTHER 3 SIDES

Load-in of the ceiling worked quite nicely. First we laid the muslin face down on the stage floor and bolted the pieces of the frame together on top of the fabric, using two bolts at every joint. Then, to make stapling easier, we picked up the fabric with the frame on top of it and slid sawhorses underneath the frame. Two teams working on opposite sides from each other moved around the sides stretching and stapling the fabric in place. Using lines they dropped from the grid, four crew members had no difficulty dead-hauling the ceiling out and tying it off above its show trim. After the walls had been erected, we lowered the ceiling into position and sprayed it with warm water to eliminate the few remaining irregularities.

FINAL NOTES

We're certainly not the first theatre to have used the built-up perimeter frame, but we have quickly learned to appreciate its advantages. It's straighter, stronger, and lighter than a wood frame could be. It's not expensive or difficult to build. And if you standardize the width of the frames and the placement of bolt holes, the frames are easily recyclable, too. The same design that worked so well in the *Candida* ceiling worked just as well for the succeeding show, *A Midsummer Night's Dream*. And the show that followed *A Midsummer Night's Dream* used not only the same framing design, but some of the same framing members. We're hooked.

❧❧❧

Despite their many advantages, 4x4 stressed-skin triscuits weigh about 80# each, a little less than a traditionally framed 4x8. The triscuit cart described here simplifies their storage, transportation, and hoisting into a second-floor loading door. Made of 1" x 2" x 0.083" tube steel, $\frac{1}{4}$" x 3" flat bar, 1" cold-rolled round stock, $\frac{3}{4}$" plywood, and four heavy-duty casters, each cart carries up to 10 triscuits and can be pushed across a level surface by one person.

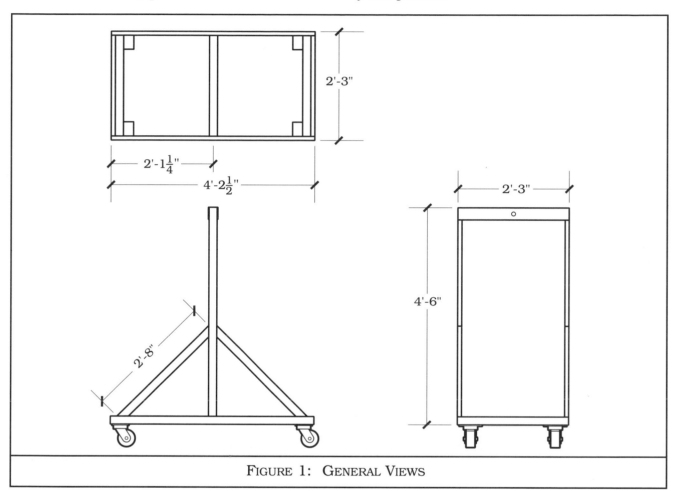

FIGURE 1: GENERAL VIEWS

THE BASE

The base is built with an outside dimension of 2'-3" x 4'-2$\frac{1}{2}$" to allow a $\frac{1}{4}$" clearance in the length and width of the cart. Three cross members, cut at 2'-1", provide support for the plywood bed and mounting opportunities for the casters. Caster choice is a key decision. Polyurethane or rubber casters don't hold up to the wear and tear that these carts will take. One good choice is the Redi-Roll Weldless caster, number 19505T15 in McMaster-Carr's Catalog 105. Though their 600# capacity and $20.29 price tag may seem excessive, these casters will stand up well under the 800# of a fully loaded cart.

CONSTRUCTION NOTES

The cart's $\frac{3}{4}$" plywood deck sits snugly within the tube steel perimeter of the base. The $\frac{1}{4}$" lip that surrounds the deck keeps the triscuits from sliding off the cart during transportation. The uprights provide hand holds and mounting locations for the cold-rolled steel rigging point. Centered on the 4'-2" sides of the base, the 4'-4" uprights are supported by 45° angle braces which measure 1'-8" on the long side. The uprights and angle braces are made of 1" x 2" x 0.083" tube steel.

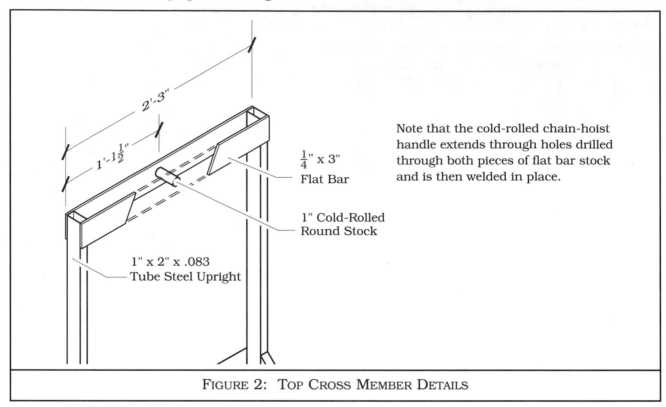

2'-3"

1'-1$\frac{1}{2}$"

$\frac{1}{4}$" x 3"
Flat Bar

1" Cold-Rolled
Round Stock

1" x 2" x .083
Tube Steel Upright

Note that the cold-rolled chain-hoist handle extends through holes drilled through both pieces of flat bar stock and is then welded in place.

FIGURE 2: TOP CROSS MEMBER DETAILS

If rigging points are not required, the cross member at the top of the uprights may also be made of tube steel. But to allow these carts to be picked up by a chain hoist, a cross member made of 2 pieces of $\frac{1}{4}$" x 3" flat bar are welded across the uprights as shown in Figure 2. A 1"-diameter hole drilled through the center of both pieces of flat bar accepts a 2$\frac{1}{2}$" length of 1" cold-rolled steel, which is welded in place to provide a handle for the hook of a chain hoist. Note that, though the design of the cross member and rigging points should be modified as necessary to accept specific chain hoist hooks, the builder is responsible for sizing materials and designing joints suitable to the total load of the cart and triscuits.

❧❧❧

The house unit in the 1998 Goodman Theatre's *Death of a Salesman* had a ceiling that was 9'-0" wide, 18'-0" long, and only 2" thick. Structurally, the ceiling was an 18'-0" beam with a 9'-0" over-hang that, because the unit rode on a turntable, could not be picked from above. Figure 1 illustrates the essentials of the problem. The ceiling couldn't be allowed to deflect noticeably, and it had to be rigid enough to maintain its integrity as the house unit rotated and drove offstage. Further, as it rotated, the unit passed beneath an upstage catwalk with only 3" to spare. Through conversations with Design Engineer Tien-Tsung Ma of Showmotion, Inc. and the Goodman's Production Manager Max Leventhal, we decided to use a cable attached 2" above the top surface to bend the ceiling back on itself like a bow.

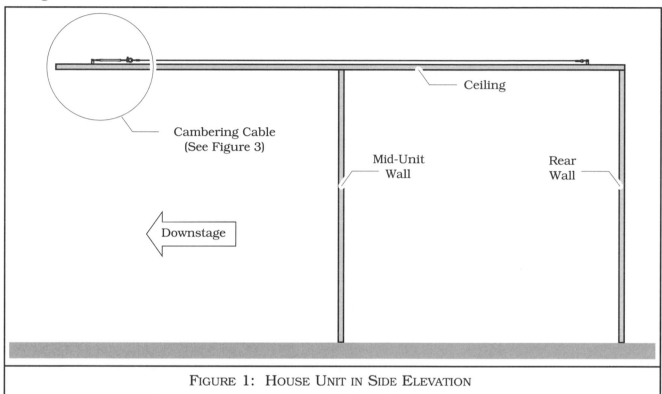

FIGURE 1: HOUSE UNIT IN SIDE ELEVATION

CONSTRUCTION DETAILS

The ceiling unit was constructed as a tube steel and plywood stressed-skin. The perimeter, made from 2" x 2" x 0.065" tube steel, surrounded a thinner frame of 1" x 1" x 0.065" tube steel. Figure 2 shows the ceiling's framing in plan view. Tabs of $\frac{1}{4}$" x 1" x 1" cut to $4\frac{1}{8}$" were welded to the inner frame a distance of 1'-0" in from the ceiling's perimeter. These tabs were drilled as shown in Figure 3 to accept the $\frac{3}{8}$" turnbuckle and $\frac{3}{16}$" aircraft cable assemblies which would counteract the ceiling's tendency to deflect. Before attaching the plywood to the inner frame with construction adhesive, we used the cables to pre-camber the ceiling in the equal but opposite direction of its predicted deflection. The construction adhesive allowed the unit to work as a stressed-skin, and the pre-cambering allowed the unit to deflect naturally into a nearly flat and level state. After the adhesive had set, we decreased the tension on the cables, but we decided against removing them altogether. They provided the ability to fine-tune the leveling, and they prevented the ceiling from sagging over time.

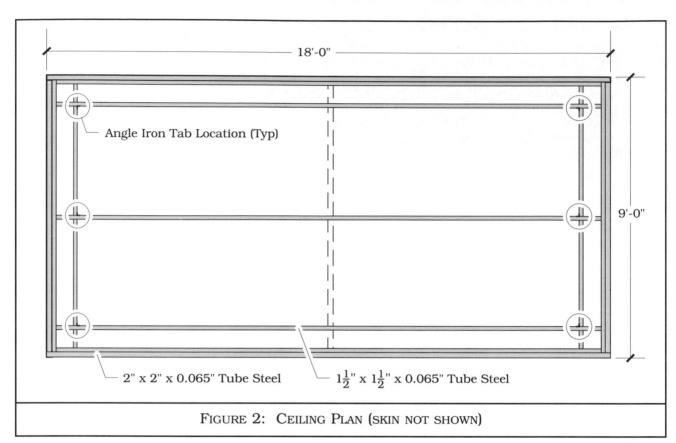

FIGURE 2: CEILING PLAN (SKIN NOT SHOWN)

Angle Iron Tab Location (Typ)

18'-0"

9'-0"

2" x 2" x 0.065" Tube Steel

$1\frac{1}{2}$" x $1\frac{1}{2}$" x 0.065" Tube Steel

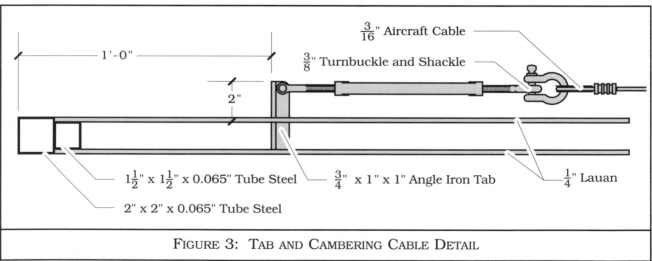

FIGURE 3: TAB AND CAMBERING CABLE DETAIL

$\frac{3}{16}$" Aircraft Cable

$\frac{3}{8}$" Turnbuckle and Shackle

1'-0"

2"

$1\frac{1}{2}$" x $1\frac{1}{2}$" x 0.065" Tube Steel

$\frac{3}{4}$" x 1" x 1" Angle Iron Tab

$\frac{1}{4}$" Lauan

2" x 2" x 0.065" Tube Steel

The set for a Yale School of Drama production of *The Golem* included two hard-covered wall sections, both 32'-0" wide. One of them was 16' tall and was dead hung 12' off the deck. The other was 12' tall and designed to fly just downstage of the first. To minimize the wall sections' weight we framed the flats with 1" x 0.065" square tube. To keep the assembled walls as flat and as thin as possible, we stiffened them with whalers — steel versions of a hogs trough. As tube steel framing has become more common, theater shops the world over have developed their own styles of whalers. Those we used for *The Golem* are detailed in Figure 1.

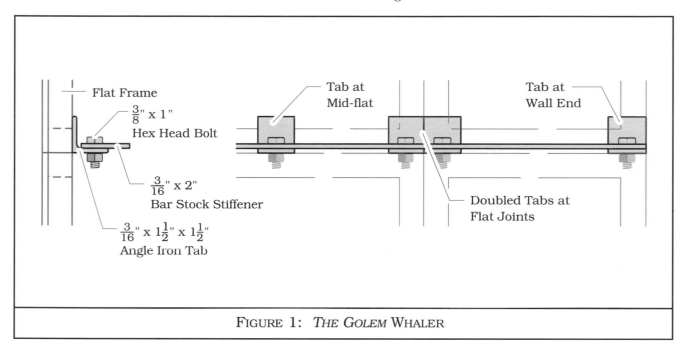

FIGURE 1: *THE GOLEM* WHALER

Whalers like these have two components — the stiffeners and the tabs that hold the stiffeners to the assembled flats. For stiffeners, we cut $\frac{3}{16}$" x 2" bar stock to lengths dictated by the wall design. We then drilled $\frac{11}{32}$" holes through the stiffeners wherever the stiffeners would cross the flat frames. Next, we made one tab for each stiffener hole by cutting $1\frac{1}{2}$" x $1\frac{1}{2}$" x $\frac{3}{16}$" angle iron into $1\frac{1}{2}$" lengths and drilling an $\frac{11}{32}$" hole through one flange of each tab. Finally, we bolted the tabs and stiffeners together with $\frac{3}{8}$" x 1" hex head bolts. To finish the whalers, we laid the flats face-down, positioned the whalers, and welded the tabs to the flats. Finally, we labeled the stiffeners and tabs, unbolted the stiffeners, and set them aside for load-in.

VARIATIONS ON THE THEME

Figures 2 and 3 illustrate alternative whaler designs. The 2" x 2" x $\frac{3}{16}$" angle-iron stiffener shown in Figure 2 makes a somewhat stronger whaler because the angle iron is less likely to buckle than bar stock. Some shops prefer to use 3" x 3" x $\frac{3}{16}$" aluminum angle as illustrated in Figure 3. It goes together faster since there are no tabs at all. The wall flats are laid out face down and pre-cut stiffeners are set in place. Then, holes for weld nuts are drilled through the whalers and the flats' framing. The whalers are set aside, the weld nuts are welded to the frames, and the flats are picked up for installation at load-in.

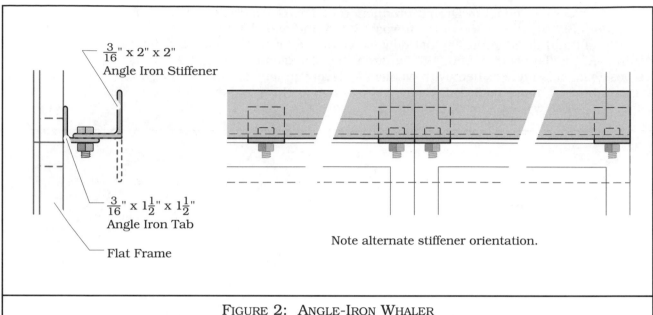

$\frac{3}{16}$" x 2" x 2"
Angle Iron Stiffener

$\frac{3}{16}$" x $1\frac{1}{2}$" x $1\frac{1}{2}$"
Angle Iron Tab

Flat Frame

Note alternate stiffener orientation.

FIGURE 2: ANGLE-IRON WHALER

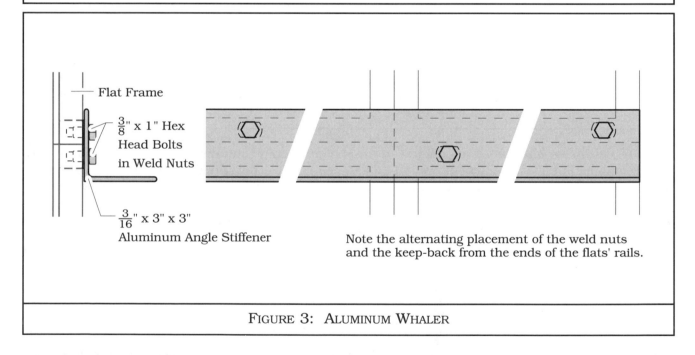

Flat Frame

$\frac{3}{8}$" x 1" Hex
Head Bolts
in Weld Nuts

$\frac{3}{16}$" x 3" x 3"
Aluminum Angle Stiffener

Note the alternating placement of the weld nuts
and the keep-back from the ends of the flats' rails.

FIGURE 3: ALUMINUM WHALER

Act III of The Yale Repertory Theatre's 1998 production of *Hayfever* required a forty-minute rain effect just upstage of an interior setting. To keep the stage as dry as possible throughout that torrent, we devised the slim-profile rain wall shown in Figure 1, whose components included a rain curtain, a delivery system, and a collection-and-recycling system.

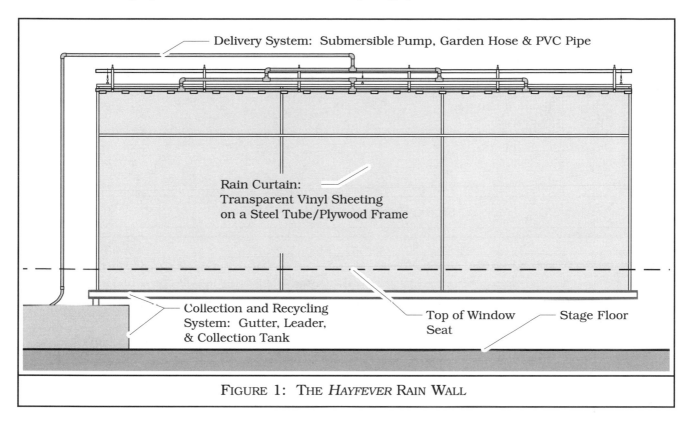

FIGURE 1: THE *HAYFEVER* RAIN WALL

THE RAIN CURTAIN

We used clear vinyl sheeting for the rain curtain. It is soft, ductile, strong, and non-reactive to both acidic and alkaline solutions. Unlike PETG, it also resists scratching. We framed the vinyl sheeting with 1" x 1" tube steel faced with $\frac{1}{2}$" plywood nailers. The frame layout and dimensions are shown in Figure 2.

THE DELIVERY SYSTEM

The delivery system included a $\frac{1}{6}$ HP submersible pump, a 1" flexible hose, a filter, a control valve, a tree-like assembly of 1" PVC pipes, and a 1" PVC drip pipe, as shown in Figure 3. The flexible hose allowed the rain wall to be flown in for the effect and out for all other scenes. The drip pipe was drilled with $\frac{1}{4}$" holes every foot. To make sure the water would continue to run down the vinyl sheeting rather than drip from the pipe as the rain slowed and ended, we inserted 1" lengths of $\frac{1}{4}$" plastic tubing into the holes and gaff-taped 2" x 3" formica diffusers between the drip pipe and the vinyl sheeting to keep the rain from streaming down the vinyl in rivulets. Figure 4 details the various pieces. The C-clamp and $\frac{1}{8}$" x 1" bar-stock hangers shown in Figure 4 allowed us to adjust the trim of the drip pipe so that the rain would be evenly distributed across the stage.

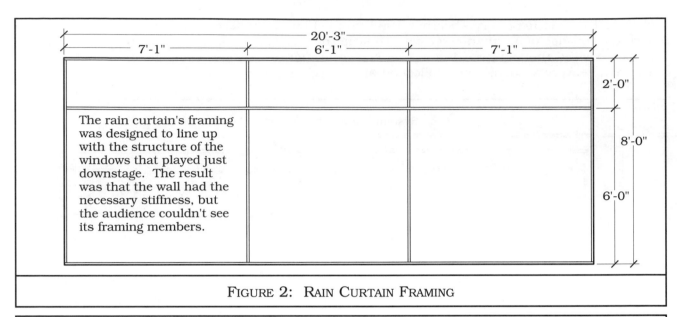

The rain curtain's framing was designed to line up with the structure of the windows that played just downstage. The result was that the wall had the necessary stiffness, but the audience couldn't see its framing members.

FIGURE 2: RAIN CURTAIN FRAMING

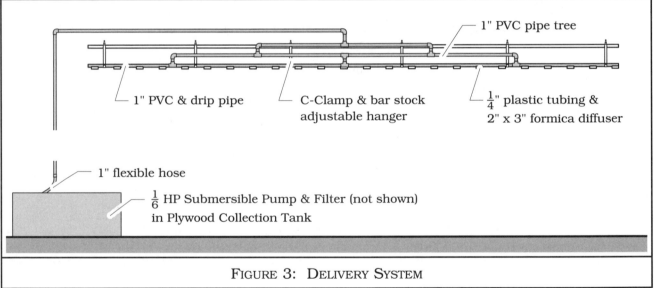

1" PVC pipe tree

1" PVC & drip pipe

C-Clamp & bar stock adjustable hanger

$\frac{1}{4}$" plastic tubing & 2" x 3" formica diffuser

1" flexible hose

$\frac{1}{6}$ HP Submersible Pump & Filter (not shown) in Plywood Collection Tank

FIGURE 3: DELIVERY SYSTEM

COLLECTION AND RECYCLING SYSTEM

We attached a 5" eaves-trough gutter to the bottom of the rain wall as shown in Figure 5. The gutter collected the rain and fed it through a leader into a 48"-long x 16"-wide x 20"-high tank made of $\frac{3}{4}$" plywood and lined with vinyl sheeting. The water was then recycled by the pump. Through calculations and experimentation we determined that we needed only about 2 gallons of water for the entire 40-minute rain effect — half of the capacity of our tank.

THE PROFILE

All the flown parts of the rain wall — the rain curtain, the delivery system's PVC pipes, and the gutter and leader of the collection system — were rigged to a single pipe. Thus, the rain wall could fly in within 8" of the window unit.

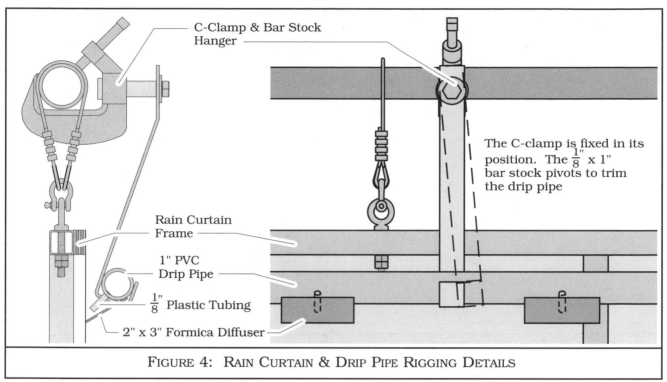

C-Clamp & Bar Stock
Hanger

The C-clamp is fixed in its
position. The $\frac{1}{8}$" x 1"
bar stock pivots to trim
the drip pipe

Rain Curtain
Frame

1" PVC
Drip Pipe

$\frac{1}{8}$" Plastic Tubing

2" x 3" Formica Diffuser

FIGURE 4: RAIN CURTAIN & DRIP PIPE RIGGING DETAILS

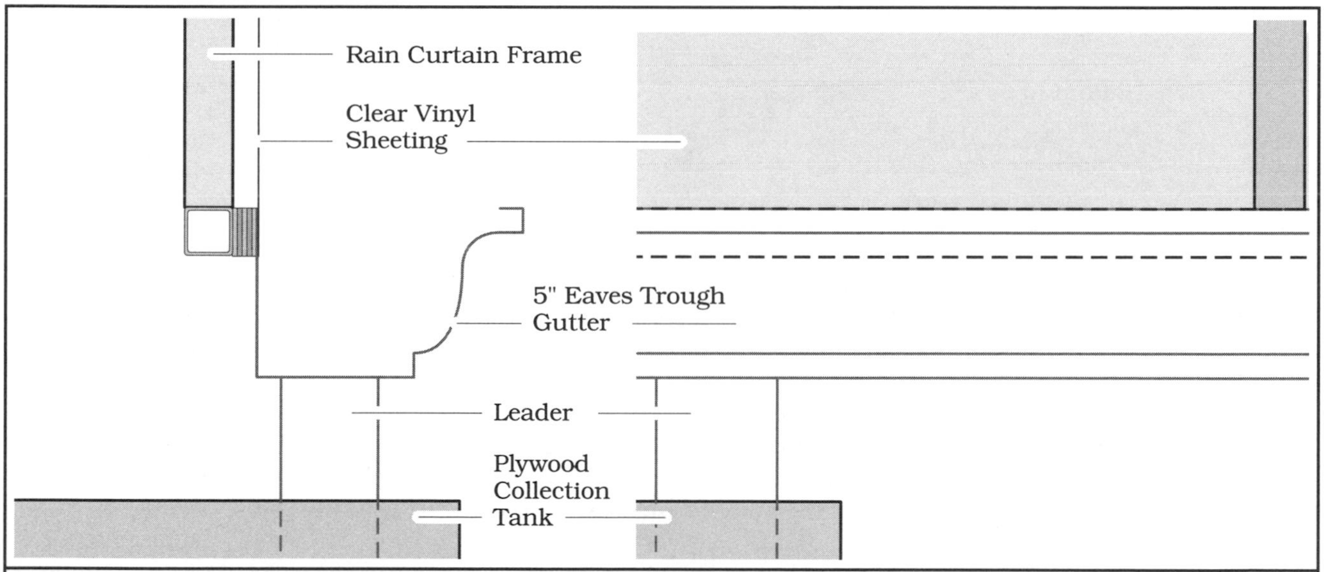

Rain Curtain Frame

Clear Vinyl
Sheeting

5" Eaves Trough
Gutter

Leader

Plywood
Collection
Tank

FIGURE 5: COLLECTION & RECYCLING SYSTEM DETAILS

For a 2000 production of *Curse of the Starving Class,* the technical design team adopted an old construction technique to enhance our use of the space frame flat. The design called for a set of leno-scrim flats that met at outside corners. We were concerned that the subtle watercolor-style painting technique and the nature of the material would result in an imperfect joint. After considering various methods of joining the space frames, we concluded that a fabric hinge could be incorporated into the space frame construction. Thus, the scenic artists could paint the leno-scrim as a single piece, and the two flats could be assembled and covered as one unit at load-in.

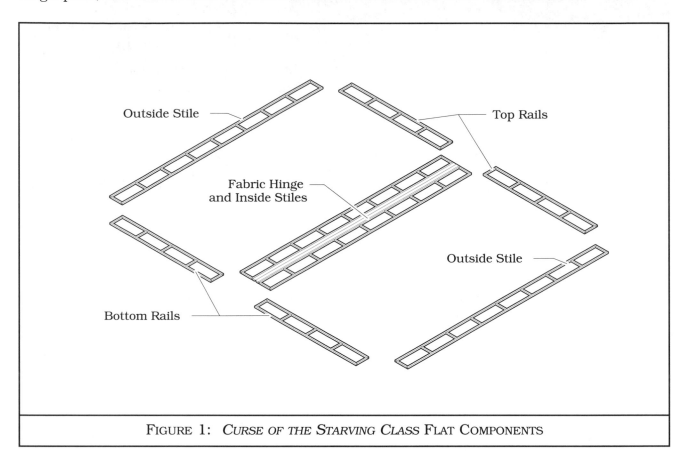

FIGURE 1: *CURSE OF THE STARVING CLASS* FLAT COMPONENTS

As the fabric hinge was not readily attachable to the tube steel frames, lengths of $\frac{5}{4}$ x 3 pine with a 45° bevel on one edge were cut to the length of the abutting space frame flats. Strips of heavy weight muslin (canvas could certainly be used as well) were glued to the lumber to form the hinge. The lumber pieces were then screwed to the space frames with pan head wood screws. See Figure 2.

Assembly in the theater involved laying out the space frames and bolting them together. The leno-scrim was then stapled to the $\frac{1}{4}$" plywood nailing strips around the perimeter on the back of the frames. Finally, the whole assembly was raised and folded into place. In one operation, we had covered and raised two large adjoining flats with no seam at the corner.

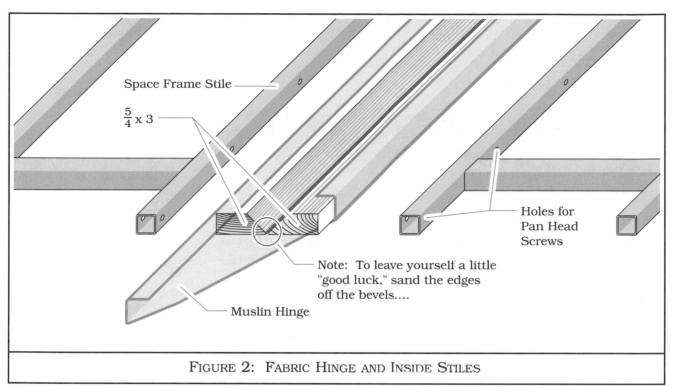

Space Frame Stile

$\frac{5}{4} \times 3$

Holes for
Pan Head
Screws

Note: To leave yourself a little
"good luck," sand the edges
off the bevels....

Muslin Hinge

FIGURE 2: FABRIC HINGE AND INSIDE STILES

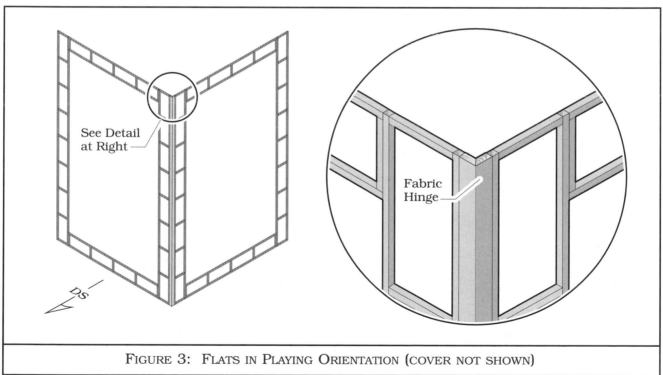

See Detail
at Right

DS

Fabric
Hinge

FIGURE 3: FLATS IN PLAYING ORIENTATION (COVER NOT SHOWN)

While polyvinyl chloride (PVC) pipe is commonly used in the "real world" for plumbing applications, its theatre applications have previously been limited to creating small diameter columns or other non-structural uses. Its modular nature and low cost make it ideal for scene shops that need inexpensive touring scenery — in our case frames for a scenic unit that can quickly be broken down for transport by unskilled workers.

FIGURE 1: PVC "BAMBOO" FRAMED SCENERY

The size of the PVC pipe chosen should be based on the needs of the scenic unit. For more rigidity use a larger diameter pipe; for greater flexibility, a smaller diameter. For example, for one set consisting of 5'-0" x 8'-0" painted panels, $1\frac{1}{4}$" PVC for the frame provided the rigidity needed to stretch painted muslin. *Comedy of Errors* required thin, curved "bamboo" frames draped with cloth. To accomplish this, the scenery was built out of $\frac{3}{4}$" PVC pipe. Figure 2 on the next page illustrates the behavior of the two examples.

Assembly of a PVC frame can be done "Erector set" style without the use of power tools, or the material can be worked with common woodworking power tools. For the painted 5'-0" x 8'-0" panels, including pipe pockets in all four sides of the muslin and inserting the PVC pipe created a lightweight frame. For *Comedy of Errors*, the frame curves had a large diameter and could be made by cold bending the pipe, allowing it to straighten out again for storage. To connect the frames together, we purchased couplers and secured them with PVC glue to one side. The other pipes connected by using a cotter pin in a $\frac{1}{8}$" hole drilled through the pipe and the coupler. See Figure 3.

In both examples, the scenery was light and could be packed quickly and stored in relatively small spaces — the entire *Comedy of Errors* set stowed away in two bags for travel.

OTHER CONSIDERATIONS

To treat the surface, sanding is required, followed by (in our case) a stain that penetrated the surface a little and did not scrape off as easily as paint.

While PVC is not the most durable material, its low cost allows you to buy replacement pieces as the need arises.

Any sanding, cutting, or drilling releases toxic fumes. If you need to heat the pipe to bend it, use indirect heat which reduces gas emission, as explained in Thurston James's book *The Theater Props Handbook*.

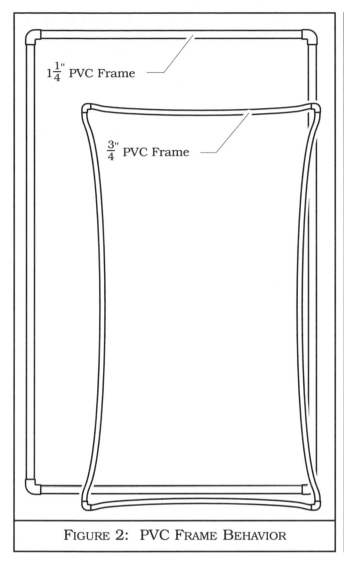

$1\frac{1}{4}$" PVC Frame

$\frac{3}{4}$" PVC Frame

FIGURE 2: PVC FRAME BEHAVIOR

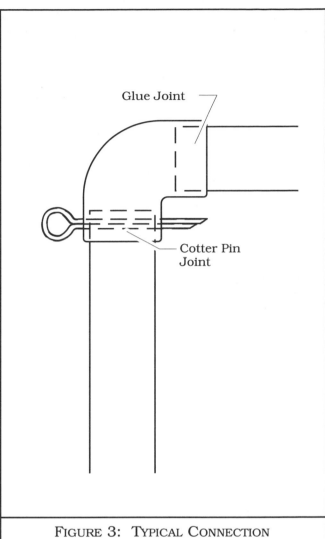

Glue Joint

Cotter Pin Joint

FIGURE 3: TYPICAL CONNECTION

In response to our need for new flexible seating in our Lab theatre, I developed a less expensive alternative for seating risers. My system cost a third of the price of commercial riser systems and can be repaired/replaced by even moderately skilled carpenters. Like traditional parallels in all other respects, this design features an all-plywood support system which, though heavier than its lumber counterpart, can be built more quickly and easily by running a flush-trim router bit around a lauan template. Keeping such a template also simplifies making replacement parts.

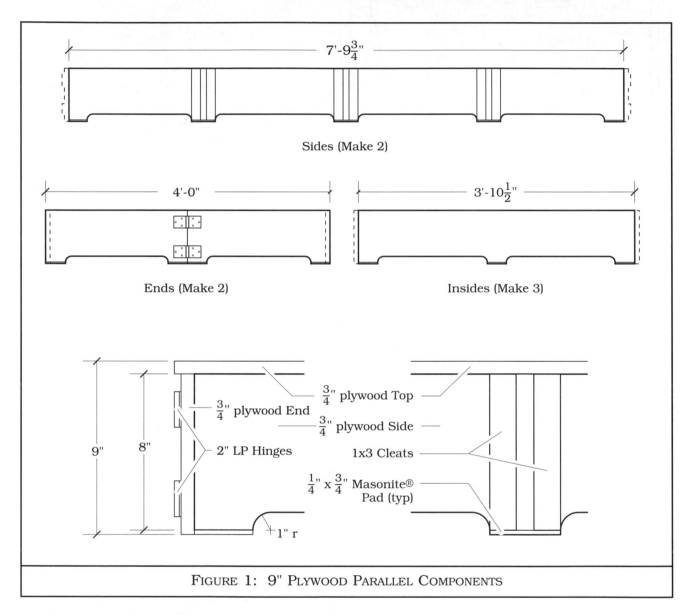

FIGURE 1: 9" PLYWOOD PARALLEL COMPONENTS

TECHNICAL BRIEF

Scenery Decks

The soft pine flooring used on our stage had started splintering, thanks to a combination of several years' misuse and an unfortunate decline in the quality of flooring materials. Our floor surface is one-inch pine T&G approximately 3" wide laid over two layers of $\frac{1}{2}$" plywood. The floor surface itself is so soft that overloaded wagons often leave temporary tracks in the surface. Splintering, which results from toenailing into the floor and from the repeated compression and decompression of wood fibers, usually affects shallow-grained boards.

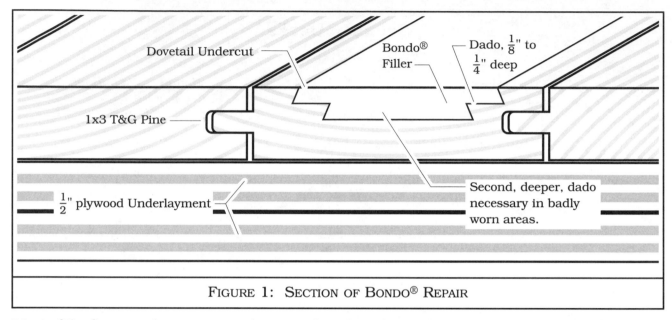

FIGURE 1: SECTION OF BONDO® REPAIR

Most of the floor-patching compounds we tried on the splintered areas became very brittle and soon broke out of the patched area under heavy wagon traffic. A fiberglass boat-hull repair compound worked fairly well but was very expensive. Bondo® autobody filler, on the other hand, flexes with the wood, is easy to mix and apply, and hardens quickly. Its only drawback as a patch is its tendency to crack around the edges, where it is feathered thin by sanding.

Dadoing the area to be patched to a uniform depth and then undercutting the edge with a dovetail router solves this last problem. As the illustration shows, in larger areas we cut a second, deeper, dado into the flooring to serve as an anchor.

❧❧❧❧

Technical Designers and technical design students rarely have the time for research that is not immediately related to a particular production. But over the years, students taking Technical Design at the Yale School of Drama have collaborated on a number of class projects designed to seek better solutions to perennial technical problems. The results are often quite good, but few of the projects have resulted in solutions as complete and as satisfying as the deck system detailed here.

SYSTEM OVERVIEW

The triscuit is a double-sided stressed-skin panel — a lightweight frame of $\frac{5}{4}$ pine covered on both sides with $\frac{5}{8}$" plywood. It was designed as a structural unit capable of carrying at least 50psf which could be used as a sub-floor under any finish layer of decking. Like other stressed-skins, triscuits cannot be legged up. They can, however, be supported on a set of ordinary 2x4 studwalls placed 4' apart. And triscuits have a distinct advantage over traditionally framed platforms in that they can be connected to their stud-walls much more easily. Each triscuit has four bolt-down holes, one in each corner. Working from above, an installer can secure each triscuit positively with four pieces of hardware, whether $3\frac{1}{2}$" lag screws, $4\frac{1}{2}$" hex head bolts, or even 3" drywall screws on washers. If the use of triscuits speeds deck assembly, it speeds strikes even more dramatically, since no one has to crawl under the deck to release connections.

CUT LIST

2 pieces $\frac{5}{8}$" CDX plywood, 3'-11$\frac{7}{8}$" x 3'-11$\frac{7}{8}$"
2 pieces $\frac{5}{4}$ x 1" (true) pine, 3'-7$\frac{7}{8}$" long
3 pieces $\frac{5}{4}$ x 2" (true) pine, 3'- 9$\frac{7}{8}$" long
2 pieces $\frac{5}{4}$ x 2" (true) pine, 3'-11$\frac{7}{8}$" long

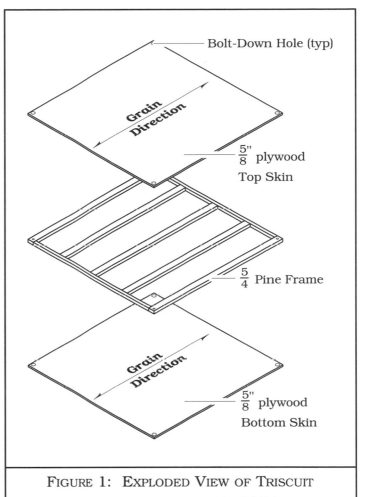

Bolt-Down Hole (typ)

Grain Direction

$\frac{5}{8}$" plywood
Top Skin

$\frac{5}{4}$ Pine Frame

Grain Direction

$\frac{5}{8}$" plywood
Bottom Skin

FIGURE 1: EXPLODED VIEW OF TRISCUIT

CONSTRUCTION NOTES

Several construction details require scrupulous attention. Two of them assure the triscuit's structural integrity. First, the surface grain of both skins must run parallel to the 2"-wide framing members, as shown in Figure 1. Grain mis-orientation reduces the triscuit's strength. Second, careless gluing or nailing will result in poor performance and will shorten the triscuit's useful life. The glue which joins skins to frame must be spread evenly during assembly, and the nails spaced no more than 6" apart. Three other construction details are only slightly less important. First, the skins are cut as squares measuring 3'-11$\frac{7}{8}$" on each side to permit an $\frac{1}{8}$" gap to be left between adjacent panels during installation. That gap insures that the deck will not squeak during use. Second, each triscuit's bolt-down holes and counterbores should be sized to suit the user's choice of hardware: the hole illustrated in Figure 2 accommodates a $\frac{5}{16}$" lag screw and washer. Third, the

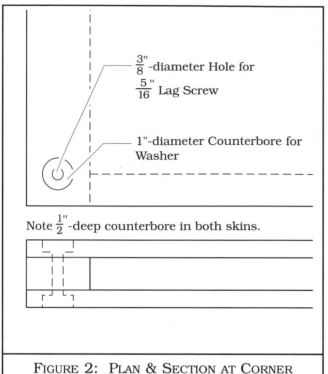

$\frac{3"}{8}$-diameter Hole for

$\frac{5"}{16}$ Lag Screw

1"-diameter Counterbore for Washer

Note $\frac{1"}{2}$-deep counterbore in both skins.

FIGURE 2: PLAN & SECTION AT CORNER

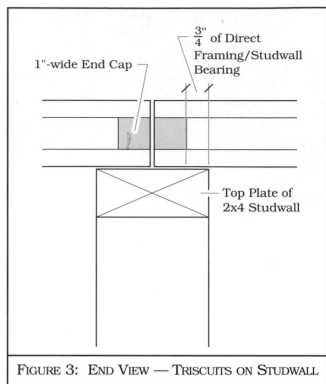

1"-wide End Cap

$\frac{3"}{4}$ of Direct Framing/Studwall Bearing

Top Plate of 2x4 Studwall

FIGURE 3: END VIEW — TRISCUITS ON STUDWALL

1"-wide framing members serve only as end caps for the triscuits. Their narrowness permits the ends of principal framing members to extend directly over the top plate of a 2x4 studwall. See Figure 3.

INSTALLATION NOTES

Triscuit decks can be installed very quickly. Each triscuit weighs only a little more than a single sheet of $\frac{3}{4}$" plywood, its shape makes it easy to handle, and it can be used either side up. Using an $\frac{1}{8}$" spacer, installers can easily maintain the desired gap between triscuits, and the ease of triscuit-studwall connection has already been established. Triscuit decks can be assembled so quickly, in fact, that installers must take care to lay each triscuit with its face grain perpendicular to the studwalls. For if a triscuit is casually installed 90° out of its intended orientation, only two of its seven framing members will be at all useful in resisting loads. See Figure 4. Painting grain-direction arrows on the skins can help avoid this problem.

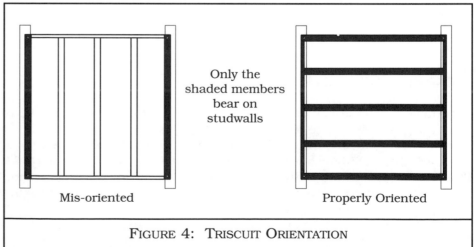

Only the shaded members bear on studwalls

Mis-oriented

Properly Oriented

FIGURE 4: TRISCUIT ORIENTATION

FINAL OBSERVATIONS

Obviously, triscuits offer several advantages, some already mentioned and a few more which deserve special note. One of them stems from the triscuit's thinness. Like some other types of decks, a triscuit deck can overhang its studwall base by 1'. But since it is only $2\frac{3}{8}$" thick, a triscuit deck can look more like a plane than like a slab, and its thinness emphasizes the overhang, heightening the sense of separation that designers so often want to establish between the stage floor and the show deck. In addition to their other advantages, triscuits are lighter than their traditionally framed 4x8 counterparts, and yet they bear just as much weight. Their size and shape make them easy to handle, and they store very efficiently. Because they are double-skinned, their framing is less susceptible to damage from the wear and tear that soon destroys other types of platforms. And, finally, at a cost of about $35 apiece, they are certainly cost-effective, especially in light of their expected life span: ours have been in use for over three years and show little if any deterioration.

Triscuits were first documented as part of an exhibit by Evan D. Gelick for USITT's 1993 Theatre Technology Exhibit.

ટ⬛ટ⬛ટ⬛

Over the long term, the most cost-effective decks may be those made of stock platforms covered with a thin show skin of Masonite® or medium density fiberboard (MDF). Each time a stock platform is re-used, its effective cost decreases; and though the show skins themselves are less likely to be useful as stock, whole sheets and larger scraps can often be used in two productions at least, as long as both faces of the material are equally "good."

On the other hand, the initial cost of such platforming is relatively high, since each platform has to be covered twice — once with a lid and once with a show skin. In an attempt to reduce the material and labor costs of the four, large throw-away decks we had to build for Arizona State University's *Crow and Weasel*, I decided to test whether a single layer of deck surface material could work in place of the usual plywood lid and MDF skin combination. Because these four decks needed to look especially clean and seamless, $\frac{3}{4}$"-thick panels of MDF seemed the best possible choice.

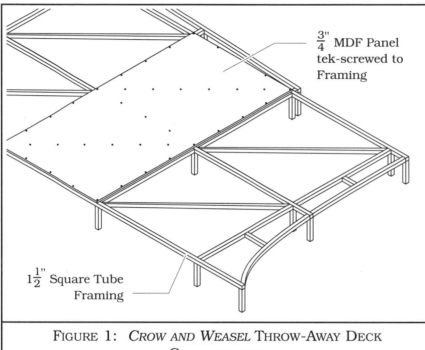

$\frac{3}{4}$" MDF Panel tek-screwed to Framing

$1\frac{1}{2}$" Square Tube Framing

FIGURE 1: *CROW AND WEASEL* THROW-AWAY DECK CONSTRUCTION

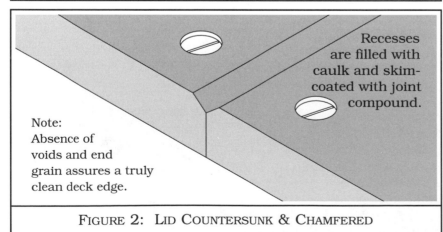

Recesses are filled with caulk and skim-coated with joint compound.

Note: Absence of voids and end grain assures a truly clean deck edge.

FIGURE 2: LID COUNTERSUNK & CHAMFERED

DECK FRAMING

Since we weren't building individual platforms, we butt-welded the $1\frac{1}{2}$" square tube steel we used as framing material into a single frame. We spaced the steel to accommodate the actual 49" x 97" size of the MDF we had bought, and included diagonal members to keep the frame in true. Legs of $1\frac{1}{2}$" square tube steel supported the horizontal framing members at nominal 4-foot o.c. increments. A view of a partly assembled deck appears in Figure 1.

THE LID

Before fastening the panels to the frame, we chamfered the edges of each panel at 45° as in Figure 2. We then tek-screwed the MDF panels directly to the frame, butting the panels tight against each other and spacing the screws about 1'-0" apart. Around the panels' perimeters, we drilled and countersank pilot holes so that the edges wouldn't break or chip, but we let all the other screws pilot and countersink themselves. Before painting the deck, we filled the screw heads and the seams between panels with latex caulk, which we smoothed with a putty knife.

For durability's sake, we skim-coated the caulk with joint compound, which we sanded to efface any hint of seams. Paint and a satin clear-coat sealer finished the surface treatment.

EVALUATION

No doubt, MDF is not a perfect deck lid material. Among its limitations . . .

Though it obviously does have some structural value, MDF has no structural rating. Using the material as a deck lid requires an especially careful and conservative load analysis.

MDF is denser and heavier than plywood. Weighing about 96#, a $\frac{3}{4}$"-thick sheet is too heavy for use as a stock-platform lid.

MDF panels are larger than most other sheet goods. Standard panels are nominally 49" x 97", but their actual dimensions (including thickness) vary from one manufacturer to the next and even from lot to lot. Prudent users will buy all the MDF needed for a project at one time before detailing or laying out any framing.

The edges of MDF panels are straight and true enough for theatrical production, but the corners are not necessarily square.

Cutting or machining standard-grade MDF releases comparatively high levels of formaldehyde.

Standard-grade MDF reacts to wide changes in humidity, and may not be suitable for use in non-air-conditioned theaters in places less dry than Arizona.

Moreover, if I were to rebuild these four decks, I would reinforce the connection between lid and frame with a bead of construction adhesive. Under moderate traffic, the tek-screws loosen after a time, and the decks became somewhat noisy.

Nevertheless, given our original objectives, MDF was perhaps the best choice for these particular decks' lids. After all, the decks' edges presented no end grain or voids to be dressed. Our seam treatment made the joints nearly invisible, and the super-smooth and hard painted finish was exactly what we wanted. Finally, the price was right: we purchased $\frac{3}{4}$" MDF at less than $21.00 a sheet — about what we pay for cdx plywood — and since we gave each deck only one cover, we saved a fair amount of our typical labor and materials costs.

¿▲¿▲¿▲

For me, one of the most intriguing things about the Yale triscuit-studwall system is its size. Here at Trinity University, we generally support platforms on 4' centers regardless of their size, so the concept of lightweight, thin-profile 4x4 stock platform units made a great deal of sense. I enthusiastically set out to make some triscuits for my theater, but finding $\frac{5}{4}$ lumber difficult to locate in my area, I decided to use thin-wall tube steel for the frames. That choice prompted the development of the triscuit described here.

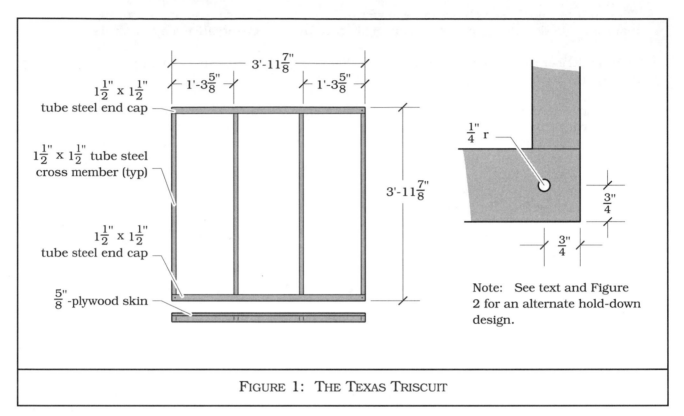

FIGURE 1: THE TEXAS TRISCUIT

The Texas triscuit has a welded frame consisting of four lengths of $1\frac{1}{2}$" x 1" and two lengths of 16-gauge $1\frac{1}{2}$"-square tube steel. Like the original, this triscuit is capable of carrying at least 50 psf, is fastened to its studwall at only four points, and can be used as a sub-floor under any finish layer of decking. It is not a double-sided stressed-skin like the original, however, and since it is skinned with $\frac{5}{8}$" plywood on just one side, it has a $2\frac{1}{8}$" profile and weighs only 56 pounds.

CONSTRUCTION NOTES

The use of steel tubing retains the strength advantages of the wood-framed triscuit and simplifies the construction process somewhat. Drilling the four hold-down holes in the $1\frac{1}{2}$"-square tube steel end caps is the first step, but the size of the holes depends on the choice of fastener to be used. Since I use 3" drywall screws, I drill $\frac{1}{4}$" holes. Those who prefer to use lag screws should drill $\frac{3}{8}$" holes instead, as Figure 2 illustrates. In either case, the holes should be drilled on the centerline of the $1\frac{1}{2}$"-square tube, $\frac{3}{4}$" from the ends as shown in Figure 1. After drilling the four holes, lay out the four cross members between the two end caps, square and weld the frame, and grind the top and bottom welds flush. Set the plywood on the frame with the grain parallel to the cross members, and attach the lid to the frame with self-tapping screws 6" apart. Turn the assembly over, and drill the four hold-down holes through the lid. Countersink or counterbore the plywood as necessary to accommodate your choice of studwall fastening hardware. See the notes in Figure 2.

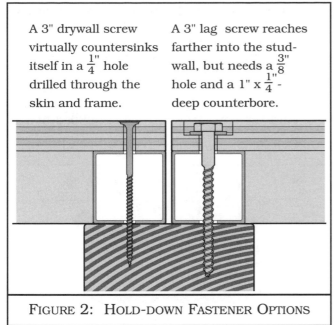

A 3" drywall screw virtually countersinks itself in a $\frac{1}{4}$" hole drilled through the skin and frame.

A 3" lag screw reaches farther into the stud-wall, but needs a $\frac{3}{8}$" hole and a 1" x $\frac{1}{4}$" - deep counterbore.

FIGURE 2: HOLD-DOWN FASTENER OPTIONS

CUT LIST

2 pieces	$1\frac{1}{2}$"-square tube steel (16-gauge) 3'-11$\frac{7}{8}$"
4 pieces	$1\frac{1}{2}$" x 1" tube steel (16-gauge) 3'-8$\frac{7}{8}$"
1 piece	$\frac{5}{8}$" plywood, 3'-11$\frac{7}{8}$" x 3'-11$\frac{7}{8}$"

INSTALLATION NOTES

Like the originals, steel-framed triscuits are to be laid out with the four cross members running perpendicular to the studwalls so that four rather than two framing members carry the load. An $\frac{1}{8}$" gap left between the triscuits prevents them from squeaking as they flex under floor traffic.

FINAL OBSERVATIONS

The steel-framed Texas triscuit is a useful option for stock platforms. Their size and shape make them easy to handle and store. The welded frame should last forever and the plywood deck can be replaced as needed. At a cost of less than $30 apiece, they offer an efficient and effective alterna-tive to traditional platforming methods.

❧❧❧

Turntables traditionally challenge theater technicians in several ways. Cutting circles out of 4x8 sheet goods is expensive; framing becomes a morass of angles; construction is slow and complicated; and turntables are difficult to modify for reuse. A production of *Beaux' Stratagem* at the Yale Repertory Theatre called for a 20'-diameter turntable to be built as inexpensively as possible while minimizing deck height for front-row sightlines. We ended up with the frameless laminated-plywood turntable this article describes. This design offered several advantages over framed and laminated-plywood turntables: the segments we developed minimized plywood waste; the turntable could be easily recycled into any diameter under 20'; and the construction was simplified by the modular design.

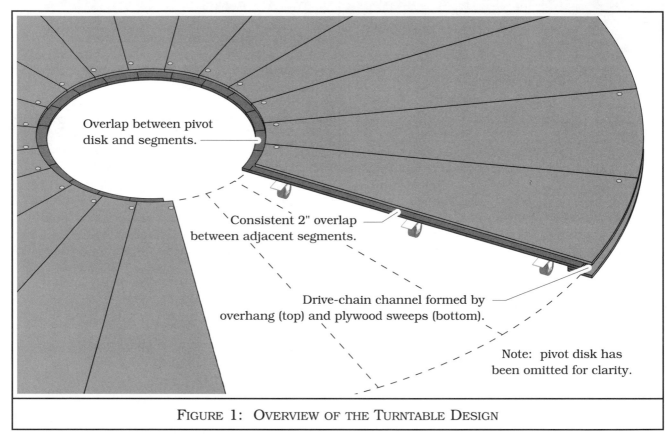

Overlap between pivot disk and segments.

Consistent 2" overlap between adjacent segments.

Drive-chain channel formed by overhang (top) and plywood sweeps (bottom).

Note: pivot disk has been omitted for clarity.

FIGURE 1: OVERVIEW OF THE TURNTABLE DESIGN

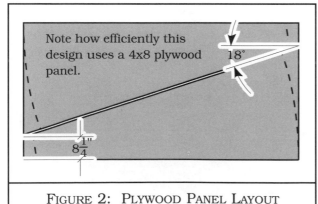

Note how efficiently this design uses a 4x8 plywood panel.

18°

$8\frac{1}{4}$"

FIGURE 2: PLYWOOD PANEL LAYOUT

The turntable consisted of a pivot disk surrounded by a twenty-segment ring, each segment a two-layer lamination of $\frac{3}{4}$" plywood wedges. To eliminate framing, the sides of the top and bottom wedges in each segment were offset to provide a 2" overlap joint, and the inside ends of the segments were joined to the laminated $\frac{3}{4}$" plywood pivot disk through a similar overlap. In designing the overlap joints, we discovered that by making the pivot disk 4'-6" rather than 4'-0" in diameter we were able to cut two wedges — a complete ring segment — from a single sheet of plywood. Figure 1 offers a general view of the turntable.

If you've designed turntables yourself, you may be asking, "How could the overlap between adjacent segments be constant? Doesn't rotating one layer of wedges result in a tapered overlap between segments?" The answer, of course, is "Yes." But we did not *rotate* any wedges. Instead, we *translated* each wedge in the upper layer of the ring 2" relative to its mate in the lower layer, keeping the factory edges of both wedges parallel. Figure 3 illustrates the resulting layout and also shows that the joints between wedges did not lie along the turntable's radii. Figure 4 more fully illustrates ring segment and pivot disk design.

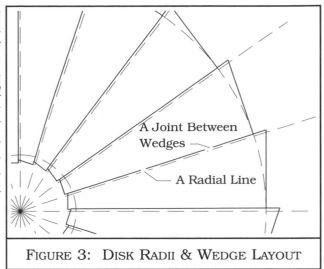

FIGURE 3: DISK RADII & WEDGE LAYOUT

CONSTRUCTION

First, we cut 40 identical wedges from 20 sheets of $\frac{3}{4}$" plywood. To allow "good luck" we were careful to cut each wedge $\frac{1}{8}$" thinner than was theoretically necessary. Next, deliberately leaving a narrow gap at each joint, we laid 20 of the wedges out on the shop floor (as in Figure 3) and tacked them down. We then routed this ratchet-shaped sub-assembly into a ring with a 10' outside radius and a 2'-4" inside radius. We filled the center of the ring with a disk made from two pieces of $\frac{3}{4}$" plywood cut as semicircles.

Next, we laid out the remaining 20 wedges on top of the first 20 and, after careful adjustment to provide the consistent offsets, we laminated each wedge in the second layer to the wedge below. That done, we routed the new layer into a ring with outside and inside radii of 9'-10" and 2'-1$\frac{1}{2}$", respectively. The smaller outside diameter of this ring would accommodate our chain-wrap friction drive. We cut the plywood for the disk in the center of the new ring and laminated it to the disk in the center of the first ring. While we had the turntable laid out upside down, we added plywood sweeps along its circumference to form a drive-chain channel (visible in Figure 1), laid out the caster pattern, and drilled holes for bolt connections in the ends of the segment overlaps.

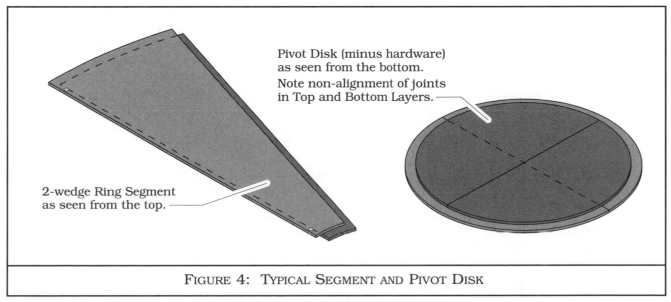

Pivot Disk (minus hardware) as seen from the bottom. Note non-alignment of joints in Top and Bottom Layers.

2-wedge Ring Segment as seen from the top.

FIGURE 4: TYPICAL SEGMENT AND PIVOT DISK

Finally, we pried the turntable off the floor and attached the casters with $2\frac{1}{2}$" flat head stove bolts. Caster connection was complicated by the overlap of the joints. Ideally, each side of a joint should be supported, but we wanted to attach casters to only one side of each joint. We decided to top each caster with a plate of 2" x $\frac{1}{8}$" steel flat stock cut long enough to extend under the non-castered side of a given joint. See Figure 5.

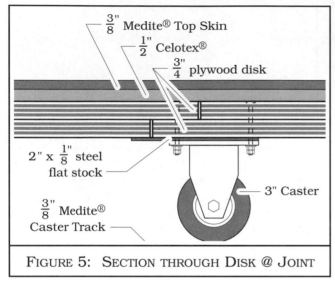

FIGURE 5: SECTION THROUGH DISK @ JOINT

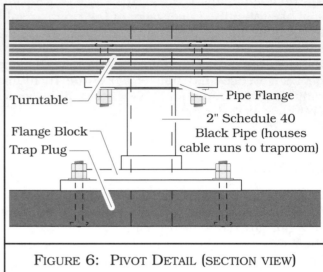

FIGURE 6: PIVOT DETAIL (SECTION VIEW)

LOAD-IN

Except for the last segment, the ring assembled quickly because of the "good luck" gaps we had left between its segments. The last piece was still a tight fit, but brute force finally won the day. We screwed the segments together through the overlaps and added a single bolt at the ends of each overlap — a step that, in hindsight, may not have been necessary. Next, we sleeved the pipe of the pivot disk into its floor-mounted flange block. See Figure 6. Finally, we screwed the pivot disk to the ring and top-skinned the turntable with $\frac{1}{2}$" Celotex® and $\frac{3}{8}$" Medite®.

NOTES

For turntables with diameters smaller than 16', a pivot disk may be optional, but having a solid structure at the center of a turntable is nearly always desirable. In all, we used 26 sheets of plywood in the rings, pivot disk, and drive channel that make up this turntable. On the other hand, that's all we used: the turntable needed no framing, and an ordinary bolt was its most sophisticated piece of hardware. The 2" overlap made the turntable acceptably stiff — though a second time around I would make it a 3" overlap. I'd also use heavier duty casters than load analysis might suggest: loading conditions change as a production is rehearsed, and caster noise is a trifling difficulty compared to changing out a caster after techs begin.

❧❧❧❧

A main element of the set for a production of *Life Is a Dream* at the Yale School of Drama was a 2"-average-depth layer of sand spread over a 42' x 29' playing area. The production team judged that handling the 15 tons of sand needed for that floor was less than desirable. Both load-in and strike would have taken a long time, and loading so much weight on the stage floor seemed unnecessary. Designer Michael Yeargan suggested a simple alternative successfully used at Hartford Stage to make a small quantity of sand look like a much larger one.

The technique involves spreading a relatively thin layer of sand over built-up dunes and an underlayment of carpet chosen to match the color of the sand. With this approach, we used 3 tons of sand at an average depth of $\frac{1}{2}$" across the stage as shown in Figure 1, a reduction of 80%. Wherever the sand happened to be brushed away during performance the carpet below was revealed, but its texture and ability to hold some sand within the fibers made it look like a packed layer of sand. The photo in Figure 1 illustrates the effect.

FIGURE 1: A SANDY FLOOR WITH DUNES

For dunes less than 8" tall like the small one on the right edge of the photo, we simply raked the sand into piles. But for taller dunes like the one visible in the background, we provided supporting structures of $\frac{1}{4}$" plywood to minimize the amount of sand needed. Though such structures could be made structural, those we built were so close to the set's walls that they were built as decorative rather than load-bearing elements.

We purchased sand known as "$\frac{1}{2}$ Jersey" from a local sand and silica supplier. This product was exceptionally clean and dust free in comparison to commonly available play sand. The grain size is larger than that of play sand and reads very well from a distance. It cost slightly more than play sand, and it came in 100 pound bags. In addition to giving us the desired color and texture, this product was virtually dustless and did not require spraying down.

Load-in began with installation of the peripheral dunes next to the set's flats. Next, we unrolled a layer of 5-mil plastic sheeting across the floor and over the dunes to keep sand from sifting into the traproom. The carpet was a commercial grade, Class-1 (fire-resistant) indoor carpet with a $\frac{1}{4}$" pile. Seams between adjacent swaths of carpet were stapled on both sides to prevent them from pulling up. Along the front of the set, where the sand was not bounded by flats, we installed an edging, as shown in Figure 2, to contain the sand. The result was a layered system of dunes, plastic, carpet, and sand with the appropriate edging.

Overall, this approach worked well for us, as it has for others in the past. The key advantages were a reduction in the quantity of sand to be handled and virtual elimination of the airborne dust that

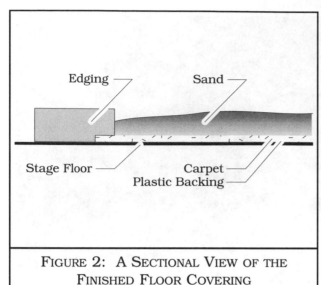

FIGURE 2: A SECTIONAL VIEW OF THE FINISHED FLOOR COVERING

other types of sand can produce. The carpet and sand together did cost about as much as the larger quantity of sand would have, but the use of carpeting saved greatly on the time needed for load-in and strike.

Incidentally, while researching ways to reduce the amount of sand we would have to handle, we discovered that in designing sand or dirt piles for the stage, the material's angle of repose must be considered. The angle of repose is the steepest angle at which a loose material will remain in a pile (*i.e.*, not slide away). According to data presented by the University of Maryland's Department of Geology (http://www.geol.umd.edu/~kaufman/ppt/chapter8/sld018.htm) the angles of repose for likely set floor materials are as follows: fine sand, 35°; coarse sand, 40°; angular pebbles, 45°.

TECHNICAL BRIEF

Scenery Electronics

The choreographer of a production I worked on asked that her dancers' handheld fans twinkle "like a starry backdrop." The size and weight limitations imposed by the project gave me the chance to devise a miniature chase control circuit. This control circuit diagrammed below fits on a 2" x 5" electronic circuit board and costs less than $10 to build. Because of its small size and light weight, this circuit is useful for many theatrical purposes.

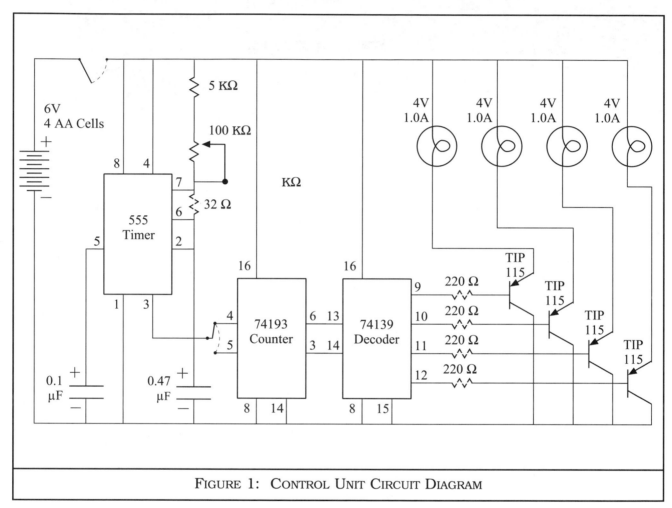

FIGURE 1: CONTROL UNIT CIRCUIT DIAGRAM

This control circuit uses three common IC chips to control the flow of electric power through light sources. The 555 timer is set up to oscillate at a relatively low frequency and to generate the square wave required by the 74193 up/down counter. The 74193 counts 4 binary digits worth of pulses. The 74139 dual 2-to-4 lines decoder is designed with four outputs, any three of which are normally high while the fourth is normally low. The binary input that the 74139 receives from the 74193 determines which one of the four outputs will be low at any time. A TIP115 transistor connected to each output boosts the decoder current to useable values. One pushbutton switch turns the unit on and off, and a second pushbutton switch changes the chase direction. The control unit's adjustable resistor alters the chase rate.

Each of the lamp loads shown in Figure 1 symbolizes one of the four chase branches controlled by the circuit. Typically, each branch consists of a number of small light sources rather than a single bulb. The control circuit could power a group of 72 light sources — either LEDs or 2-volt incandescent lamps (#49). In a fan like the one I built, for instance, that would allow for each of the 9

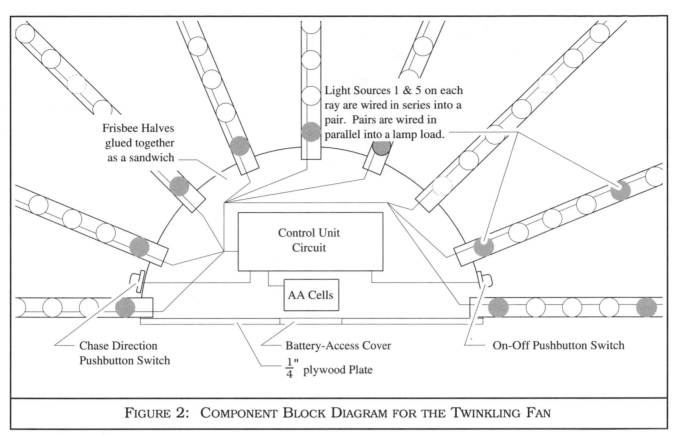

FIGURE 2: COMPONENT BLOCK DIAGRAM FOR THE TWINKLING FAN

plastic-tubing rays to contain 8 light sources, series-wired into 4 sets of 2 lamps each. See Figure 2. This arrangement would keep one pair of light sources on each of the 9 rays (a total of 18 light sources) lit at the same time.

In building the fans, I cut a Frisbee® in half and joined the halves as shown in Figure 2. The Frisbee® sandwich provided a housing for the electronic components and a base for the feathers and plastic-tubing rays. A $\frac{1}{4}$" plywood plate and battery-access cover sealed the open side of the sandwich.

FIGURE 1: SYSTEM CONTROLLER

Stage managers always need direct control over cue lights and the practical sound cues that directly affect the timing of a show. Yet, lighting control systems do not always include enough non-dim circuits to meet all such needs. In such instances, the cue light system described in this article may be particularly useful. A version of this system has served in many Delaware Theatre Company productions, starting with *Trip to Bountiful* in October, 1993. The system is inexpensive, easy to build, and can quickly be adapted to new cue light control and placement needs.

This cue light system uses toggle switches to control six low-voltage alternating current (AC) cue lights and momentary pushbutton switches to control two low-voltage AC doorbell or buzzer devices. The complete system is made up of three shop-built components: the system controller (seen in Figure 1), a distribution network, and a set of cue lights. The parts needed to construct all three components are available at most Radio Shack stores.

THE CONTROLLER

The first step in constructing the controller is to drill holes in the front and rear of the controller box for the power indicator light, switches, fuse holder, power cord, and controller output connector. Measure each component type for hole sizes, and space the holes for the switches $\frac{7}{8}$" apart. Mount the power indicator lamp, switches, and fuse holder on the box and attach the power cord, providing appropriate strain relief where the power cord enters the box. During this process, be sure to orient the toggles so that "up" is "on."

Pre-assemble the multicable connector before mounting it on the box. Cut nine 6" pieces of 18 AWG wire and crimp an AMP socket (AMP 66504-9) on one end of each piece. Use different color wires so that each control channel can be identified easily. Once the sockets have been crimped to the wires, push the sockets into the AMP connector housing until they click into place. Finally, mount the transformer and terminal blocks inside the box and complete the wiring. Figure 2 shows a completed controller with its cover removed, and Figure 3 diagrams the circuitry.

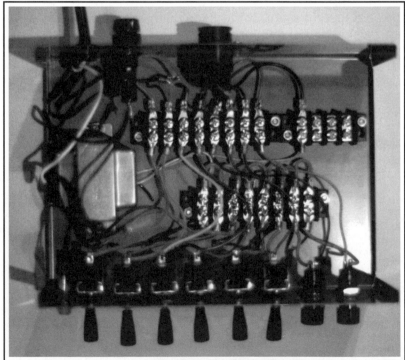

FIGURE 2: THE INTERIOR OF THE CONTROLLER

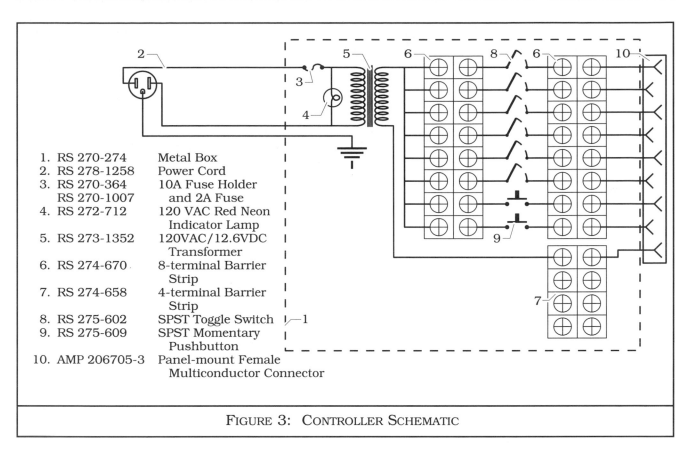

1. RS 270-274   Metal Box
2. RS 278-1258   Power Cord
3. RS 270-364   10A Fuse Holder
    RS 270-1007   and 2A Fuse
4. RS 272-712   120 VAC Red Neon
    Indicator Lamp
5. RS 273-1352   120VAC/12.6VDC Transformer
6. RS 274-670   8-terminal Barrier Strip
7. RS 274-658   4-terminal Barrier Strip
8. RS 275-602   SPST Toggle Switch
9. RS 275-609   SPST Momentary Pushbutton
10. AMP 206705-3   Panel-mount Female Multiconductor Connector

FIGURE 3: CONTROLLER SCHEMATIC

THE DISTRIBUTION NETWORK

The distribution network consists of lengths of multicable containing at least nine 18 AWG conductors and a number of barrier strips with at least 9 terminals each. In the control booth, the cue light controller's usual location, the multicable terminates in a male AMP multi-conductor connector which plugs into the controller. Because this is a low-voltage system, the distribution network does not need to be run through conduit. Instead, the multicable is simply snaked backstage along the simplest route.

Backstage, the multicable terminates at a barrier strip mounted on the back of the proscenium wall. Figure 4, a diagram of the basic distribution network for a proscenium house, shows the use of a 12-terminal barrier strip. But the combination of an 8-terminal and a 4-terminal barrier strip as shown in Figures 2 and 3 would work equally well.

Another length of multicable joins this first barrier strip to a second one mounted on the opposite side of the stage. Additional branches of multicable and barrier strips may be added to expand the basic network as desired.

THE CUE LIGHTS

For redundancy's sake, each cue light consists of a pair of 12VAC Hi-brightness red lamps connected in parallel and mounted on a small piece of lauan (about 4" x 6") that can be screwed or clamped to scenery pieces. The cue lights can safely be connected to the barrier strips with zip cord.

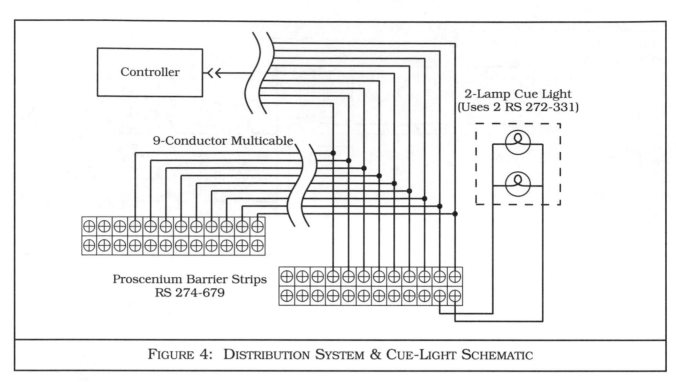

FIGURE 4: DISTRIBUTION SYSTEM & CUE-LIGHT SCHEMATIC

In installation, one conductor from each cue light is connected to a toggle-switch control channel terminal. The cue light's second conductor is connected to the common terminal. Doorbells or buzzers are similarly wired, but to momentary switch terminals rather than toggle terminals.

NOTES

Though this cue light system is simple, it can be tailored to satisfy varying control and cue-light placement needs and it can be adapted to suit various types of performance spaces. Because the distribution multicable plugs into the controller, the controller isn't locked into a particular location. With enough multicable extension cord, the controller could be readily moved into the house for technical rehearsals, or quickly set up backstage or elsewhere as necessary.

The system's parts are quite affordable — the controller, barrier strips, and AMP connectors total less than $100 — and all are generally available, if not from local vendors, from mail-order companies like Digi-Key.

ୡୡୡୡ

The Yale School of Drama's new flexible theatre needed cue lights for its inaugural production, *The Skriker*. Not happy with the look of our stock pigtail cue lights, I designed the custom cue lights shown in Figure 1. These cue lights are easy to build and install and, most importantly, they can be focused to mask the bulbs from most seats in the house. Figure 1 shows a finished unit.

MATERIALS

Though the spare parts and scrap material I used were free, cue lights like these could be made of materials totaling not more than $25.00. The necessary parts are listed below.

CONSTRUCTION

To build the housing, I cut the aluminum tube to length, drilled $\frac{3}{8}$" holes on both sides for the yoke, and milled a 2"-long, $\frac{5}{16}$"-wide slot in the bottom for the sled. Once the housing was finished, I made the yoke by bending the $\frac{1}{8}$" x 1" bar stock into a "U" whose bottom measured $4\frac{1}{4}$" — enough to accommodate two $\frac{1}{8}$"-thick washers between the hanger and the housing. I finished the yoke by drilling a $\frac{3}{4}$" C-clamp hole and two $\frac{3}{8}$" yoke bolt holes.

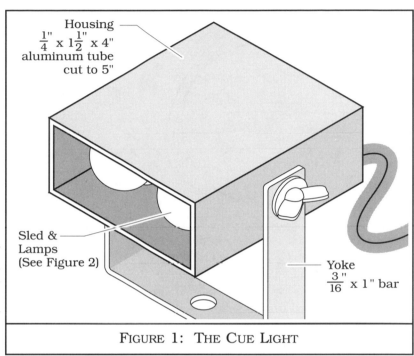

FIGURE 1: THE CUE LIGHT

Quantity	Material	Part
1 ea.	$1\frac{1}{2}$" x 4" aluminum tube, 5" long	Housing
1 ea.	$\frac{1}{4}$" x $1\frac{1}{4}$" UHMW, $3\frac{1}{2}$" long	Sled Plate
1 ea.	$\frac{1}{8}$" x $1\frac{1}{4}$" x $1\frac{1}{4}$" angle iron $\frac{1}{2}$" long	Sled Clamp
1 ea.	$\frac{5}{16}$" x $\frac{3}{4}$" shouldered thumb screw	Focus Knob
1 ea.	$\frac{3}{16}$" x 1" flat bar, 1'-0" long	Yoke
2 ea.	$\frac{5}{16}$" x 1" round head stove bolts	Yoke Bolts
2 ea.	medium lamp bases (Leviton 167)	
2 ea.	15-watt red indicator lamps	
2 ft.	18-gauge zip cord	
1 ea.	3-pin stage plug	

Building the sled plate (shown in Figure 2) was no more difficult. After cutting the UHMW to size, I drilled the two evenly spaced $\frac{1}{4}$" holes to receive the studs of the lamp bases and two more $\frac{1}{4}$" holes near one end for the zip cord. Finally, I drilled two $\frac{3}{16}$" holes in the center of the UHMW plate for the machine screws that would connect an angle-iron sled clamp to the UHMW plate. Rounding off the edges of the UHMW completed the sled plate.

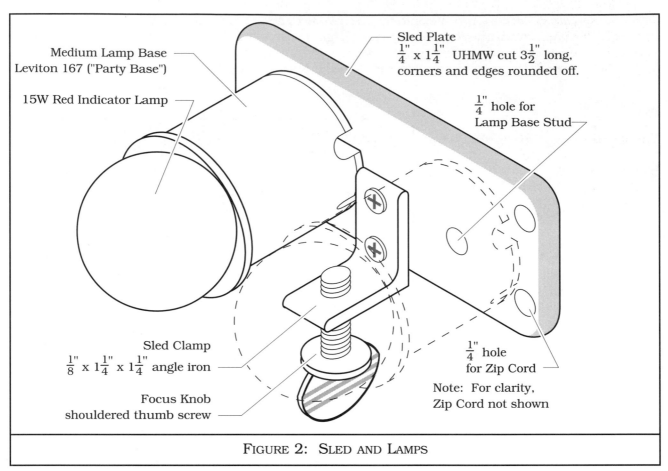

Medium Lamp Base
Leviton 167 ("Party Base")

15W Red Indicator Lamp

Sled Plate
$\frac{1}{4}$" x $1\frac{1}{4}$" UHMW cut $3\frac{1}{2}$" long,
corners and edges rounded off.

$\frac{1}{4}$" hole for
Lamp Base Stud

Sled Clamp
$\frac{1}{8}$" x $1\frac{1}{4}$" x $1\frac{1}{4}$" angle iron

Focus Knob
shouldered thumb screw

$\frac{1}{4}$" hole
for Zip Cord

Note: For clarity,
Zip Cord not shown

FIGURE 2: SLED AND LAMPS

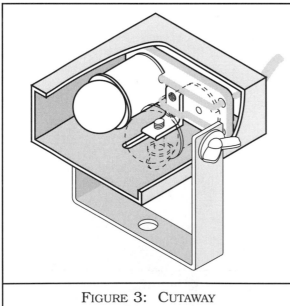

FIGURE 3: CUTAWAY

To build the sled clamp, I drilled two $\frac{3}{16}$" holes in one leg of the angle iron. They were spaced $\frac{1}{4}$" in from the end of the angle-iron stock and as far apart as the corresponding $\frac{3}{16}$" bolt holes in the UHMW. I then drilled and tapped a $\frac{5}{16}$" thumbscrew hole in the other leg, also $\frac{1}{4}$" in from the end, and cut the angle iron to its finished $\frac{1}{2}$" length.

In assembly, I first bolted the sled clamp and the bottoms of the lamp bases onto the UHMW plate. Then, after splitting the last 4" or 5" of the zip cord into single leads, I pushed the leads through the back of the plate, laid them in place in the lamp base bottoms, and screwed on the tops of the lamp bases. Finally, I installed the lamps, slid the sled into the back of the housing, and attached the yoke. Figure 3 illustrates the relationship between the focusable cue light's components.

TECHNICAL BRIEF

Scenery Hardware

The *Technical Brief* article "An Elevator Door Hinge" describes one way to link two flats so they will move like the paired panels of an elevator door. Because that drive is made up of rigid lever-arms it takes up a fair amount of space beside the frame of the door opening. Whenever enough clear space isn't available the sheave-and-cable alternative presented here can be used instead.

Figures 1A and 1B illustrate the drive, which uses a principle of double-purchase rigging to move one panel twice as far as another within a given time. To avoid clutter, the illustrations show only the drive's components.

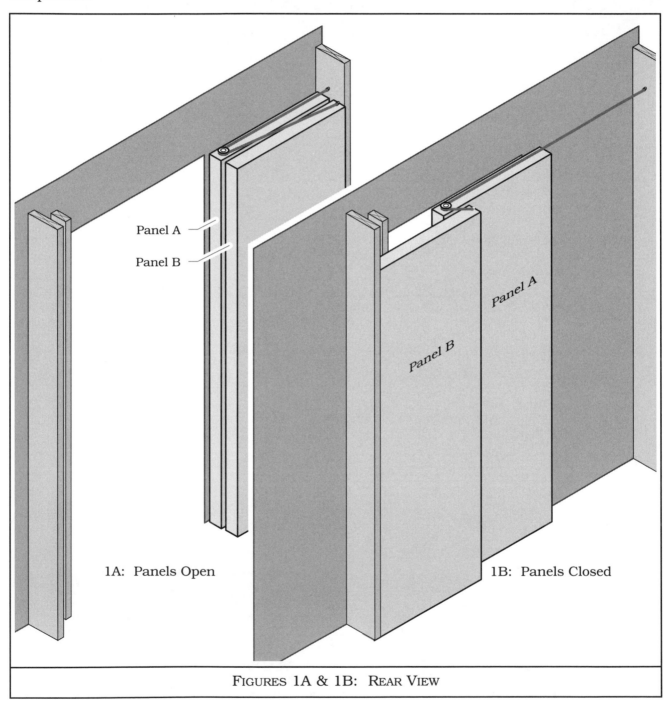

Panel A
Panel B

1A: Panels Open

Panel B
Panel A

1B: Panels Closed

FIGURES 1A & 1B: REAR VIEW

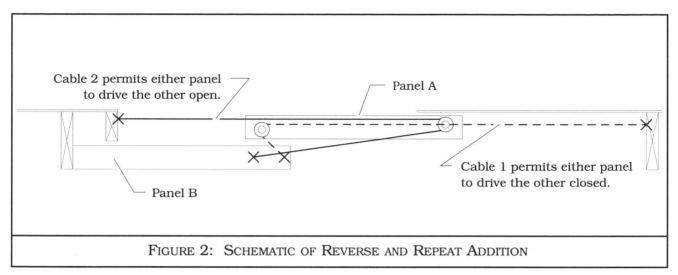

Cable 2 permits either panel
to drive the other open.

Panel A

Panel B

Cable 1 permits either panel
to drive the other closed.

FIGURE 2: SCHEMATIC OF REVERSE AND REPEAT ADDITION

Figures 1 and 2 show that Panel A's leading edge is fitted with a sheave. The ends of the cable that passes around this sheave are fixed at the door's frame and at the trailing edge of Panel B. As Panel A moves toward its door-closed destination halfway across the door opening, the cable pulls Panel B twice as far, into its destination at the opposite jamb. As long as the panels can alternate as master and slave, Figures 1A and 1B represent a complete system, for Panel A can drive B closed and Panel B can open A. The reverse-and-repeat addition shown in Figure 2, however, eliminates the need for such master-slave switching.

This system's design offers several advantages. First, it imposes no limits on the size of the panels; it could be used on portal-high flats as easily as on elevator doors. Second, it takes little shop time to pre-rig and it loads in quickly. Third, applied to both sides of a pair of panels, it could be used to drive them vertically rather than horizontally. And, finally, it takes up little space offstage.

જાજાજા

What better way for a fireman to enter the scene in a farce than by sliding down a fire pole that has just come plunging through the ceiling of the set? None, apparently, for that's exactly how the script describes the action in Pavel Kouhout's *Fire in the Basement*. But what if the fire pole needs to be over 20' long and there's only 9' of usable headroom above the set? Dennis Dorn and Chuck Mitchell faced that exact problem in the University of Wisconsin-Madison's 1991 production of the play. Figure 1 at the right offers an overview of their solution: a telescoping fire pole that is extended rather than simply flown in.

The rig they designed included a pneumatic cable cylinder mounted above the set, and three sections of schedule 40 black pipe of different diameters that, like sections of a telescope, nested one inside another. The largest of the pipes, $2\frac{1}{2}$" in diameter, did not move. But the two smaller pipes, 2" and $1\frac{1}{2}$" in diameter respectively, descended simultaneously until the middle pipe stopped at its low trim some 6' off the stage floor, leaving the bottom pipe to travel on alone. During reset, the cylinder lifted the bottom pipe off the floor; and as the bottom pipe rose, it was drawn up inside the middle pipe, which it carried along until both pipes had fully retracted into the fixed top pipe, at which time a new paper-covered plug was installed to repair the ceiling.

HARDWARE DETAILS

Figures 2A, B, and C illustrate the various fittings. A shop-built channel (Figure 2A) made from angle iron and three lengths of steel bar and bolted to the upper 6" of the $2\frac{1}{2}$" pipe held the pole's top pipe in place. For this particular installation, the channel was capped by a fourth length of steel bar which secured it directly to the theater's ceiling. The legs of the channel supported two $\frac{1}{4}$" rods. One of these rods served as an axle for a pair of 2" wire-rope sheaves mounted just above the top pipe; the other kept the cables seated in the grooves of the sheaves. A $\frac{5}{16}$" hex head bolt through the assembly joined the fixed pipe to the channel and stopped the travel of the other two pipes before they could hit the sheaves.

The sheaves mounted in the channel guided two $\frac{1}{8}$" wire-rope lift lines along the pole's axis. As Figures 2B and 2C illustrate, one of these lift lines picked up the middle pipe at a $\frac{1}{2}$" steel rod near the pipe's upper end; and the other picked up the bottom pipe at a similar rod through the pipe's lower end.

The pneumatic cylinder lifted both traveling pipes. The middle pipe's loft line was lightly counterweighted so that it would be drawn out of the pole during retraction, but the rig was nevertheless left deliberately stage heavy so that the middle pipe would ride in with the bottom pipe. As the pipes flew in, the middle pipe's lift line stopped the middle pipe at its low trim while the bottom pipe moved on. At the stage floor, the chamfer at the lower end of the bottom pipe guided the base of the pole into a 2" socket drilled into the floor of the stage.

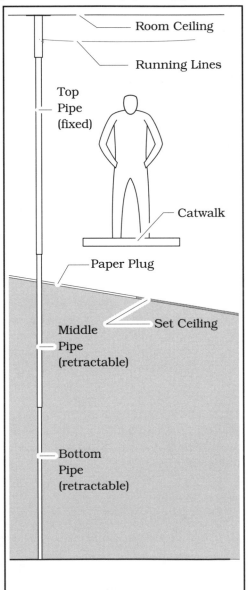

Room Ceiling

Running Lines

Top
Pipe
(fixed)

Catwalk

Paper Plug

Set Ceiling

Middle
Pipe
(retractable)

Bottom
Pipe
(retractable)

FIGURE 1: PARTIAL SECTION
LOOKING LEFT

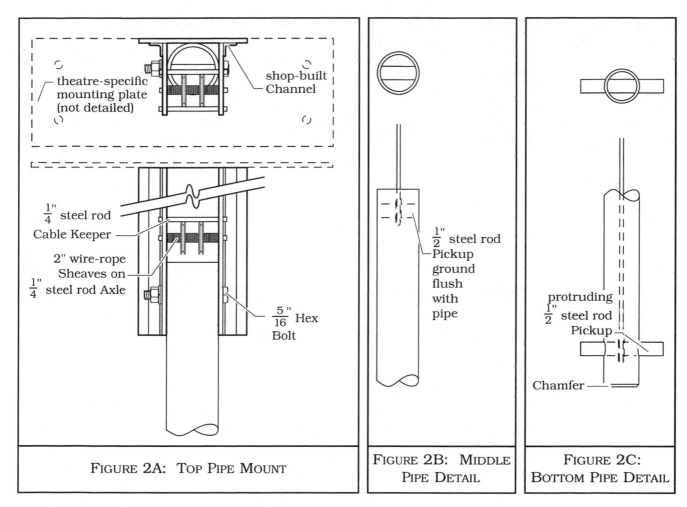

FIGURE 2A: TOP PIPE MOUNT

FIGURE 2B: MIDDLE PIPE DETAIL

FIGURE 2C: BOTTOM PIPE DETAIL

STABILITY

The solid built connection at the pole's top and the relatively deep socket connection at its base gave the pole a great deal of stability, and the designers enhanced that stability by leaving generous amounts of overlap between the sections of pipe. As a result, the first actor down the pole each night was not at all nervous about the prospect of grabbing the pole and sliding blithely — and somewhat blindly — downward, through the paper plug in the ceiling of the set.

❧❧❧

Distributing power to a wagon or slip-stage is problematic at best. When the distribution system includes a mix of fluid-power hoses and electrical, control, and audio cables, paging the bundle as the wagon moves can be a challenge. Some traditional methods, particularly those that use carrier chains or self-retracting cable reels, are expensive. Others, like festooning, require complex rigging, which is not always an option especially if the scenery is too low to hide the system. A simple, inexpensive solution suitable in many situations is the self-paging cable tray described here. It can be built with simple hand tools and from materials commonly found around the shop: a few boards, a couple of strap hinges, a caster, and miscellaneous nuts and bolts.

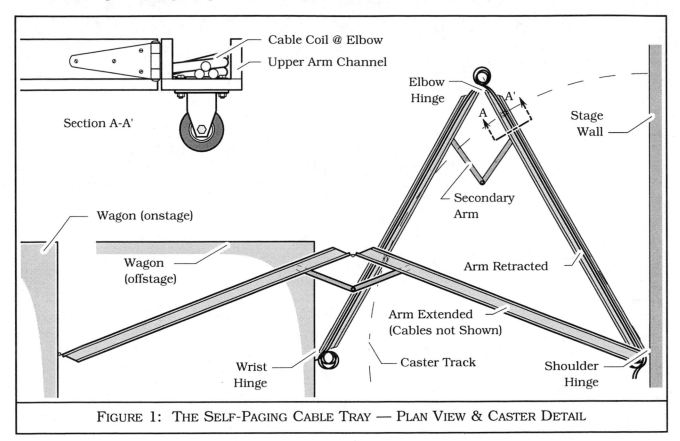

FIGURE 1: THE SELF-PAGING CABLE TRAY — PLAN VIEW & CASTER DETAIL

As shown above in plan view, the tray is nothing more than a pair of wooden channels joined by a strap hinge and two pieces of steel bar to form an articulated arm. At the "wrist," the arm is hinged to the wagon; and at the "shoulder," to a convenient point offstage. The width and depth of the channels depends on the size and quantity of the cables or hoses that will ride in the tray. The length of the two arm segments combined should be about 10% longer than the wagon's travel so that the arm will not straighten completely. A fixed caster mounted near the elbow on the "upper arm" supports the elbow. Since the caster needs to describe a circular arc as it moves (see Figure 1), its axle should point directly toward the pin in the shoulder hinge to prevent the caster from scrubbing. Additionally, at the back of the elbow, the ends of the arm segments should be trimmed at 45° to prevent pinching the cables when the arm is near full extension.

The secondary arm assures that the elbow moves properly when the angle between the primary arm segments is small. It can be made of wood, but $\frac{1}{4}$" flat steel is preferred because it allows the use of simple washers as spacers. Without this secondary arm, it is possible for the wrist to move while the elbow remains stationary — a condition which can damage the hinge joints. The length of the

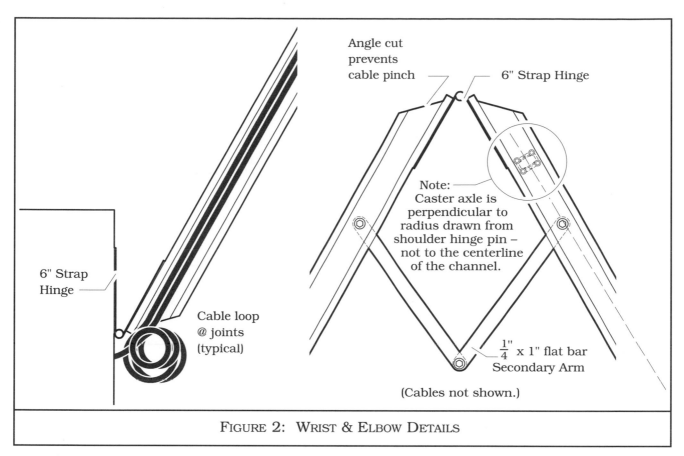

Angle cut
prevents
cable pinch

6" Strap Hinge

Note:
Caster axle is
perpendicular to
radius drawn from
shoulder hinge pin –
not to the centerline
of the channel.

6" Strap
Hinge

Cable loop
@ joints
(typical)

$\frac{1}{4}$" x 1" flat bar
Secondary Arm

(Cables not shown.)

FIGURE 2: WRIST & ELBOW DETAILS

secondary arm segments is not critical — 10% of the primary arm's total length seems about right. Thus, if the total length of the primary arm is 10', the length of each secondary arm segment should be about 1'. The secondary arm attachment points should be located in such a way that the secondary arm cannot straighten completely. If it could, it would bind the system. Flat head machine bolts fitted with washers and self-locking nuts provide a sliding surface and keep the segments of the secondary arm from loosening during movement.

Once the cable tray has been assembled, the cables and hoses are laid in the channels. If necessary, they may be secured with gaffers' tape. Looping the cables and hoses at each joint, including the elbow, provides greater flexibility as the arm moves.

Outdoor use or the need to shield audio cables from AC signals may require cable trays made of steel or aluminum. Wooden channels, which should suffice for most applications, are certainly cheap and easy to make. Whatever the materials used, the self-paging cable tray is a simple, reliable method of paging cables connected to moving scenery.

ᑫᐁᑫᐁᑫᐁ

This article, describing a variation in nylon roller design, was prompted by the needs of a particular project: a sturdy, serviceable pallet not more than $1\frac{1}{4}$" thick, made from $\frac{3}{4}$" plywood covered with $\frac{1}{4}$" Masonite®.

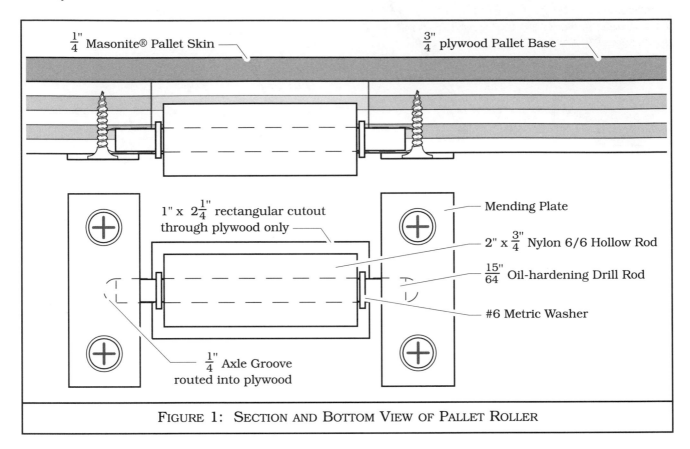

$\frac{1}{4}$" Masonite® Pallet Skin

$\frac{3}{4}$" plywood Pallet Base

1" x $2\frac{1}{4}$" rectangular cutout through plywood only

$\frac{1}{4}$" Axle Groove routed into plywood

Mending Plate

2" x $\frac{3}{4}$" Nylon 6/6 Hollow Rod

$\frac{15}{64}$" Oil-hardening Drill Rod

#6 Metric Washer

FIGURE 1: SECTION AND BOTTOM VIEW OF PALLET ROLLER

At first, following the earlier designs, I started by cutting stock 5' lengths of 6/6 hollow rod into 2"-long pieces that would work as wheels. Then I cut stock 3' lengths of $\frac{15}{64}$" oil-hardening drill rod into 2"-long axles. In assembling the rollers, I sandwiched the nylon rod between #6 metric washers, just as in the earlier design. But then I made some pallet design changes that allowed me to avoid the potentially destructive welding.

Given the anticipated loading conditions, I decided to give my 4' x 7' pallets 15 rollers each, arranged in 3 rows of 5 rollers. After cutting the plywood to size and marking the rollers' locations, I routed the fifteen $3\frac{1}{2}$" long roller axle grooves into the bottom of the plywood, using a $\frac{1}{4}$" rabbeting bit set at a depth of about $\frac{15}{64}$". Then I cut fifteen 1" x $2\frac{1}{4}$" rectangles into each piece of plywood, centering the rectangles on the roller-axle grooves. After placing each roller-and-axle assembly in its groove, I simply screwed a store-bought mending plate over the ends of each axle.

Once I had the rollers fastened down, I flipped each pallet over, brad-nailed the $\frac{1}{4}$" Masonite® skins on, and beveled the edges of each pallet at 45° to emphasize how thin they were — 1" thick units that cleared the stage floor by a scant $\frac{1}{4}$".

NOTES

We all know that no solution is perfect. But if you plan well the imperfections you're stuck with won't matter. The rollers were a little noisy, for instance, but since we were building these pallets for a musical, we knew that scene-shift music would cover any noise the rollers might make. And the simplicity and cost of this nylon roller design were just too attractive to pass up. Routing the axle grooves was the most complicated step in construction, and the total per-pallet hardware cost was less than $35.00.

❦❦❦

I recently had the opportunity to repeat a technical solution that worked so well in both instances it seemed time to write about it. The technical solution was a $\frac{3}{4}$" ball-bearing placed at the end of a $\frac{1}{2}$" schedule 40 black pipe to create a low-profile and low-friction pivot.

The first application occurred at the American Repertory Theatre for a production of *The Chairs*, designed by Anita Stewart. See Figure 2. Anita had designed a very tall and almost free-standing set of double doors that needed to open DS magically. Because there was no place to hide an operator the doors needed to be activated remotely. I also didn't want there to be any visible lever arms or strings. What I needed, I surmised, was a shaft attached to the hinge side of the door that could be rotated to open and close it. That shaft turned out to be a piece of $\frac{1}{2}$" pipe, lightly sanded to fit snugly inside a 1" x 1" x 0.065" square tube that was the outside framing member of the door.

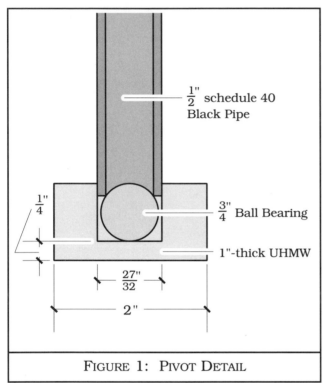

$\frac{1}{2}$" schedule 40 Black Pipe

$\frac{3}{4}$" Ball Bearing

1"-thick UHMW

$\frac{1}{4}$"

$\frac{27"}{32}$

2"

FIGURE 1: PIVOT DETAIL

There were two pieces of pipe for each door panel, one that extended above and one below. The pipe at the floor barely protruded from the framing and rested on a $\frac{3}{4}$" ball-bearing in a cup bored from UHMW. Because the O.D. of a $\frac{1}{2}$" pipe is 0.84" and the I.D. is 0.62", the ball-bearing was smaller than the outside of the pipe but not so small that it slipped inside. The pipe at the top of the door was connected to the mechanism that rotated it. I should add at this point that it was possible to drive the doors from above because they were set back from the wall (by a mere $1\frac{1}{4}$", the thickness of lauan and 1" square tube). The $\frac{1}{2}$" pipe at the top of each door had a short piece of $1\frac{1}{2}$" pipe welded around it to increase its diameter. Then an $\frac{1}{8}$" cable was wound clockwise around one door shaft and counterclockwise around the other creating a figure eight. The two ends of the cable were joined together by a $\frac{1}{4}$" turnbuckle. Finally, the body of the turnbuckle was bolted to the clevis of a small cable cylinder that actually powered the door. Because of the figure eight, when the cable was moved, the two door halves rotated in opposite directions and thus opened and closed together.

While the mechanism certainly worked well enough, the cable cylinder had a difficult time overcoming inertia (it was a $\frac{3}{4}$"-bore cylinder) and then once the door did start to move, slowing it down became the problem. If there had been a deeper reveal, it would have been possible to increase the diameter of the drive pipe which would have improved the start-up torque, but adjusting the air (or nitrogen in this case) to prevent the doors from banging open or closed would always have been a matter of operator finesse. If I had the problem to do again, I would look more closely at adding a linkage that would build in deceleration in at least one direction.

The second application was for a production of *The Crucible* at Brandeis University. The designer, Kathy Arfken, wanted a hidden panel in the wall to pivot during a scene shift, bringing with it a cupboard that was attached to the backside. We called it the "Batman door." The wall itself was made of rough cut planks. See Figure 3. The hidden panel, therefore, was 2" thick, or two layers of rough-cut. This time the $\frac{1}{2}$" pipe shaft was continuous and passed through the center member of a 1" square tube steel frame creating butterfly wings on either side. The frame and pipe were

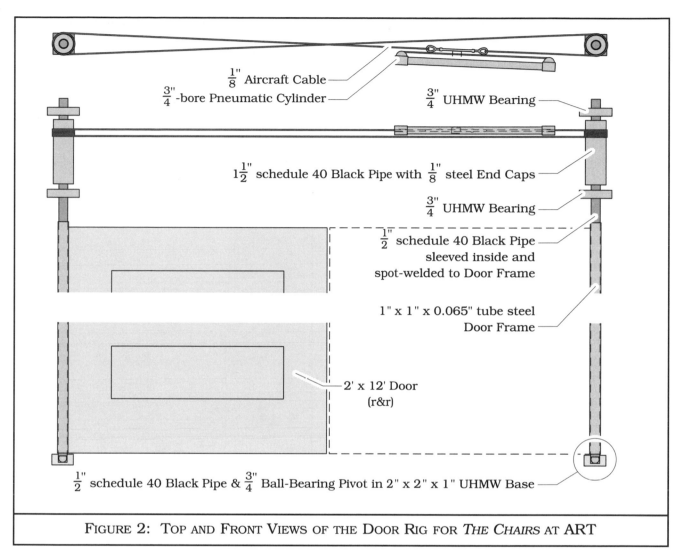

FIGURE 2: TOP AND FRONT VIEWS OF THE DOOR RIG FOR *THE CHAIRS* AT ART

routed into and sandwiched between the two layers of rough-cut to help keep the panel flat. The panel itself was, not surprisingly, quite heavy, and then we added the cupboard. But when we placed the pipe on the ball-bearing, it still spun effortlessly.

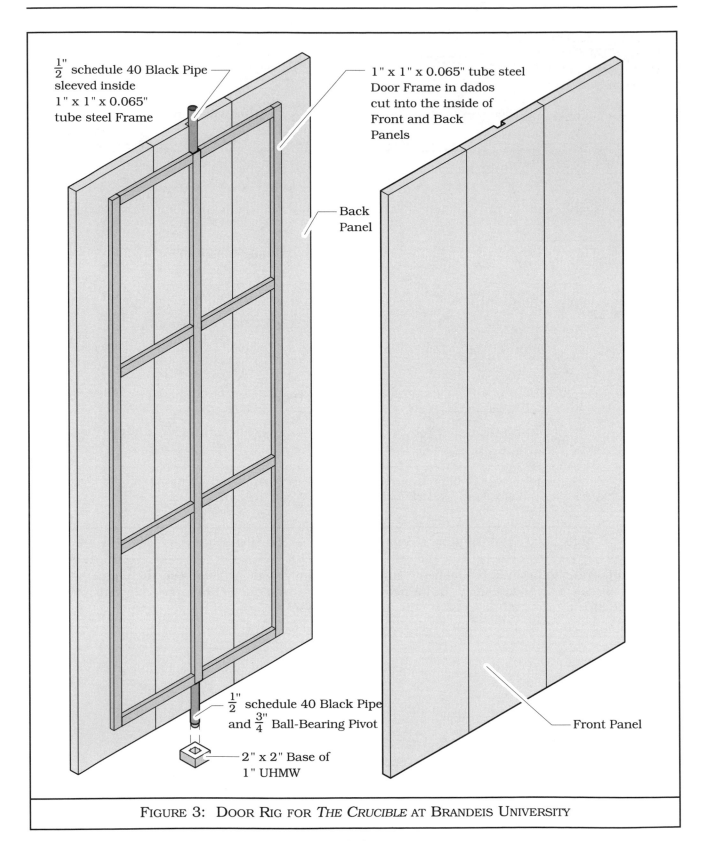

$\frac{1}{2}$" schedule 40 Black Pipe sleeved inside 1" x 1" x 0.065" tube steel Frame

1" x 1" x 0.065" tube steel Door Frame in dados cut into the inside of Front and Back Panels

Back Panel

$\frac{1}{2}$" schedule 40 Black Pipe and $\frac{3}{4}$" Ball-Bearing Pivot

2" x 2" Base of 1" UHMW

Front Panel

FIGURE 3: DOOR RIG FOR *THE CRUCIBLE* AT BRANDEIS UNIVERSITY

During a production of *Life Is a Dream* at the Yale School of Drama, the technical staff was faced with recycling 8x8 hard-covered, steel-framed flats from a previous show. Because changing the shape of some of the flats made many of the original bolt connections useless, the staff decided to "weld on new holes."

The technique was suggested by a student who had worked in a theatre where the standard method of connecting steel-framed flats was to weld small pieces of box tube to the back of the flats and connect them with $\frac{5}{16}$" hex head bolts as illustrated in Figure 1.

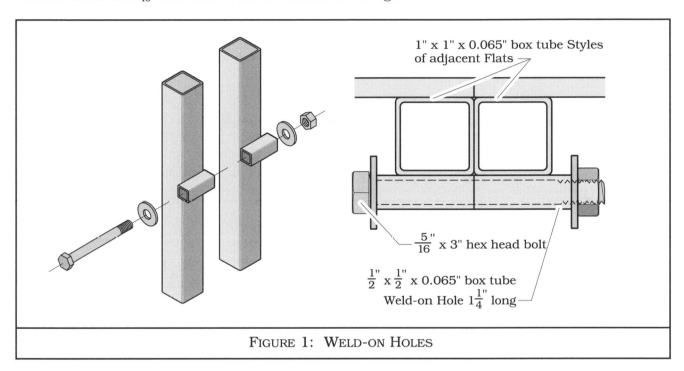

1" x 1" x 0.065" box tube Styles of adjacent Flats

$\frac{5}{16}$" x 3" hex head bolt

$\frac{1}{2}$" x $\frac{1}{2}$" x 0.065" box tube
Weld-on Hole $1\frac{1}{4}$" long

FIGURE 1: WELD-ON HOLES

After a couple of test samples had been made, pieces of $\frac{1}{2}$" x 0.065" square tube were cut to a length of $1\frac{1}{4}$", deburred, and bolted tightly into pairs (all faces flush) with 3"-long $\frac{5}{16}$" hex head bolts. At load-in, after the flats had been laid out face down on the stage floor, a single carpenter spaced the holes at convenient intervals along the framing and welded them in place. Installation was incredibly quick and simple.

Weld-on holes offered two distinct advantages in this particular situation. First, relatively unskilled labor was easily able to mass-produce them. Second, the flats were sent to the paints department much sooner than they would have been otherwise, since building weld-on holes is not part of the critical path during a build.

¿▲¿▲¿▲

The Laguna Playhouse mounted a production of Alan Ayckbourn's *Communicating Doors* which required a small rotating unit containing two walls, each including a door. This unit acted as a "time machine" transporting the actor to different time periods. Since the director and the designer did not want to build a false floor to accommodate a revolving platform, we needed to construct a revolving unit that was as thin as possible and level with the show floor. Since it was impossible to find a wheel small and strong enough to accomplish this, I created a design for a revolve that was only $1\frac{1}{2}$" tall, ran smoothly, was virtually noiseless, and had no wheels.

I have often used Ultra High Molecular Weight plastic (UHMW) for guides and glides and thought why not as a surface for a revolve? The revolve was only 6'-0" in diameter and it didn't have to sustain a great deal of weight; at most only the weight of the two wall/door units and two actors. The revolve was constructed of four layers of $\frac{1}{4}$" plywood and one layer of $\frac{1}{4}$" UHMW for an overall thickness of $1\frac{1}{4}$" as shown in Figure 1.

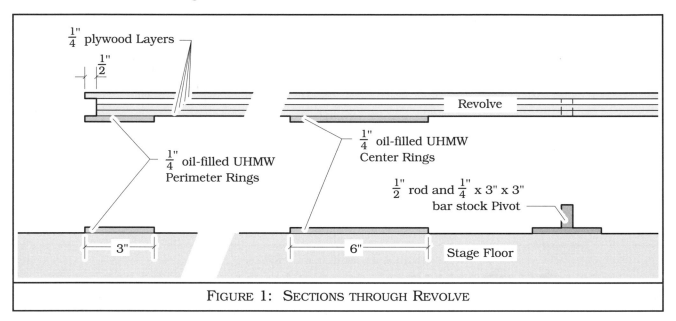

FIGURE 1: SECTIONS THROUGH REVOLVE

The top layer was a full 6'-0" in diameter. The remaining layers of plywood were 5'-11" in diameter to accept the roller chain that would drive the revolve. Given an overall revolve diameter of 6'-0" each plywood layer consisted of two semicircles. When the layers were glued together with flooring adhesive, the seams of adjoining layers were offset 45°.

A 3" perimeter ring of oil-filled UHMW (McMaster-Carr Catalog #84945K413) was mounted to the bottom of the plywood layup. The UHMW ring's outer diameter measured 6'-0" and its inner diameter, 5'-6". The ring was cut from six 24" x 24" x $\frac{1}{4}$"-thick pieces ($32.29 each). I used the first method illustrated in Figure 3 to cut sweeps from the UHMW squares. Figures 3.4 and 3.5 illustrate an alternate approach.

It takes nine full-size sweeps and one smaller one trimmed to about 5" long to complete a ring 6'-0" in diameter. I used four 24"-square UHMW pieces to make two complete rings — one for the revolve, and one for the floor. The UHMW rings were drilled and countersunk to receive the flathead wood screws joining them to the revolve and the stage floor. Adding the rings made the overall thickness of the revolve $1\frac{1}{2}$".

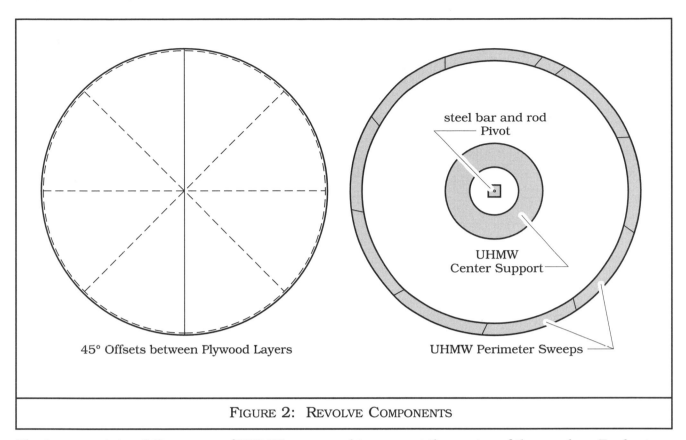

45° Offsets between Plywood Layers   UHMW Perimeter Sweeps

FIGURE 2: REVOLVE COMPONENTS

The two remaining 24" squares of UHMW were used to support the center of the revolve. Each piece was cut into a 2'-0" ring with an inner diameter of 1'-0" to accommodate the pivot point. I pre-drilled and countersunk a few holes in each piece and screwed one to the floor and one to the bottom of the plywood layup.

The pivot point for the revolve was a 3" square piece of $\frac{1}{4}$" steel plate with a 1"-long piece of $1\frac{1}{2}$" round steel bar welded to it. The plate had pre-drilled holes and was fastened to the stage floor with $1\frac{1}{4}$" x $\frac{1}{4}$" lag screws. At the center of the revolve I drilled a $\frac{1}{2}$" hole through the bottom three layers of plywood to accept the pivot point. When the revolve was placed on the pivot point, its UHMW rings lined up with those on the stage floor.

A #35 roller chain was placed in the groove created by making the revolve's top layer of plywood and perimeter UHMW ring 1" wider than the middle layers of the revolve. The chain went through a small hole cut in the upstage wall of the set, passed through a series of idler sprockets and was connected to a variable-speed motor drive, which revolved the disk on cue. In the end, the revolve made a half-turn in about 10 seconds. When we tested the revolve by having six stagehands stand on it and turning on the motor drive, it worked without any hesitation or slipping.

To help hide the fact that the revolve was higher than the rest of the set, we added a small ramp around its perimeter. The ramp was made by cutting many small wedges out of scrap pine and fastening them to the floor around the revolve and covering them with Masonite®. Since the incline of the wedges was minimal, there was no discernible difference between the height of the revolve and the height of the carpeted stage floor.

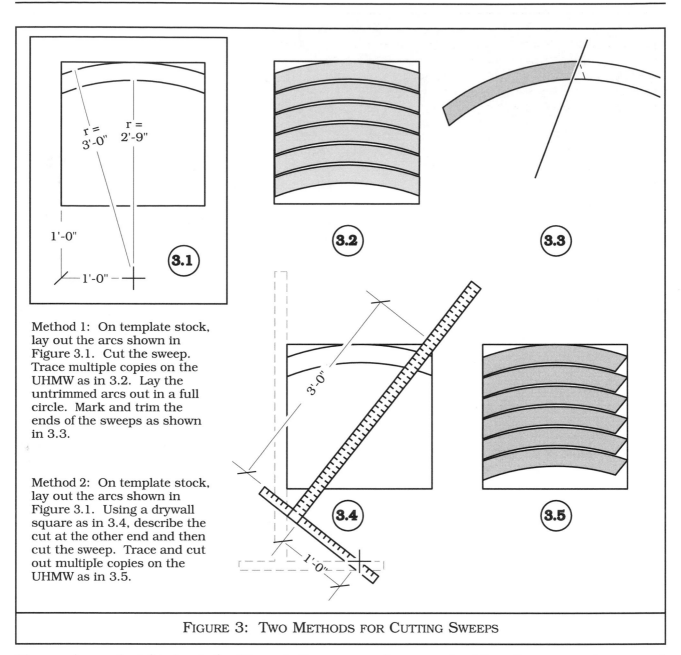

Method 1: On template stock, lay out the arcs shown in Figure 3.1. Cut the sweep. Trace multiple copies on the UHMW as in 3.2. Lay the untrimmed arcs out in a full circle. Mark and trim the ends of the sweeps as shown in 3.3.

Method 2: On template stock, lay out the arcs shown in Figure 3.1. Using a drywall square as in 3.4, describe the cut at the other end and then cut the sweep. Trace and cut out multiple copies on the UHMW as in 3.5.

FIGURE 3: TWO METHODS FOR CUTTING SWEEPS

The revolve worked flawlessly for 15 revolutions per performance for 40 performances plus several tech rehearsals. When the set was struck, the revolve showed few signs of wear and the UHMW still had traces of oil.

❧❧❧

While working in the machine and automation shop at Hudson Scenic Studios I was charged with the task of building a tensioning sheave for a winch-driven wagon system. The main concerns in a deck winch system are transmitting the movement of the drum to the wagon and reducing noise created by the cable slapping in the knife track. A tensioning sheave addresses these concerns by preventing cable slippage and keeping the cable properly reeved through the system components, *i.e.*, the winch drum or other sheaves.

This tensioning sheave is easily built and installed, and its design affords the user simple maintenance of the system. Though the details and material choices described here are specific to this system, the basic design could be modified for use in any cable-driven system.

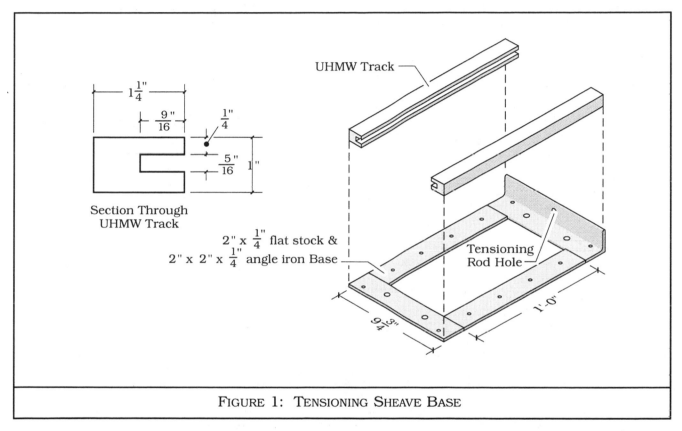

FIGURE 1: TENSIONING SHEAVE BASE

The first component of the unit is the base, shown in Figure 1, in which the sheave plate travels. The flat stock and angle are welded together so that the two lengthwise pieces of flat stock lie flat within the shorter pieces, making the outside dimensions 16" x $9\frac{3}{4}$". Flathead wood screws through a line of $\frac{5}{16}$" holes bored through the base and countersunk from the bottom hold the sheave-plate track in place. The track is made from two custom-milled pieces of UHMW. The $\frac{5}{16}$"-wide groove is milled $\frac{9}{16}$" deep along the length of the UHMW. A $\frac{1}{2}$" hex nut (not shown) welded to the hole in the vertical leg of the angle accepts the $\frac{1}{2}$" threaded tensioning rod of the sheave plate.

As for the sheave plate itself, the materials, dimensions, and functions of the parts are shown in Figure 2 and are based on our use of a 6"-diameter $\frac{3}{8}$" steel wire-rope sheave. Components of other sizes can be used, of course, but in each case they must be sized to suit a given system's loading conditions.

In our design, the rod measures approximately 12". During assembly, it is threaded through the $\frac{1}{2}$" hex nut that has been welded to the back of the base's angle iron, and then through a second $\frac{1}{2}$"

hex nut — this one left to rotate freely until the sheave's installation. Finally, hex nuts are welded to both ends of the rod, and the tensioning sheave is complete.

After the drive cable has been reeved through the tensioning sheave during load-in, torque is applied to the hex nut at the free end of the tensioning rod. The rod pulls on the sheave plate and sheave, adding tension to the cable. For routine maintenance, the rod is turned counterclockwise, releasing cable tension.

This tensioning sheave is very useful for fine tuning a cable system. It requires minimal technical skill and can be built in a short amount of time. The materials required are affordable and readily available. But the real beauty to this hardware is the ease of installation and maintenance in an under-deck cable system.

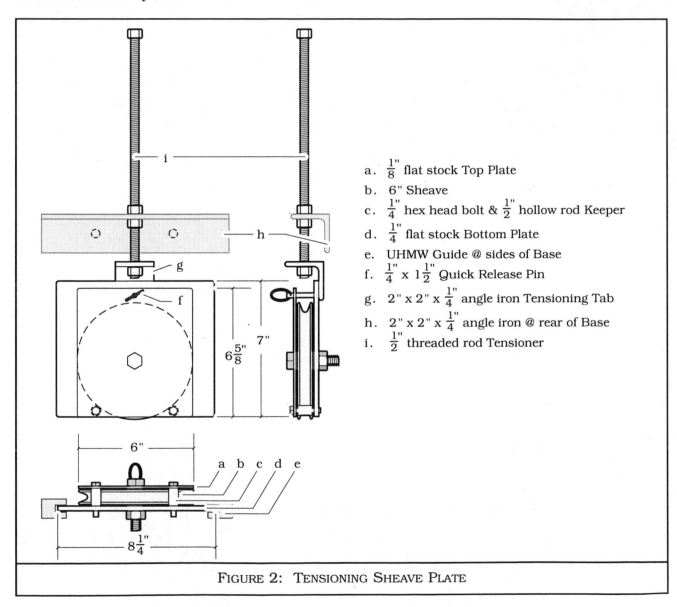

a. $\frac{1}{8}''$ flat stock Top Plate

b. 6" Sheave

c. $\frac{1}{4}''$ hex head bolt & $\frac{1}{2}''$ hollow rod Keeper

d. $\frac{1}{4}''$ flat stock Bottom Plate

e. UHMW Guide @ sides of Base

f. $\frac{1}{4}''$ x $1\frac{1}{2}''$ Quick Release Pin

g. 2" x 2" x $\frac{1}{4}''$ angle iron Tensioning Tab

h. 2" x 2" x $\frac{1}{4}''$ angle iron @ rear of Base

i. $\frac{1}{2}''$ threaded rod Tensioner

FIGURE 2: TENSIONING SHEAVE PLATE

At the climax of Martin Sherman's *Bent*, the main protagonist — a prisoner in a German prison camp — commits suicide by walking into an electric barbed-wire fence. The director of the Hong Kong Academy for Performing Arts wanted to see real sparks at this crucial moment in the action. Since the fence had to be set up during an intermission during a heavy scene change, the effect we needed had to be portable and quick to rig. Limited by budgetary considerations and Hong Kong's restrictive pyrotechnics laws, we settled on using a 12V car battery to generate a dramatic but safe low voltage spark.

FENCE DESIGN

Our effect included two fences, a "prop fence" visible to the audience and an electrified fence. The "prop fence" was made of appropriately painted twisted string which the actor could touch without any risk of being burned by the sparks. The second fence, the electrified one, was made as unnoticeable as possible and played a safe 6" farther upstage.

The electrified fence was powered by three 12V car batteries wired in series. This combination gave us a 36V, 55-amp-hour source — powerful enough to supply the six spectacular "spark points" the director wanted, yet not so powerful as to threaten electrocution. The fence consisted of two 18' lengths of black-plastic-coated $\frac{3}{16}$" aircraft cable strung between two 1x2 uprights and pulled taut to "shadow" the prop fence. We pared the plastic away to expose the aircraft cable for electrical contact and connected these cables to one terminal of the battery series. We connected the other terminal to four more lengths of intermittently stripped plastic-coated $\frac{3}{16}$" aircraft cable rigged to rub against the horizontal cables, as shown in Figure 1. We fixed small lead weights to the ends of the vertical leads to keep them tensioned. Pulling the off-stage end of the vertical leads brought the bare sections of wire together and created a half-second of sparks.

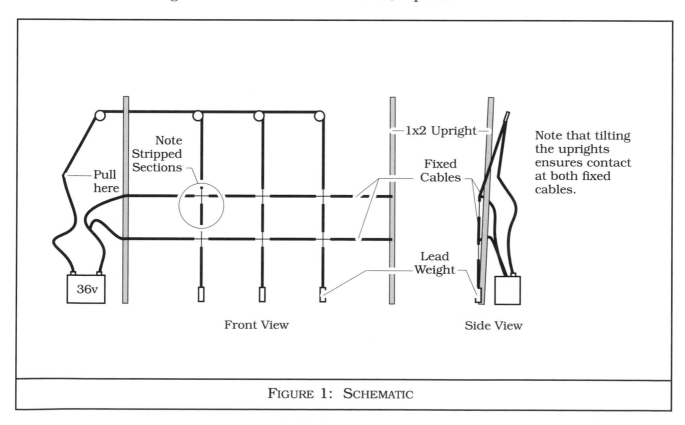

FIGURE 1: SCHEMATIC

REFINING THE OPERATION

During rehearsal, we learned that the operator had to pull the vertical leads out in one swift, continuous movement. If the operator pulled too slowly or paused at all, the wires were in danger of welding together. Offstage, we marked "in" and "out" trims on the vertical leads, ganged them together with a metal ring, and looped the ring over appropriately positioned cup hooks.

SAFETY

There is very little danger of electrocution in a 36V system, but there is a potential fire hazard. Though the sparks our fence generated lasted only a half-second or so, they flared in a 6" diameter circle, and the nearest piece of soft-goods (a scrim) was only 4' away. We made sure the scrim was treated with proprietary flame-proofing. Most significantly, to prevent accidentally triggering the effect, we wired a normal open momentary switch and a contactor into the system as a dead man's switch. Unless a second operator held the switch closed as the wires were pulled, the system would not operate. Domestic switches cannot handle such high currents (they melt!), and a suitably rated contactor is essential in switching currents as high as 55 amps.

A NOTE ON VISIBILITY OF THE WIRES

In the past, I have found that wires with a reflective surface are less visible than those with a matte finish. Since black-plastic-coated aircraft cable has a reflective surface, it is difficult to detect against a black background if a little care is taken with the lighting. If you paint the same wire with a matte black finish, it will immediately become far more visible, though that would appear to defy logic. I believe the reason is that a matte surface reflects light in all directions, while a gloss surface reflects like a mirror, *i.e.,* in one direction only with only a very thin reflection line visible, while with a matte black wire, they will more likely see the whole surface of the wire. Our reflective wires were nearly invisible to a studio audience sitting within 20 feet.

Originally, we also painted the weights at the bottom of the wire with a gloss black finish. That, however, made them clearly visible against the stone-colored floor. Repainting the weights and bottom 6" or so of wire to match the floor made them much less noticeable.

EVALUATION

The scene change could not have been simpler. The two horizontal cables were pre-attached to the two battens of 1x2, which were carried on stage and then fixed top and bottom with loose pin hinges. The vertical wires, stored in their out position with the weights tucked up under the header, were simply pulled down by hand and laid against the horizontal wires. Job done!

Finally, the effect worked very well. It was 100% reliable, and the batteries did not have to be recharged once throughout a total of twelve dress rehearsals and performances. Combined with sound effects, audience-blinding lighting, and precise cueing, the effect created a suitable and satisfactory climax to the play.

༄ༀ༄ༀ༄ༀ

TECHNICAL BRIEF

Scenery Mechanics

There are many solutions to the problem of locking rolling units in place following a scene change (see Mark Stevens's *Technical Brief* "A Simple Lift Jack" for one method). However, the solution to this problem becomes more difficult when all sides of the unit must be faced, the unit must be moved quickly and easily by a single person, and the unit must remain stationary under the movement of actors performing stage combat. We faced this set of conditions in a production of *Romeo and Juliet* at East Tennessee State University. The solution we selected was a pneumatic floor lock system.

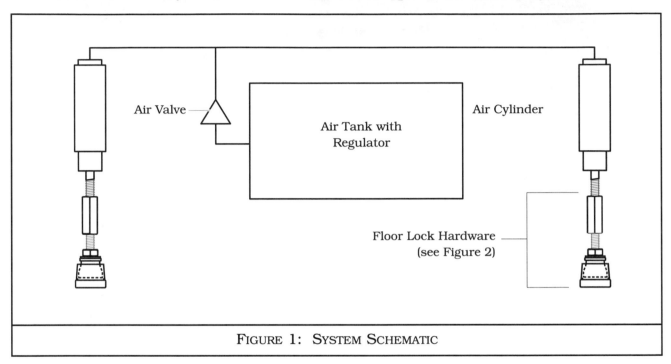

Air Valve

Air Cylinder

Air Tank with Regulator

Floor Lock Hardware (see Figure 2)

FIGURE 1: SYSTEM SCHEMATIC

Floor locks, unlike lift jacks, do not lift the unit. Instead, a non-skid pad on the bottom of the floor lock applies downward pressure on the floor, serving as a brake. Commercial toe-operated floor locks, which are used in pairs, have been available for many years. However, since our unit had to be faced on all sides, a toe-operated device was impractical. Instead, we used air cylinders to construct floor locks which could be operated by a single valve, recess mounted on the face of the unit. An air tank mounted inside the rolling unit supplied the air for the cylinders. Our system used two locks on each rolling unit.

The dimensions of our 18"-tall rolling unit were 2'-6" x 6'-0". These dimensions influenced some of our component choices — particularly the size of the air tank. We used a 6-gallon air tank because it was in stock. We have experimented with smaller tanks constructed from $2\frac{1}{2}$" schedule 40 black pipe, and plan to use them on lower rolling units.

MAJOR COMPONENTS FOR ONE ROLLING UNIT

2 ea. $1\frac{1}{2}$" bore, adjustable-stroke, single-acting Air Cylinders

1 ea.   3-way, 3-port, 2-position Toggle Valve

1 ea.   6-gallon Air Tank with regulator

2 ea.   1" Crutch Tips (the brake pads)

2 ea. $\frac{1}{2}$" x $\frac{3}{8}$" galvanized Reducer Couplings

2 ea. $\frac{7}{16}$" x 2" Hex Head Bolts

2 ea.   Long Nuts for $\frac{7}{16}$" Threaded Rod

Appropriate lengths of $\frac{1}{2}$" Copper Tubing and a number of $\frac{1}{8}$" NPTF fittings.

CONSTRUCTION DETAILS

One air cylinder was mounted on the inside of each end of the unit so that the extended foot would apply pressure to the floor. The air tank was mounted inside the unit, the air valve was recess-mounted on one face of the unit, and all components were connected by $\frac{1}{8}$" copper tubing. We found that 40psi provided enough pressure to keep the unit from rolling, even under the most strenuous actor traffic. It should be noted that the unit was built to be very heavy. A lighter prototype had been lifted off the floor by 40psi air pressure. We used rubber crutch tips as the non-skid surface on the foot of each lock: they were easy to apply and worked well enough that we tried no other materials or designs for brake pads.

The system worked very efficiently and made it possible for an actor to reposition the unit during scene changes. We were very satisfied with the system's operation and plan to use it on both larger and smaller rolling units in future productions.

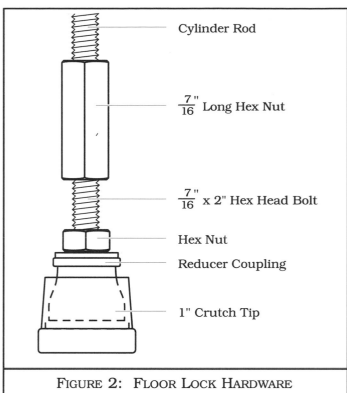

Cylinder Rod

$\frac{7}{16}$" Long Hex Nut

$\frac{7}{16}$" x 2" Hex Head Bolt

Hex Nut

Reducer Coupling

1" Crutch Tip

FIGURE 2: FLOOR LOCK HARDWARE

A simple, reliable, practically free source of hydraulic power is available right out of your sink faucet. Using tap water is a great way to get into hydraulics without the expense of buying pumps, filters, reservoirs, and lengths of special hosing. And because most municipal water companies pump water at pressures of about 45 to 90psi, tap-water hydraulic power systems are much safer than oil-based, industrial hydraulic power systems, which work at pressures of 500 to 2000psi or more.

Industrial hydraulic power systems typically have six components: a liquid, usually hydraulic oil; a reservoir for storing the liquid; a pump to pressurize the liquid; a valve to control the flow of the pressurized liquid; some kind of tubing to transport the pressurized liquid; and an actuator to convert the hydraulic power of the pressurized liquid into mechanical power.

A tap-water hydraulic power system substitutes water for the oil and eliminates the pump and reservoir, usually the most expensive parts of any system. The use of $\frac{5}{8}$" reinforced garden hose for the transport tubing leaves the valve and actuator as the only major expenses in a tap-water system.

It is possible to rig up a series of low-cost ball valves for use in a tap-water system, but I recommend an industrial-model 4-way, 3-position pneumatic valve — especially if double-acting actuators are used. Yes, I said "pneumatic" valve, rather than a hydraulic valve. The "off" or center position of a 3-position pneumatic valve stops the fluid at the valve's inlet port. The "off" position of a hydraulic valve allows the fluid (highly pressurized oil in a "real" hydraulic system) to pass directly through the valve and back to the reservoir. If you use an industrial hydraulic valve in a tap-water system, you're going to waste a lot of water. A good pneumatic valve is the Speedaire Hand Control Throttle Valve available from W. W. Grainger, Inc. (Catalog #5A5456 — about $110.) This valve's $\frac{1}{2}$" NPT ports allow a good flow of tap water.

The other major expense in a tap-water system is the actuator. Fluid power actuators come in several different forms, but perhaps the most common is the cylinder, a long rod attached to a piston which moves inside a tube. Industrial hydraulic cylinders, especially those with long rod strokes, are very expensive and can corrode if used with tap water. But you can build your own large-bore double-acting cylinders from non-corroding, easily available components using regular scene shop tools and fabricating techniques. See Figures 1 and 2. By using PVC pipe with a diameter of 3 inches or more, this shop-built cylinder will convert the relatively low pressure of your faucet water into a surprising amount of mechanical force.

COMPONENTS

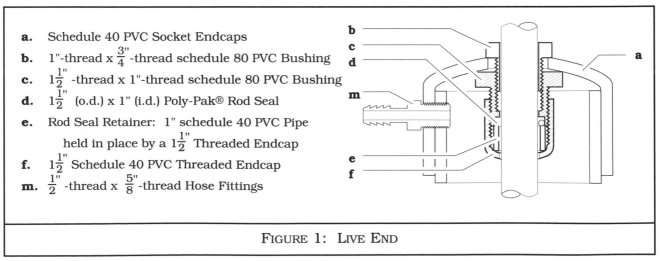

a.   Schedule 40 PVC Socket Endcaps

b.   1"-thread x $\frac{3}{4}$"-thread schedule 80 PVC Bushing

c. $1\frac{1}{2}$"-thread x 1"-thread schedule 80 PVC Bushing

d. $1\frac{1}{2}$" (o.d.) x 1" (i.d.) Poly-Pak® Rod Seal

e.   Rod Seal Retainer: 1" schedule 40 PVC Pipe
       held in place by a $1\frac{1}{2}$" Threaded Endcap

f. $1\frac{1}{2}$" Schedule 40 PVC Threaded Endcap

m. $\frac{1}{2}$"-thread x $\frac{5}{8}$"-thread Hose Fittings

FIGURE 1: LIVE END

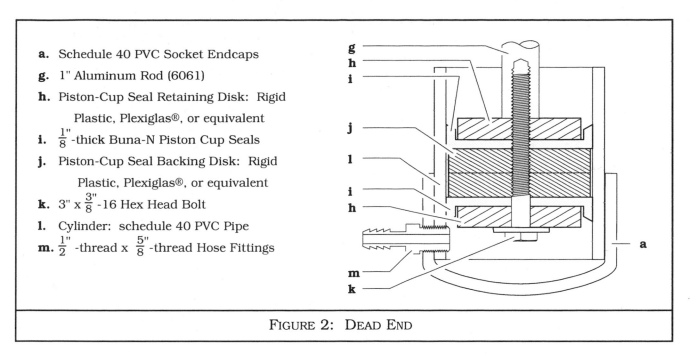

a. Schedule 40 PVC Socket Endcaps

g. 1" Aluminum Rod (6061)

h. Piston-Cup Seal Retaining Disk: Rigid Plastic, Plexiglas®, or equivalent

i. $\frac{1}{8}$"-thick Buna-N Piston Cup Seals

j. Piston-Cup Seal Backing Disk: Rigid Plastic, Plexiglas®, or equivalent

k. 3" x $\frac{3}{8}$"-16 Hex Head Bolt

l. Cylinder: schedule 40 PVC Pipe

m. $\frac{1}{2}$"-thread x $\frac{5}{8}$"-thread Hose Fittings

FIGURE 2: DEAD END

CONSTRUCTION NOTES

It is, of course, essential that all holes, bores, and taps be exactly centered and squared. Ream out the inside of bushing **b** with a 1" hole saw and drill through the center of threaded endcap **f** with a 1" hole saw to accommodate rod **g**. Ream out the bottom $\frac{1}{2}$" of bushing **c** with a $1\frac{1}{2}$" hole saw to accept rod seal **d**. Cut piston cup seal retaining disks **h** $\frac{1}{2}$" smaller than the inside diameter of cylinder **l**, and drill a $\frac{3}{8}$" hole at the center of each disk. Drill a $\frac{3}{8}$" hole at the center of each piston cup seal **i**. Cut piston cup backing seal disks **j** slightly smaller than the inside diameter of cylinder **l**, and drill a $\frac{3}{8}$" hole at the center of each disk. Drill and tap the bottom of rod **g** to accept hex head bolt **k**.

Glue the endcaps to cylinder **l**. Apply a thin bead of silicone sealant on the outer edge of rod seal **d**, and then push **d** into the reamed-out bottom of rod seal housing **c**. Slide rod seal **d** and rod seal retainer **e** onto rod **g**. Slip endcap **f** onto rod **g** and screw it onto bushing **c** to effect a rod seal. Apply silicone sealant to the top of bushing **c** and assemble it and bushing **b** to the top of endcap **a**. Coat the mating surfaces of rod **g**, piston cup seal retaining disks **h**, piston cup seals **i**, piston cup seal backing disks **j**, and bolt/washer assembly **k** with silicone sealant. Assemble parts **g** through **k** to complete the piston. Slide the piston into cylinder **l**, and glue endcaps **a** in place with PVC cement. Finally, drill $\frac{11}{16}$" holes through endcaps **a** and the cylinder for hose fittings **m**. Use a $\frac{1}{2}$"-14 NPT tap to cut threads for the fittings.

FINAL NOTES

In hydraulics, the mechanical **F**orce the cylinder can apply is equal to the **P**ressure (psi) of the liquid multiplied by the **A**rea of the cylinder's piston: **F=PA**. For example, a 4"-diameter, double-acting cylinder with a 1"-diameter rod, using tap water at a pressure of 50psi, will exert a push force of over 600 pounds on the outstroke, and a pull force of over 550 pounds on the instroke. (The pull force is smaller because the 1" rod reduces the overall area of the piston on the instroke.)

You can build cylinders up to 20 feet long, the standard length of most large-bore PVC pipe, enabling you to move even heavy scenery wagons smoothly and quietly. A 4"-diameter cylinder costs about $4 per foot of stroke plus $50 for the other parts. PVC pipe and fittings are available from any well-stocked plumbing supply house, and the seals can be ordered from a rubber products supplier or from a hydraulics repair shop.

ක්‍රියාව

The principal scenic feature in the East Carolina University production of *A Chorus Line* was a row of nine 14'-6" tall periaktoi set parallel to plaster. Since *A Chorus Line* is about dance, it was essential that our periaktoi rotate from spike mark to precisely located spike mark in perfect synchrony, regardless of their speed. As Technical Director for the production I considered and ruled out several means of rotating the units: friction drives, worm gear drives, and chain drives with a sprocket on each periaktos — all would be too expensive or time-consuming. But finally, after batting some ideas around with Pete Feller, Jr. of New York's Feller Precision, I devised the cable-and-drum system detailed here.

In this system, each of our nine periaktoi was mounted on its own shop-built cable drum and rotated on two pivots, one attached to the bottom of the drum and the other to a plywood plate fastened to the top of the periaktos. Figure 1 illustrates one periaktos' assembly and shows it in position with the others.

PERIAKTOS AND DRUM DETAILS

Each drum consisted of a core disc of $\frac{3}{4}$" plywood sandwiched between two $\frac{1}{4}$" plywood flange discs. Setting the diameter of the flange discs at 3'-11$\frac{1}{2}$" allowed us to cut two flanges from a single sheet of plywood. The 3" difference between the diameter of the flange discs and the 3'-8$\frac{1}{2}$"-diameter core disc left a 1$\frac{1}{2}$" groove all around. See Figure 2.

Since the faces of the periaktoi were 4'-0" wide, the points of the periaktoi overhung their drums by 4", as shown in Figure 3. We blocked each periaktos up on a set of $\frac{3}{4}$" plywood pads so that it would easily clear its neighbor's drum during rotation.

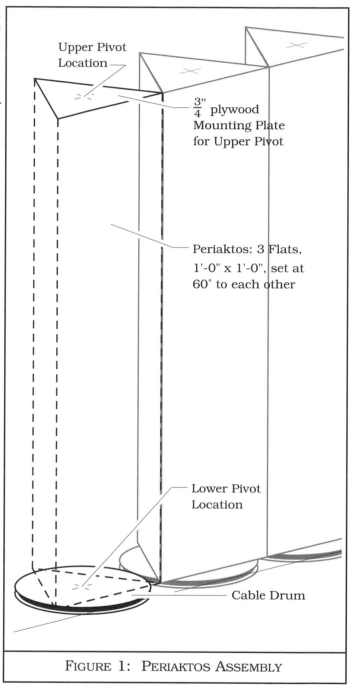

Upper Pivot Location

$\frac{3}{4}$" plywood Mounting Plate for Upper Pivot

Periaktos: 3 Flats, 1'-0" x 1'-0", set at 60° to each other

Lower Pivot Location

Cable Drum

FIGURE 1: PERIAKTOS ASSEMBLY

THE DRIVE DRUM

A tenth drum, identical in size and construction to those under the nine periaktoi, served as a drive drum. We bolted a sturdy 3'-6"-diameter pedestal table to its top. By turning the table, the operator had no difficulty at all in making the 16 scene-shift rotations required for each performance.

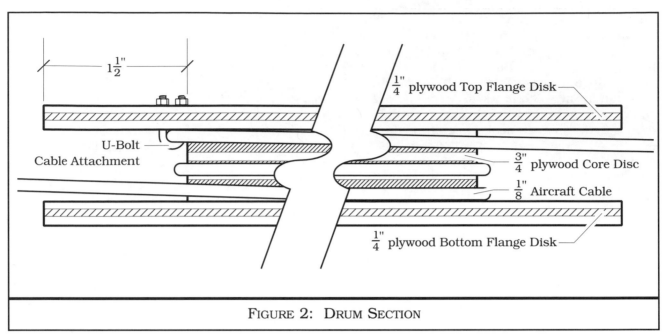

FIGURE 2: DRUM SECTION

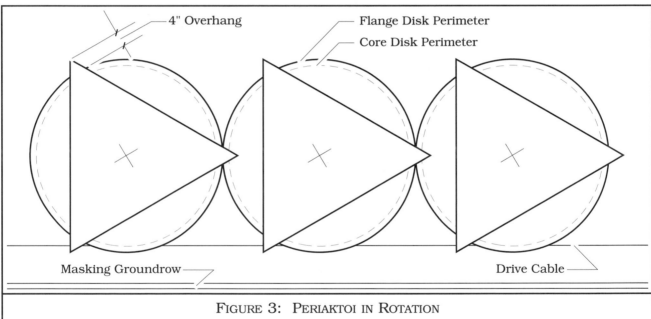

FIGURE 3: PERIAKTOI IN ROTATION

THE CABLE RUN

Figure 4 illustrates the linkage of all 10 drums. We attached plastic-coated $\frac{1}{8}$" aircraft cable to the drive drum at point **AD** and wrapped it twice, counterclockwise, around the drum. We then ran the cable to periaktos drum #1, where we wrapped it twice, counterclockwise, and secured it at point **A1**. After repeating this sequence of double wraps and attachment at each of the remaining drums, we reeved the cable through two floor-mounted muling sheaves (**M1** and **M2**), wrapped it once more past point **AD** on the drive drum, and attached it to the drive drum at point **AE**. Though it limited our rotation options, attaching the cable to the drums assured synchrony.

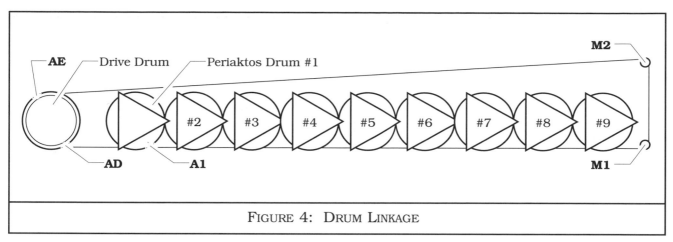

FIGURE 4: DRUM LINKAGE

At each point of attachment to a drum, we stripped the cable of its plastic coating and bolted it to the plywood flange with the u-bolt side of a cable clamp, as shown in Figure 2. Before installing the cable, we took care to align the periaktoi and to lock them in position temporarily. As we ran the cable, we simply pulled it as tight as possible by hand — an approach which worked well enough that no subsequent tension adjustment was necessary.

As the drums rotated, the cable would occasionally "walk across itself" as it served onto a drum, but the flange discs kept the cable seated properly, and the drums were large enough in diameter that the cable never jammed.

A NOT-UNCOMMON PROBLEM

Set Designer:	So then a large moon rises from behind the rake. But we don't want to see any of the machinery to lift it.
Tech Director:	No Problem. If we use black-nylon-covered cable, no one will see it behind the scrim.
Set Designer:	Well, actually, the moon box is in front of the scrim.
Tech Director:	In front of the scrim?
Set Designer:	Yeah — but you can just put it on a big piston or something, right?
Tech Director:	Maybe. How big is this moon box?
Set Designer:	Well, in the model, it's 18' wide . . . .

A GOOD SOLUTION

Prevented from rigging aloft to pick up the 18' x 14' x 22" moon box Douglas Rogers had designed for the Yale School of Drama's production of *Waiting for Godot*, we could only install a lifting device in the trap room beneath the stage. Further, because the moon box would have to sit flat on the trap room floor in order to be masked from view, we would have to lift the unit from behind rather than from below. Our solution was the telescope-stabilized lift rig detailed here. Figure 1 depicts the upper ends of the three vertical components we built and installed near either end of the moon box: a sheave column with two sheaves, a telescoping stabilizer, and a bumper.

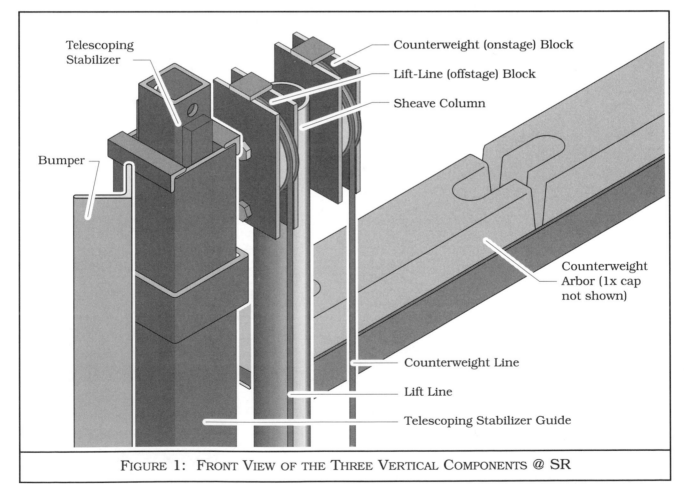

FIGURE 1: FRONT VIEW OF THE THREE VERTICAL COMPONENTS @ SR

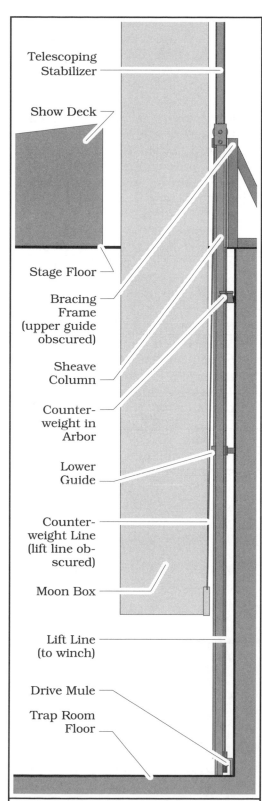

Telescoping
Stabilizer

Show Deck

Stage Floor

Bracing
Frame
(upper guide
obscured)

Sheave
Column

Counter-
weight in
Arbor

Lower
Guide

Counter-
weight Line
(lift line ob-
scured)

Moon Box

Lift Line
(to winch)

Drive Mule

Trap Room
Floor

FIGURE 2: CENTERLINE SECTION
LOOKING RIGHT (BUMPER OMITTED)

LIFT AND COUNTERWEIGHT

The fully loaded moon box weighed about 550 pounds. In order to lighten the load on our Goddard-controlled 5-hp winch and to keep the load on all the $\frac{1}{8}$" aircraft cable lift-line's segments within safe working load limits, we counter-weighted the unit by means of the specially designed arbor illustrated in Figure 1. The arbor was made from two 12' lengths of 2" x 2" x $\frac{3}{16}$" angle iron and reinforced with side plates of 2" bar stock. It carried a number of regular stage weights, laid end-to-end and capped with a 1x3 held in place by plumbers strap. The counterweight lines ran from pick-up plates at the bottom of the moon box's frame, over the onstage sheaves at the top of the sheave columns, and then to the arbor.

The lift lines ran from those same pick-up plates, over the offstage sheaves at the top of the sheave columns, and then back downward and through drive mules welded near the bottoms of the sheave columns before connecting to the winch drum. Figure 2 illustrates both lines' paths.

The sheave columns were secured to the trap room floor by concrete screws and welded to bracing frames lagged to the stage floor. Pipes welded between the bases of the sheave columns and between the columns and the winch frame countered the lateral forces created by the weight of the raised moon box.

THE BUMPER

Because the moon box's top was held steady by the tele-scoping stabilizers and the unit's center of mass was for-ward of the lift points, lifting the moon box tended to swing its bottom upstage. To keep its rear bottom edge from foul-ing on other components, we installed a traproom-tall angle-iron bumper offstage of each telescoping stabilizer as shown in Figure 1. We fastened the bumpers in place with their leading edges just downstage of the stabilizers.

THE TELESCOPING STABILIZERS

To keep the top of the moon box from falling forward as it rose, we fitted either end with a stabilizer made from two 14' lengths of 11-gauge square tube steel sleeved together, the inner sleeve measuring $1\frac{3}{4}$" square, and the outer measur-ing 3" square. We attached the top of each inner sleeve to the top of the moon box with a $\frac{1}{2}$" x 6" hex head bolt, and through this connection the moon box lifted the telescoping sleeves, which in turn stabilized the moon.

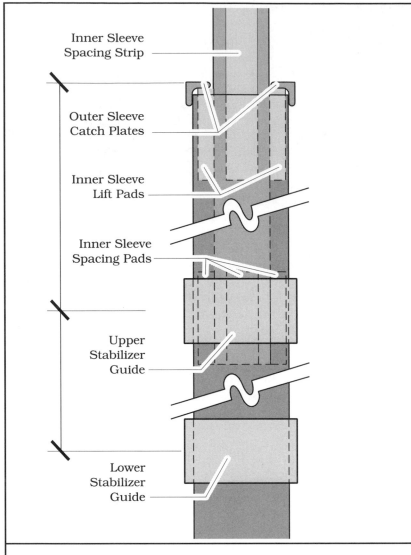

Inner Sleeve
Spacing Strip

Outer Sleeve
Catch Plates

Inner Sleeve
Lift Pads

Inner Sleeve
Spacing Pads

Upper
Stabilizer
Guide

Lower
Stabilizer
Guide

FIGURE 3: THE STABILIZER SLEEVES IN FRONT VIEW

The moon box was to rise 14'. When it (and the inner telescope sleeve) had been lifted 7', two "blue plastic" (HDPE) lift pads Tek-screwed to the inner sleeve came to rest against a pair of angle iron catch plates welded to the top of the outer sleeve. As soon as contact had been made, the inner sleeve picked up the outer sleeve, sliding it smoothly through two bent-bar-stock guides fastened 7' apart along the telescope's line of travel, one guide secured to the bracing frame at stage level, the other to a permanent pipe structure in the trap room.

In addition to the lift pads, we Tek-screwed several other pieces of HDPE to the inner sleeves. All the pieces are shown in Figure 3. The two 7'-long spacing strips at the top of the inner sleeves' upstage and downstage faces and the four smaller spacing pads at the bottom of the inner sleeves simultaneously reduced friction and filled the gap between the sleeves. As a result, the telescope operated smoothly and kept the moon reliably in plane.

Many thanks to Alan Hendrickson and Eric Sparks for their contributions.

John Lee Beatty's designs for our *East of the Sun and West of the Moon* included a small, wagon-mounted revolve which allowed one of the play's characters to disappear quickly. This revolve rotated through only 180° each performance; but carried a 180-pound person and the backing wall that hid him. Its spin began with enough snap to make the disappearance convincing, but didn't stop with an absolute jolt.

A torsion-spring seemed the ideal motor for this trick. Self-contained and lightweight, torsion springs start unwinding at full torque and lose effectiveness as they unwind. That characteristic gave the revolve the sudden start and the controllable deceleration it needed. To establish the correct start and stop points, I built a cam-like version of the notched disks used on locking-swivel casters. Figure 1 shows the parts of the revolve we built.

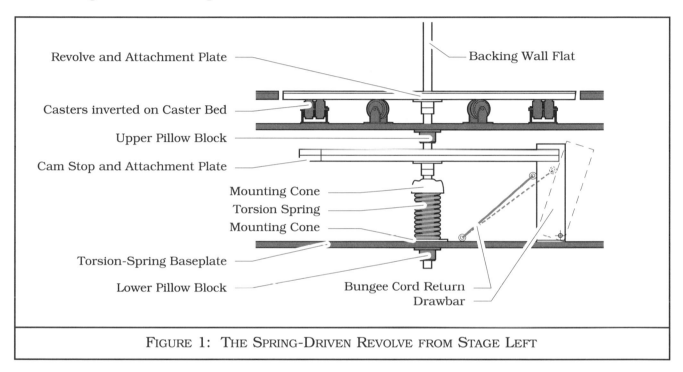

FIGURE 1: THE SPRING-DRIVEN REVOLVE FROM STAGE LEFT

THE SPRING MOTOR

Torsion springs, which are made from various wire sizes, come wound as right- or left-hand coils available in a number of different inside diameters. Extrapolating from a table supplied by the Bloomington (Minnesota) Door Company, I determined that I would need a $2\frac{1}{4}$" I.D. x 0.250" wire size garage-door spring. Springs like the one I bought come with two mounting cones designed to sleeve over the shaft they turn. One cone bolts to the supporting structure; the other grips the shaft, usually by means of a pair of set screws.

The first of two modifications we made to the unit we bought was to substitute a 1" shaft for the supplied 1" tubing. The second was to cut the spring to the length we needed. My calculations indicated that a spring as short as $2\frac{1}{2}$" would turn the revolve through 180° at speed. But torsion springs last only so many cycles before breaking, and the longer they are, the longer they last. Besides, I wanted more speed options than a $2\frac{1}{2}$" spring would offer. Wedging screwdrivers between the coils to spread them far enough apart, we saber-sawed the spring to 5", a length that allowed the revolve a full turn and a half. During techs, we used the extra length to accustom the actor to the spinning motion gradually, starting from the slower speed produced by a half-turn and subsequently increasing the speed by winding the revolve one full turn and finally the full turn-and-a-half. By the time the show moved into its run, the revolve was working to everyone's satisfaction, and I chose not to shorten the spring further.

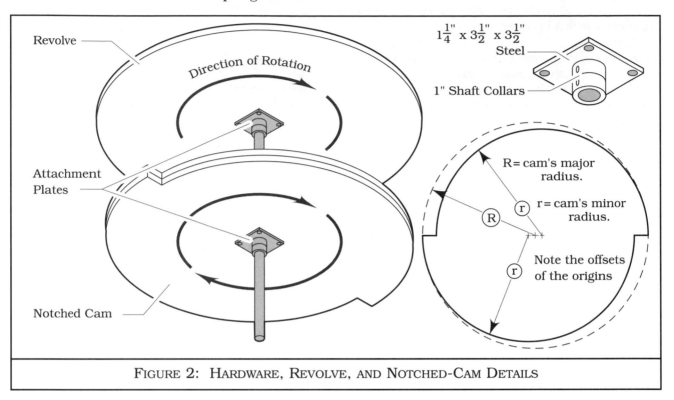

FIGURE 2: HARDWARE, REVOLVE, AND NOTCHED-CAM DETAILS

THE NOTCHED-CAM STOP

Figure 2 illustrates the revolve and the parts of the notched cam stop we made from a double layer of $\frac{3}{4}$" plywood. The notches were designed to catch the end of a 2x4 drawbar, hinge-mounted on the spring's baseplate. A bungee cord between the baseplate and the middle of the 2x4 pulled the drawbar toward the center of the cam. Members of the wagon's frame braced the drawbar horizontally so that it would not be torn away by the cam's impact. The plywood cam was bolted to one of two attachment plates we built to sleeve over the revolve's shaft. The second attachment plate bolted the revolve to the top end of the shaft. We soon discovered that the two set-screws in the attachment plates' shaft collars would not keep the cam or the revolve from spinning on the shaft, so we welded the attachment plates directly to the shaft.

OPERATION

Stagehands wound the spring for each performance by spinning the revolve backwards. When the notched cam reached its preset, the bungee cord return pulled the 2x4 drawbar into the cam's notch, locking the revolve in place. As soon as a stagehand tripped the drawbar, the bungee cord pulled the drawbar back into position to catch the next notch, and the stagehand helped brake the revolve so that it did not stop too abruptly.

CONCLUSION

The $2\frac{1}{4}$" spring and two mounting cones cost \$42.60; the 1" shaft collars, \$1.08 each; the 1" flange blocks, \$23.25 each; and everything else was on hand in the shop. This \$100 drive worked out extremely well — so well that I would not hesitate to adapt a torsion spring to power other kinds of machines built for productions. I can easily imagine, for instance, a torsion-spring-powered car: a larger version of the child's toy that is pulled backwards for a distance then let go to move forward the same distance. Such a solution would be relatively inexpensive, compared to the likely alternatives, and would be quiet, lightweight, and cordless, to boot.

	Length(")	Active Coils	Total Coils	Torque Inch-Pounds per Turn	Maximum Turns	Spring Weight(#)
Turning Force:	2.5	5	10	902.8	0.4	1.1
	3.0	7	12	644.9	0.6	1.3
Torque = $\dfrac{4514}{\text{Active Coils}}$	3.75	10	15	451.4	0.8	1.6
	4.0	11	16	410.4	0.9	1.8
	5.0	15	20	300.9	1.2	2.2
Maximum Torque 370"#	6.0	19	24	237.6	1.6	2.6
	7.0	23	28	196.3	1.9	3.1
	8.0	27	32	167.2	2.2	3.5
	9.0	31	36	145.6	2.5	3.9
	10.0	35	40	129.0	2.9	4.4
Weight per Linear Inch 0.4385#	11.0	39	44	115.7	3.2	4.8
	12.0	43	48	105.0	3.5	5.3
	13.0	47	52	96.0	3.9	5.7
	14.0	51	56	88.5	4.2	6.1
	15.0	55	60	82.1	4.5	6.6

TABLE 1: DATA FOR A $2\frac{1}{4}$" X 0.25" TORSION SPRING

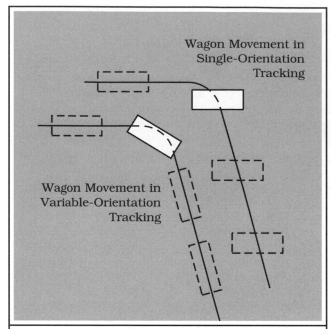

FIGURE 1: VARIABLE-ORIENTATION AND SINGLE-ORIENTATION TRACKING, COMPARED

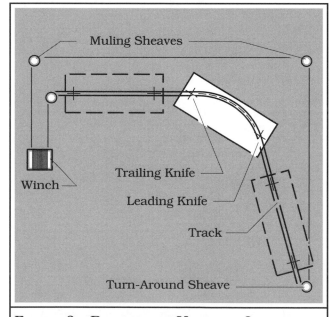

FIGURE 2: RIGGING FOR VARIABLE ORIENTATION

Of the several curved-track sets designed for the Pittsburgh Public Theatre's tight, extended thrust stage, Ray Recht's *Old Ladies Guide to Survival* in 1992 was the first to require single-orientation wagon movement. The wagons used in earlier productions had, like the unit drawn at the left in Figure 1, turned to face in a new direction as they rounded their tracks' curves. Ray wanted the type of travel depicted on the right in Figure 1: single-orientation tracking. For instance, if a park bench sat facing downstage in its storage position, it needed to track onstage, around the curve, and into its playing position, all the while continuing to face downstage. We answered his requirement by adding a second track to the deck, offsetting it from the first, but with the same geometry as the first track.

ORIENTATION CONTROL

Most units that run on curved tracks have two guide knives. Whether both are attached to the drive cable or not, the two knives typically ride in the same track, one travelling along behind the other. Because the leading knife moves into a curve before the trailing knife, the wagon being driven takes the curve almost like a car turning right or left. Figure 2 shows a more complete schematic of such a system.

A two-track, single-orientation system works by establishing and maintaining a desired offset between a unit's two guide knives. The tracks are identical, down to the radius of their curves, but the distance between them varies. If, as in Figure 3 for instance, knife **A** must be 11" upstage and 3'-5" stage left of knife **B** when the wagon reaches its playing position, then the center point **C** of the curve in Track 1 must be set 11" up and 3'-5" left of Track 2's center point, **C'**. Consequently, the downstage straight sections will be farther apart than the upstage straight sections since the straight sections simply extend tangents erected at the ends of curved track sections. See Figure 4.

THE HARDWARE

The single-orientation tracking system described here uses two drive cables, two tracks, and twice as many muling sheaves as its variable-orientation counterpart. But there, the hardware doubling stops: both cables in this system are driven by a single winch so that the knives move synchronously and stay properly oriented to each other.

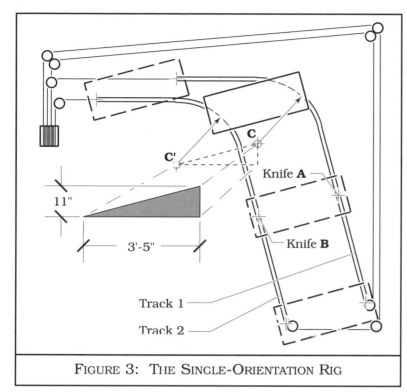

FIGURE 3: THE SINGLE-ORIENTATION RIG

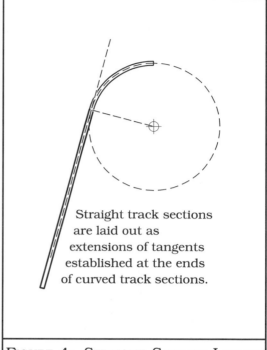

Straight track sections
are laid out as
extensions of tangents
established at the ends
of curved track sections.

FIGURE 4: STRAIGHT-SECTION LAYOUT

A FINAL NOTE

This approach to single-orientation tracking can be used with many types of gear. For the record, a description of the Pittsburgh Public Theatre's shop-built track and hardware appeared in the 1991 USITT *Theatre Technology Exhibit Catalog* and was reprinted in the Summer 1991 issue of *TD&T*.

The design for LA Shakespeare Festival's traveling production of *Taming of the Shrew* included a row of ten rotating doors. One side of each door was paneled for use in exterior scenes; the other side was painted to form part of a 30' long mural for interiors. Each of the doors needed to spin individually for actor entrances, but at seven moments during the show, all ten doors had to be quickly linked so that an unseen operator could open them simultaneously. The director described this movement as similar to the starting gates at a horse race. The action of the play left plenty of time to link the doors, but the release time had to be kept under five seconds. In two scenes, actors rushed through pairs of doors almost immediately after the entire row had turned.

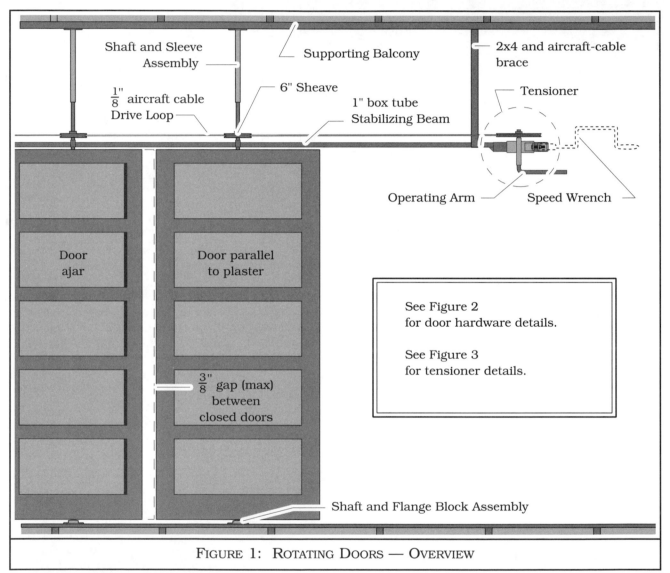

FIGURE 1: ROTATING DOORS — OVERVIEW

Several factors influenced the design of the rig. First, the doors had to rotate through 90°, 180°, and 360°. Second, since the production was to play at four different venues, the mechanics had to assemble quickly and easily, and the rig had to be sturdy, dependable, and simple. With the show performing as far as 60 miles away from the shop, even basic repairs would prove extremely challenging. Finally, the height of the balcony under which the rig would be mounted could not be determined until load-in at the first venue. Thus, the rig's height had to be made adjustable to fit a range of possibilities.

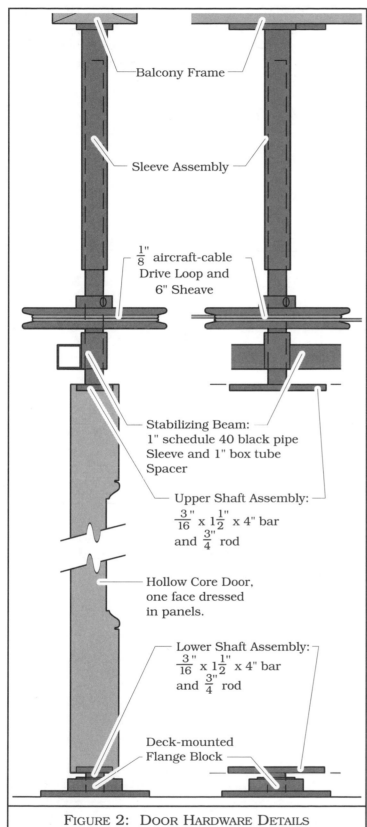

Balcony Frame

Sleeve Assembly

$\frac{1}{8}$" aircraft-cable
Drive Loop and
6" Sheave

Stabilizing Beam:
1" schedule 40 black pipe
Sleeve and 1" box tube
Spacer

Upper Shaft Assembly:
$\frac{3}{16}$" x $1\frac{1}{2}$" x 4" bar
and $\frac{3}{4}$" rod

Hollow Core Door,
one face dressed
in panels.

Lower Shaft Assembly:
$\frac{3}{16}$" x $1\frac{1}{2}$" x 4" bar
and $\frac{3}{4}$" rod

Deck-mounted
Flange Block

FIGURE 2: DOOR HARDWARE DETAILS

Figure 2 shows the doors' hardware. Each door spun freely on a $\frac{3}{4}$" shaft in a deck-mounted flange block. At the top of each door, short sleeves of 1" schedule 40 black pipe welded to a 31' long beam of 1" box tube stabilized the doors' upper shafts and guaranteed their exact spacing. Above the stabilizing beam, long sleeves of 1" schedule 40 black pipe held the 20" upper shafts in place. A 6" sheave was mounted on each door shaft and a 10" sheave was mounted to the tensioning hardware offstage. A nicopressed drive loop of $\frac{1}{8}$" aircraft cable was wrapped once around each 6" sheave and, to augment friction, twice around the 10" sheave.

Figure 3 shows the tensioner: a short piece of $2\frac{1}{2}$" box tube sliding on a longer piece of 2" box tube welded to the end of the 1" beam. The 10" sheave itself was mounted on a $\frac{3}{4}$" shaft held in a sleeve of 1" schedule 40 black pipe that was welded to the $2\frac{1}{2}$" box tube. One short "clip" made of 2" angle iron was welded to the $2\frac{1}{2}$" box tube; another, to the 2" box tube. A $\frac{1}{2}$" bolt welded to the angle iron on the $2\frac{1}{2}$" box tube passed through holes in clips and was nutted at the offstage end. Tightening or loosening the nut with a speed wrench quickly adjusted the cable tension by moving the carriage. When slack, the cable would slip on the sheaves and the doors could spin independently. When tensioned, the cable caused all the doors to open or close simultaneously in response to movement of the operating arm. It took only about seven turns of the wrench to tension or slack the cable sufficiently. Since the audience was 30' away, they did not notice that the operator walked behind the doors and dressed them into alignment before linking them.

The rig held up well during performances and transport, and its operation required only one crew member's part-time attention. The motion of the cable running on itself caused an audible "swoosh," but the director was actually pleased by both the spectacle and the sound it made.

‌‍ﭠﭠﭠﭠ

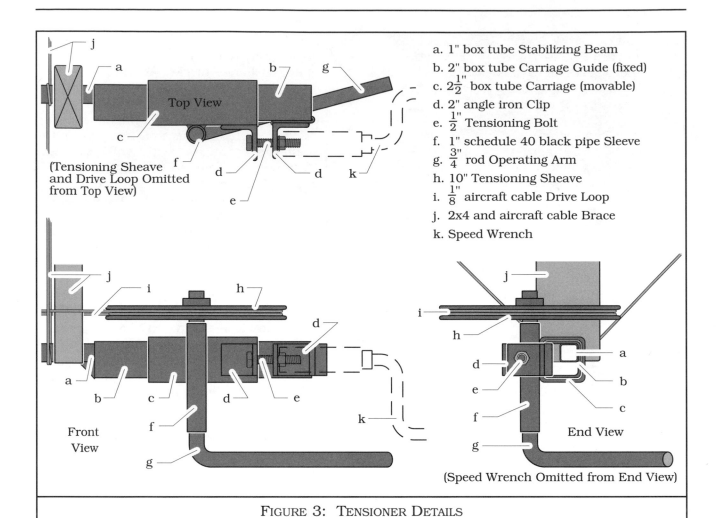

a. 1" box tube Stabilizing Beam
b. 2" box tube Carriage Guide (fixed)
c. $2\frac{1}{2}$" box tube Carriage (movable)
d. 2" angle iron Clip
e. $\frac{1}{2}$" Tensioning Bolt
f. 1" schedule 40 black pipe Sleeve
g. $\frac{3}{4}$" rod Operating Arm
h. 10" Tensioning Sheave
i. $\frac{1}{8}$" aircraft cable Drive Loop
j. 2x4 and aircraft cable Brace
k. Speed Wrench

Top View

(Tensioning Sheave and Drive Loop Omitted from Top View)

Front View

(Speed Wrench Omitted from End View)

End View

FIGURE 3: TENSIONER DETAILS

The masking for the Seattle Rep's *Jolson Sings Again* in 1995 included two 4'-6" x 12' velour tabs that played perpendicular to plaster between the first and second portals. The tabs effectively blocked the audience's view of equipment and crew backstage, but they also blocked the passage of two winch-driven wagons that entered from the wings. Prevented from tripping the tabs out of the way because of overhead lighting positions, we decided to rig them to turn back against the back of the first portal for scene changes. Since seeing the run crew move the tabs was undesirable, we built two pneumatic tab turners as described here, and put their control in the hands of the winch operator.

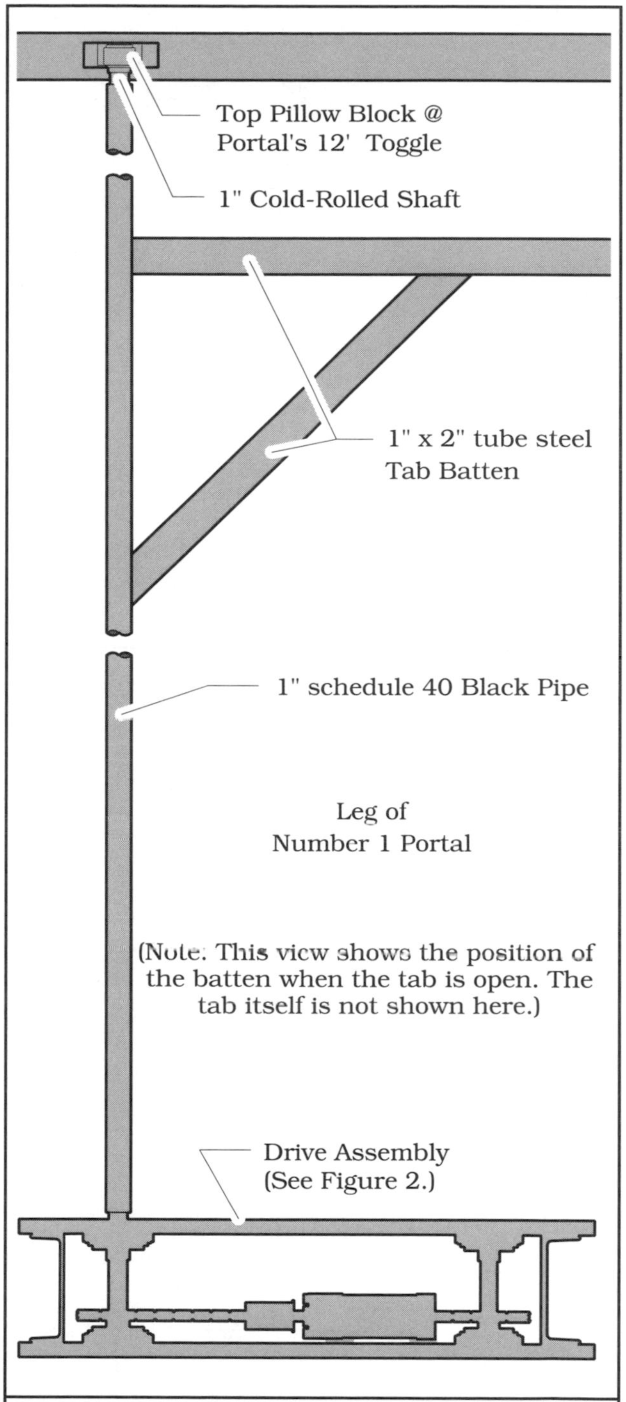

THE BATTEN

Each tab hung on a 5' arm-like batten of 1"x 2" tube steel welded to an 11' length of 1" schedule 40 black pipe as shown in Figure 1. Short pieces of 1" cold-rolled keyed shaft welded into the ends of the pipe accommodated the tab's main chain sprocket and the three pillow blocks that held the pipe vertical. The top pillow block was bolted to the back of the first portal. The lower two pillow blocks were incorporated into the tab's drive assembly.

THE DRIVE ASSEMBLY

Each drive assembly was designed as a self-contained unit for quick prep and installation. The working components — a short loop of #40 roller chain, two 24-tooth, 40-pitch sprockets, and a $1\frac{1}{2}$" bore, 3"-stroke Speedaire® pneumatic cylinder — were bolted in place inside an open frame made of two short pieces of 6"-wide aluminum channel and four pieces of half-height Unistrut®.

CONSTRUCTION

Before load-in, we welded the tube steel batten and brace to each of the 1" pipes. We also welded the upper shaft into each pipe and fitted it with a pillow block. With that much of the batten done, we began

Top Pillow Block @ Portal's 12' Toggle

1" Cold-Rolled Shaft

1" x 2" tube steel Tab Batten

1" schedule 40 Black Pipe

Leg of Number 1 Portal

(Note: This view shows the position of the batten when the tab is open. The tab itself is not shown here.)

Drive Assembly (See Figure 2.)

FIGURE 1: TAB TURNER IN OVERVIEW

work on the drive frames, mounting a cylinder, four pillow blocks, and two shafts in each frame. The "short shaft" (at the right in Figure 2) carried the chain's turnaround sprocket. The "long shaft" (at the left in the illustration) was welded into the bottom end of the batten's pipe during load-in.

To connect the cylinder rod to the chain, we cut a "clip" — a 1"-wide piece of $2\frac{1}{2}$" x $2\frac{1}{2}$" x $\frac{1}{4}$" angle. We drilled one $\frac{11}{16}$" hole for the $\frac{5}{8}$" cylinder rod in one leg of the clip, and two $\frac{1}{4}$" holes for 10-32

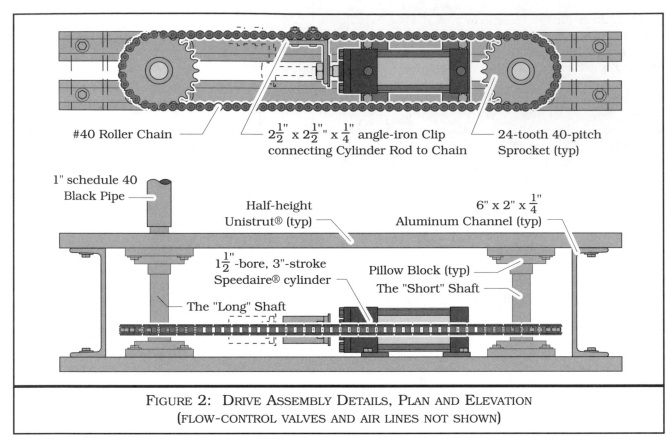

FIGURE 2: DRIVE ASSEMBLY DETAILS, PLAN AND ELEVATION
(FLOW-CONTROL VALVES AND AIR LINES NOT SHOWN)

machine screws in the other. The $\frac{1}{4}$" holes were set far enough apart that the machine screws passed between links in the chain. Once all the drive components had been mounted in the frame, we installed and tensioned the chain and adjusted the cylinder's position in the frame to fine-tune the relationship between the holes in the clip and the openings between chain links. After joining the chain to the cylinder rod with the clip, we plumbed and bench-tested the setup. Later, at load-in, we easily pulled the "long" shaft out of the drive assembly, welded it into the bottom of the batten pipe, and then re-installed it in the frame. For safety's sake, we gave the drive frames a lauan cover.

PLUMBING AND CONTROL

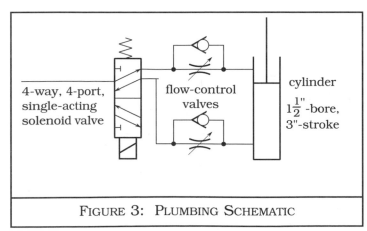

FIGURE 3: PLUMBING SCHEMATIC

Along with a pressure regulator setting of about 40psig, meter-out flow controls installed on both cylinders let us optimize the tab turners' movement so that they turned quickly and discretely. We mounted the flow controls on the cylinders themselves, where they would be accessible yet protected from damage. We ran the air lines from the flow controls to exhausts and to two solenoid-actuated valves that we installed in the basement to reduce operational noise. Figure 3 details the plumbing connections. The valves we used insured that the cylinders would be pressurized whether the tabs were open or closed. The winch operator controlled the tabs' movement by means of a pair of toggle switches mounted near the winch controls offstage.

$1\frac{1}{2}$"-bore, 3"-stroke, double-acting cylinder	$85 ea.
4-way, 5-port, 2-position, single-acting solenoid valve	$70 ea.
24-tooth, 40-pitch sprocket, fixed-bore	$20 ea.
#40 roller chain	$20 per 10' length.
flow-control valve, $\frac{1}{4}$" NPT	$15 ea.
1" cold-rolled keyed shaft	$2 per foot.

A RECOMMENDATION

The Seattle Rep has a large inventory of mechanical components and scrap, and these tab turners were built with no cost to the show. The components would, however, be useful in so many small applications that they would be good additions to any theater's stock. Grainger's prices for the essential components for one tab turner add up to less than $250.

ଽଈଽଈଽଈ

One traditional method of driving a turntable is to use an endless loop of cable wrapped around the sheaves of a drive machine and the edge of a turntable. This method results in a turntable that can turn infinitely in either direction. Friction between the drive sheaves and the cable and between the cable and the turntable edge transmits power from motor to turntable. While this system works well, it does have some disadvantages. The drive mechanism is basically a set of driven and idler sheaves. The high part count of sheaves, a shaft, and a pair of bearings results in a machine that is relatively expensive, somewhat difficult to construct, and often awkward to reeve cable through. Also, the long loop of drive cable must be spliced together. Few of us have experience in making long splices in wire rope, and finding a company that can do this, and do it quickly, is difficult. Finally, once you have the spliced cable, you are locked into a fixed distance between the drive and the turntable.

The following system uses the same friction drive principle as the endless loop cable drive, but was designed to eliminate the cable drive's disadvantages. ANSI standard roller chain is used in place of the wire rope cable. Unlike cable, roller chain can be easily spliced into a loop of any desired length with just a connecting link. At the drive machine, one roller chain sprocket replaces the cable drive's array of driven and idler sheaves — a single sprocket is inexpensive, requires no machining, and is almost trivial to reeve.

Turntables and the loads on them vary widely. The drive described here will run a 20' to 24'-diameter, 5000-pound total load turntable to a speed of about 3 rpm. The cost of the parts for this machine, including a typical chain loop, would be around $1400 (this does not include any of the electric and electronic components needed to control the motor's speed and position). Drives for other sizes, loads, or speeds will, of course, use different components, but the parts layout will remain essentially the same. The turntable drive consists of seven main components: brakemotor, gear reducer, chain sprocket, chain, manual backup crank, tensioning frame, and idlers.

The brakemotor, a 2-hp, 1750-rpm, 208-volt, 3-phase, NEMA C-face (Lenze 145010, call 201-227-5311), couples directly into a 20:1, double end output shaft worm gear reducer (Winsmith model 930, available from Grainger). The C-face mounting between motor and reducer simplifies a connection that would otherwise involve both a frame to hold the motor and reducer in precise rigid alignment and a shaft coupling between the motor and reducer shafts. The reducer mounts into the drive machine frame so that its output shaft is vertical. A 60-tooth #40 roller chain sprocket (Browning 40Q60, available from Grainger) is mounted onto the lower reducer output shaft, while an emergency backup hand crank is made so that it can key into the upper output shaft.

The chain loop that goes around both sprocket and turntable is formed from a long length of ANSI #40 roller chain. Chain is available in 100 foot coils from many sources — Grainger's, for instance, at $185 per 100 feet — as are connecting links. When you splice a long chain, put some paint on the connecting link so you can find it easily during strike. For a 24'-diameter turntable, a loop of about 85' would be typical:

> approximate loop length = turntable circumference + 2 x distance between table edge and reducer shaft

$$85' = (\pi \times 24' \text{ diameter}) + (2 \times 5')$$

The strength of the chain determines the maximum pull that it can exert on the turntable edge. ANSI standard chain is manufactured with a minimum breaking strength specification. Number 40 chain has a minimum breaking strength of 3125 lb, and therefore, with a standard 5:1 safety factor for non-life-threatening situations, a working strength of 625 lb. This is roughly equivalent to the strength of a spliced $\frac{3}{16}$" aircraft cable drive loop.

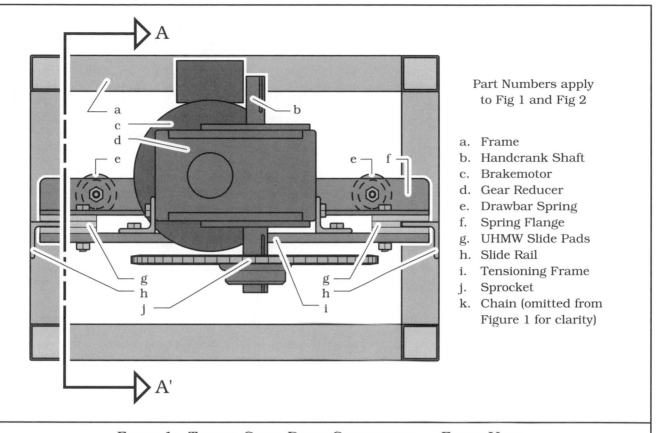

Part Numbers apply
to Fig 1 and Fig 2

a. Frame
b. Handcrank Shaft
c. Brakemotor
d. Gear Reducer
e. Drawbar Spring
f. Spring Flange
g. UHMW Slide Pads
h. Slide Rail
i. Tensioning Frame
j. Sprocket
k. Chain (omitted from
　　Figure 1 for clarity)

FIGURE 1: TYPICAL CHAIN DRIVE COMPONENTS — FRONT VIEW

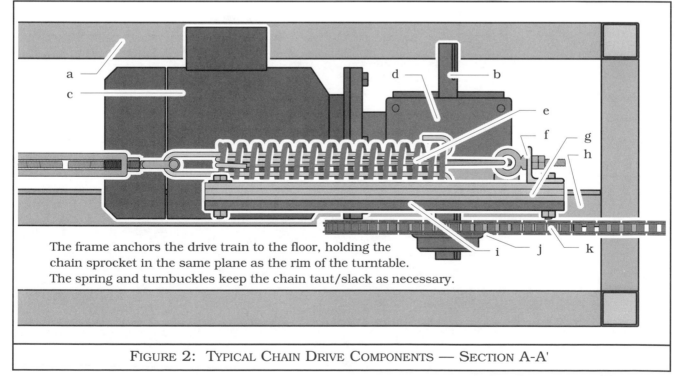

The frame anchors the drive train to the floor, holding the
chain sprocket in the same plane as the rim of the turntable.
The spring and turnbuckles keep the chain taut/slack as necessary.

FIGURE 2: TYPICAL CHAIN DRIVE COMPONENTS — SECTION A-A'

In order to prevent the chain from slipping, and yet allow for out-of-round turntables, spring-actuated tensioning is built into the drive machine. An inner frame holding the motor, reducer, and sprocket is built to slide on rails that are part of an outer stationary frame. A pair of drawbar springs (McMaster-Carr, 9630K2) pull the inner frame away from the turntable, and hence tension the chain. Turnbuckles pulling on the springs allow the tension to be adjusted to the roughly 100 to 200 pounds of tension typically needed, while still allowing the inner frame to slide to accommodate for slightly out-of-round turntables.

At a location just off the edge of the turntable, the roller chain passes through a pair of idler sprockets, as shown in Figure 3. These act to increase the contact of the chain around the turntable, and the friction developed between chain and turntable increases exponentially in proportion with the amount of contact between them. The idlers (Browning HB40A17, available through Grainger) are mounted into their own small frame which gets lagged down to the stage floor.

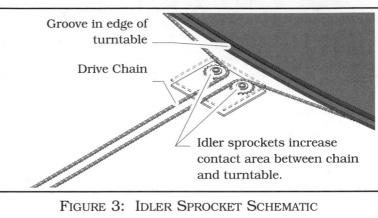

Groove in edge of turntable

Drive Chain

Idler sprockets increase contact area between chain and turntable.

FIGURE 3: IDLER SPROCKET SCHEMATIC

There is no special construction difference in the turntable edge between cable and chain drive except perhaps that chain, being wider than cable, needs a wider edge-groove. For both drive methods, high friction between cable or chain and turntable groove surface is essential. A textured vinyl anti-slip tape (McMaster-Carr 6243T31, 1" wide, 60 ft long, $20 — enough for a 20'-diameter turntable) was laid into the groove to increase friction without being abrasive as some sandpaper-like anti-slip tapes would be.

This technique has worked well on several shows at the Yale Repertory Theatre, but it does have one inherent disadvantage. Unlike cable, roller chain can bend in only one plane, and so the driving sprocket and turntable edge must be coplanar. Hiding the drive upstage of scenery or in the trap room keeps it out of sight, but certain designs might preclude the use of chain.

One person turning a handcrank can easily move a lightly loaded turntable, and a turntable driven by an endless-loop cable can rotate clockwise or counterclockwise any number of times. The device described here embodies both of those principles in a simple, inexpensive turntable drive.

SYSTEM COMPONENTS

The welded tube steel drive frame shown in Figure 1 holds a handcrank about 3 feet off the floor, a comfortable working height for most people. With this frame, a stagehand might typically be expected to turn a foot-long handcrank at about 60 to 90 rpm.

To allow the use of a simplified endless loop, all the sheaves in the drive frame are standard cast-iron A-size V-belt sheaves. In most endless loops, the ends of a piece of wire rope are joined in a long splice. In this one, the ends are simply Nicopressed together. The swages travel easily, if a bit inelegantly, through the large grooves of the V-belt sheaves. These sheaves' groove profile is hard on the wire-rope loop, but most productions will come and go long before the loop needs replacing.

The cable tensioner (detailed in Figure 2 along with a handcrank) can move the handcrank-shaft's pillow blocks back and forth to adjust cable tension; and the two muling sheaves, those on the lowest shaft, can be moved up and down to adjust the drive loop's height off the floor.

The muling sheaves must be free to spin in opposite directions because of the way the loop serves into the frame, and the four idler sheaves may be left unkeyed. But the four drive sheaves on the handcrank shaft must be keyed in place in order to increase the wrap friction on which this system relies.

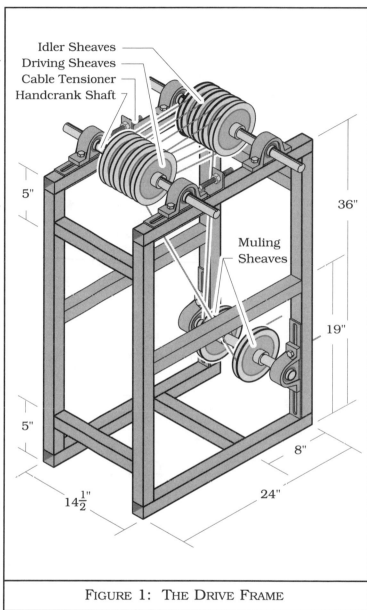

Idler Sheaves
Driving Sheaves
Cable Tensioner
Handcrank Shaft

Muling Sheaves

5"

36"

5"

19"

8"

$14\frac{1}{2}$"

24"

FIGURE 1: THE DRIVE FRAME

MULTIPLYING USEFUL FRICTION

Many things — rope cleats, capstan winches, and clove-hitches, for instance — rely on multiple-wrap friction to hold a load. In turntable drives too, a little more wrap means a lot less chance of slipping. In fact, increasing the amount of wrap between cable and turntable, and between cable and driving sheaves exponentially increases the effects of friction and decreases the likelihood of slipping. Figure 3 schematically illustrates how wrap is maximized with this system.

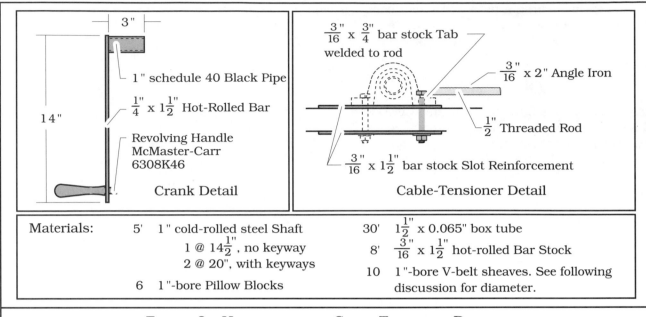

Crank Detail

3"

14"

1" schedule 40 Black Pipe

$\frac{1}{4}$" x $1\frac{1}{2}$" Hot-Rolled Bar

Revolving Handle
McMaster-Carr
6308K46

Cable-Tensioner Detail

$\frac{3}{16}$" x $\frac{3}{4}$" bar stock Tab
welded to rod

$\frac{3}{16}$" x 2" Angle Iron

$\frac{1}{2}$" Threaded Rod

$\frac{3}{16}$" x $1\frac{1}{2}$" bar stock Slot Reinforcement

Materials:

5' 1" cold-rolled steel Shaft
1 @ $14\frac{1}{2}$", no keyway
2 @ 20", with keyways

6 1"-bore Pillow Blocks

30' $1\frac{1}{2}$" x 0.065" box tube

8' $\frac{3}{16}$" x $1\frac{1}{2}$" hot-rolled Bar Stock

10 1"-bore V-belt sheaves. See following discussion for diameter.

FIGURE 2: HANDCRANK AND CABLE TENSIONER DETAILS

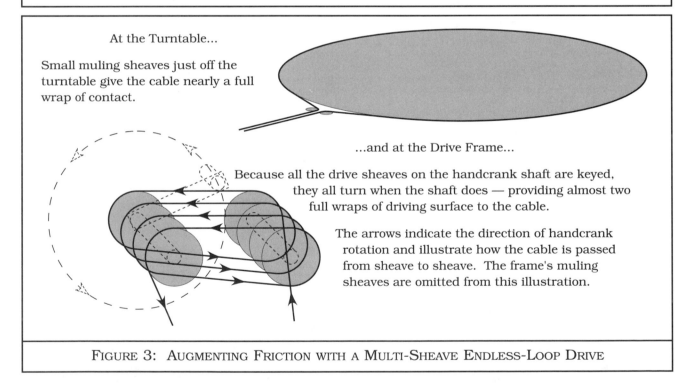

At the Turntable...

Small muling sheaves just off the turntable give the cable nearly a full wrap of contact.

...and at the Drive Frame...

Because all the drive sheaves on the handcrank shaft are keyed, they all turn when the shaft does — providing almost two full wraps of driving surface to the cable.

The arrows indicate the direction of handcrank rotation and illustrate how the cable is passed from sheave to sheave. The frame's muling sheaves are omitted from this illustration.

FIGURE 3: AUGMENTING FRICTION WITH A MULTI-SHEAVE ENDLESS-LOOP DRIVE

CALCULATING DRIVE SHEAVE DIAMETER

Estimating how fast a turntable must spin is essential in determining drive sheave diameter. One estimate of top rotational speed comes from consideration of edge speed, or the linear speed at the edge of a turntable:

$$\text{rpm} = (9.55 \times \text{edge speed}) \div \text{radius}$$

where: rpm = top rotational speed of the turntable (rev per min)
edge speed = top linear speed at turntable edge (ft per sec)
radius = (ft)

If an actor must move gracefully onto or off of a moving turntable, edge speeds must be limited accordingly. A stroll covers about 1.5 ft/sec; a brisk walk, about 3 ft/sec.

Another estimate of the top rotational speed relates the needed degree of rotation to the amount of time available, for example, a 180° turn in 14 seconds:

$$\text{rpm} = (0.333 \times \text{degrees}) \div \text{time}$$

where: rpm = top rotational speed of the turntable (rev per min)
degrees = total turn from start to finish (deg)
time = total time taken for move from start to finish (sec)

This formula assumes that half the time for the move will be spent in acceleration and half in deceleration — the gentlest type of move possible to accomplish the rotation in time. Faster acceleration and deceleration would permit reducing the top rpm by as much as half.

The total reduction ratio between power source and turntable is:

$$\text{ratio} = \text{rpm source} \div \text{rpm turntable}$$

where: ratio = reduction ratio (unitless)

rpm source = top rotational speed of the power source — usually a motor or handcrank — (rev per min)

rpm turntable = top rotational speed of the turntable, as obtained from the formulas above (rev per min)

Example: A person turning a handcrank at 60 rpm is driving a turntable 20 ft in diameter to a top edge speed of 1.5 ft/sec. What diameter are the driver sheaves?

Solution: First find the top speed of the turntable: rpm = (9.55 x edge speed) ÷ radius
rpm = (9.55 x 1.5) ÷ 10 = 1.43 rev per min

Now calculate the reduction ratio: ratio = rpm source ÷ rpm turntable
ratio = 60 ÷ 1.43 = 42.0 (or "42:1" or "42 to 1")

The ratio of turntable diameter to driving sheave diameter equals the total reduction ratio, so: ratio = turntable dia ÷ driving sheave dia
42 = 20 ÷ driving sheave dia
driving sheave dia = 0.48' (or $5\frac{3}{4}$")

❧❧❧❧

Creating an effective raft was an obstacle to Theatre Memphis' 1989 opening production, *Big River*. The director wanted the feel of a real raft, but budget and labor constraints ruled out any elaborate, mechanized tracking system. After some discussion, we opted to have the actors pole the raft just as they would a real raft. Our raft, shown in Figure 1, rolled on a row of rigid casters mounted from side to side across the center of the raft, and a set of four small swivel casters, one in each corner. This configuration allowed the raft to pivot on its center like a real raft or to move in a straight line to almost any location on stage. It also required that the actors steer the raft as well as propel it, thus helping to achieve the illusion of poling. In fact, this approach left only one small problem: how to keep the raft from shifting once it had reached a spike.

FIGURE 1: THEATRE MEMPHIS'S *BIG RIVER* RAFT

To solve that problem, we chose a locking system that I had inherited from Dan Hall, the previous Technical Director at Theatre Memphis. Though its ultimate origins are somewhat obscure, this medium-duty locking system is an elegant and quick way to secure rolling units. It is self-contained (no external hoses are needed), it can be reused, and it can be built out of parts that are reasonably priced if not already a part of most shops' stock parts. The system we built consisted of a PVC-pipe accumulator, a standard valve-and-nylon hose delivery/control system, and a shop-built lock: a pneumatic cylinder and a strap-steel caster shoe.

THE ACCUMULATOR

Our accumulator was a 3' length of 4" schedule 40 PVC (rated at 250 psi) that could be easily concealed under low wagons. We used PVC glue to secure the end caps, then drilled and tapped the pipe for pneumatic fittings. Pressurized at 100 psi, our accumulator held enough air to lock and unlock four brakes through one act.

THE DELIVERY AND CONTROL SYSTEM

We "teed" four cylinders off the feed/exhaust line. See Figure 2. The needle valve we added to the feed/exhaust line kept the locks from "clunking" when the valve was thrown. We used $\frac{1}{4}$" OD nylon air hose for delivery from the accumulator to the cylinders. The 3-way, 2-position normal-closed control valve was located at one end of the raft where its extended lever could be thrown by a rafting pole. We added a muffler to the exhaust port of the valve to minimize hiss.

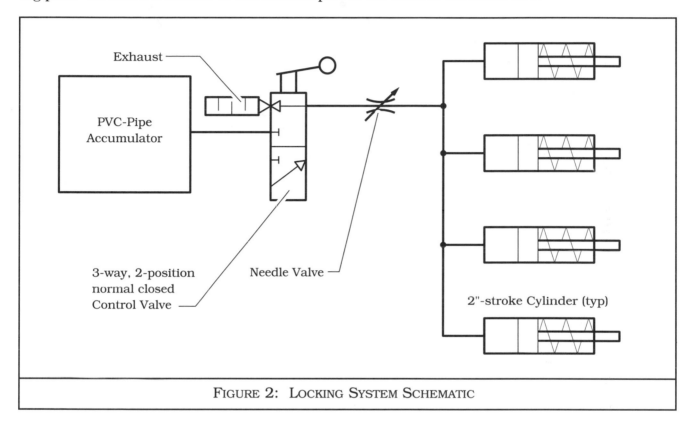

Exhaust

PVC-Pipe
Accumulator

3-way, 2-position
normal closed
Control Valve

Needle Valve

2"-stroke Cylinder (typ)

FIGURE 2: LOCKING SYSTEM SCHEMATIC

THE LOCK

Each lock consisted of a 2"-stroke spring-retracting cylinder and a hinged strap-steel shoe. See Figure 3. The cylinder's spring insured that the shoe would stay clear of the caster wheel when the system was exhausted. In designing a lock like this, calculating the angle of the cylinder in relation to the shoe is tricky. The legs of the angle iron that formed the cylinder's bracket were splayed to approximate the desired angle. Leaving the connection between the cylinder and the bracket somewhat loose provided "wiggle room" for further assembly and operation.

The strap steel we used for our lock's shoe was as wide as the caster wheel and moved freely in the yoke. We drilled a $\frac{1}{4}$" cylinder-shaft hole in what would be the curved end of the shoe. We then hand bent the strap to fit the caster wheel, welded a small hinge to the straight end of the strap, and glued a piece of an old inner tube in the area where the strap would meet the caster. Then, prior to installation, each shoe was passed through its caster and nutted to the cylinder shaft as shown in Figure 3.

There is no clear way to describe the placement of the cylinder and shoe. When the cylinder and shoe are connected the whole unit must be "fiddled with" to find the proper placement. Once this is done the shoe cylinder assembly can be screwed down.

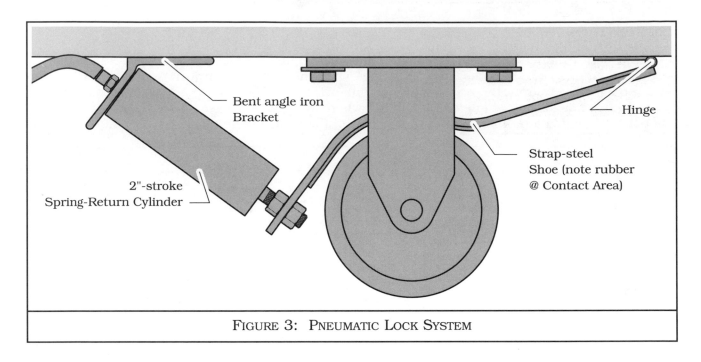

FIGURE 3: PNEUMATIC LOCK SYSTEM

Bent angle iron
Bracket

Hinge

Strap-steel
Shoe (note rubber
@ Contact Area)

2"-stroke
Spring-Return Cylinder

The banquet in the 1997 LA Shakespeare Festival production of *The Tempest* had to appear quickly and without any help onstage. Budget, time, and the fact that the production toured required that the trap be easy to build, quick to install, and simple to operate. To meet these needs, we designed a flipping trap unit that could unlock, flip, and re-lock. One side of the trap was used as the stage floor. Props representing the banquet were attached to the other side. The trap, plug, and mechanism were built as a unit to simplify movement and installation.

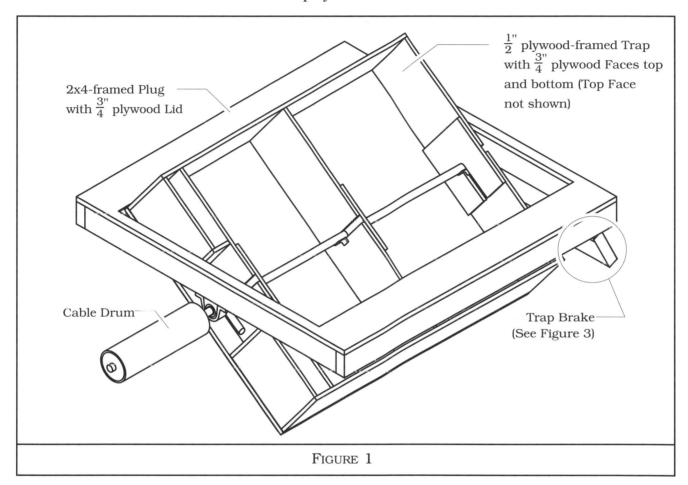

2x4-framed Plug with $\frac{3}{4}$" plywood Lid

$\frac{1}{2}$" plywood-framed Trap with $\frac{3}{4}$" plywood Faces top and bottom (Top Face not shown)

Cable Drum

Trap Brake (See Figure 3)

FIGURE 1

CONSTRUCTION

The plug that carried the trap was a basic 4' square 2x4 framed platform. The $11\frac{1}{2}$"-deep double-faced trap, which measured 2'-11" x 3'-8", sat in a 3' x 3'-9" cutout in the center of the plug. The trap's thickness required every bit of the $\frac{1}{2}$" good-luck gap we left all around between the trap and the plug. To minimize weight, the trap's internal framing was $\frac{1}{2}$" plywood. Although only one face of the trap needed to bear weight, we used $\frac{3}{4}$" plywood on both sides to help balance the weight. The depth of the 2x4 plug framing combined with the axle-to-base dimension of the pillow blocks we used dictated that our trap would have to be $11\frac{1}{2}$" thick for both sides to be flush with the stage floor. Figure 1 shows the slot cut down the center of the framing to allow the axle to be installed after the trap had been framed. Keeper plates of $\frac{1}{2}$" plywood added after axle installation held the axle in place and reinforced the frame.

The axle, as shown in Figure 2, was a 5'-6" long 1"-diameter piece of cold-rolled steel with $1\frac{1}{2}$" angle iron tabs welded along its length to bolt the shaft to the trap and the cable drum. To limit trap

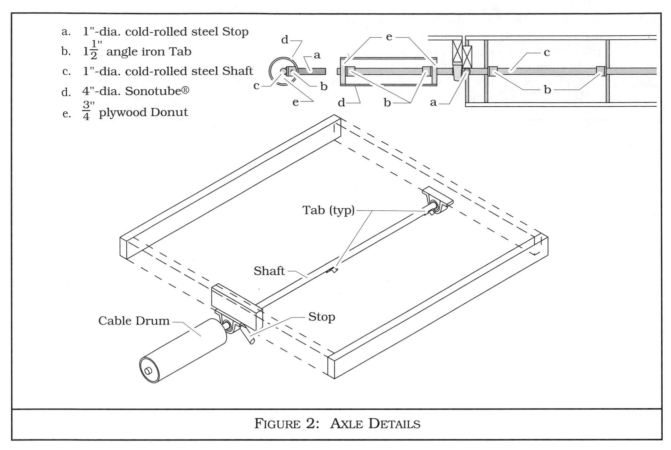

a. 1"-dia. cold-rolled steel Stop
b. 1½" angle iron Tab
c. 1"-dia. cold-rolled steel Shaft
d. 4"-dia. Sonotube®
e. ¾" plywood Donut

Tab (typ)

Shaft

Cable Drum

Stop

FIGURE 2: AXLE DETAILS

movement to 180° a 6"-long stop of 1"-diameter cold-rolled steel was welded perpendicular to the axle. The cable drum was made from two ¾" plywood donuts bolted to two of the axle's angle iron tabs and sleeved over with a piece of 4"-diameter Sonotube®.

Though the stop was strong enough to keep the trap from flipping more than 180°, we did not design it to support the live load of actor traffic. To hold the trap securely in position, we added a U-shaped brake made from 1½" angle iron welded to two spring hinges that bolted to the plug as shown in Figure 3. No matter which face of the trap was up, the spring hinges forced the brake into contact with the sides and bottom of the trap, preventing movement. This brake safely held 400# for the duration of the run.

OPERATION AND CONTROL

Trap operation was nearly foolproof. The stop welded to the trap's axle limited rotation to 180°, and a few turns of an offstage hand winch flipped the trap completely in about 1.4 seconds. The move required only one operator, whose first step was to free the trap for flipping by pulling the brake control line into a jam cleat. After releasing the brake, the operator cranked the hand winch a few turns to flip the trap. The hand winch drove an endless loop of manila rope passed through a number of muling sheaves under the deck and then wrapped around the trap's cable drum. After the flip was complete, the operator released the brake control line from the jam cleat, and the spring hinges snapped the angle back under the trap. Releasing the brake made a noticeable amount of noise. We did not find the noise objectionable, however, and chose to mask it with a sound cue. Padding the brake with felt would probably have reduced the noise just as satisfactorily.

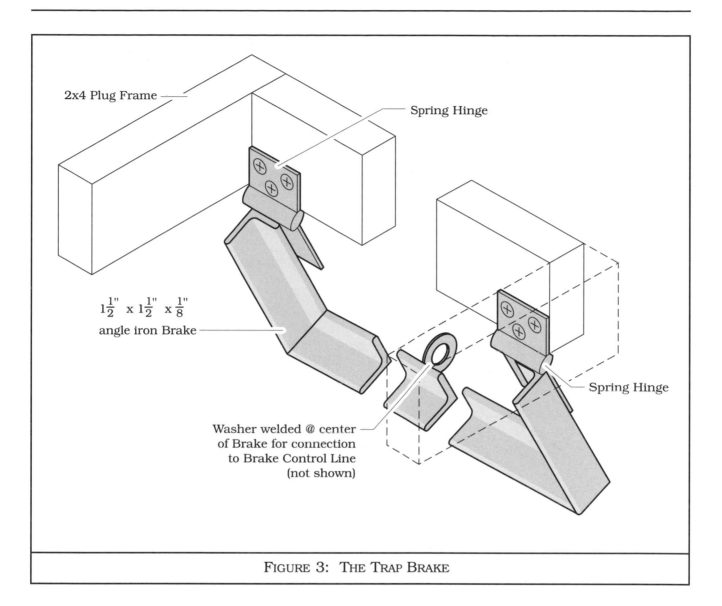

2x4 Plug Frame

Spring Hinge

$1\frac{1}{2}"$ x $1\frac{1}{2}"$ x $\frac{1}{8}"$
angle iron Brake

Spring Hinge

Washer welded @ center
of Brake for connection
to Brake Control Line
(not shown)

FIGURE 3: THE TRAP BRAKE

A Control Rig for a Down-Opening Trapdoor

Randy Steffen

A 1999 production at the Yale Repertory Theatre required a large, down-opening trapdoor that could open and close quickly. Its 175# weight and its size — 7'-0" on the hinge side by 3'-0" — made manual operation awkward without some mechanical advantage. Since the trapdoor was part of the show deck, it had to lock quickly and securely. Figure 1 illustrates the solution described in this article: a fast, reliable approach to locking, and a custom counterweight arbor.

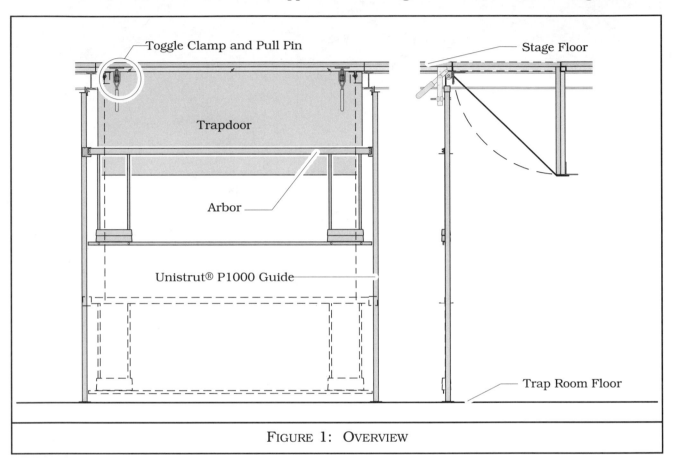

FIGURE 1: OVERVIEW

THE LOCKING SYSTEM

See Figure 2 for details of the locking system. The door was locked in place by three quick-release pull pins that passed through the angle-iron frame of the door and its surrounding plug. Vertical toggle clamps mounted next to the pins at the ends of the door facilitated pin removal. On a first cue from the stage manager, the operators pulled the pins while the toggle clamps were still locked. On a second cue, they released the clamps and kept hands on the arbor as it rose to ease the trapdoor open. To close the trapdoor, they pulled the arbor down, locked the clamps, and then inserted the pins. Because the toggle clamps momentarily support the weight of the trapdoor, they are load rated.

THE COUNTERWEIGHT SYSTEM

The arbor was installed along the door's downstage side (opposite the hinge) so that the operators could easily reach the toggle clamps and pull the pins. To give the operators a hand-hold on the arbor no matter which pin or lock they were operating, the top of the arbor was built as a handrail

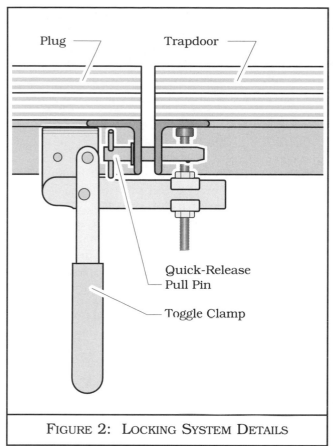

FIGURE 2: LOCKING SYSTEM DETAILS

Plug

Trapdoor

Quick-Release
Pull Pin

Toggle Clamp

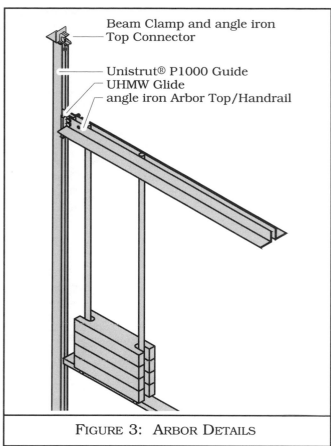

FIGURE 3: ARBOR DETAILS

Beam Clamp and angle iron
Top Connector

Unistrut® P1000 Guide
UHMW Glide
angle iron Arbor Top/Handrail

the full width of the trapdoor. The availability of stock hardware and rigging components dictated the rest of the arbor's design. See Figure 3. In place of T-track, two lengths of P1000 Unistrut® were cut to length, tap-conned to the trap room floor at the ends of the arbor, and clamped to I-beams overhead during load-in. Stock UHMW glides like those described in "A Quiet, Glide and Unistrut Traveler System" joined the arbor to the Unistrut®. The top of the arbor consisted of two 7'-4" lengths of 2" x 2" x $\frac{1}{8}$" angle iron. Between these, four $\frac{3}{4}$" rods, oriented vertically, were spaced to allow separate counterweight stacks at either end of the arbor. The bottoms of the four rods were joined by a single piece of 1" x 2" channel, oriented legs down.

For this production, the arbor itself was heavy enough to counterweight the door without the addition of counterweights. Proper counterweighting for a trapdoor is never a one-to-one ratio of door weight to counterweight. As the door swings open, the amount of force it exerts on the counterweight decreases. The trapdoor is "in weight" when the arbor must be resisted as the trap is unlocked and assisted as it approaches full open. While this weight is most easily determined through trial and error, it will never exceed the weight of one-half of the door.

¿▲¿▲¿▲

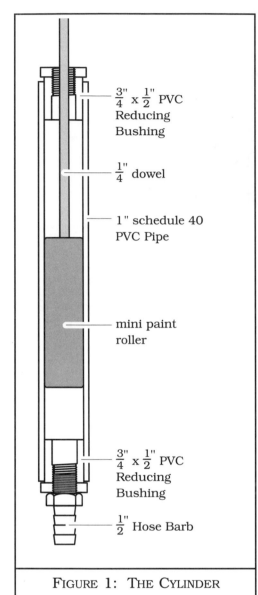

$\frac{3}{4}"$ x $\frac{1}{2}"$ PVC Reducing Bushing

$\frac{1}{4}"$ dowel

1" schedule 40 PVC Pipe

mini paint roller

$\frac{3}{4}"$ x $\frac{1}{2}"$ PVC Reducing Bushing

$\frac{1}{2}"$ Hose Barb

FIGURE 1: THE CYLINDER

At the denouement of San Diego State's production of *Triumph of Love*, a cardboard carriage rolls up to the door of a fairytale castle, high on a storybook hill, and five fluttering pennants rise suggestively from the tops of the castle towers. Single-acting, shop-built pneumatic cylinders powered each pennant — cylinders whose pistons are mini paint rollers.

These inexpensive cylinders are quick and easy to build from materials typically found around the scene shop: 1" schedule 40 PVC pipe, $\frac{1}{4}"$ dowel, miniature paint rollers and a little hot glue. (For strokes greater than three feet, $\frac{1}{4}"$ fiberglass rod may be substituted for the dowel.) Simply hot glue a dowel into the shaft opening of a miniature paint roller. Then cut a length of 1" schedule 40 PVC pipe slightly shorter than the length of the paint roller/dowel combination, insert the paint roller and dowel into the PVC pipe, and cap the pipe with threaded reducing bushings. When fully inserted into the pipe, the dowel should project a little past the bushing. Screw a hose barb or other suitable connector into the other end of the PVC pipe and connect to a convenient regulated air supply. The cylinder is now ready for use.

We used an air supply regulated to 40 psi for our application, which provided a theoretical piston force of around 35 pounds. Despite some leakage through the porous paint roller piston, the cylinders tested to over 30 pounds of force at 40 psi. We also discovered that the paint roller makes an ideal muffler, making the sound of airflow nearly inaudible. If the remaining hiss is objectionable, an O-ring slipped around the dowel where it enters the roller will seal the cylinder once it reaches its full stroke.

The type of valve used to control the cylinder is not critical, but since there is some leakage past the paint roller piston, it should be large enough to pass air freely. We used a Grainger valve, part number 2G527, with $\frac{1}{4}"$ ports, which provided enough air to run five cylinders simultaneously.

A double-acting system can be constructed from a pair of cylinders placed head to head, sharing a common dowel. The paint roller piston is so simple, so easy to build and so inexpensive, technicians will find the design useful for numerous applications besides propelling pennants.

ಜಜಜಜ

TECHNICAL BRIEF

Scenery Tools

A Swivel Caster Bolt-Hole Jig

Bonnie McDonald

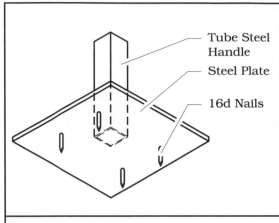

FIGURE 1: PICTORIAL

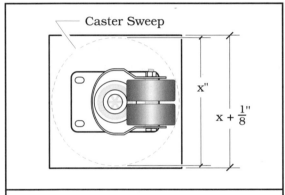

FIGURE 2: CASTER SWEEP CLEARANCE

Tired of spending too much time tracing bolt holes for stock casters? Try this simple jig, commonly used at the Santa Fe Opera, and your tracing days are over.

CONSTRUCTION

Place the caster upside down on the steel plate. Rotate the caster on its base, and mark both the wheel's sweep and the caster plate's bolt holes on the steel. Next, around the sweep circle, draw a square whose sides are $\frac{1}{8}$" larger than the sweep circle. See Figure 2. This larger size assures caster clearance. Cut out the square, and drill $\frac{11}{64}$" holes at the bolt hole markings. Snip the tops off the nails so that $\frac{1}{2}$" protrudes through the "bottom" side of the steel, and weld the nails to the steel. Now cut a handle from a four- or five-inch length of tubing or pipe (whatever you feel comfortable gripping) and weld this to the center of the steel's "top" side. Test the jig to assure that the nails fit through the caster plate's bolt holes.

USE

Place the jig in position on the bottom of a platform and strike the handle with a hammer. Drill bolt holes in the indentations left by the nails, and bolt the stock caster in position.

When a recent project found our shop in need of an adjustable router fence, we fabricated an adjustable jig out of materials we had on hand. As illustrated below, the jig incorporates a pivoting fence and a replacement baseplate for a router.

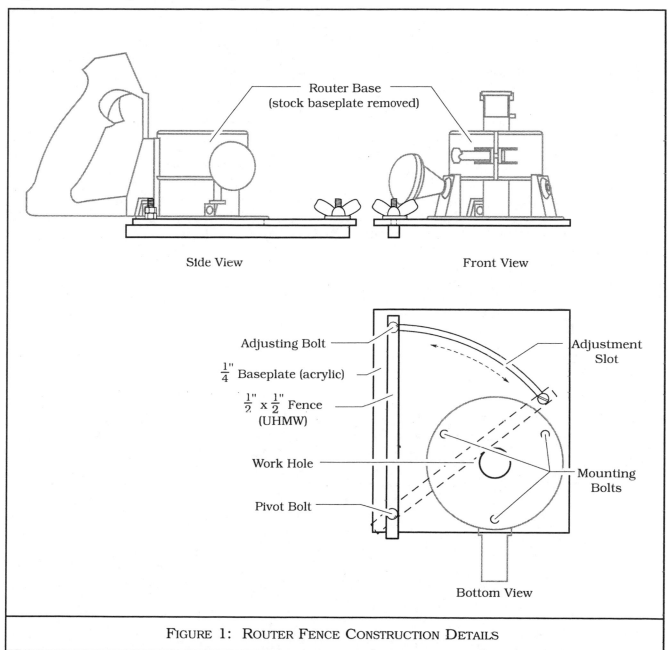

FIGURE 1: ROUTER FENCE CONSTRUCTION DETAILS

MATERIAL CHOICES

The baseplate material we used is probably the best choice: $\frac{1}{4}$" clear acrylic provides excellent work visibility and is thick enough to accept countersinks. The fence material, on the other hand, can be wood, plastic, or metal, as long as the stock is thick enough to take a countersink. We used a $\frac{1}{2}$"-wide strip of $\frac{1}{2}$"-thick UHMW.

CONSTRUCTION AND ASSEMBLY

Obviously, the dimensions and some of the hole-to-hole distances used in building a jig like this depend on the design of a particular router and on personal preference. But, as the construction sequence we followed illustrates, those measurements are not entirely arbitrary.

First we cut a piece of the acrylic into an 8" x $9\frac{1}{4}$" rectangle and used our router's stock baseplate as a template to mark the location of the mounting holes and work hole in one corner of the rectangle. Near the other corner along the 8" side, we marked the location of the pivot bolt hole.

Cutting the fence itself and drilling its two bolt holes was the next step. We made the fence 9" long and drilled its holes $7\frac{3}{4}$" apart — far enough that the wing nut on the adjusting bolt would clear the router's base when the fence pivoted in close to the work hole. That $7\frac{3}{4}$" distance determined the radius of the adjustment slot, whose arc we next scribed into the acrylic with a compass.

With layout now complete, we drilled the various holes in the baseplate, countersank all the bolt holes, and used a saber saw to cut the $\frac{1}{4}$"-wide adjustment slot centered along the arc we had scribed. One end of the slot had to allow the fence to pivot under the work hole, the other had to allow the fence to swing parallel to the baseplate's longer sides.

We attached the fence to the baseplate with $\frac{1}{4}$" flat head bolts, double-nutting the pivot bolt so that it wouldn't vibrate loose and providing a lock washer and wing nut on the adjusting bolt for ease of adjustment. Once we had attached the assembled jig to the router with the router's stock mounting screws, we were ready to go back to work.

FINAL NOTES

So why not just buy the manufacturer's stock fence for one of your routers? This jig has two advantages worth considering. First, other sets of mounting holes can be drilled around the work hole so that this jig can be made to fit many different router models and brands. Second, the jig was fabricated in 30 minutes from salvaged materials — much faster and much cheaper than taking a trip to the store.

Homasote® brickface is often used to simulate realistic brick surfaces on scenery in both regional and educational theater. The tool described in this article dramatically reduces the time and skill required for mass-producing Homasote® brickface.

This splitter has a stationary blade. See Figure 1. The operator inserts a blank into the guide channel and strikes down repeatedly on the ram, forcing the Homasote® blank into the blade until the shearing is complete and the brickfaces fall through the escape hole in the base of the tool. The enforced alignment of the blanks keeps the splitting consistent. The ram's travel is limited in order to prevent contact with the blade. Splitting a blank usually requires two or three strokes. The whole operation is safe, simple, and fast — normal operation can produce over a hundred square feet of brickface per hour.

CONSTRUCTION NOTES

The splitter is constructed mostly of wood. A metal ram might last longer, but the $\frac{1}{2}$" plywood rams of all the models built to date have worked well. The only necessarily metal component is the blade, which may be made of any flat stock or angle iron thick enough to resist deflection.

The blade edge must be double-beveled so that "blank drift" is minimized. Grooving the edge of the ram so that it does not touch the blade will help keep the blade sharp. As Figure 2 illustrates, the guide channel must stop short of the tip of the blade to allow the blanks to spread apart as they are sheared. The sides of the guide channel, which are initially set a little more than $\frac{1}{2}$" apart, have to be be aligned periodically to ensure a consistent splitting path.

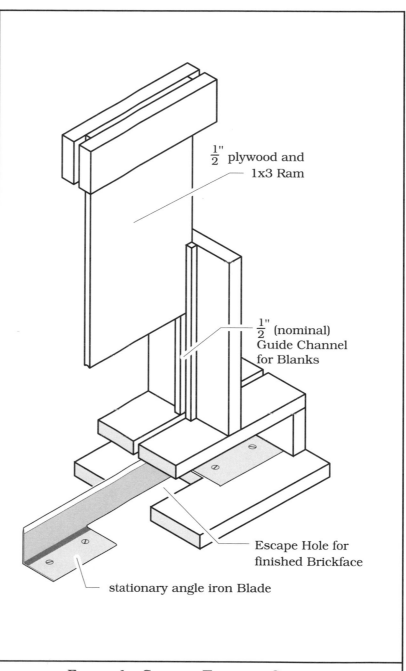

$\frac{1}{2}$" plywood and 1x3 Ram

$\frac{1}{2}$" (nominal) Guide Channel for Blanks

Escape Hole for finished Brickface

stationary angle iron Blade

FIGURE 1: SECTION THROUGH SPLITTER

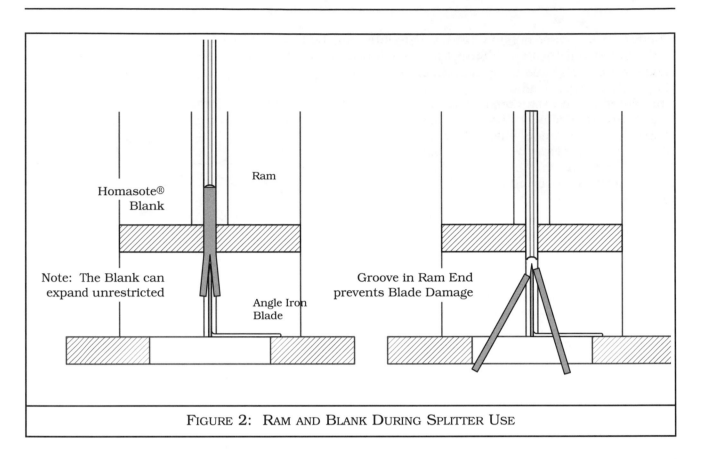

Homasote®
Blank

Ram

Note: The Blank can
expand unrestricted

Angle Iron
Blade

Groove in Ram End
prevents Blade Damage

FIGURE 2: RAM AND BLANK DURING SPLITTER USE

Whether or not we've actually tried it ourselves, most of us know that a carefully guided hot wire can cut blue foam slabs and blocks into elaborate cornices and other architectural details very efficiently. The technique takes so little time and the resulting pieces are so feather-light that some shops have virtually abandoned the much more tedious process of assembling lumber, plywood, and veneer of one sort or another into complex and heavy mouldings. The simply built hot-wire bow described in this article, the descendant of an earlier version developed at the Santa Fe Opera, could be a valuable tool for any scene shop.

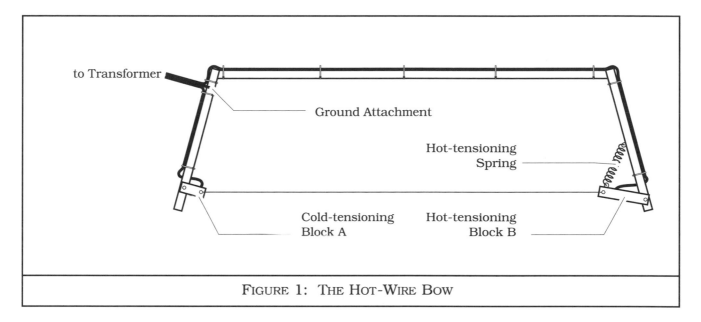

to Transformer

Ground Attachment

Hot-tensioning
Spring

Cold-tensioning
Block A

Hot-tensioning
Block B

FIGURE 1: THE HOT-WIRE BOW

CONSTRUCTION

The bow, pictured in Figure 1, consists of a 1" square tube steel frame, two blocks of $\frac{3}{4}$" plywood, a spring, a length of 22-gauge nichrome wire, and a length of 14-gauge SO cable. The long side of the tube steel frame measures 3'-10" overall, with both ends mitred at 15°. Two 18" lengths of box tube welded to those ends give the frame a rough "C" shape. Other frame sizes are possible, of course, but a bow built to these dimensions can cut foam slabs nearly 4'-0" long.

The plywood blocks attached to the ends of the completed frame with $\frac{1}{4}$" bolts insulate the frame electrically and thermally from the cutting wire and also provide a means for tensioning the wire. During setup, the $1\frac{1}{2}$" x 3" plywood block (Block A in Figure 1) is rotated to tension the wire lightly and then is locked down securely to the frame. The spring and the $1\frac{1}{2}$" x 6" plywood block (Block B) maintain wire tension during the bow's use. Two washers between the frame and block B allow it to pivot fairly easily. No washers are used between the frame and block A. The spring is attached to both the frame and block B by means of eye bolts.

The nichrome wire, chosen because it heats more evenly than other types of wire, is tightly wrapped around 1"-long $\frac{1}{4}$" bolts and then bolted securely to the free ends of the plywood blocks. Each end of the wire is then attached to one of the leads of the SO cable. The bow is run from a step-down transformer that is itself plugged into an autotransformer. The step-down transformer performs the essential safety function of isolating the exposed nichrome wire from ground, while the auto-transformer allows the power sent to the wire to be varied. Any 120-volt AC-primary transformer that will supply 15 amps or more at 12 to 24 volts at the secondary will work as the step-down. (One surplus transformer dealer, C&H Sales Co., Pasadena, CA, 1-800-325-9456, sells several different ones for around $40 each.) The SO cable's ground wire is screwed or bolted directly to the bow's tube steel frame and attached to the grounding pin of the plug powering the autotransformer. See the schematic in Figure 2.

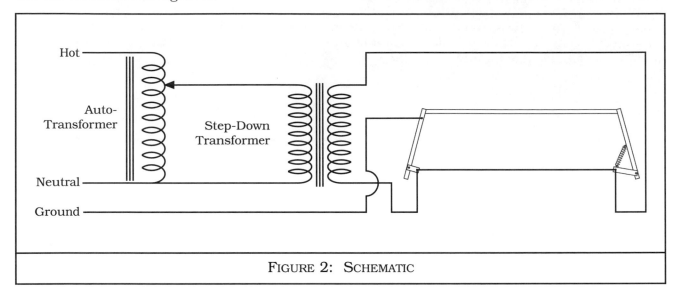

FIGURE 2: SCHEMATIC

OPTIONS FOR USE

This bow can, with practice and patience, be hand-held and used to sculpt shapes from blocks of foam. More commonly it can be mounted vertically and used like a band saw or scroll saw, or it can be mounted horizontally and used to slice a thick slab of foam into thinner slabs or to plane a slab down to a desired thickness. Used in combination with shop-built guides or jigs, it can quickly turn out identical lengths of cornice or other moulding, ready for covering and painting.

SAFETY AND HEALTH CAUTIONS

Despite the electrical isolation provided, under no circumstances should anyone touch the nichrome wire, and the bow should be unplugged except when actually being used. Further, since the wire is so exposed, it is quite susceptible to breakage and replacement. Users must be doubly careful — before each use and periodically during each use — to check the circuit for continuity and to make sure that all connections are secure and protected from mechanical damage. Users must also take care to avoid contact with the hot wire itself and to warn others to keep away. And, finally, using any heat source to shape foams produces a number of noxious gases, including potentially deadly isocyanates. Consequently, use of this bow requires that the work station and adjacent areas be appropriately ventilated, that all workers wear respirators fitted with the proper filters, and that frequent work breaks be scheduled and taken to limit exposure to harmful chemicals.

❧❧❧❧

Cutting sizable holes in plywood may be easy, but cutting them in plate steel is certainly not. And while this is not a common problem in the entertainment industry, there are times when we need to cut circles in steel. For example, we may need to allow access to caster locks through a hole in a steel caster plate, or to make steel mounting plates for zero-throw casters. The oxyacetylene torch is the only appropriate tool for such purposes, but using it to freehand regular, accurately sized holes is a skill few scene shop carpenters have. The compass-like torch guide described here can help.

I learned about this tool from Frederick W. ("Call me Fred") McAllaster, who loaned it to me to speed the job of cutting access holes in the caster plates of some heavy-duty Santa Fe Opera wagons. Fred had seen his father use one while working on the family farm in Kansas. A fancier version of the same device can be purchased at welding shops for around $100, but the one described here costs about $5.00 and takes only an hour or so to build.

PARTS

Figure 1 illustrates all of the tool's parts. Though many of the design details can be modified to suit individual preferences, the choices indicated by the illustration were deliberate, and a few points are worth mentioning:

1. A $\frac{1}{2}$" hex nut is just the right size for a torch tip.

2. At 18", the rod is just about as long as a torch's body — long enough to be held easily and short enough not to get in the way. See Figure 2.

3. The $\frac{1}{2}$" rod sleeves reasonably snugly into $\frac{1}{2}$" schedule 40 black pipe.

4. Mounting the thumbscrew on the sleeve's side makes it accessible and yet keeps it out of the way.

NOTES ON CONSTRUCTION

Most of the construction steps are simple: welding the nut to the end of the rod is no problem; and drilling and tapping the pipe for the thumbscrew and the center offers no real challenge either. But grinding the end of a $\frac{1}{4}$" bolt into a good point can be tricky, especially if you first cut the bolt to length and attach it to the pipe as I did in making the guide shown in the photos. I had thought that once I had screwed and tack-welded the bolt into the pipe I could use the pipe as a handle during

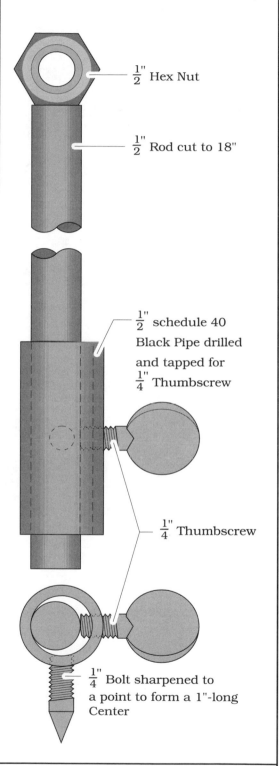

$\frac{1}{2}$" Hex Nut

$\frac{1}{2}$" Rod cut to 18"

$\frac{1}{2}$" schedule 40 Black Pipe drilled and tapped for $\frac{1}{4}$" Thumbscrew

$\frac{1}{4}$" Thumbscrew

$\frac{1}{4}$" Bolt sharpened to a point to form a 1"-long Center

FIGURE 1: TORCH-GUIDE PARTS TOP AND END VIEWS

FIGURE 2: GRIPPING THE GUIDE ROD

FIGURE 3: GUIDING THE CUT

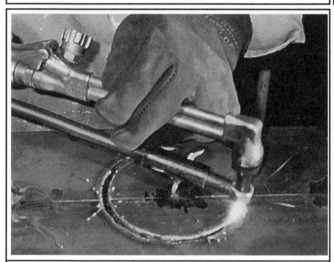

FIGURE 4: THE NEAR-FINISHED CUT

grinding; but the bolt was so short that the pipe got in the way of the bench grinder's stone. Pointing the end of a much longer bolt first and then cutting it off and touching up the threads with a die if necessary before attaching it to the pipe might be easier.

USE

Once you have punched or drilled the center of the circle you are about to torch, cutting a circle is not much different from making any other torch cut. The only difference is that the torch hand also grips the guide's rod (as in Figure 2) and the other hand bears down gently on the torch (as in Figures 3 and 4) so that the guide stays properly centered.

ૐૐૐ

Using a tuffet, a combination creeper and stool, is more comfortable than squatting or sitting on the floor for low work. The Seattle Repertory Theatre's shop developed the style described here, which uses a zero-throw caster to facilitate movement.

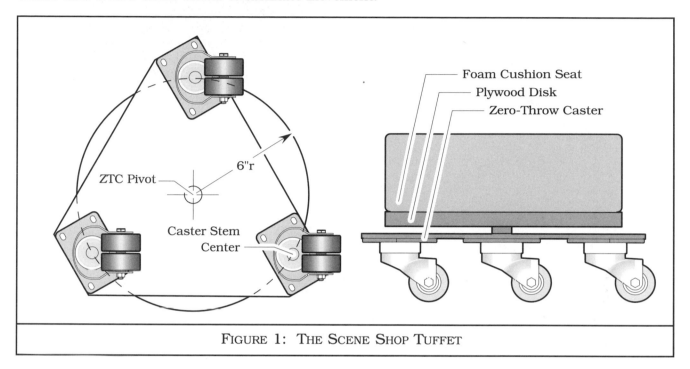

FIGURE 1: THE SCENE SHOP TUFFET

Normal swivel casters would cause the stool to lurch when changing direction. For a person sitting so low, these lurches are difficult to control. A Zero Throw Caster (ZTC) like the three-caster model shown here eliminates any lurch. Any size swivel casters can be used for a ZTC, but for stability the caster stems should be aligned with the edge of the seat as shown in Figure 1. For the cushion, upholster a foam pad at least four inches thick to a one-foot-diameter plywood disk. Finally, attach the cushioned plywood disk to the ZTC.

Things to keep in mind when designing and building your tuffet.

1. It can be used for moving materials or buckets that you need to keep near at hand.
2. Different fabrics could be used in upholstering to create tuffet individuality.
3. A backrest would not allow approaching or sitting from all directions.

As Steve "Lars" Klein notes, scene shop tuffets have been of great use in general shop operations at Seattle Repertory Theatre and are widely embraced by our artisans. However, we are concerned to note that Mr. Klein has (inadvertently?) used an older and highly unstable tuffet design. The three-wheel design indicated is not recommended for the type of rigorous stress and variable dynamic load configurations found in Tuffet Ball. We have found through extensive field testing that when employed in a standard Tuffet sprint, the rotation of the two lead casters will bring their axles into parallel alignment within inches of the center of the Tuffet. This will almost guarantee a spill for the rider — or for the 5-gallon bucket of unsorted stage hardware.

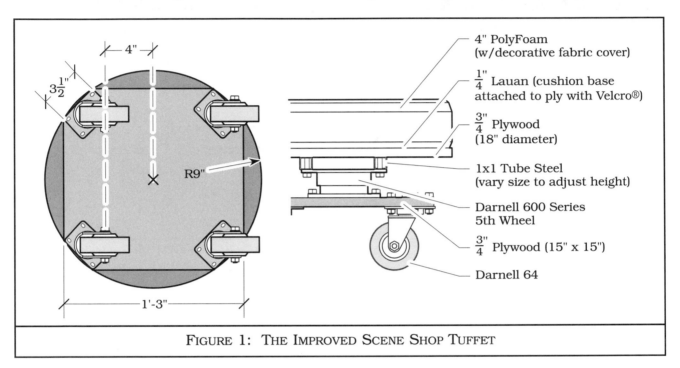

FIGURE 1: THE IMPROVED SCENE SHOP TUFFET

We urge you to abandon the three-wheel Scene Shop Tuffet Design. I have included here our most recent Tuffet design. While still susceptible to the dreaded Norbert Herriges "dismount-maneuver," it is fast, responsive, and stable.

Things to keep in mind:

1. Tuffet research by the SRT scene shop; Tuffet engineering and drafting by T. Furr; Tuffet construction by the SRT scene shop; Tuffet maintenance by M. Boulanger.
2. Tuffet text by M. Immerwahr.
3. Inspirational Tuffetry by the SRT prop and paint shops.
4. Inspirational Tuffet playing by M. Gustafson and J. Law.

A gauge design developed at the American Repertory Theatre offers an efficient method for measuring and marking standard steel shapes. The tool comprises two 6" lengths of angle iron, one $\frac{3}{4}$" x $\frac{3}{4}$" and the other 1" x 1", arranged in a pinwheel configuration. See Figure 1. These pieces overlap along their exterior faces by $\frac{1}{2}$". Spot welds on each end hold the gauge together. In its various orientations, this gauge provides measures of $\frac{1}{4}$", $\frac{1}{2}$", $\frac{3}{4}$", or 1", making it particularly useful for marking much of the tube steel, angle, and bar stock used in theatrical construction. This particular gauge is, of course, only a suggestion; different sizes of angle iron can be arranged to yield whatever measurements are required by a project. For quick and reliable measurement, one need only choose the appropriate side of the gauge and pass a scribe along its edge. See Figure 2.

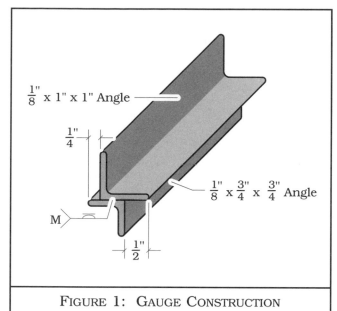

FIGURE 1: GAUGE CONSTRUCTION

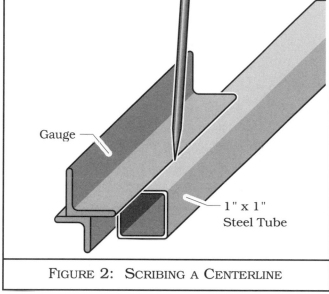

FIGURE 2: SCRIBING A CENTERLINE

Use of this gauge can noticeably speed construction, but the tool's real benefit is its ability to establish regularity among pieces marked by several different people. For this reason, each shop's set of gauges must be made in an identical fashion. At the American Repertory Theatre, the staff used a piece of $\frac{1}{4}$" x 1" bar stock to align the gauge's pieces for the $\frac{1}{4}$" measurement; the components were then clamped in place and welded together. The gauges were spray painted a bright color to prevent them from being thrown away, and each face was labeled so that the tool could be turned like an architect's scale rule to find the proper side quickly. Although any gauge is only as accurate as the procedures used for its initial construction, using this tool as a steel shop's measuring standard will ensure consistency among the many parts of a scenic element.

꒰꒱꒰꒱꒰

For the Boston University School for Theater Arts' production of *The House of Bernarda Alba*, the set design was very simple — principally a large, elliptical raked deck. The ellipse's major and minor axes measured 32'-0" and 26'-0", respectively. The major axis sat at a 30° angle to the stage centerline, but the slope of the rake was parallel to the centerline. To speed up load-in, I decided to build the deck of as many 4x8 platforms as possible that could be installed parallel to the centerline. The most straightforward construction approach was to lay out and cut the $\frac{3}{4}$" plywood skins and then frame the platforms. Still, cutting an ellipse of that size was a challenge.

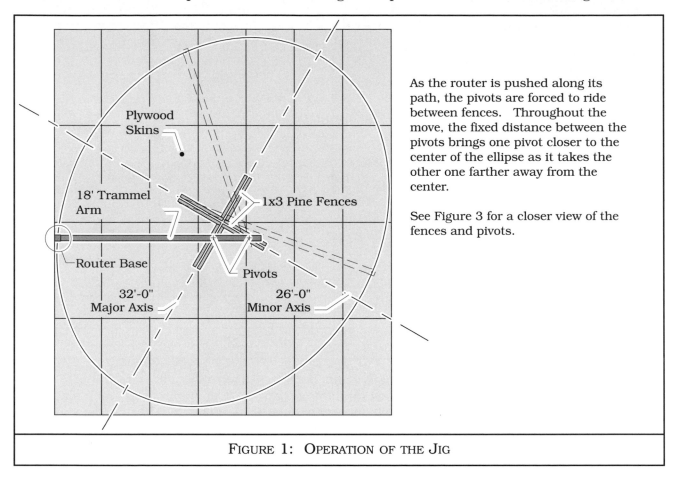

As the router is pushed along its path, the pivots are forced to ride between fences. Throughout the move, the fixed distance between the pivots brings one pivot closer to the center of the ellipse as it takes the other one farther away from the center.

See Figure 3 for a closer view of the fences and pivots.

FIGURE 1: OPERATION OF THE JIG

Given the tight schedule and the relative inexperience of the staff, the likelihood of cutting a clean ellipse with a saber saw seemed unlikely. Using a line anchored at the ellipse's foci to guide a router seemed no less promising — even aircraft cable stretches. The likeliest approach involved mounting a router on a two-pivot trammel arm. I had seen a jig like this used successfully to cut elliptical sweeps for moulding, and though that ellipse had been much smaller (its major axis measured only about 6'-0") the approach had worked well. Figure 1 illustrates the jig's operating principles.

Figure 2 details the construction of the trammel arm we built, essentially a nominal 1x6 and 1x3 hogs' trough with a $\frac{3}{4}$" plywood router base attached to one end and two pivot blocks bolted near the other end, still able to pivot. For our purposes, a 16'-long 1x6 was just barely long enough since the distance between the inside cutting edge of the router bit and the center of the further pivot must be equal to one-half the length of the major axis: 32'-0" ÷ 2 = 16'-0". So that we could leave 1'-0" between the further bolt hole and the end of the 1x6, we oversized the long dimension of the plywood router base by 1'-0".

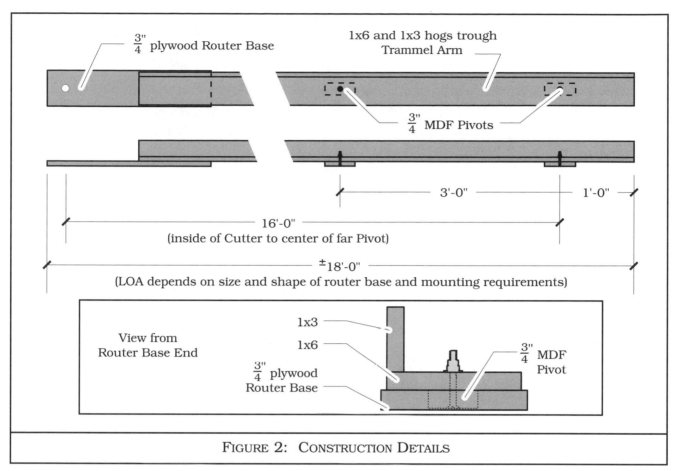

FIGURE 2: CONSTRUCTION DETAILS

The pivots were 2" x 5" rectangular blocks of $\frac{3}{4}$" Medite® (MDF), and the distance between them was set according to the formula "distance equals one half the length of the major axis minus one-half the length of the minor axis": (32'-0" ÷ 2) minus (26'-0" ÷ 2) = 3'-0". Math located the pivots' bolt holes at 13'-0" and 16'-0" from the inside of the cutting edge of the straight-flute plunge router bit.

With the trammel-arm built, we laid out 28 sheets of $\frac{3}{4}$" plywood in a 32'-0" x 28'-0" rectangle. We then laid the axes in with a chalk line and screwed 4'-long nominal 1x3 pine fences to the plywood as in Figure 3, leaving a 2"-wide track and a little extra space between them so that the MDF pivots would slide easily.

Operation of the jig required three people: one person spotting each pivot point as it rode in between the fences, and one person operating the router. On our first pass, we learned that the pivots needed to ride more snugly between the fences than we had thought: the first pass with the router left a 1" variance between the start and end of the cut. By bringing the fences closer together and then coating them with butchers wax to counter the friction, we reduced our initial variance by half.

Although this jig seemed somewhat cumbersome at times, it was inexpensive, took little time to build, and, for a one-time use, served its intended purpose quite well.

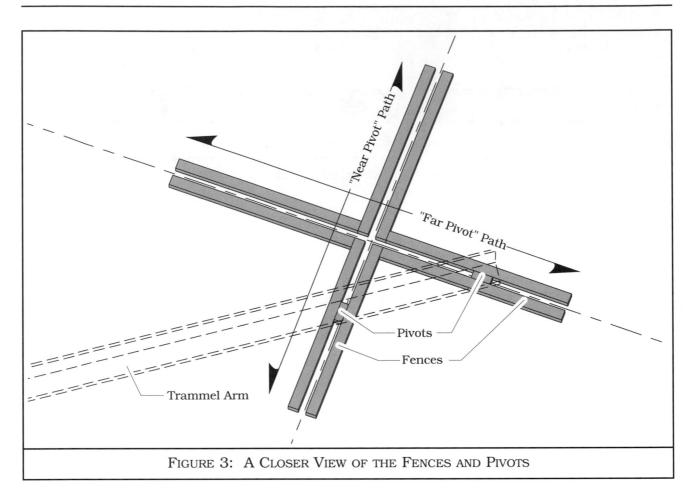

FIGURE 3: A CLOSER VIEW OF THE FENCES AND PIVOTS

TECHNICAL BRIEF

Sound

How to Use Your Headset as a Page Mic

Darren Clark

This article describes a simple adapter box that allows an intercom headset with a dynamic mic to function additionally as a page mic. With the adaptation, a Stage Manager can make backstage and in-house pages without having to pick up a second microphone.

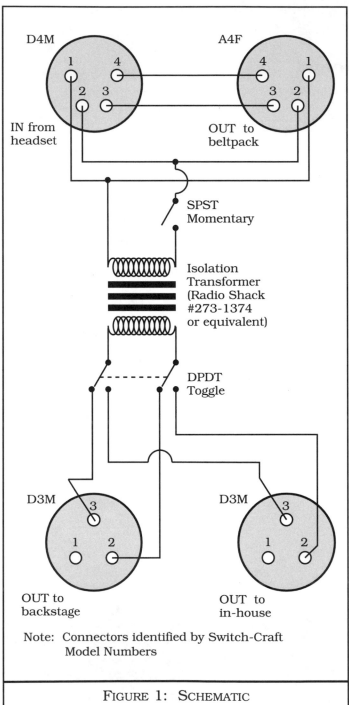

FIGURE 1: SCHEMATIC

The device acts somewhat like a direct box in an orchestra pit. The mic signal from the headset is split and then fed to both the intercom beltpack and (through a balancing transformer) to any external amplifier with microphone inputs.

CONSTRUCTION

Any small metal project box can be used as an adapter enclosure. On one end of the box, drill holes for and mount the two D3M connectors that will serve as outputs to your page system. On the opposite end of the box, drill holes for and mount the D4M and install strain relief for a short cable tail between the adapter and your beltpack. Install the two switches.

Mount the transformer in the box. Solder a 12" piece of cable to the A4M connector. Wire the connectors, switch, and transformer as shown in the schematic.

USE

The headset plugs into the D4M connector, and the tail with the A4F connector plugs into the beltpack. Normal beltpack to base station connections must be made. Mic cables are then used to attach the two D3M connectors to your page system. The output can be connected to any low-impedance mic input on a page system.

The toggle switch is used to select backstage or in-house paging. The momentary switch is used as a push-to-talk (page) button.

With this device, all standard headset functions are normal. When you want to make a page, you select in-house or backstage and push the momentary switch.

The audio equipment in theaters offers enough inputs and outputs to accommodate most production needs. Occasionally, however, it may be necessary to feed an amplified output into a line-level input. The simple solution described here is within the resources of most production organizations.

The amplified-to-line signal circuit illustrated below uses a resistor and an audio transformer to convert the low-impedance, high-current output of the amplified signal to the low-impedance, low-current signal required by a line-level input. A switched, passthrough ground is included to help eliminate ground loops. Connectors and their wiring are matched to the hardware and polarity of existing equipment.

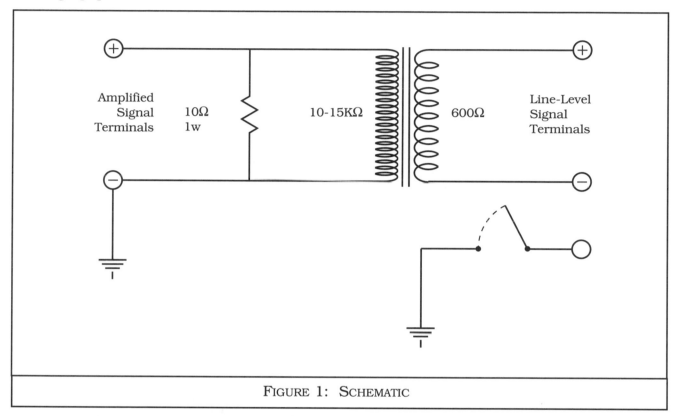

FIGURE 1: SCHEMATIC

The resistor, rated for 10 ohms at 1 watt, is connected in parallel to the amplifier's output terminals. If the output of the amplifier cannot be limited to 1 watt or less, a resistor with a larger power capacity must be used. The audio transformer is also connected in parallel to the output terminals. The transformer must be capable of handling the full audio frequency range without distortion. Appropriate transformers cost $20 to $50 and are available from Newark Electronics and similar suppliers.

The converter's operating principle is quite straightforward. The 10-ohm resistor loads the amplifier to keep it operating normally. The transformer performs electrical isolation and reduces the amplifier's output voltage to a level usable as a line-level input signal for semi-professional equipment.

While not required frequently, this particular amplified-to-line converter provides an inexpensive solution to what might otherwise become a show-stopping problem.

❧❧❧

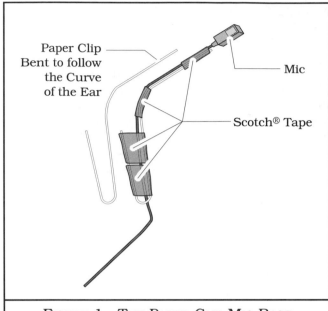

Paper Clip Bent to follow the Curve of the Ear

Mic

Scotch® Tape

FIGURE 1: THE PAPER-CLIP MIC BASE

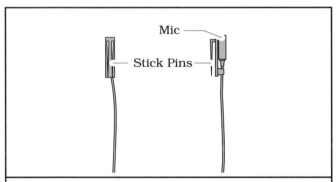

Mic

Stick Pins

FIGURE 2: A MIC AND VIPER CLAW HEADBAND ATTACHMENT

Sound designers and engineers are often plagued by the problem of securing wireless body microphones to a performer's head, which is important for providing consistent sound pickup. You can hide most body mics fairly well in the hair of the performer. But simply attaching mics to the hair by using bobby pins often provides too little stability. The microphones frequently fall out of the hair or twist the wrong way, resulting in poor pickup for directional microphones.

One good solution to the problem involves providing a larger base for bobby pins to attach to. As Figure 1 illustrates, an ordinary paper clip partly unfolded and molded to fit around the performer's ear creates a stable base for bobby pins. Taping the mic wire securely to a bent paper clip in this manner also helps improve pickup by keeping the microphone from twisting.

A different approach is particularly useful with short or particularly fine hair. Most body microphones come with the kind of viper-claw accessory shown in Figure 2, a plastic microphone holder backed with two stick pins. A mic and its viper claw can be easily pinned to a headband made of a piece of the clear elastic (found in most costume shops), as long as you're careful not to tear the elastic. You can further secure the viper claw by taping it to the headband with Scotch® tape or clear Band-Aids®. The microphone will be well hidden if worn on the side of the head, just above the ear.

Maintaining the same polarity among several speakers is absolutely critical to the successful performance of large-scale public address systems, musical reinforcement systems, page/monitor systems, and the like. The circuit described in Figure 1 provides a reference signal to the input of a sound system, and the circuit described in Figure 3 decodes that signal as it comes from a speaker, indicating whether polarity through the system has been maintained or reversed. Commercial devices cost upwards of $350, but this device can be built for around $30.

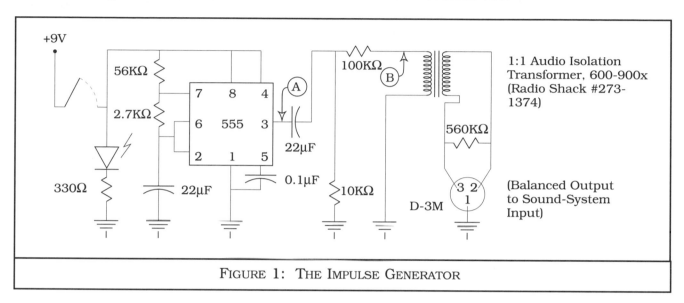

FIGURE 1: THE IMPULSE GENERATOR

The impulse generator's 555 timer chip generates positive and negative impulses of a known time relationship. Connected to the sound system input, this circuit produces recognizable excursions and incursions at a speaker's cone. The impulse decoder uses an electret mic positioned in front of the speaker to detect those excursions and incursions. The succession of positive and negative pressures is translated into digital pulses, revealing whether an excursion or an incursion happened first. If polarity is maintained, the green LED lights up; otherwise, the red LED lights up.

Each circuit is powered by a 9-volt battery and a power-supply circuit like that shown in Figure 2. Both circuits and their power supplies can be mounted in small project boxes for portability.

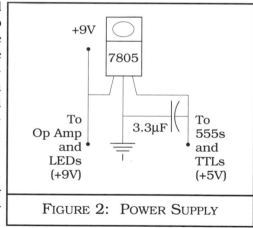

FIGURE 2: POWER SUPPLY

Figure 4 presents a comparison of waveforms obtained at the points A through I in Figures 1 and 3 when system polarity is correct. If polarity is reversed, waveform C would be inverted, and D, F, and H would switch with E, G, and I.

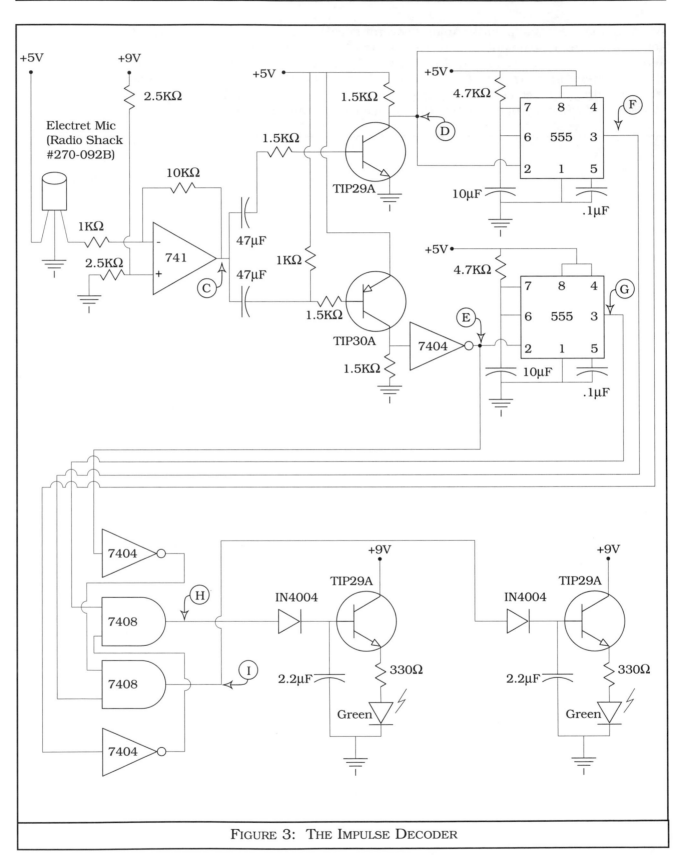

FIGURE 3: THE IMPULSE DECODER

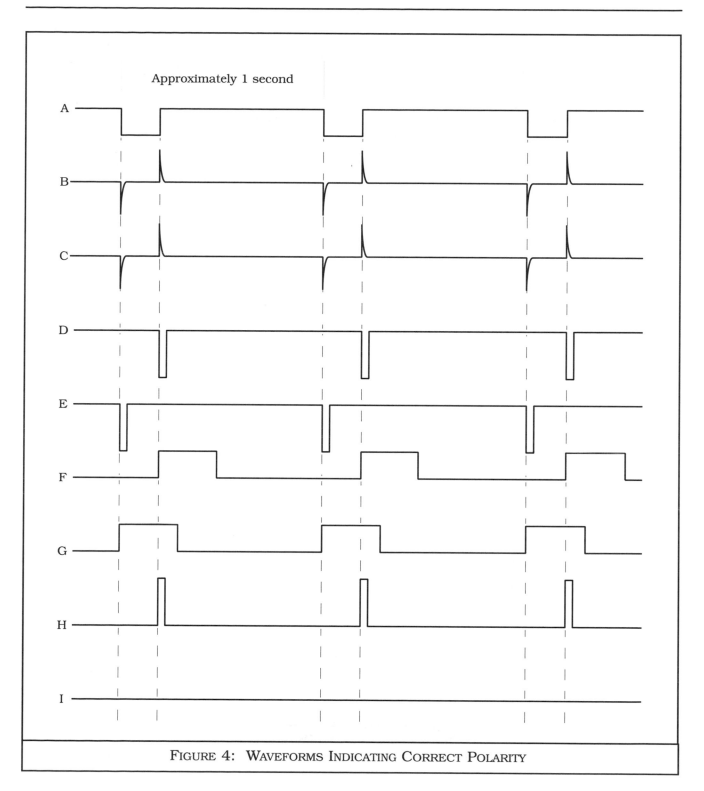

FIGURE 4: WAVEFORMS INDICATING CORRECT POLARITY

The sound quality of an inexpensive cassette tape player was a key element in a production of *Antigone in New York* at the Yale Repertory Theatre. Wanting to make a prop tape player sound as realistic as possible without sacrificing cueing or volume control, Sound Designer Kevin Hodgson came up with the idea of putting a wireless receiver in the tape player that the actors would use and transmitting a signal to it from the sound board. The wireless unit we found, the NADY 151 VR, is primarily used as a remote sound pickup for video camcorders. The NADY package contains two parts: a radio transmitter with a small lavalier mic, and a receiver with both line-level and headphone output jacks. I added some parts to make the transmitter take a balanced line input, and built an amplifier to boost the signal from the receiver and send it to the speaker. With advice from electronics specialist Alan Hendrickson, I designed the circuits described below.

PARTS

NADY 151 VR Wireless
    Camcorder Microphone System
Tape player with an 8Ω speaker
Sescom MI 109
    5kΩ to 600Ω Audio Transformer
3-pin XLR connector
LM386 N-4 Op-Amp
Potentiometer - 10kΩ
Resistors - 1 @ 10Ω, 3 @ 560Ω, 1 @ 56Ω

Capacitors - 1 @ 250µF, 1 @ .5µF, 1@ 22µF,
    2 @ 1µF
On/off switch
Three 9v batteries, one battery terminal
LED
22AWG wire
Two small circuit boards
Mounting screws
One project box

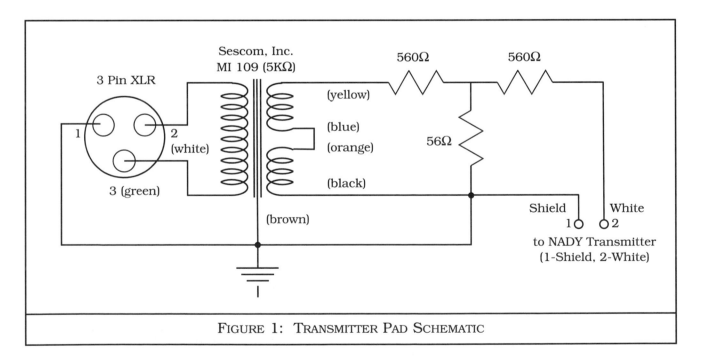

FIGURE 1: TRANSMITTER PAD SCHEMATIC

NOTES ON THE TRANSMITTER

Figure 1 shows the circuit that steps down from line level to mic level. The transformer isolates a balanced line-level signal from the unbalanced output, and the resistors form a T-pad which attenuates line level to mic level.

The NADY's lavalier mic is not used in this application and needs to be cut off. But since the mic cable doubles as the transmitter's antenna, make the cut as close as possible to the mic. To get the greatest clarity of signal, place the transmitter near the stage to cut down on signal interference, and let the input/antenna wire between the transmitter pad and the transmitter itself extend as far as possible. Send a balanced signal to the pad's XLR.

NOTES ON THE RECEIVER

The NADY receiver's output appears at both a line-out jack and a headphone jack. I found that using the headphone jack worked better than using the line-out jack. A single 9v battery powers the one-watt op-amp I added to the receiver to drive the tape player's speaker.

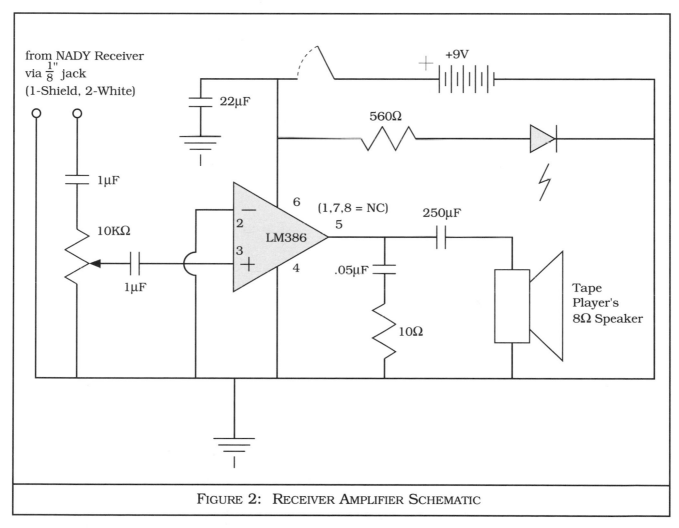

FIGURE 2: RECEIVER AMPLIFIER SCHEMATIC

Trial and error determined the size of the capacitors between the signal input and the 10KΩ potentiometer. These capacitors maximize the strength of the input signal before clipping. I used the 8-pin DIP socket to protect the op-amp from the heat of soldering.

It took me some time to replace the tape player's parts with the new circuitry, and each tape player is different, so you may have more or less room than I did. Constructing your parts efficiently will save you headaches. In the same vein, screw down all the loose parts and pad the receiver circuit well. As careful as we all can be, the tape player will almost certainly get knocked off a counter at some point in its life. Oh, yes, and be sure to hide the kill switch inside the tape player so that actors won't accidentally turn it off during the show.

MISCELLANEOUS NOTES

Sound quality depends partly on speaker quality, of course. We found that the CDs we needed to use sounded too good, so we purposely drove the tape player's speaker a little hot to get an acceptably tinny sound. Volume was maximized using three controls: the 10KΩ potentiometer, the output volume on the receiver, and the input signal on the board. Maximizing the tape player's gain while using the fader on the board to adjust levels was the most practical way of keeping the volume consistent.

The indicator LED is useful — especially during techs — because it shows when the op-amp's battery is running low. The 9V battery will not last more than six hours in continuous operation, and its strength affects the cassette's volume. We replaced all the batteries before each performance to guarantee the same volume every night. A rechargeable battery pack for the op-amp would be a cost saver for a long-running show, but if you choose not to use one be sure to put your power supply in an easily accessible area, since someone will have to change batteries every day.

The total cost of this device depends on what you have in stock. The tape player can be in any condition as long as the director likes it and its speaker works. The 9 volt batteries cost a dollar apiece, and except for the NADY camcorder microphone system, everything else costs around $20.00 all told. The NADY, though, costs about $150.

ea·ea·ea

Few discoveries are more frustrating than discovering that the long cable you just finished snaking through cramped, dirty quarters does not work. Many technicians learn this lesson the hard way; the smart ones make sure it doesn't happen twice. Though testing each conductor in a cable is tedious and time-consuming, checking and maintaining a cable inventory saves time in the long run.

Commercially available XLR cable testers aren't expensive: Markertek sells one for about $40. On the other hand, building a tester isn't all that difficult or time-consuming. The parts used in the unit described here are readily available and can be assembled in a few hours.

The tester, shown in Figure 1, checks 3-pin XLR cables for continuity. The numbers beside the rotary switches represent the cable's pins. If a cable is good (and the tester is working), the lamp lights when and only when both switches are set to the same pin number. If the lamp doesn't light (and the tester is working), then the circuit between the selected pins is broken. If the lamp lights when the switches are set to different numbers, then there is a short between the pins involved.

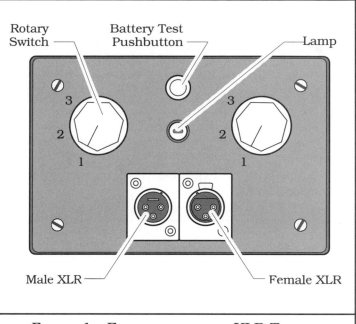

FIGURE 1: FACEPLATE OF THE XLR TESTER

PARTS LIST

The middle column in the list below represents part numbers. "RS" means "Radio Shack" and "SC" means "Switchcraft."

1 small 6-volt lamp (an E-5, for instance)	RS 272-1142	$1.19 pkg/2
1 mountable lamp holder	RS 272-340	$1.99 pkg/2
2 single-pole, three-position rotary switches	RS 275-1386	$1.69 each
2 knobs for the switches	RS 272-407	$1.39 pkg/2
1 momentary-on pushbutton (for Battery Test)	RS 275-609	$2.79 pkg/2
1 battery holder for 4 AA batteries	RS 270-383	$1.39 each
4 AA batteries		$5.00 pkg/4
1 panel-mount female XLR connector	SC d3f	$4.29 each
1 panel-mount male XLR connector	SC d3m	$4.29 each
1 project box (3" x 6") with a metal faceplate	RS 270-627	$2.79 each

FACEPLATE DESIGN AND ASSEMBLY NOTES

Lay out the faceplate design with user convenience in mind. The layout shown in Figure 1 is a good model, for a cable being tested is not likely to foul on the lamp or get in the way of the rotary switches.

Once the faceplate layout is set, drill or punch the necessary mounting holes: $\frac{5}{16}$"-diameter holes for the lamp holder and the rotary switches; a $\frac{1}{2}$"-diameter hole for the pushbutton; and one $\frac{3}{4}$"-diameter hole and two $\frac{1}{8}$"-diameter holes for the XLR connectors.

During assembly, orient the rotary switches logically. If the clockwise-most position on one switch selects pin 3, for instance, then the clockwise-most position on the other switch should also select pin 3. If one switch's position 3 is "at 10 o'clock," the other switch's position 3 should be "at 10 o'clock" as well. Label the position numbers on the faceplate.

CIRCUITRY

The main circuit is shown at the left in Figure 2. To build it, solder a lead from the battery holder to the common pole of one rotary switch. To that switch's three selectable poles, solder leads long enough to reach the female XLR connector, using different colored leads to distinguish the poles from one another. Then solder the lead from switch pole 1 to the female connector's pin 1, the lead from pole 2 to pin 2, and the lead from pole 3 to pin 3. The rest of the main circuit is only slightly different. Solder the second lead from the battery holder to one pole of the lamp holder. To the lamp holder's second pole, solder a lead to the common pole of the second rotary switch. Solder color-coded leads from the three selectable poles of this switch to the male XLR. The battery-lamp test circuit shown at the right in Figure 2 simply joins a momentary-on pushbutton to the tester's battery and lamp.

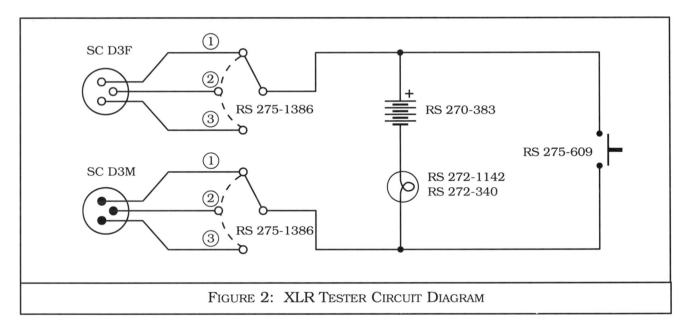

FIGURE 2: XLR TESTER CIRCUIT DIAGRAM

CHECKOUT AND USE

Install the lamp and batteries. Test your work by shorting between the corresponding pins of the XLR connectors. Make sure that the lamp lights when pin 1 of the male XLR is shorted to pin 1 of the female XLR, when pin 2 is shorted to pin 2, and when pin 3 is shorted to pin 3. After the checkout, install the parts in the box and screw the faceplate on.

Testing a 3-pin XLR cable involves checking 9 combinations of rotary switch settings. First, make sure the tester's batteries and lamp are working. Then, after plugging a cable into the tester, set one of the rotary switches to position 1. Rotate the other switch through each of its positions. The lamp should light when the second switch is set to position 1, and it should not light when the second switch is rotated to position 2 or position 3.

Once you've checked each of these possibilities, set the first switch to position 2 and again rotate the second switch through its three positions. This time around, the lamp should light only when the second switch rotates to position 2. After you've finished testing pin 2, set the first switch to position 3 and repeat the tests a third time.

ADD-ON POSSIBILITIES

This design can easily be altered to accommodate various connectors. Simply install the appropriate connector in place of (or in addition to) the XLR jacks. If the connectors you want to test have more than three pins, of course, you'll need to "upgrade" your rotary switches. For example, to test a 5-pin control cable you'd need to replace the 3-position rotary switches with single-pole 5-position switches.

ᒪᒪᒪ

For sound designers with modest computer-based digital audio setups, digital noise reduction requires an expensive investment in high-end software from companies such as Digidesign. However, anyone who has internet access can achieve quality noise reduction (removal of tape hiss, hum, etc.) using inexpensive shareware. One such program is SoundHack®, a Macintosh application written by Tom Erbe, faculty member at Cal Arts. SoundHack® performs a spectral analysis of an input file and resynthesizes elements of that file as an output file based on user-defined variables. In eliminating tape hiss, for example, SoundHack® identifies spectral components below a certain threshold and excludes them during resynthesis. This technique works well for removing any noise which is fairly constant and not too loud.

To practice using SoundHack®, you will need a soundfile with some audible tape hiss. For your first experiments, choose a fairly percussive track which has pronounced staccato transients between quieter sections of hiss. First, use your editing software to create a separate short sample of the background noise you wish to remove. This sample should be a second or two long clip between notes or phrases. If your original soundfile is longer than five seconds, you will also want to copy a short section to experiment with before working with the entire soundfile. SoundHack® has many user-defined variables with which you will have to experiment to get good results.

Next, launch SoundHack® and open the soundfile you want to process. Type <command+D> to bring up the Spectral Dynamics Dialog Box, shown in Figure 1. Use the settings shown as a start-

The first pop-up dialog box selects the type of spectral dynamic process: Gate, Expander, Compressor. "Bands" sets the number of filter bands the audio file will be divided into. Select a lowest band of zero and a highest band equal to the number of bands set. "Gain/Reduction (dB)" determines the decibel gain/reduction for the bands above/below the threshold identified in "Affect Sounds: Below Thresh./Above Thresh." The next box "Thresh. Above File (B)" sets the threshold in decibels relative to the trigger soundfile threshold.

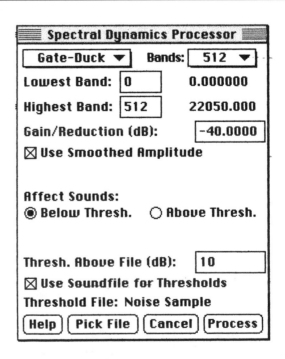

FIGURE 1: SoundHack® Dialog Box Options

ing point. Click on the PICK FILE button and select the short noise sample you saved earlier as the reference or "trigger" for your original sound "input." When you click PROCESS, SoundHack® creates a spectral analysis of the input file, performs a spectral gate based on the trigger file, and builds a new output file. In this non-destructive process, the original remains unchanged.

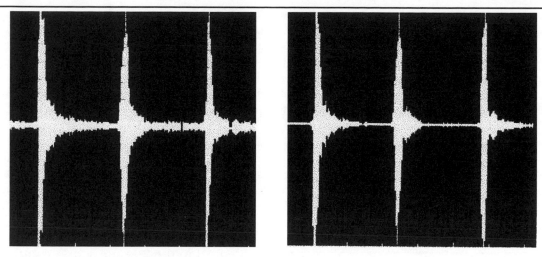

The original file (left) shows the noise sample selection. The soundfile is approximately one second long. The tall spikes represent desirable sound. The horizontal base line represents the time between desirable sound. The thicker the horizontal line, the noisier the file. Note the significantly thinner line in the "after" sample.

FIGURE 2: BEFORE AND AFTER

Getting the best results takes practice and requires experimentation with different settings. For example, you'll find that using fewer bands (8, 16, 32, 64) works well for cleaning up soundfiles with fast transients such as drums, and using a higher number of bands (>512) works well with the legato sounds of strings or speech. You'll also find that while raising the "Thresh. Above File" value improves noise reduction, it also affects the sound you want to keep.

SoundHack® is certainly a useful addition to the sound designer's toolkit.

❧❧❧❧

The sound design I created for the Yale School of Drama's Experimental Theatre production of *The Tempest* consisted of two beds of sound that I wanted to play almost continuously for more than 2 hours. I wanted to be able to fade component sounds in or out within these beds as needed, so that, for example, during a marsh cue, the sound of buzzing insects could become temporarily more prominent. I also wanted the changes between the beds of sound to be smooth, and I wanted to be able to do some relatively sophisticated speaker reassignments on the fly. But the available playback system didn't even have a matrixed sound board. How could I get the control I needed?

I have always admired the intuitive arrangement of the 2-scene preset lighting control board. What if I could handle my sound a little like light? Running sound through a controller styled after a light board would mean that the volume levels, the equalization, and the speaker assignments of the upcoming cue could be preset, waiting to be crossfaded in, while the volume levels of the current cue could be adjusted even during playback. The 2-scene sound controller is what I came up with. It is configured out of a standard sound board and a readily available multi-track disk recorder.

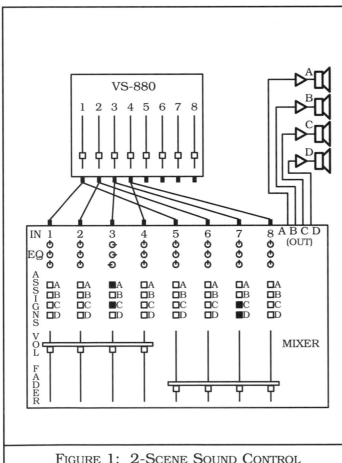

FIGURE 1: 2-SCENE SOUND CONTROL

Central to the 2-scene sound controller is the Roland VS-880 Virtual Studio or its equivalent. The VS-880 is a small ($17\frac{1}{8}$" wide x $12\frac{1}{2}$" deep x $3\frac{1}{2}$" high 8-lb 14-oz) digital disk recorder with, among many other features, 8 tracks of sound available for playback, volume level controls for each track, and the output of each track assignable to any of 4 outputs. If 8 tracks and 4 outputs make you think of the number 2, you are getting the idea, because, by organizing the sound on the VS-880, it is possible to make it function as though it were 2 synchronized 4-track recorders playing through the same outputs.

To organize sound beds for 2-scene sound, alternate recordings back and forth between these two "4-track recorders." For example, "the marsh cue" could be recorded on tracks 1-4 with nothing on tracks 5-8, and the "Prospero's cave" cue on 5-8 with nothing on 1-4.

Since it is possible to adjust the volume of tracks 1-4 using the VS-880's faders, you can turn the volume up or down on the insects or the other sounds that make up the marsh cue even while that cue is playing. At the same time, the volume levels for Prospero's cave can be preset on tracks 5-8.

To achieve playback of more than 2 hours without stopping, you have to do some tricks. By using a 1-gigabyte portable disc drive attached by SCSI to the VS-880, more than 2 hours of 4-track playback is possible (note: the Jaz drive makes a repeating ratcheting-type sound during use). But it is also possible to create more than 8 hours of 4-track playback while using only a few minutes of the VS-880's own on-board memory by assigning loop points to the tracks. It takes only 30 seconds of memory to make 20 minutes of playback if you loop it 40 times. Short loops are also a lot easier to edit than 2-hour recordings.

Moving from cue to cue is done by using counter memory markers. By placing start points in the VS-880's memory, it is possible to skip forward or backward to different cues at the push of a button. This skipping creates an approximately one-quarter-second break in the playback. I covered them with either mixer fades or brief bridging sounds from another source.

If you've organized your recorded sound properly, moving to your next cue means that sound is now recorded on tracks 5-8 and nothing is on tracks 1-4. Thus, the volume levels preset on 5-8 will come into use with the start of "Prospero's Cave," while the faders of the empty tracks 1-4 become available for presetting for the Banquet scene. Of course, with a 2-scene sound controller, you cannot preview your cues.

Once the volume control faders of the mixing board have been ganged together into two groups, speaker assignment and crossfading can be performed by the mixing board after it is connected to the VS-880.

Figure 2 shows how the 4 outputs of the VS-880 are Y-ed into 8 of the inputs of the mixing board. This arrangement means that the mixing board's channels 1-4 and 5-8 are receiving identical input from the VS-880.

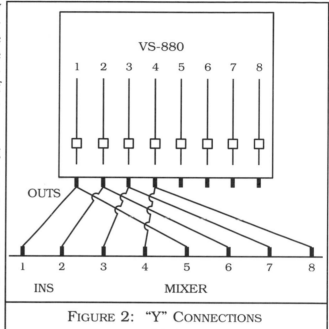

FIGURE 2: "Y" CONNECTIONS

Ganging the board's volume control faders is done with 2 dowels and some tape. Attach the slider knobs of faders 1-4 so that they move simultaneously and do the same for 5-8. These are now the "x" and "y" crossfaders. Let's follow a sound through Figure 1 to see how.

The sound we'll follow comes out of the VS-880's output #3. The Y connector sends the sound into the mixing board's inputs 3 and 7. The sound now goes through the mixer channel, and anything that's turned on there will affect the sound. In our case, channel 3 will perform some equalization on the sound, while channel 7 will not. Next the sound goes on to the volume control fader. Right now the volume of the "x" group is turned up, so the sound in channel 3 is attenuated. Our "y" faders are pushed all the way down, however, so the sound in channel 7 stops right there. The sound in channel 3 makes its way out of the mixer through the output assigns (we're sending our sound to speakers A and C) and is finally heard by the audience.

In crossfading "x" and "y," the "x" volume control faders are pushed down at the same time that the "y" volume control faders get pushed up. So our sound can now pass through 7, but is choked off in 3. Because there are differences between the settings of 7 and 3 the sound that reaches the audience will be quite different now. It will have no EQ, and it will play through different speakers (C and D). Such big changes would be quite startling if they were made abruptly, but the 2-scene sound controller crossfaded these changes, so they are heard as very smooth.

≈≈≈

Recreating an Acoustic Space with Discrete-6 Recording

Brian MacQueen

For the Yale School of Drama's production of *The Misanthrope*, director Lisa Channer wanted to suggest that the title character was aware of a beauty that all the other characters were not. This beauty was represented by Vivaldi's *Sposa son disprezzatta*, performed on a piano at key moments. To create these distinctly different cues, I used discrete-6 recording and playback techniques not only to capture the cue itself, but also to recreate the ambience of a recording hall.

The first step in recording in discrete-6 is locating six microphones in the recording hall in the same relative positions that 6 individually channeled playback speakers will occupy in the theatre. In other words, before you can place the microphones in the recording hall, you have to know within plus or minus 2' where you are going to hang your speakers in the theatre.

I was able to establish available speaker locations before the set was built by Xrefing the technical director's AutoCAD plans and sections. I then created a circle centered on "the ideal seat" in the

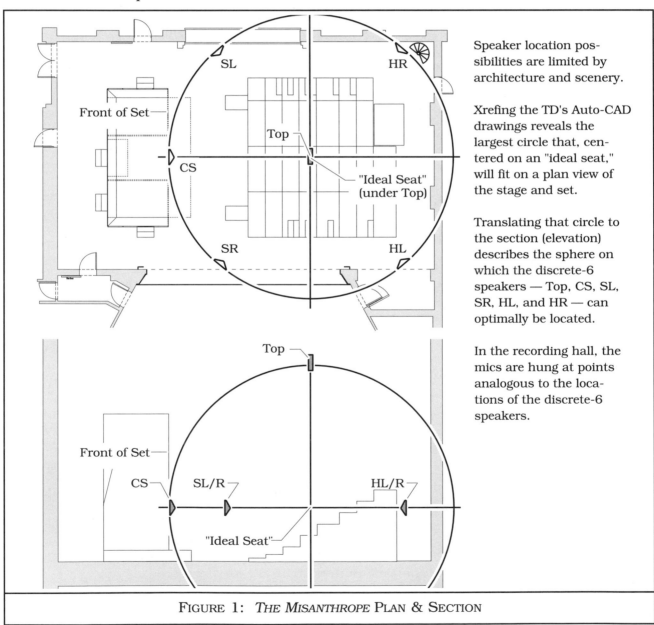

Speaker location possibilities are limited by architecture and scenery.

Xrefing the TD's Auto-CAD drawings reveals the largest circle that, centered on an "ideal seat," will fit on a plan view of the stage and set.

Translating that circle to the section (elevation) describes the sphere on which the discrete-6 speakers — Top, CS, SL, SR, HL, and HR — can optimally be located.

In the recording hall, the mics are hung at points analogous to the locations of the discrete-6 speakers.

FIGURE 1: *THE MISANTHROPE* PLAN & SECTION

audience, adjusting it until I found one that gave me the six discrete-6 microphone/speaker positions I needed. See Figure 1. By placing scale templates of the Apogee AE-2 speakers I planned to use onto this circle, I could measure the distances between the speakers in order to determine the placement of the microphones in the recording hall.

In the recording hall, the Center Stage (CS) microphone was placed closest to the sound since I wanted the sound to come from in front of the audience. Four microphones were placed in relation to the first microphone that the proscenium and house speakers had to the CS speaker. Note: these five microphones should all fall on the circumference of a circle. The sixth microphone was directly above the center of that circle, placed as high in the air as the other 5 microphones are from the center of the circle. This creates a "hemisphere" of microphones centered, not around the stage, but around the ideal seat.

Ideally, the microphones that you record discrete-6 with are all matched and all omnidirectional. "Flat response" reference microphones are best. (I had five Bruling Kjer 4006 omnidirectional microphones and one Bruling Kjer 4011 cardioid microphone. I used the one 4011 for the top microphone and pointed the center of the pickup pattern directly up toward the ceiling.) Each microphone is then recorded as directly as possible onto its own separate track of tape. I recorded PFL through a Neeve console onto a Tascam DA38 eight-track digital recorder.

The discrete-6 recording process is very simple. You set the microphone gains so that they are the same for all the microphones — that is, if the hottest microphone gain is set for minus 20dB then all of the microphone gains are set to minus 20dB — and then you just let the music happen.

Do not adjust microphones individually! All 6 microphones must be allowed to record exactly what they are "hearing" from their own positions. The loudness and softness of each microphone are accurate representations of the sound in the recording hall at each of the 6 points. When put together in playback, they will recreate the complex patterns of reverberation and direct sound that make up the sound of the recording hall. So be forewarned: track by track, a discrete-6 recording is not the kind of recording that you are used to listening to, because all of the tracks are meant to be played back together.

The CS microphone recorded the loudest signal by far and had very little "hall" in the sound. The SR and SL microphones sounded distinctly off-axis, but the direct sound was clearly the strongest part of the signal, with brief, clear secondary reflections. Even though the HL Rear and HR Rear mics were 31'-4" and 34'-2" from the stage, respectively, their signals had more gain than did those at SR and SL. Nonetheless, the direct sound at HR and HL was wrapped in rich reverberations. The Top microphone was almost eerily quiet, with an even, pristine sound. (The lighting boom I used to elevate the Top mic only extended to 17'-8" — short of the ideal, but in the end not an issue.)

Once the recording was done, the DA38 recording was dumped onto six tracks of ProTools via an O2R digital mixer, and edits were done with all six tracks grouped together, so that an edit made on one track was made on all. Any edits that required butting different parts of the recording together sounded clear and clean on the CS track, but in the reverb-rich HL Rear and HR Rear tracks there would be a slight slur, an unevenness of reverb, as the excised portion of the recording's reverberation died away. This was not enough to be noticeable in my situation, but the ideal would be to not alter the performance by excise editing.

Because the set was so tall (26'), I had my engineer hang the CS speaker at the top of the set. I then used AutoCAD to "tip the brim," as described in Figure 2. Tipping the brim would, I hoped, help keep the sound image from floating above the heads of the audience. And it did.

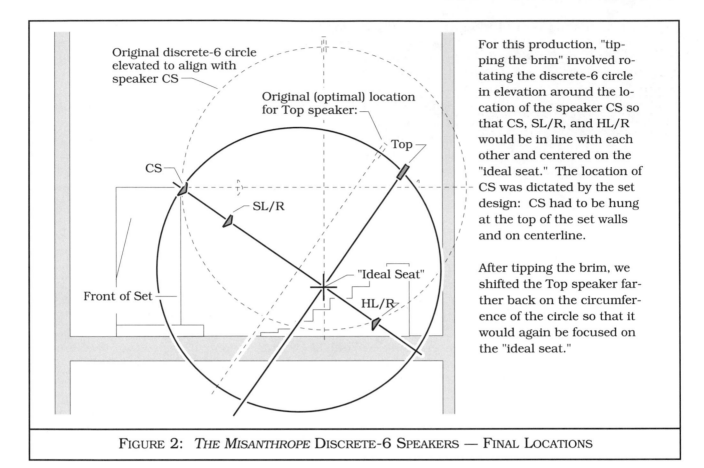

Original discrete-6 circle elevated to align with speaker CS

Original (optimal) location for Top speaker:

Top

CS

SL/R

"Ideal Seat"

Front of Set

HL/R

For this production, "tipping the brim" involved rotating the discrete-6 circle in elevation around the location of the speaker CS so that CS, SL/R, and HL/R would be in line with each other and centered on the "ideal seat." The location of CS was dictated by the set design: CS had to be hung at the top of the set walls and on centerline.

After tipping the brim, we shifted the Top speaker farther back on the circumference of the circle so that it would again be focused on the "ideal seat."

FIGURE 2: *THE MISANTHROPE* DISCRETE-6 SPEAKERS — FINAL LOCATIONS

Playing back the recording, particularly at volume levels low enough not to excite the reverberations of the theatre, sounded wonderful and created a distinctly different set of acoustics than those of the theatre. The sound was so natural that walking from the front rows of the theatre to the back rows gave one the clear impression of walking away from the piano. Even the audience seats that were within a few feet of HR and HL perceived the sound as coming from center stage.

Combined Topical Index: Volumes I and II

PAINTING

PROPS

Rigging Techniques

Safety

Scenery

Scenery Electronics

Scenery Hardware

Scenery Materials

Scenery Mechanics

Scenery Tools

Sound